MW01001728

THE STORY OF PSYCHOLOGY: A THEMATIC HISTORY

ROBERT C. BOLLES

UNIVERSITY OF WASHINGTON

THE STORY OF PSYCHOLOGY

A THEMATIC HISTORY

Brooks/Cole Publishing Company

Pacific Grove, California

Brooks/Cole Publishing Company
A Division of Wadsworth, Inc.

Printed in the United States of America
10 9 8 7 6 5 4 3 2 1

Library of Congress Cataloging in Publication Data
Bolles, Robert C.
The story of psychology: a thematic history / Robert C. Bolles.
p.   cm.
Includes bibliographical references and index.
ISBN 0-534-19668-3
1. Psychology—History. I. Title.
BF95.B57 1993
150′.9—dc20   92-34713

Psychology Publisher: *Kenneth King*
Editorial Assistant: *Gay Meixel*
Production Editor: *Karen Garrison*
Cover and Interior Designer: *Cloyce Wall*
Print Buyer: *Randy Hurst*
Art Editor: *Donna Kalal*
Permissions Editor: *Peggy Meehan*
Copy Editor: *Cheryl Ferguson*
Compositor: *Graphic World, Inc.*
Printer: *R. R. Donnelley & Sons, Crawfordsville*

Contents

Chapter 15 The Diversification of Psychology

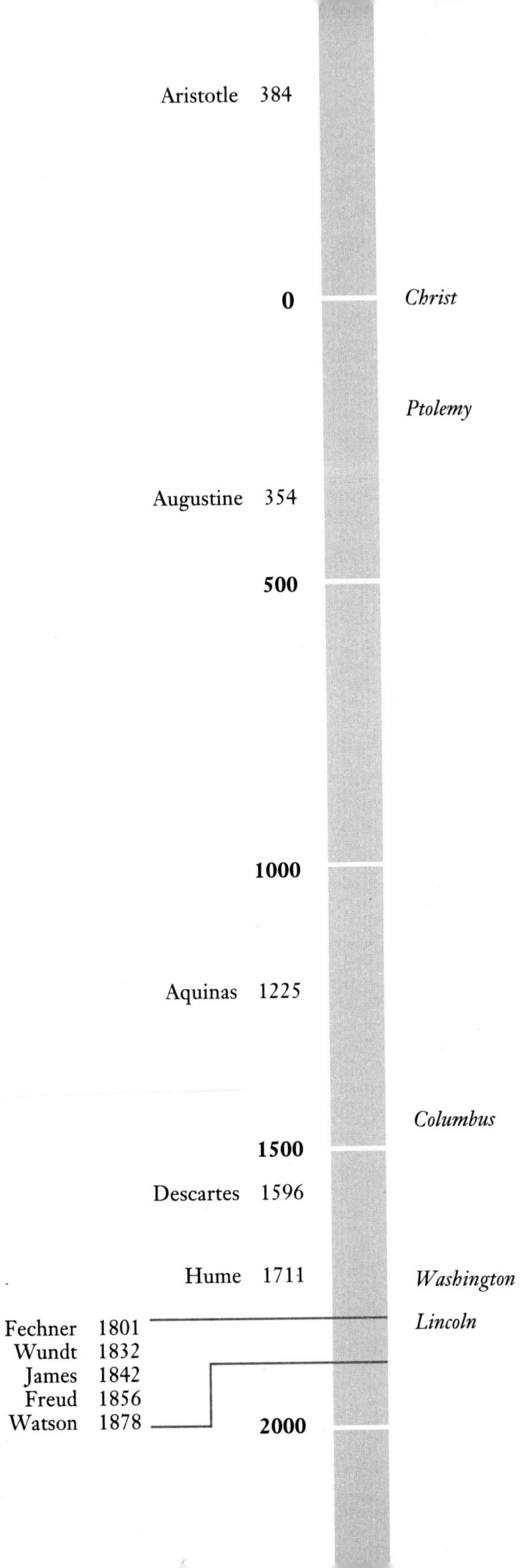

Aristotle 384

0   *Christ*

                               Ptolemy

Augustine 354

500

1000

Aquinas 1225

                               Columbus

1500

Descartes 1596

Hume 1711   *Washington*

Fechner 1801   *Lincoln*
Wundt 1832
James 1842
Freud 1856
Watson 1878   **2000**

Preface

A TEXT ON THE HISTORY of psychology ought to accomplish a few simple objectives. It should give the student some sense of history. It should give the student some feel for the story, the movement, and development of psychology. It should give students a better perspective of the entire field. And it should give them new things to think over and worry about. In my experience, however, even the better textbooks do not meet these objectives very well. So I have tried to write a book that does.

To foster a sense of historical time I have related the principal psychologists to kings, wars, literary figures, and other historical contexts. Special topics, such as the entrance of women into psychology and the development of the modern university, also help create a historical perspective.

In telling the story I have emphasized the plot and tried to indicate how crucial events were developing at a given time. The story is basically about people and their adventures. It tells of good people who never seemed to get anywhere, and a few dubious characters who succeeded marvelously. It tells of lucky breaks and misfortunes, logical developments and ironic twists, good times and times of trouble. To keep the storyline clear I have simplified it in some ways. First, by beginning the story with Descartes I can pass over most of the earlier scholars, who made little direct contribution to psychology. Second, the story passes over a lot of the great philosophers and the big problems they worried about, and draws on them mainly to present a few central philosophical themes.

This is a *thematic* history because it stresses certain recurring concepts that help hold the story together; the themes are woven all through it. In 1970 I had been teaching the history of psychology (without an adequate text) long enough that I wanted to do it differently. So I taught it backwards. For a few classes my students and I worried about how to characterize psychology as it appeared at that time. We finally agreed on four different adjectives: Atomistic, mechanistic, empiricistic, and associationistic. Cumbersome words, but they seemed to describe psychology as of 1970. I then followed these themes backward in time for my students. That journey took us to Descartes and his contemporaries. Before his time there were major breaks in the record. So here we merely unwind the process and start with that remarkable Frenchman and his contemporaries.

In recent years there has been a healthy growing interest in what is called the historiography of psychology. How should one approach the history of psychology, and how should one teach it and write about it? (Higard et al., 1991, nicely introduce this literature.) For example, should one attribute the significant advances in psychology to the great innovators or to the spirit of the times? I generally look at both the individuals and their times. For example, Descartes was certainly a great innovator, but he also had some remarkable friends. Freud was a great innovator, but most of his key concepts were already quite familiar to German scholars. I believe that rarely are there easy answers to the really interesting questions of historical causation.

I am indebted to my editor Kenneth King who began with no more than my idea of a history book, and hung in there until it became a reality. I was blessed by the efforts of some outstanding reviewers: Charles L. Brewer, Furman University; Samuel Fillenbaum, University of North Carolina at Chapel Hill; Edward J. Haupt, Montclair State College; Tracy B. Henley, Mississippi State University; Merle J. Moskowitz, University of Pittsburgh; Kenneth E. Smoot, University of Wisconsin–Eau Claire; and W. Scott Terry, University of North Carolina at Charlotte. I am obliged to Karen Garrison and Cheryl Ferguson and all the Wadsworth production people who did what they do so very well. And I want to thank Shigeko Ikari for her unique portrait of Freud.

The reason I teach is rather selfish: I teach so that I can get my own thoughts organized. As a bonus I sometimes learn from my students; I get ideas from them that I had not thought about before. Certainly they learn from me too, but from my selfish viewpoint that is secondary. This book also makes me get my thoughts in order, and it lets me reach out to students other than my own. I have no doubt that some of my readers will in time make their marks on the history of psychology. And then I can learn from them! I therefore dedicate this book to its readers, the students that make the whole process work.

THE STORY OF PSYCHOLOGY: A THEMATIC HISTORY

Chapter One

The Beginnings of a Science

TODAY PSYCHOLOGY has many faces. It is a science, an academic discipline, one of the healing professions, and one of the branches of human engineering that tries to cope with social and personal problems. But historically it had to become a science before it could develop any of its other faces. Most of our story will be concerned with how psychology became a science and a profession, and we will only briefly sketch how the other aspects of psychology came to be. In this chapter, however, we will look at other sciences and science in general. We might understand the beginning of psychology a little better if we can see how other sciences began. We might also get a better perspective on how psychology fits in if we go back in time to when science as we now know it got started.

What Science Is Not

WE START OUR examination of science in general by considering some of the common myths and misconceptions that even today tend to surround science. One might suppose that in the modern world everyone would be familiar enough with science to know what kind of an enterprise it is. But no, there are still common misconceptions. So we begin by considering some of the things that science is not.

Science Is Not Technology

The distinction can often be made with regard to scale and scope. Consider that it cost about $20 billion dollars to put astronauts on the moon. The great expense of the moon adventure suggests immediately that it was not science; that kind of money is not available for a scientific project. We already knew about rockets and trajectories. We already had the fuels and the know-how to shoot payloads into space. What was new was the technology of setting off

1

Galileo Galilei

a rocket big enough to carry men and their life-support systems. The development of that technology may have been wonderful. All the electronic control and communication systems were surely impressive. The political and military payoffs may have been great. The economic benefits to the Cape Canaveral and Houston areas may have been tremendous. But as science it was nothing, certainly nothing that justified the cost. NASA attempted to blur the line between science and technology by publicizing the scientific aspects of the project. A few experiments were even carried out on the moon. But that is not what it was all about.

There are several connections between science and technology. For one thing, the scientist often depends on new and better instruments, tools, and measuring devices that only technology can provide. Classical physics advanced enormously with the development of precise clocks and thermometers; astronomy leapt ahead when Galileo improved the telescope. Technology in its turn often depends on scientific advances. The moon rocket was only possible once factors such as rocket fuels and the earth's atmosphere had been carefully studied and worked out scientifically.

Furthermore, the line between science and technology is obscured by the fact that some people engage in both. We have seen that the scientist Galileo also designed and perfected instruments—all the better for measuring things. The great mathematician–astronomer Karl Gauss was also the inventor of the telegraph; he laid out the first short telegraph line. And today, as it becomes increasingly difficult to get research grant money, more scientific researchers are turning to applied and practical problems, everyday problems of a technological nature.*[1]

---

*In what follows, an asterisk will refer the reader to the bottom of the page for some immediate clarification, personal comment, joke, or other professorial digression. A number will refer the reader to the end of the chapter for further

But there remain essential differences in spirit between science and technology. Part of it is a difference in purpose. Scientists are not primarily interested in making an immediate contribution to human welfare, but rather in advancing their own understanding of scientific principles. Technologists want immediate solutions to practical problems; they want some practical, useful applications of their work. Part of the distinction reflects a difference in time scale. Technologists seek to achieve results right now, or as soon as possible. Scientists might well believe that their work will make a useful contribution, but they are in no hurry for that to happen. Moreover, they are usually willing to let someone else find the useful applications; they are not very concerned with that part of it. Time scale is a large part of the difference between experimental and clinical psychologists. The experimenter can defend a study of rat behavior on the grounds that someday someone will find how to apply it to the real world. The clinician, by contrast, wants to see something accomplished in the "50 minutes" with the client.

Science Is Not Just a Collection of Facts

Science is more orderly than some facts here and some data there, all piled together. It seeks lawfulness and general principles. Data and theory have to be coordinated. To look only at data or think only about theory would be to ignore what scientists spend most of their time doing, which is relating data to explanatory principles and modifying the principles when the data make that necessary. Science is the interaction of data and theory. We sometimes get a distorted view of a science by looking at its "official" history. The usual history of some sciences is little more than a chronology of discoveries. In chemistry, for example, we find that Lavoisier discovered oxygen in 1777, Galton discovered atomic weights in 1803, Marie Curie discovered radium in 1898, and so on. But chemistry is much more than a string of discoveries. Its history includes the gradual evolution of explanatory concepts, the development of theories, and the search for findings to test its tentative theories. Science is the interaction of data and theory.

Science Is Not a Finished Product

Science is not a set of solutions to a particular set of problems. One might get that impression from looking at a modern textbook where the explanatory principles are all laid out with assurance and elegance. An introductory physics books, for example, indicates on page one that the student must learn to think about grams, centimeters, and seconds. There is a short account of

---

details and reference material. With this system citations and references are gathered together in one place rather than being scattered throughout the text to distract the reader.

the extraordinary accuracy with which these fundamental units can now be measured using crystals and lasers. What the text does not say is that every few years the second and the centimeter change a tiny bit as new and more accurate ways of measuring them become standardized. On page four we have a picture of Isaac Newton, and a summary of his three laws. This homage to Newton has the effect of creating an illusion of the antiquity of physics, the near immortality of the noble science. It also implies that Newton was a brilliant scholar, and that subsequent physicists have been brilliant to recognize the fact. The truth is that it took a long time for physicists to agree on Newton's laws of motion, to see them as basic, to redefine such terms as momentum and force, and to couch them in a convenient notation. Newton's laws changed a lot over the centuries. So the citation of them at the outset of the textbook serves essentially a persuasive or rhetorical function. It lends authenticity, respectability, and a sense of immortality to the material covered in the textbook.

After 700 pages of a physics textbook we find that, sure enough, it is all grams, centimeters, and seconds. And it is all very elegant, logical, and impressive. But it is not physics as a science, it is textbookery. The beauty of the text comes not from the neatness of the science but rather from 300 years of polishing and perfecting physics textbooks. However, textbooks do not reflect the current status of a science. Psychology is a new science, but it can already boast a number of texts suggesting that all the basic principles are now known, and that it only remains to develop a technology in order to build a better world. This is not a very accurate picture of psychology as a science today.

There is a more basic sense in which the scientist's job is never completed. Consider a student embarking on a thesis project after diligently looking for an answerable question. We can expect that even with a well-framed question the student is not going to find an unequivocal answer. Instead the student finds two new questions that now need to be answered. The professor, an old-timer, usually has the same fortune of not finding answers, but knows how to restructure the situation, reformulate the question, and parlay it into a new research grant. It is clear that the researcher does not want to answer all the questions—that would put them out of business. The scientist is always pursuing new findings, just as the business person is always looking for new profitable deals.

Science Is Not an Objective Search for Truth

Science does not try to straighten everything out. Its purpose is certainly not to remove the myths and misunderstandings that surround our first primitive understanding of things. Psychology textbooks often feature experimental findings that run counter to common sense, or to what is commonly accepted. Thus, a social psychology text might pose to the reader the question "True or false, people tend to be attracted to people who are different from themselves?" Then an experiment is cited to show that this cultural myth is false. This introduction to the matter might appeal to the beginner, but it is bad science because it ignores the complexity of interpersonal attraction. It is only textbookery again.

The search for truth is certainly a noble activity, but that is probably not what motivates most scientific work. Many noble searchers for truth appear to know already what is true before they set out to find it, and all too often they merely confirm what they already believed. In any case, science is not a body of truths that will be revealed to us when the misconceptions and errors are stripped away. It is a much more creative activity that involves the formulation of better interpretations, gradually evolving concepts, and the slow discovery of better ways to measure things. It is not so much that we uncover nature's secrets as that we gradually learn how to understand nature in new ways.

The search for truth is also not entirely objective, because it is so dependent on our prior assumptions and concepts. Consider how a psychologist would react to new data demonstrating extrasensory perception (ESP): The data would probably be dismissed out of hand because "it does not belong" in experimental psychology. Most psychologists would feel it a waste of time to look at such data, and so they would not assess it objectively.

Science Does Not Grow Continuously

A science grows by fits and starts and moves awkwardly in different directions. It changes shape as it gets bigger. It grows in one direction for a while and then appears to angle off in a new direction for a time. This concept is embodied in the idea that science is not just the collection of data—if it were, then it would grow more evenly and continuously. For a number of years physiological psychologists did a great deal of work on the behavioral effects of brain lesions. About twenty years ago that kind of research slowed down sharply, and physiological psychologists turned much of their attention to neural transmitters. We seem to see trends and fads throughout science. The history of a science is to a large extent the story of its fads.

The Personal and Political Character of Science

WE HAVE BEEN LOOKING at science rather negatively, because we have been considering some of the idealistic characteristics that science lacks. We have noted a number of negative points, but each point also has a positive side. Thus, if science is something other than technology and not very interested in serving humanity immediately, then perhaps it can find nobility in its search for general explanatory principles. Perhaps in standing apart from everyday problems and mundane applications science becomes free to examine all sorts of data and entertain all sorts of theories. If science is not interested just in collecting facts or answering questions, then perhaps it can serve the higher mission of seeking broad and powerful generalizations. If the object of science is not to produce a finished product, then perhaps it attains greatness by always searching for new things to explain. If science is not an objective search for truth, perhaps it is more important in the long run that it search for certain kinds of effects and test certain sorts of theories. And if a science can dramatically change direction, perhaps that means it is free to pursue what is seen as an important new phenomenon or new theory.

There is a basic ambiguity here. From some points of view, such as whether it can be applied to practical problems, science does not look very good. But if science is therefore free to range far and wide, that does look good. People have the same sort of ambiguity to them—good points and bad. And that is the point. Science is not an abstract thing that transcends normal human activity—on the contrary, science is more than anything else a normal human activity. It is cursed with all the human frailties, such as the desire for power and fame, and it is blessed with all the human virtues, such as honesty, integrity, and imagination.

Political Parallels

In politics, when a government is overcome by problems it cannot handle, those in power may be put out of office in the democratic manner by the voters, or in the traditional manner by revolutionary forces. Science is much the same; when a science confronts problems it cannot handle, there may be a scientific revolution. Let us pursue this parallel. We can picture a king sitting on his throne, levying taxes, controlling legislation, and generally running the country. We can also picture trouble breaking out. There is a famine and the people are hungry. Or there are oppressive taxes, or workers want higher wages. If the trouble is great enough, a popular revolt might do away with the king and his government. So the king prepares for trouble with an army to control the people and a police guard to protect the palace. Most of the time a few troops can deal with the rebels and take care of any popular uprising. But sometimes the king misjudges the seriousness of the trouble. The army cannot cope with all the rebels. Because the rebels have such a just cause they win converts; maybe they start winning over the army. The trouble that started in the hills spreads to the valleys and into the cities, so what started as a minor matter becomes widespread. Occasionally, a revolt succeeds in overwhelming all the people, the army, and the government. The revolution is complete when a new government is put in the place of the old one.

Scientific Revolutions

There can be analogous revolutions in science also. In peaceful times there will be an "establishment" that serves as a sort of government. The establishment controls the important journals, writes most of the textbooks, and pretty well dictates how the science is conducted. It determines what sort of problems the science can deal with, what kind of technical language it can use, and what the proper research methods are. It determines what kind of data the science can concern itself with and what kind of theory it can entertain. In effect, the establishment organizes and governs the science. But sometimes there will appear a body of data or a set of ideas that does not fit. The establishment would like to ignore such troubles but it cannot because they continue to attract the attention of scientists. The problematic ideas or phenomena continue to attract attention, and begin to change the shape of the science. In time there might be what amounts to a revolution that causes the demise of the old establishment and the beginning of a new one. We can then refer to such dramatic events as a scientific revolution.

When Copernicus proposed that the earth was not the center of the known universe, but was revolving around the sun, that sowed the seeds of a scientific revolution. When the idea of a moving, off-center earth was supported by precise data and tied together with some elegant theory, that showed the revolutionary movement in its full fury. Eventually, after more than a century of controversy, the Copernican view became the centerpiece of a new science, modern astronomy.

When Charles Darwin proposed that all the species of animals had not been divinely created, but instead had gradually evolved as their environment changed, he was unleashing a scientific revolution. Although there was, and still is, considerable debate, most biologists rather quickly came to accept Darwin's idea of **natural selection,** and this idea has given rise to another new science, modern biology. A revolution does not necessarily result in a new science, of course; there were astronomers before Copernicus and biologists before Darwin, but such revolutions can totally alter their respective sciences and make them look new.

The Structure of Scientific Revolutions

ONE OF THE FIRST scholars to stress the human character of science, and the analogies between political and scientific developments, was Thomas Kuhn. His book *The Structure of Scientific Revolutions* (1962) presents a useful analysis of revolutions—how they start, gather momentum, and what consequences can be expected if they succeed.[2]

Normal Science

Most of the time, Kuhn says, a science will be at a stage that he calls **normal science.** There is a well-entrenched establishment that defends and elaborates what Kuhn calls a **paradigm.** A paradigm is not a theory, it involves much more than that. The accepted paradigm dictates what kinds of theories are acceptable; theorists can disagree and fuss over this detail or that mechanism but they all have to be working with the right kind of theory. The paradigm also dictates all the rules and procedures by which the science conducts itself. It clearly indicates what kinds of phenomena can be studied, how experiments are to be designed, and how data are to be treated statistically. All the day-to-day business of the science is guided by its paradigm.

In psychology we find that counting how many lever presses a rat makes for food is quite acceptable, but that experimenting with telepathy would not be. In psychology we can talk about stimuli and responses, but there are a host of things we are not supposed to talk about. Associations, traits, attitudes, and a variety of other basic concepts are all right in some areas of psychology, but transpose one of these concepts into an inappropriate area and you are likely to be in trouble! The journals and the textbooks play an important part in keeping the language of psychology in proper order. They also help to ensure that young psychologists getting into the field will be properly indoctrinated, will work on appropriate problems, and will use acceptable methodology.

Puzzles

Normal science is not an entirely closed business, however. One of the chief occupations of normal scientists is to extend the existing paradigm to new phenomena, and thereby give it greater power and generality. Sometimes a phenomenon just does not seem to fit in with the way everything else is structured. For some reason the paradigm does not seem to encompass it. It is like the king having a recalcitrant nobleman. Kuhn calls such a situation a *puzzle,* and he stresses that much of the work of normal science is addressed to working out puzzles. The phenomenon has to be redefined and reinterpreted, new data have to be collected, a new theoretical wrinkle has to be worked out. Sooner or later, we assume, the puzzle will be resolved, and the troublesome phenomenon will be brought into line with everything else the paradigm covers. The establishment has strengthened its position, the paradigm looks better and more powerful than ever, and we have a new phenomenon we can work on. Everyone benefits when the king gets that recalcitrant nobleman to behave.

Crises

From time to time, however, there are puzzles that do not get resolved. The establishment then has a couple of options. It may simply dismiss the puzzle and exclude it from further consideration. Or it may do just the opposite and increase its efforts to resolve the puzzle. It becomes a fad; professors start putting all their students to work on it; they go at it with a greater variety of approaches. Conferences are held on it and books get written about it. If the puzzle still fails to work out, there might be a sense of malfunction. Scientists begin to note that something is wrong. Kuhn calls it a *crisis*. The ordinary conservative rules of the game may be set aside and all sorts of new concepts, peculiar theories, and creative methods brought to bear on the problem. Uneasy alliances might form as scientists begin to look at the problem in new ways. They might start wondering how a geologist or an oceanographer would look at the problem. It is like when the king calls on allies in a neighboring country to help his troops put down a rebellion. This is a dangerous game indeed, because the game gets hard to control and the stakes can get uncomfortably high.

At this point we have a crisis, but not yet a revolution. In order for a revolution to begin there has to be a focusing point, a place where crystals can form and start to grow. There has to be an alternative way to look at the whole field. Kings rarely abdicate just because their governments have fallen to pieces. And theories are rarely discarded just because they are inadequate. Paradigms, too, have great staying power, and are usually abandoned only when there seems to be a more attractive alternative. The establishment risks this danger when it undertakes the all-out war on the troublesome puzzle. When the establishment loosens the rules of the paradigm and encourages so many scientists to attack the problem in new ways it is inviting disaster. If some clever scientists can propose a neat way to deal with the puzzle, and handle a lot of what the old paradigm handled as well, then we might witness a scientific revolution. The old paradigm might collapse and be replaced by a new one. Then we have what Kuhn calls a paradigm shift.

Paradigm Shifts

The old paradigm goes grudgingly. And we are likely to see a lot of acrimonious contention. The old-timers, who rode the old paradigm to their present positions of power and influence, are understandably disconcerted by the new developments, and are usually not willing or able to participate in them. The new paradigm will usher in new journals, new journal editors, and new textbooks, and those who defended the old paradigm are likely to be left behind. The old-timers are also likely to be lacking in the new research skills that are called for by the new directions research is taking, and again they will be left behind. As the old research, at which the old researchers were so proficient, gradually disappears, they are left stranded as everyone seems to be moving off in new directions. Characteristically, the revolutionaries are younger scientists who are full of energy and new ideas, while the defenders of the old faith tend to be older and more conservative in that they tend to hang on to what power and position they can. The transition can be a long, bitter battle.

A successful revolution depends on the recruitment of believers to the new cause. One's fellow scientists have to be persuaded to look at new phenomena, and to regard them in new ways. One's colleagues have to be convinced that the new perspective is important and valuable. Like a political revolution, a scientific revolution depends on getting popular support. The ideas that come to prevail in the new paradigm find their success not necessarily in their greatness but in their popularity. Some of these ultimately successful ideas are not necessarily new; they might have been in the background for some time before they suddenly became popular. Thus, Copernicus was by no means the first astronomer to propose that the earth moved about the sun. The idea was widely discussed much earlier by Greek philosophers. It was the authority of Aristotle, backed up by the authority of the Church, that fixed the earth at the center. Copernicus merely revived an old concept, but because he did so at a critical point in our history, he began a scientific revolution and started a paradigm shift. With most scientific revolutions it is possible to find anticipations of what would later be epochal ideas.

A paradigm shift brings with it a new set of problems. These problems might overlap with some of the old problems, but even the traditional sorts of problems will have a new flavor. New phenomena and new methods for studying them always emerge. New explanatory concepts become popular; scientists begin to talk about things they could not talk about before. Even more importantly, a paradigm shift is likely to change completely our picture of a science. The old and the new paradigms are incompatible, both logically and conceptually, as well as politically. There was no way to compromise between the earth being at the center and the sun being at the center. Thus, the acceptance of the new generally implies a total rejection of the old. If it had been possible to have it both ways, then there would have been a solution to the puzzle rather than a revolution.

The paradigm shift, the new way of looking at the science, can bring with it a total change in our world view, according to Kuhn. For example, before Darwin the human was something different from the animals; we were separated from them by possession of an immortal soul, free will, and rationality. After Darwin the human was simply a part of nature, part of the big biological picture, part of the mindless evolution that had produced the diversity of creatures we see around us. In this case the paradigm shift produced a complete break with earlier theological doctrine and cultural tradition. After the break it was reasonable to look for intelligence in animals and for instinct in humans. Before Darwin's revolution such ideas were unthinkable.

The Case of Psychology

There is a problem if we want to apply Kuhn's analysis to the history of psychology. He says that psychology and all the other social sciences have no established paradigm at the present time. We are all in a **preparadigmic** state where there is a great diversity of theories and a multitude of different explanatory concepts, but none of the unifying discipline that a paradigm provides in a mature science. This seems like a fair judgment, but perhaps Kuhn is needlessly strict on this point. Although experimental psychology came into being in the absence of any scientific paradigm, there was a body of widely accepted truths, a consensus world view, about the human mind and human behavior. Perhaps when John Watson launched the behavioristic revolution in 1913 he was not rebelling against a prior scientific psychology paradigm, but rather against all the psychological traditions and folklore that existed in our society.

A comparison could be made to Darwin's argument for natural selection. There was no unifying theory or data on evolution—no paradigm—before *Origin of Species*, although various kinds of evolutionary ideas were widely discussed. So perhaps we should think of Darwin's revolution as a rebellion against the traditional biblical account of creation rather than a revolution within biology. Just as most of the opposition to Darwin's ideas came from the clergy and not from biologists, most of Watson's opposition came from other intellectuals and not from psychologists. And if Kuhn's analysis can be applied to Darwin, perhaps it can be applied to Watson as well. Perhaps there can be revolutions in psychology.

Lavoisier and the Beginning of Chemistry

BEFORE WE GET into the serious business of the beginning of psychology, it will be helpful to look briefly at a different case, the beginning of chemistry. Modern chemistry derived from a series of experiments with gases. The key experiment was carried out by the French chemist Antoine Lavoisier (1743–94) just before the French Revolution. His discovery of oxygen in 1777 forced chemists to think about their science in new ways. Today chemists are inclined to ignore everything prior to Lavoisier or else to dismiss it as alchemy or magic or nonscience. What we will see here, though, is that the scientists prior to Lavoisier who worked on chemical problems were not charlatans; they were earnest and often brilliant researchers who had worked

11

Antoine Lavoisier

out what seemed to be a very adequate way to account for Lavoisier's results, and their earlier paradigm worked quite well. Let us see how the critical events unfolded.

Lavoisier's Experiment

Lavoisier's experimental situation consisted of a dish of mercury that was covered by a glass container. Lavoisier heated the whole business for a day or two. Under the glass he found a mass of dark red, cruddy-looking stuff floating on the mercury. He also found that the air in the container was partly depleted. Scientists would now say that when the liquid mercury was heated it was oxidized by the oxygen trapped in the container, forming mercuric oxide—the dark red, cruddy stuff floating on top. In modern notation, $O_2 + 2Hg \rightarrow 2HgO$.

Lavoisier proposed an explanation that was very close to the modern account. He suggested that ordinary air consists of two parts, and that one of these parts (what we call oxygen) had combined with the mercury to form the cruddy-looking stuff. This proposal accounted nicely for the depletion of air in the container. Later, when Lavoisier was able to weigh gases accurately, he showed that the loss of weight of the trapped air just matched the gain in weight of the oxide. That should have settled any controversy, but on the contrary, Lavoisier's discovery of oxygen did not go at all smoothly. When his contemporaries heard of Lavoisier's 1777 experiment they were probably puzzled by the apparent loss of air, but they were much more bothered by his strange notion that air (which was very hard to detect) is really composed of two kinds of air (both of which were very hard to detect). That looked like magic, particularly since they had already worked out a rather adequate theory of how things burn. Very similar experiments had already been done by Priestley and others, and their results were entirely consistent with their theory.*

Phlogiston Theory

Joseph Priestley (1733–1804) was a distinguished British chemist and clergyman who later came to America and brought the Unitarian Church with him. Priestley and his friends believed in **phlogiston,** an interesting old concept that present-day chemists tend to be rather embarrassed about. It had been noted that except for a rare glitter of gold, one almost never sees metal lying about. So metals are the strange and unnatural substances. The fundamental stuff is minerals and ores, some of which we now recognize as oxides. Phlogiston is a property of matter, the property of being burnable. It was burnability.

You start with an oxide, such as rust. If you add burnability to it you get iron, which is hard, shiny, and burnable. It was noted that the different metals look a lot like each other, whereas the ores are all different. This shows that when you add phlogiston to an ore, the phlogiston gives you hardness, shininess, and burnability. The formula is: Ore + burnability → metal. The phlogiston concept gave a neat, simple account of all sorts of oxidation and reduction experiments. The shrinkage of air in Lavoisier's glass container was a problem because it seemed to suggest that phlogiston had negative mass. But that was not the critical consideration. Priestley and his fellow phlogistonists had too many reasons to hold onto their position.

The New Paradigm

Part of the reason Lavoisier's work was not immediately decisive is that it took him some time to understand just what he had. Like Christopher Columbus, he did not know quite where he was. At first he spoke about his gas (oxygen)

---

*About this time the French government decided it would not do the unpopular thing of collecting taxes, so a private company was set up to carry out the ugly job. Lavoisier invested a good deal of money in the stock of the new company— so much money, in fact, that he was made an officer in the new company. At this juncture the president of the company married off his daughter to the young chemist. She was only 14, but she turned out to be extremely important in Lavoisier's work. He did not know English, but she was fluent and translated his writings into English, as well as putting Priestley's papers into French so her husband could read them. She also kept his lab notes and did the illustrations for his publications. So was the tax business a good thing for Lavoisier? Not really. As the revolution rolled along, taxation became exceedingly unpopular, and in 1794 they trumped up some charge against Lavoisier, found him guilty, and sent him to the guillotine.

as though it had "potential heat" and some kind of chemical principle. It wasn't phlogiston, but it wasn't really oxygen either. The modern view of the gases was developed over a number of years, and what proved to be decisive were two relatively incidental considerations rather than any direct test of the new theory against the old one.

One consideration was that the chemical equations of the phlogiston theorists contained both substances and properties, oxide plus burnability (and they had a number of other properties too). Lavoisier's equations involved only substances. The mechanistic philosophy pervading science at that time convinced the chemists that they only wanted to measure substances. Properties did not count, because they could be inherent in the different substances. Iron burns, and it does so without burnability being added to it. It was really the nicety of equations with nothing but substances in them that carried the day. And so we see that a new paradigm can come to prevail for aesthetic reasons, because it is more elegant, or prettier, or cuter than the old alternative.[3]

Another decisive consideration was quantification. First, it is impossible to quantify properties and substances at the same time. More importantly, when they were able to weigh gases accurately, some marvelous relationships were discovered. Consider carbon monoxide, CO, and carbon dioxide, CO_2. The first is 58 percent oxygen, by weight, while the second is 72 percent. Now, unfortunately, the two numbers, .58 and .72, do not have any kind of relationship to each other; to most of us they would appear to be just ugly empirical numbers. But not so for John Dalton (1766–1844), the great English chemist. Dalton loved numbers, and was always fiddling with his data. He was also obsessed with the idea of atoms; he was always thinking about atoms and drawing pictures of them. One day around 1803 it occurred to him to look at the oxygen to carbon ratios. If CO is .58 oxygen, then it is .42 carbon and the ratio (.58/.42) is 1:3. For the other gas we have .72 and .28, and the ratio is 2:6. Wow, there it is; 1:3 and 2:6 *are* related, and suddenly everything snaps into place. Molecules are made up of atoms just as Dalton suspected, and they combine in simple ratios. Moreover, we know that an oxygen atom weighs 1.3 times as much as a carbon atom. And we can go on from there. If hydrogen is 1 then oxygen is 16 and carbon is 12. All at once we had about half of what we now find in freshman chemistry. All at once it became obvious that Lavoisier was a great pioneer and that he had discovered oxygen.

Music of the Spheres

IN THE HOT, dry lands around the eastern end of the Mediterranean Sea one can see the stars in all their glory. And back when Western civilization was just getting going there, the stars were an important and exciting part of it.

If you sat out under the stars you would soon learn, partly on your own and partly with the help of your elders, that there are patterns. The stars fall into patterns that become familiar, and these patterns are full of seasonal significance. If Aries rises in the evening, you know it is autumn. If you see the dog star coming up at dawn, then you know you are in the dog days, the bad part of summer. The stars provide an unfailing calendar because they never change. The reassuring predictability of the stars contrasts with earthly matters like the weather, crops, and local politics. The stars are wonderful.

The sun rises and sets, which gives us our days, and it is quite predictable as it rises higher in the long days of summer and sinks in the south in the short days of winter. It has a discernable rhythm. And so does the moon, although it may surprise you by when and where it rises on any given night. Nonetheless, it has its own off-beat predictability. The problem is the "wanderers," the five planets that display really strange patterns. For example, Jupiter usually moves a trifle to the east every night, but every 13 months or so, when it has moved into the next sign of the zodiac, it stops and moves west for a while. It also wanders up and down a little. Your uncle tells you that a few summers ago Jupiter was sitting right on top of Saturn. But your grandmother insists that years ago, in the spring, Jupiter was right underneath Saturn. Mars gets around the sky quickly, taking just over two years. Somewhere in the cycle it also moves in the wrong direction for a while, but Mars is unique in brightening greatly at that time. Venus dazzles you in the evening for several months, then disappears, and then dazzles you in the morning for several months. Mercury rarely gets high enough in the sky to be seen at all. The wanderers act strangely indeed.

Early Greek Astronomy

The Greek philosopher–scientists, whose work was pulled together by Aristotle, had a scheme to explain it all. The fixed stars were simple enough; they were attached to a large spherical shell that rotates around the earth. It goes around us once a day. Actually it gets slightly ahead of itself so that it rotates 366 times in a year. That lets the stars move with the seasons. The sun sits on its own big crystalline sphere that moves almost in time with the stars, but it is also made to wobble up and down with the seasons. The moon is on another crystalline sphere (it has to be crystal so we can see through it to the stars beyond), which gives it its particular motion in the sky. The planets are a little more complicated; to account for the occasional "backward" motion of Mars, there is a big Martian sphere that goes around every two years or so. Attached to it is not Mars itself but another, smaller sphere that carries Mars. Then when that small sphere swings toward us it makes Mars move backward, and of course it is brighter because it is closer. With Mars in motion, a couple of further spheres have to be attached to Mars to *undo* its motion and provide a stationary base for generating the motion of outlying Jupiter. And so on with the other planets.

This scheme was described in detail by Aristotle, and it became the prevailing view, the paradigm prior to Copernicus, one might say. The music of the spheres was created by the slipping and sliding of all those crystalline balls around the earth. This model of the heavens was cumbersome; there was all that machinery and gears and stuff out there, but it was workable, at least in principle. All the critical parts were spherical, and that was vitally important. And it was naturalistic; indeed, it was all very mechanistic. It was not Zeus moving his planet around as he saw fit, it was mechanical.

Ptolemy's Model

Around A.D. 200 there emerged an important variation on this paradigm that preserved much of the Aristotelian model but that also altered it in some ways. This was the work of Ptolemy, the last of the great Greek (or Hellenistic) astronomers. Ptolemy was less concerned about the three-dimensionality of the machine than with a two-dimensional model that would predict where everything was at any given time. He had each planet swinging around the earth in a large "major" cycle. Then riding on that was a smaller "epicycle" that carried the planet. Mars had a large epicycle so that it would, once in a while, get quite close to us and move backward, just as the spherical model maintained (see figure 1.1). It was already known in Ptolemy's time that a simple epicycle system was not adequate. Changes in movement and in brightness did not correspond very well, and the planets failed to stick to their schedules. Corrections had to be made: Tiny epicycles were added to the standard ones to deal with the errors. The centers of the major cycles were

FIGURE 1.1

Ptolemy's conception of how Mars moves about the earth, showing an epicycle and an offset center.

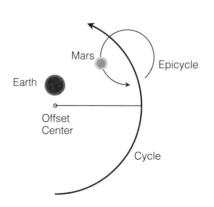

offset, moved away from the earth, and different planets even had different centers. It had gotten rather messy, and the Greek ideal of concentric circles was badly compromised. Instead of music of the spheres we had a bunch of noisy egg beaters. But appearances had been saved; Ptolemy and his followers could predict rather accurately where the planets and everything else were in the sky. To that extent, the old paradigm had solved the puzzle. Accounting for the odd behavior of the wanderers had been a major intellectual achievement.

The Calendar and the Cosmos

In the late 1400s there was a small problem, a really quite minor matter, just a practical detail, but the Church had been worried about it for some time and decided to do something about it. It seemed that the Julian calendar (set by Julius Caesar in 46 B.C.) had gotten a little ahead of the seasons. Easter, the anchor of the Church's calendar, was coming perhaps 10 days too late. A 10-day error after a millennium and a half might look to some to be pretty good, but no, it had to be fixed. The pope instructed certain scholars to look into the matter and straighten everything out. It was a small problem, but working it out would bring about all sorts of trouble. Aristotle would be replaced as the authority on science. Modern science, science as we know it, would begin. Several new sciences would arise. Philosophy would also change dramatically. The Church would no longer have much to say about either science or philosophy. The calendar would change, yes, but so would everything else in the Western world.

The trouble began innocently enough when a German astronomer was established in Nuremberg to make accurate observations of planetary motion. Scientists of that time often assumed scholarly Latin names, and his was Regiomontanus. In everyday life he was Johannes Müller (1436–76), and a nice monument now stands in Nuremberg to celebrate his work there. He collected a good deal of data, and then his findings made their way into the hands of the famous Polish scholar Nicholas Copernicus (1473–1543). Copernicus had become enamored of the old idea that the sun was the center of the known universe and that the earth and everything else revolved around it. As Copernicus pored over Regiomontanus's data he became convinced that the Aristotelian–Ptolemaic model of the heavens would not work. Even when it was patched up with further epicycles, it would not describe the movement of the planets as accurately as they were then known.

Notice that Copernicus's sun-centered model was not really any more accurate; it had problems too. Indeed, there was little grounds for deciding between the two models. It was simply more convenient to work out the mathematics doing it his way. Nor did he claim that his model reflected reality; he told the Church that it permitted one to derive a more accurate calendar. Copernicus made it look more like a practical, engineering sort of matter rather than a challenge to the authority of Aristotle. Of course the Church is not very concerned with planetary motion per se. But it is very deeply concerned with questions of authority, and having committed to the Aristotelian view it would have been obliged to defend it. The Church had a vested interest in vested interests, and surely would have attacked Copernicus if it had understood what was at stake or seen what was going to happen next.

Johannes Kepler

Johannes Kepler (1571–1630), a German scholar and mathematician, entered the scene about fifty years after the death of Copernicus. He was something of a mystic and he believed in geometry. For a number of mystical reasons he put the sun at the center. And then he argued that rather than concentric spheres holding the planets, the planets were circumscribed around a set of nested regular solids—tetrahedron, cube, dodecahedron, and so on. The spacing of these solids would then determine the relative distances of the planets from the sun. Then the whole mystery of the heavens would be solved. To work it out quantitatively he had to have data, and for data he turned to Tycho Brahe (1546–1601), the Danish astronomer who had a way with machines and had built the largest and most precise sighting instruments anywhere. There were no telescopes yet, but a sighting instrument indicated precisely where a visible object, such as Mars, was in the sky at a given time.

The more Kepler crunched his numbers the clearer it became that the problem could not be solved by offsetting centers and adding epicycles. With minimal real theory, and with the crudest of mathematical tools, and with 10 years of struggling with the problem, Kepler discovered that the planetary orbits had to be ellipses. Mars did not move in a circle at all, but in an ellipse! It is incredible that Kepler solved the problem. Ellipses are very messy to deal with mathematically, but Kepler developed ways to do so. He developed an equation that said it all but unfortunately was not solvable, and then he developed ways to solve it. He worked mainly on the orbit of Mars, and published a book about it in 1609. He had impeccable data from Brahe, and he worked it over and over until it fell into a beautiful pattern. He abandoned his geometric fancies when he discovered a much simpler and more elegant relationship between the distance of a planet and the speed with which it moves around the sun in an ellipse.

Kepler published his book on Mars just in time. That same year one of the greatest of scientists, Galileo Galilei (1564–1642), made a momentous discovery. In 1609 Galileo began experimenting with different lenses, and soon had a primitive 20-power telescope, which he played with day and night. One day he saw spots on the sun and observed that they moved as the sun rotated. One night he saw the craters on the moon. He saw that the planets had visible disks, whereas even the brightest stars did not. He was

Johannes Kepler

most fascinated by the finding that Jupiter had its own little moons. Certainly the earth could not conceivably be the center of the universe if things were revolving around Jupiter. It was clear to anyone who cared to look through his telescope (and there were many who were so accustomed to getting their knowledge from authority that they did not dare to look) that the ancient account of the heavens was wrong on all counts. When Galileo wrote his defense of the Copernican paradigm in 1632, the evidence was overwhelming.[4]

But the battle was still not completely won. For one thing, the Church had finally become alarmed at all this heresy. Copernicus might claim he was only fixing the calendar. But Galileo could not pretend innocence; his astronomical work, along with much of his other research, was pointed directly against the word of Aristotle. Surprisingly, few scientists had previously had trouble with the Church. The astronomer Giordano Bruno was burned at the stake in 1600, but that was not because of his Copernican ideas; it was because of his stated views on the Trinity. Then in 1632 the Church forced Galileo to recant his views. But the Church's actions against Galileo were too little and too late. They could not stop the development of science that had been set in motion.[5]

Galileo and Gravity

The Copernican revolution had also left scientists in a quandary because it was mainly descriptive. Kepler had done little more than let us predict accurately where Mars would be in the sky at any particular time. He had a hypothesis about what made it move—there were supposed to be forces emitted from the sun that pushed the planets around—but it is not clear how seriously this idea was taken. Aristotle's crystal shells all geared together at least gave us a plausible and familiar kind of machinery. The best part of

Kepler's model, its real advance, was its ability to predict where the heavenly objects were, and not the mechanism that got them there. The Copernican revolution would not be complete until we either had some mechanical substitute for all the gears and levers, or had learned to live without that kind of machinery.

The Copernican revolution is easy to conceptualize and talk about because it appears to involve a question of fact; namely, whether the earth or the sun is at the center of things. But there have been other questions that have more to do with outlook, attitude, and the way we conceptualize things that have been just as revolutionary, and just as important in the long-term fortunes of a science. We saw that Lavoisier's contribution to chemistry was not so much to *discover* oxygen as to reconceptualize what it meant for a substance to burn. In the same way, Galileo reconceptualized the planet problem. He began by asking what it meant for an object to fall.

Aristotle had asserted that heavy objects had a greater power than lighter ones to move toward the earth, which is their natural resting place. For Aristotle the critical thing for the falling object was how far from the ground it is, because it speeds up as it approaches its goal. This is what everyone believed before Galileo started doing experiments and measuring things. Galileo's fascination with falling objects began, so the story goes, when as a young man he was in the great cathedral in Pisa (which is just across the street from the leaning tower). He noticed that for some reason the candle lamps that lit the cathedral swayed back and forth from their long chains. He wondered what force could make them swing like that. One might think of that moment of contemplation as the beginning of modern science (I was in the cathedral in 1988, about 400 years later, and was thrilled to see those old lamps still hanging there).

It is said that Galileo dropped objects from the leaning tower and found that light wooden things fell just as fast as heavy metal things. It is doubtful that he ever did such an experiment, but what he did do was roll objects down inclined planes (to slow their descent and make timing them easier). And what he found was that the speed with which an object falls depends only on how long it has been falling. That was the only variable. If you measure speed of falling and plot it against the duration of the fall you get a lovely straight line. Wonderful, orderly data. Now the Aristotelians would never get orderly data like that, first of all because they did not measure things. But even if they did, they would not have gotten much because they would have had the yardstick going the wrong way; they would have measured how far it had to go to reach the ground rather than how far or for how long it had fallen. This incident provides a nice illustration of the principle that one's presuppositions, whether they be philosophical or scientific, can dictate what you see out there in the world. It also illustrates the principle that what science requires more than anything else is nice orderly data.

Isaac Newton

Isaac Newton (1642–1727) understood the primary importance of orderly data quite well. He took the laws of motion that Galileo and he had discovered and put them into sophisticated mathematical form. He was then able to describe the motions of all sorts of different things: falling rocks, bullets, pendulums, and planets. These powerful laws were all mathematical, and they were all based on the concept of gravitation. Newton clearly recognized that the concept of gravity was a mathematical abstraction, and difficult to comprehend in physical terms because it seemed to require forces operating over empty space. How does the earth hold onto the moon to keep it from flying away? How does the sun hang onto the earth so that it does not wander off into space? Calling it gravity does not indicate how the machinery works. In an often-quoted passage at the end of the *Principia* (1687) Newton says alas, he has no hypothesis to explain the phenomenon, but he does have some equations that can describe it, and perhaps these equations will prove useful in the development of science. They certainly have been useful.

Galileo's and Newton's idea that a mathematical description of a phenomenon could provide an explanation of it did come to prevail, but there was considerable discussion at first. The great French philosopher René Descartes was typical. He died too early to know of Newton, but he did know of Galileo's early work and he knew that Aristotle's notions would soon be replaced by a gravitational concept. And because Descartes was so thoroughly mechanistic, he did not like the idea of gravity operating from a distance without there being some sort of machinery to make it work. Thus, he proposed his theory of *vortices*, which filled space with currents of subtle fluid swirling around. This fluid swirls around on the other side of the moon and pushes it toward us just the right amount so that it stays in orbit. We can sympathize with Descartes and his allies because, indeed, it would be nice to have some sort of machinery that produced gravitational effects.

Here we had mainly mechanistic philosophers on one side of the issue, and mathematical scientists on the other. The philosophers lost, and the scientists had their way. As children we learn about the physical world by pushing, pulling, and feeling things, by interacting with things directly. And those experiences give us an early sense of a mechanical world. But then later we become more sophisticated and feel as though a phenomenon is explained when we can describe it in a systematic manner. If we can quantify the effect with an equation, particularly if the equation is elegant, simple, and apparently universal, then that is what we will do. We become content and satisfied by such equations, and ask for no more.[6]

Perhaps we can begin to see what kind of activity science is. It starts with someone making observations and measuring something; it starts perhaps with Galileo dropping objects from the leaning tower, and timing their fall. Then other people measure further phenomena, and someone begins putting the pieces together. Pretty soon the whole thing starts to unfold. We will see that psychology too started that way. Someone started measuring something.

Summary

SCIENCE IS NOT a matter of discovering some hidden reality out there; it is the business of carefully measuring some phenomena, and then organizing the data in meaningful ways. It is the business of observation and conceptualization. What is wonderful about science is that over time people discover new things to measure and new ways to measure them. And scientists are also constantly discovering new ways to reorganize their thinking and reconceptualize what they have got.

We are indebted to Thomas Kuhn for calling attention to the fact that science is not an external sort of ideal realm that transcends human activity, it *is* a human activity. Science therefore suffers from all the human frailties. But it also reflects all the best that is in us, our ability to seek out new knowledge, to build something beautiful, to create something valuable, to help make the future.

Kuhn also observed that as a science grows and matures, it does not do so in a smooth and continuous manner. Rather, it seems to go by fits and starts and to change its direction as it goes. That is because science, being a human activity, has many of the properties of a political arena. If these changes of direction are serious enough, then we can think of them as scientific revolutions. Kuhn describes a number of symptoms that let us diagnose a revolution. Normal science is always looking for problems to solve or puzzles to work out, and most of them do get worked out. But sometimes a puzzle arises that cannot be resolved, and that may lead to a crisis. Sometimes a crisis cannot be resolved, even with intensified efforts, and then there may be a revolution. Some revolutions arise from a new discovery that challenges the old order, as did Lavoisier's discovery of oxygen. When all the difficulties were finally worked out there was a new science—chemistry. Copernicus did not discover anything, he only thought of the world in a new way, and when that was ultimately settled we had a new science called astronomy. Revolutions totally change our view of the world, and when Galileo was done measuring things, the Aristotelian view of the world was lost, and in its place stood the science we call physics. What all these new sciences shared was the isolation of a phenomenon, and the discovery of how to measure it in a way that could be described usefully and elegantly.

Notes

1. There are many good histories of technology up to about 1900, such as Derry and Williams (1961). After 1900 it is hard to gain much perspective on the explosion of new materials, plastics, and so on, that have enriched our world. It is also hard to grasp the vast impact on science of the new things we take so much for granted, such as the wide use of electricity, electronics, or the new thing, computers.

2. Thomas Kuhn's *The Structure of Scientific Revolutions*, first published in 1962, was something of a revolution itself. It rocked a lot of boats and was widely criticized, particularly by philosophers of science. The second edition, in 1970, answered some of the critics, but was not fundamentally different from the first edition. It was mainly more complicated. A lot of the criticism and rebuttal has been gathered together in two books by Suppe (1970) and Lakatos and Musgrave (1970). The heart of the matter is that for a long time philosophers had been proclaiming that science was defined by its *method*, which might be inductive or deductive or something else. Others had argued that science was defined by its commitment to objectivity, or positivism, or some other slick label. Kuhn rejects all that, and while his stress on scientific revolutions is interesting, the most important thing in his analysis is the idea that science is fundamentally what a community of scientists do. It follows that scientists are much like business people, or politicians, or artists, or anyone else, in that they are folks who are trying to convince their colleagues to think about things as they do. Science is like everything else, it is mainly a matter of persuasion. So while we want to keep an eye open for any possible revolutions, our main task here will be to watch people pushing their ideas.

3. Lavoisier's revolution is discussed briefly by Kuhn (1962) and Jaffe (1957), and in more detail by Conant (1950).

4. The Copernican revolution has been described many times before. Kuhn (1957) is most cogent, and Dreyer (1953) is the classic account. The landmark publications in this story are Copernicus, *De Revolutionibus* (1543); Kepler, *Commentaries on the Motion of Mars* (1609) and *Harmony of the World* (1619); Galileo, *Dialogue on the Two Chief Systems of the World* (1632); Newton, *Principia* (1687). I will note here that I will consistently give English translations of titles when the works themselves are readily available in translation. But it should also be noted that by some curious custom a few works are invariably cited by their original Latin titles, even when your library shows them to be conveniently translated into English. Newton's *Principia* is one example.

Galileo's work on falling objects is described (originally in Italian) in *Dialogues on the Two New Sciences* (1636). There is a welcome new translation of Galileo's *Sidereus Nuncius* (*Sidereal Messenger*) (1610). Galileo was stunned by what he saw in his little telescope and knew at once that the intellectual world would never be the same. Hurriedly and excitedly he wrote this little book, which is mostly about the moons of Jupiter.

5. When I teach the history of psychology I do it from a Kuhnian perspective, and one of the first things confronting my students is a paper due in a few weeks for which they will choose some major event in the history of science, excluding psychology, and examine it to see if it meets the criteria for being a Kuhnian revolution. Was there a prior paradigm, a puzzle, a crisis, a time of turmoil? The student has to figure out what these criteria are, and then match up the historical events to document them. Thus, the students find out something on their own about science and how it changes and develops. I get to read about Alfred Wegener and continental drift, Darwin and natural selection, Albert Einstein and relativity, and more. What we find is that while some of these major turning points look rather Kuhnian, many of them do not. Gregor Mendel's genetics is not very Kuhnian, nor is Wilhelm Roentgen's discovery of X-rays, even though both discoveries greatly changed the way scientists looked at their world. We begin to suspect that there are some problems with Kuhn's analysis.

6. There are a lot of good books on the history of the sciences, as well as surveys of science in general. In the latter category my favorite is Singer (1959) because he is particularly sensitive to the issue just discussed, namely, the empirical as against the mechanistic character of science.

Chapter Two

Physiological Background

Psychology came in part from philosophy, as we will see in the next chapter, but it also came from physiology. Philosophy provided the way psychologists would think about things, but physiology provided the original subject matter. As we continue our story we will see that psychology has always occupied some kind of middle ground between philosophy and physiology, being itself neither the one nor the other but something in between. We will not see psychology beginning in this chapter, but we might be able to see it lurking in the background as we watch physiology get going in the modern era. We will see that some points at which psychology *might* have gotten started were dead ends. We begin the chapter with Descartes, the great French intellectual. There was physiological research before Descartes, of course, particularly in the study and practice of medicine, but we have to begin somewhere, and Descartes gives us a salient and important landmark.

Descartes, Mathematician and Philosopher

René Descartes was born in 1596, so he was a teenager at the time Kepler and Galileo were solving the problem of the wandering planets. In 1650, just as Descartes was at the prime of his intellectual life, Queen Christina of Sweden invited him up north to tutor her. Her invitation was irresistible (she sent the navy down to pick him up), but he should have resisted, because it was a terrible winter up there and he got pneumonia and died before he could teach the good queen much of anything.[1]

Descartes made brilliant contributions to mathematics, philosophy, and physiology. There is a story that one day early in the 1630s Descartes was lying in bed watching a fly make its way slowly across the ceiling. It occurred to the great mathematician that if the fly's distance from the corner along this wall was called x and its distance from the corner along that wall was called y, then the fly was walking out a parabola. The algebra of the path and the

René Descartes

geometry of the thing were closely related. And thus the idea of analytic geometry was born. There had been many clever algebraists who could solve all sorts of difficult equations. And there had been a lot of ingenious geometers who had vastly extended Euclid's work. But before Descartes these two branches of mathematics had not been related to each other; he brought them together and called it analytic geometry. Without analytic geometry there could not have been a useful calculus; without Descartes's insight no one today would have heard of Isaac Newton. It was an important discovery. The basic concept of how to connect geometry and algebra was presented in his *Discourse on Method* in 1637.

The *Discourse* presented not only some of Descartes's mathematical ideas but also much of his philosophical thinking. Here is where we find him wondering if anything is really the way it appears, and wondering what one can believe in, in view of all the illusions we know of. His famous answer to this dilemma, the philosopher's dilemma, was that he could believe in his own doubts, his own thoughts. He said, *"I think, therefore I am."**

Descartes's Mechanist Physiology

Descartes's thoughtful conclusion nicely epitomized his faith in the rationalistic approach. But even more than rationalism (thinking), he believed in machinery; Descartes was first, last, and always a mechanist. He was

---

*Actually, although the book was in French he is usually quoted in Latin: "Cogito, ergo sum." The "cogito" conclusion tells us something about Descartes himself. He was a very thoughtful person, so much so that thinking really was his existence. Hanging on the wall of my office is a cartoon that shows Descartes' dog wondering about such matters and thinking to himself, "I bark, therefore I am." If we can believe what Descartes said about himself, then we probably should believe his dog, too.

familiar with William Harvey's work (published in 1628) on the circulation of the blood, and he was no doubt influenced by that work. It meant that the body was a purely mechanical system, with little need for Galen's (Roman physician c. 130–c. 200) scheme of vital spirits, animal spirits, and so on that had dominated physiological thought for centuries. But probably even more important in forming Descartes's thoughts about how the body works was a Disneyland sort of enterprise that had recently been constructed near Paris. In the hills just west of Paris lies the town of St. Germain, and that is where they built a park for the entertainment of the royal family, which included the boy king Louis the 13th. The park contained a number of animated statues that were activated by water power. Hidden treadles buried in the lawn opened valves that made water flow into an intricate system of pipes that activated the statues. A nymph along the path moved off into the bushes when approached. If visitors followed her, they inadvertently stepped on a new treadle that activated the great god Neptune, who charged forward with his trident raised to scare them out of their wits. Just like Disneyland.

Descartes was fascinated by it all. It must have been obvious to him that if statues, fake bodies, can move around realistically because of fluid flowing through their pipes, then real human bodies might work the same way. Our limbs move because fluid of some sort is flowing through our nerves. (It would be another 200 years before anyone would understand what actually happens in the nerves. In Descartes's time the nerves were often assumed to be tubes that carried spirits of some sort.) The basic mechanism seemed clear: As fluid flows from the nerve into a muscle the muscle gets pumped up. It gets bigger around. It gets shorter, too, of course, when it is working, but Descartes had a bias about that. He thought the fattening was more important than the shortening. Besides, he knew that the muscle gets firmer when it is working. So it is obviously getting pumped up. Wonderful! He had a mechanism that could account for movement, with no mysterious essences or animal spirits involved. Just like in the park, water or something ran through the pipes, or something. The reason for uncertainty here is that Descartes sometimes thought of it like a plumber, but sometimes he subscribed to the view that the sensory nerves contained very thin fibers that reach up into the brain so they can operate the valves there.

Descartes understood that some of our movements are automatic. If I stick my finger in a flame, you can bet that I will quickly withdraw it. The finger in the flame will be impressed with certain painful sensations that cause certain fluids to flow in the nerves. Then when this flow gets to the brain, specifically, into the ventricles of the brain, the flow will be "reflected" back into the muscles that withdraw the finger. This "reflection" is quick and automatic, and purely mechanical—we call it a "reflex." Here Descartes gave us something almost as valuable as analytic geometry; that is, the idea of reflexive behavior. It is a mechanical sort of behavior, which was important

reflex behavior,

in Descartes's view because it is the only kind of behavior there is besides voluntary.

Voluntary Behavior

Descartes tells us that only humans are capable of voluntary behavior; animals do not have volition. They are just automatons, cute machines that are forever bound by reflexive, mechanistic principles. Descartes said that there are two sorts of evidence for believing that animals have no awareness, or rationality, or voluntary control over what they do. One sort of evidence is that they cannot learn from experience, and the second is that because they do not communicate with us what they are thinking, they cannot be thinking. It would appear that Descartes never had a dog, but actually he did, one he called Monsieur Grat.

The important thing here, according to Descartes, is that people have voluntary control over their behavior, and thus are not constrained and restricted by the machinery of their bodies. The flow of nervous fluid to the muscles does not have to be just a reflection of the input flow, but can be voluntarily diverted to flow in other directions. He thought this was accomplished by subtle tilting of the pineal body, which lies right there in the central ventricle near the center of the brain. Whereas most brain structures occur in pairs, one on each side, the pineal body sits neatly in the middle and there is only one of it. So that must be where the soul sits, Descartes reasoned. By voluntarily moving the pineal body slightly this way or that, the machinery of the body could be induced to do this or that. The mind could control the body.

The distinction between mind and body had been widely discussed as far back as we know of. Descartes surely did not invent the distinction. What he did do was attract attention to a peculiar problem that has become known as the **mind–body problem.** The difficulty is this: If the machinery of the body really is like a machine, which Descartes believed, then how can anything going on in the mind affect it? How can we control the machinery just by thinking about it? You cannot stop your car just by thinking about it—you also have to do something mechanical to it, like stepping on the brake. How then is it possible to do things with your body just by deciding to do so? This is much more of a problem for Descartes than for any of his predecessors because of his emphasis on the machinery of the body, and his insistence that people at least have voluntary behavior. Because Descartes firmly believed in the reality of both mind and body he is classed as a dualist (see chapter 3).

His solution to the dilemma was with a conceptual trick that we might call the Cartesian ploy. If you decide to kick a ball, your mind does not have to impel a large quantity of spirits down the nerves to pump up your big leg muscles. The mind only has to tilt the pineal body, and it only has to tilt it a tiny bit because it is right at the center of things. The mind enjoys a lot of leverage. The mind only has to violate the mechanical rules on a very small scale in order to be effective. That's the ploy. The mechanical laws are still mainly valid, the machine is basically a machine, and the mind has only a tiny effect on it, even if it turns out to make a big difference in what the machine is doing.

Descartes made a number of other important contributions of a psychological nature. He wrote a book on emotion, in which he developed the idea that emotions were agitations of the body that are violent enough to stir things up in the brain, so that we become aware of them. He wrote about instincts, too, suggesting that instinct coordinates behavior in several different ways. It makes us have certain feelings, and it puts certain behaviors in readiness so that we are ready to fight, or eat, or make love, or whatever is appropriate for the particular instinct. In addition, it makes the body ready to participate in appropriate ways, and all of this is accomplished mechanistically, through the machinery of the body. He had a rather plausible theory of motivation more than 300 years ago.

It is important to note that the great French philosopher could not bring himself to be a 100 percent mechanist. As mechanistic as he was, he seems at the last moment to back off from where he is going. When he describes the machinery of the body, he concludes by telling us that this is the way it would be *if* the human were just a machine. For reasons that remain unclear, it was important for him to keep the mind in there, where it could control the machine. Animals might be just machines, but we are not. Descartes wanted to keep the mind intact, and that is why he encountered the dilemma of how mind and body interact.[2]

It would be a century later before the enterprising French scholar J. O. La Mettrie would write a totally mechanistic philosophy, thus finally realizing the potential so clearly suggested by Descartes. La Mettrie's book *Man a Machine* (1748) would be important in its own time. But all such mechanists who came along later owed a tremendous debt to Descartes, who had led the way. Descartes stirred up a lot of the physiological research that occurred in the years immediately following his demise in 1650. Moreover, he got a host of other scholars thinking about behavior, what causes it to occur, and what it means in the overall scheme of things. And to put the machinery idea and the behavior idea together, he gave us the very simple and compelling concept of the reflex.

Reflexes

IT SEEMS THAT psychology suffers from a peculiar curse. The trouble is that it is very difficult to test any kind of psychological hypothesis, and very easy to test any kind of mechanical hypothesis. Descartes's ideas illustrate the point. It is tough to test whether the pineal body moves when we exercise our will. We can measure where the pineal body is very accurately with modern technology, but it is much tougher to tell when our subjects are exercising their will because we do not know how to measure that. So the psychological part of Descartes's theory remains untested 300 years later. (And since we still do not understand what the human pineal body does, it seems unethical to remove the thing just to see if our subjects would or would not retain voluntary control of their behavior.) On the other hand, the purely mechanical part of Descartes's theory was tested almost immediately by several experimenters. Thus, in 1670 Francis Glisson could report that muscle contraction did not result from the muscles being pumped up. Descartes was clearly wrong about that. Glisson's subject immersed his hand and arm in a bucket of water. The water level was measured while he was lightly touching an object in the bucket. Then the level was measured again while the subject squeezed the object in his fist. The water level did not change, so the muscles were not any larger. The fattening of the muscles was exactly canceled by their shortening. Descartes the mechanist had been wrong. But regarding Descartes the psychologist, we may still wonder, because there are no data.

The Evolution of the Reflex Idea

THERE WAS OTHER early research on muscle contraction besides Glisson's. In 1668 Jan Swammerdam, a comparative anatomist, made the first nerve–muscle preparation and, taking a very empirical approach, worked out in detail how much a muscle would contract as a function of how hard the nerve was pinched. Thomas Willis, the mathematician–anatomist, got involved with reflexes with a book in 1664 that followed in the tradition of Galen in distinguishing animal spirits and vital spirits. For no good reason, he put the former in the cerebrum and the latter in the cerebellum. An interesting feature of Willis's book is that the illustrations in it were drawn by Christopher Wren, who is thought of today as the master architect who rebuilt London, including the great church, after the terrible fire of 1666. In his own time, however, he was known primarily as a scientist, and he was a member of the Royal Society. Today, of course, everyone is a specialist, and physiologists are rarely also artists or architects.

As the physiologists of the time continued to pursue their understanding of the reflexes, the issues became rather complicated. About a century later, Albrecht von Haller was arguing that muscles have their own power of contractibility, which does not depend on the nerve. His view stood in opposition to the prevailing doctrine that muscles were inert and could do nothing unless activated by something coming from their nerves. Just a few years later, in 1763, the physiologist Robert Whytt pulled together an impressive mass of observations. He had noted, for example, that quite a number of reflexes required that the spinal cord be intact, although isolated nerve–muscle preparations might give contractions in the absence of any kind of central involvement. In the century or so after Descartes, a large treasure of experimental findings had been gathered together, but unfortunately no one understood what they meant. There was no unifying theory. Whytt cataloged all the available facts, but he obviously had little idea of what it was all about. Part of the problem was that nerve impulses are electrical events, and at that time there was no understanding of electricity and very little understanding of how the nerves actually functioned.[3]

So experimental psychology might have started with the experimental study of reflexes. Just such studies would much later (with Charles Sherrington's work in 1906) be very important in helping psychologists understand behavior, but that later development had no bearing on how psychology got started. There is no historical connection. It could have happened that way, but it did not work out like that.

An incident occurred in 1853 that decisively severed any tie that there might have been between the earlier work following Descartes and the subsequent work of Sherrington's time. In 1853 the German physiologist Eduard Pflüger proposed that the study of reflexes was central to the understanding of all behavior. The reason for that, he said, is that all nervous action is conscious, at least to some degree. There is no sharp line, he said, between the spinal cord that is involved in reflex behavior, and the brain that is involved in voluntary behavior. Moreover, both sorts of behavior are adaptive, and useful for solving different kinds of problems. Had anyone believed Pflüger's argument, some sort of behaviorism might have begun back there in 1853. However, that same year the philosopher Hermann Lotze was able to convince everyone that they should not take Pflüger's position seriously. Lotze contended that while reflexes are adaptive in solving ordinary, customary problems that we can handle without thinking about them, consciousness lets us solve new problems and adapt to novel situations. So there is a fundamental distinction to be made, and the study of reflexes is not important psychologically, he said. Lotze was decisive, and had it all his way. Psychology might have started with Descartes and the reflex, but it did not turn out that way. As much as we might like to trace our ancestry back to the brilliant Frenchman who never understood his dog, there is no direct connection, even though he was terribly important in the history of psychological ideas. It looked promising, but it was a dead end.[4]

The Nervous System

ONE OF THE EARLIEST achievements in the understanding of the nervous system was the discovery of a "law" that began to clarify how the brain was organized. The law was named after the two men who each discovered it about the same time. One of them was the English physician and researcher Charles Bell. His 1803 book on physiology was the standard English language reference for a number of years. The other person was the French physiologist François Magendie. His most important research was published in 1822, and it described numerous studies of reflexes using dogs. Magendie would make small surgical lesions, sometimes in the spinal cord of dogs, and observe how their reflexive behavior was altered by such intervention. Modern researchers could not get away with his procedures, doing surgery on unanesthetized dogs, but he did, and his results were extremely valuable. Bell was more humane with his animals and literally knocked them out, but as a consequence he got a distorted picture of what was happening. What Magendie and Bell found is that sensory and motor nerves are different, mainly because they are anatomically different. Looking at the spinal cord grossly, one can see that the large nerve trunks coming from the arms and legs split just before they get to the cord and enter the cord either toward the front of it (ventrally) or on the backside of it (dorsally). The anatomical distinction is born out by an important functional distinction. The **Bell–Magendie Law** states that the dorsal root, as it is called, is sensory. If you cut that root you get an animal that will not respond in any way to being pricked, poked, or pinched. On the other hand, if you sever the ventral root you get an animal that is obviously distressed by being pricked or pinched, but is unable to move the hurt part of its body. Sensory nerves go in the back of the cord, and motor nerves come out the front of it. That is the basic law. It was historically important, first because it indicated that sensory and motor nerves are not functionally different, nor do they operate differently (as Descartes sometimes supposed) but rather are located differently. It was also important because it provided a clear correlation between where neural structures are located and how they function. The location of neural structures suddenly became important.

The Localization Problem

Upon examination, the human brain appears to be a bunch of bloody grey mush. And that is about what it is. There are some lumps here and there, and a number of strands of congealed mush, but by and large it is pretty hopeless to figure out by examining the brain how it is put together or how it works. Magendie is probably largely responsible for starting people to think about a more functional sort of analysis. He was cutting nerves here and there in dogs and looking to see what effect these cuts had on his animals' behavior. By the early part of the 1800s there was increased interest in the problem of localization, what the different parts of the brain were doing, where all the different nerves went, and so on. Some of the interest in localization may have arisen from the enormous popular interest in **phrenology**, which was not the science of but rather the profitable business of reading bumps on the head. If your skull was a little convex right over here, that meant you had a lot of imagination, a bump over there meant a lot of artistic ability, and so on. There were said to be a couple dozen such traits. In the early 1800s a lot of people in France and England paid a lot of good money to get their personalities assessed by the phrenologists.[5]

But finding out how the brain works and what its important parts are was a slow and difficult enterprise. Magendie did not get very far. The localization experiments were tedious and often frustrating (they still are). It is easier out in the periphery, but ever more challenging as one approaches the brain itself. Some of the best experiments turn out to be those done by accident. In a hospital near Paris there lived for many years a man who was more or less normal except for one peculiarity—he could not talk. He was intelligent, and could communicate in other ways, but he could not talk. Fortunately, he was in good hands when he died, and Dr. Paul Broca did the autopsy and reported in 1861 that only a small part of the brain showed any damage. Broca tentatively concluded, more or less correctly, that the part of the cortex that controlled speech was right smack there below and in front of the central sulcus on the left side. Today we call it Broca's area (see figure 2.1). But good data of a clinical sort are hard to come by, so the localization problem turns out to be a tough one. The brain yields its secrets grudgingly.

The localization problem might have given rise to experimental psychology, *if* the experiments could have been done, *if* the functional differences were clearer, *if* there had been more substantial support for the phrenologists. But the correlations turn out to be almost hopelessly difficult

FIGURE 2.1
The left side of the human cortex.

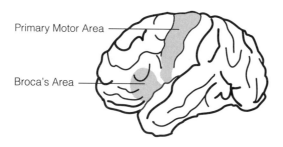

33

to find. Broca had been very lucky. Bell and Magendie had been lucky, too, because they had found one of the few gross functional–locational relationships. Little progress could be made on the localization problem in the 19th century because the things they were trying to localize were so complicated. Suppose Kepler had tried to work out the orbit of the moon instead of Mars. He would never have come close to solving the problem. The moon has an ugly, complicated orbit that even today is tough to resolve. There is so much luck in this business. The localization approach might have given us an experimental psychology, but it did not turn out like that. The localization approach is good and important, and we have made a great deal of progress on it, but it did not give rise to psychology. It was another dead end.

Electricity

I DIGRESS NOW to note a great discovery. It was, I claim, the greatest, the most important discovery of all time. It was the most momentous thing humankind ever stumbled onto. I do not know the details of the discovery, so I will make up a story about it. The year was 1791, more than a century after Descartes had stirred up interest in reflexes and after Swammerdam had started preparing gastrocnemius muscles with a stub of nerve attached. The discoverer was an Italian gentleman named Luigi Galvani, who obviously puttered with other projects besides muscle–nerve preparations. Thus, his workbench was cluttered with all kinds of stuff. On this day in 1791 he noticed that a frog muscle, which was just lying there, was twitching. He touched it and it quit moving. He moved things around carefully and it twitched some more. It seemed that the muscle twitched whenever its attached nerve touched two pieces of metal that were themselves lightly touching. If Galvani had not had such a messy workbench, he would never have encountered such a thing, but there it was. The two pieces of metal, barely touching, made a primitive battery. Nerves are more sensitive to electricity than anything else, and the muscle provided Galvani with a handy measuring instrument. In no time at all he had developed workable batteries, ones that made sparks, tasted sour, and made muscles jump all over the place.

Prior to Galvani there were two sources of electricity. One was lightning, which is not very useful because it comes all at once in billion-volt packages. The second was static electricity, which you can get by walking with leather shoes on a rug on a dry winter day. You walk across the room to give your sweetheart a kiss, but you give her a charge instead. You can also get a lot of static by peeling off a rayon shirt (do it in the dark some night and you will be amazed at all the sparks), or by rubbing a cat with a glass rod. The classic method of making static was rubbing an amber rod on a silk cloth, but today it is hard even to find amber rods and silk clothes. And none of these methods is very useful either. It turns out that Galvani did not understand very well what he had discovered (we remember that Lavoisier had that same problem). Galvani kept trying to pile up frogs' legs to make a battery because he believed in "animal electricity." The person who figured it out was Alessandro Volta (we commemorate him with *volt*), who piled up metals and figured out how to isolate the metals (there should be wet, salty paper, or something of the sort, between the different metals), to make practical batteries.[6]

By 1800 Volta had it all worked out, and soon we had lots of batteries in various sizes and shapes. We had lots of electricity, and we had it in an easily manageable and controllable form. We had it in delicate doses that would make muscles twitch; we had it in massive amounts that would turn powerful motors. In time we would have it in AC as well as DC, and eventually we would have it all over the countryside. Ultimately almost everything in our lives would be run with electricity, all thanks to Galvani. For most of us, it was his momentous discovery of how to control electricity that mattered. But a gentleman named Johannes Müller was different; for him the important thing was Galvani's discovery that a muscle twitches when its nerve is stimulated electrically.

Professor Müller the Physiologist

Johannes Müller (1801–58) had the same name as Regiomontanus but was not related to him. He was the professor of physiology at the University of Berlin. Of the several scholars and scientists we have encountered so far, very few were professors. In the early days science was dominated by amateurs and gentlemen scientists rather than professionals. Müller's professorship is most important because he had students, and some of his students were extremely important in the history of psychology. He founded an academic empire. His professorship was also important because in his own time he was the authority on all matters physiological. Indeed, he wrote the book on physiology. His *Handbook of Human Physiology*, which came out in pieces between 1833 and 1840, was a large work that embodied virtually everything known about physiology at that time. It rapidly became the standard reference and text, and was soon translated into English. When English-speaking scholars of the next generation or so sought a reference for some physiological datum, they cited the *Handbook*. For example, Darwin cited it rather frequently. Müller believed that neural activity was electrical. Nothing was known at that time about the nerve impulse, so Müller's position was little more than a conjecture. But of course he was right; neural activity is electrical. Müller was also lucky in having a number of brilliant students, whom we turn to now.

The Mechanists

Emil du Bois-Reymond (1818–96) went to work verifying Müller's conjecture, and it was largely through his efforts that neural activity finally came to be seen as electrical. Du Bois-Reymond's intellectual triumph on this matter was marked by his election to the presidency of the Royal Academy in 1858. A number of Müller's students, and most especially du Bois-Reymond, were ardent, militant mechanists. They were deeply opposed to the poetic, romantic **nature philosophy** that had dominated German science earlier in the 1800s (which we will encounter in chapter 4).

Du Bois-Reymond's commitment to the mechanistic philosophy was so strong and so noteworthy that there are some stories about it. It is said that he took the opportunity of his presidential address to assail the romantic, human-spirit types, the *nature-philosophers*, with the following intriguing puzzle. Suppose you encountered a person, and at the same time a robot, a machine that had been cleverly designed to clone the person. This robot is so ingeniously constructed that it not only looked like the person in all respects, it also spoke and acted just as the person did. So when you encounter these two, the person and the machine, you smile and they both smile back. You speak and they both reply to you. You look at their dark brown eyes, and they both look back at you. But while you are looking back and forth between the two sets of eyes it occurs to you that only one pair is really seeing you. The great puzzle is which one is seeing you. Behind one pair of eyes is a human spirit, an immortal soul. But which eyes? They look so much alike you cannot tell. That is the puzzle: How can you determine which is the human and which is just a complicated machine? Du Bois-Reymond's answer to the puzzle was, of course, that both of them are machines, they are merely constructed of different kinds of parts.[7]

There is another story about du Bois-Reymond that involves a pledge. A group of four young men, all students or protégés of Müller, were said to be gathered together at a beer garden one day in 1845. We may suppose that they sealed their pledge with a hearty clanking of mugs and the downing of beer. What was the pledge? No more vitalistic, spiritual, poetic kinds of explanations in physiology; henceforth all explanations in their science would be in physical or chemical terms. They were dedicating themselves to the mechanistic philosophy. Who were these four beer drinkers? One was Emil du Bois-Reymond, who would ultimately become the professor of physiology at Berlin after Müller died. Another was Hermann von Helmholtz, without doubt the greatest of all sensory physiologists. Another was Carl Ludwig, who became the professor at Leipzig. He did a lot of important work and trained countless students, but is perhaps best known for having invented the kymograph (a paper rotating on a drum so that it can record the time course of some measured event, such as a muscle contraction). One of his students, an intense young foreigner named Ivan Pavlov, would carry Ludwig's

Johannes Müller

mechanistic beliefs back to Russia to bolster the materialistic cause there. The fourth of the famous beer drinkers was Ernst Brücke, who went on to become the professor of physiology at the University of Vienna. One of his students was young Sigmund Freud. What an incredible bunch of guys to have beer with![8]

Müller's Doctrine of Specific Nerve Energies

Professor Müller's *Handbook* was full of interesting things, and much of it is still current. But we must remember that physiology concerns itself with lungs and kidneys and other body parts that are of minor interest to psychologists. Our interest tends to focus on the nervous system, and that was perhaps what Müller knew the least about in 1833. But even so, he proclaimed a doctrine about the nervous system that has subsequently become quite famous and has proved quite useful in understanding how to think about it. This is the doctrine of **specific nerve energies**. Basically, it is the idea that the information conveyed by a nerve depends on where the nerve comes from, but the impression the information makes depends on where it goes to. Suppose it were possible to do the delicate surgery necessary to cross-connect the auditory and visual nerves so that the information coming from the ear went to the visual part of the cortex while the impulses originating in the eye ended up in the auditory part of the cortex. If the surgery could be done, then we would have a person who would hear lightning and see thunder. The flash comes from the external world, to be sure, and that is what we see. But the nerves that convey the information are just nerves, just like any other nerves. There is nothing visual about the optic nerve fibers, except that they connect to the visual part of the brain. Lead them somewhere else, such as to the auditory area, and we would not see the flash, we would hear the roar of lightning, and then momentarily later see the color of thunder.

Even dressed up in such a colorful illustration, it is not obvious why this doctrine should be very important. Part of the reason relates to the earlier history of neural activity in which it was widely believed that something visual moves through the optic nerve to make itself known to us, to be literally "seen" by the brain. The Greek atomists, Isaac Newton, and David Hartley (all of whom we will meet later) had envisioned the physical vibrations of light going through the eye and traveling on through the nerves to the brain where they were, somehow, detected by the mind. Müller was saying, no, that is not the way to think of it. Today we have the handy notion of *information*, and we can say that information is conveyed from external object to the eye and to the brain, even though it is coded in different ways as it goes along. Müller was the first to understand clearly that our perception is governed by the decoding process that occurs wherever in the brain the information finally comes in.

Helmholtz and Sensory Physiology

WE TURN NOW to Hermann von Helmholtz (1821–94), the most illustrious of all Müller's associates and probably the greatest sensory physiologist of all time. Helmholtz studied medicine in a program that obliged him to serve for several years as a surgeon in the army. Fortunately, he was stationed in Berlin and had enough spare time to visit the university. This was when, in the 1840s, he worked with Müller and became a friend of du Bois-Reymond. He also worked with Magnus in the physics department. In 1849 he went to Königsberg as professor of physiology. After seven years there, he went to Bonn for two years, and then spent thirteen profitable years at Heidelberg. Finally, in 1871 he completed the cycle by returning to the University of Berlin, succeeding Magnus as the professor of physics.

Helmholtz had diverse skills and wide-ranging interests. Before turning to his work on the sensory systems, it is instructive to note some of the other matters he worked on. He was always proud of a paper he presented to his friends at the Berlin Physical Society in 1847 that dealt with the conservation of energy. Energy can change form, but it cannot be destroyed or created, he argued. If it could be created then we would be able to build a perpetual-motion machine, which we know to be impossible. In 1849 he sought to measure the speed of the nerve impulse. The problem was conceptually plausible but technically beyond reach at that time. There was no way to measure it, and at that time they had no idea what sort of a thing a nerve impulse was. Du Bois-Reymond was just beginning to convince people that it was some sort of electrical event, but no one knew how to measure it yet. Helmholtz figured out a way to measure, not the impulse itself, but how fast it traveled. He trained a subject to respond as fast as he

Hermann von Helmholtz

could on a key to a touch on the foot, and he measured the subject's reaction time. Then he measured the reaction time when he touched the subject on the thigh; it was slightly quicker. The length of the guy's leg divided by the difference in reaction times gave a speed that was not far from that found with modern high-tech methods. The speed of neural transmission was somewhat slower than the speed of sound, and this was a very important finding because it meant that there was nothing magical or mysterious about the neural process; it was a physical phenomenon with parameters, and presumably mechanisms, very like those found in other physical phenomena. Helmholtz had not forgotten the pledge.

There is something about eye color that everyone has observed, but almost no one thinks about. We readily understand that the colored part of the eye, the iris, may be some shade of blue, or green, or brown, or mixed like hazel. Our eyes provide a great range of different colors. And yet everyone has black pupils! Why is that? How is it possible that although skin and hair and iris can be all sorts of different hues and shades, we all have black pupils? So do all of our vertebrate friends, unless they are albino. How do we explain that? We take it so much for granted that hardly anyone ever wonders about those ever-constant black spots. Helmholtz thought about it and arrived at a simple explanation. You look at my pupil and it is black; that is, no light is reflected from it. While you are doing that, I am looking at your pupil, and the light rays from my eye to yours are all nicely focused on points on your retina, and there is no light reflected from there, either. There is no light anywhere in the system—the point on my retina, the spread out light on my pupil, the parallel rays to your pupil, the focused rays falling on your retina—nowhere in that whole system is there any illumination. So no wonder it all looks black. If you had a small lamp in your eyeball, I could see it in there, or if I had a tiny candle inside my eye we would each be able to see inside the other's eyeball. Helmholtz figured that the way to introduce some light into the closed system was with what we now call an ophthalmoscope, a small mirror-like thing with a light source and a lens that a doctor can wear on the forehead. The doctor looks through a small hole in the mirror right into your eyeball and sees all the arteries and other things, including disease processes, you might have in there. All at once Helmholtz had begun the special medical science of ophthalmology!

Helmholtz and Vision

The study of vision goes way back in time, back to and beyond the time of Arab domination of science following the great Islamic empire building. Subsequent physiologists added what was new in their time. Thus, Müller's *Handbook* had a lot to say about vision, but its main function was to stimulate an explosion of vision research in the middle of the 1800s. And Helmholtz was right at the center of this vigorous research activity. To understand the achievement of a couple of decades, note that while Müller's *Handbook*, finally published in 1840, had several chapters on vision, Helmholtz's *Physiological Optics*, which was finished in 1866, presented three full volumes on vision. Helmholtz's great book was definitive for many years; indeed, after more than a century it is still an extremely useful reference. The English edition, which is actually quite close to the original 1866 edition, is still widely used.[9]

Although Helmholtz was largely self-taught, he was well-skilled in a number of disciplines, and this breadth is apparent in the *Physiological Optics*. He begins like an optician, using his own recently invented ophthalmometer to measure visually the curvature of the lens and other parts of the eyeball. He becomes an anatomist when he describes the rods and cones of the retina. He is a mathematician when he is working out equations for the horopter (no one needs to know what that is, but Helmholtz knew all about it), and for focusing and accommodation.

Color Vision

Perhaps Helmholtz's greatest single achievement was his thorough analysis of color vision. Back in 1802 the English physician Thomas Young had proposed that just as artists do not need an infinite array of pigments on their palettes because they can mix paints to obtain intermediate colors, so one does not have to have color detectors for all possible perceived hues. If the eye has a red detector and a green detector, for example, the balance of activity in the two receptors will change according to whether the stimulus is red, or orange, or yellow, or whatever. Only three basic color receptors sensitive to quite different colors are needed to appreciate the whole spectrum of colors. That was Young's theory, but it was basically just theory because he did not have much evidence for it. Helmholtz had the evidence. He studied light mixtures and paint mixtures, he studied afterimages, he studied color-blindness, and he was able to pull all the threads together into a tough and durable fabric. We call it the **Young–Helmholtz color theory.**

The color theory can be regarded as an extension of Müller's doctrine of specific nerve energies. The latter says that color itself is not conveyed by the nerves—you will not see red and green in there—but rather the color information is coded in some way so that impulses going to the color part of the cortex will be interpreted as red if they are coming from a red receptor. What the color theory says is that you do not need to transmit the color, nor do you need a spectrum of receptors, one for each discernable hue. You only need three sorts of receptors. Color is appreciated because of how color information is transmitted to the brain. Moreover, Helmholtz's exhaustive analysis of the matter indicated that there really are only three basic receptors.[10]

Audition

Not content with his *Physiological Optics*, Helmholtz brought out a similar analysis of audition in 1863, *On the Sensations of Tone*, which has appeared in several revised editions in both German and English. A wonderful book, it looks at the physics of sound vibrations, the physiology of the ear, the psychology of tonal perception, and the structure of music. It talks about different kinds of musical instruments, pentatonic and other sorts of scales, and different varieties of harmony. It answers all sorts of questions. For example, if you bang out a D and a D-sharp on your piano, you will hear the individual notes, you will hear dissonance, and you will also hear something wobbling back and forth about six times a second—what we call a beat. Is such a beat a physical entity—is there something going on six times a second in the ear—or is it psychological, something that the perceiver constructs? The mechanist Helmholtz was looking for a physiological answer. The answer, according to Helmholtz's extensive analysis of the question, is yes and no. There is indeed something happening in the ear. The organ of Corti is vibrating six times a second in the vicinity of where the two similar notes are detected, but on the other hand, we do not hear this six-cycle event directly because nowhere on the organ of Corti is there any sensitivity to such an event. Our perception is therefore central. What we hear is the D-note getting louder and softer six times a second.

It is important to notice that Helmholtz had a vested interest in the question. He had a strategy in such questions. He wanted the answer to be physiological. He wanted to find the correlate of the beat in the ear because he did not want it to be psychological. Physiology is science, the physical, chemical forces that control everything in nature. Psychological matters are strange and weird and rather uncomfortable for the mechanist. So he wanted to find something physiological in the ear to which he could relate the perception of beats. And he finds it. We have to keep in mind that Helmholtz was basically a physicist; he was never happier than when he ultimately got to Berlin and could be a full-time physicist.[11]

Helmholtz's Quandary

Physiological Optics was organized in three volumes. The first dealt with physical things, such as the optical, that is, physical, properties of the eyeball. This discussion found Helmholtz in his most natural element. To the extent that physiology is a mechanistic science, he was pretty comfortable in the second volume discussing matters of color perception, because he had been able to work out the explanation of color in terms of physiological properties of the color receptors. And that is one of his great contributions, the reduction of an important psychological dimension, color, to purely physiological mechanisms. And reductionism is what the physiological approach is all about. The third volume of the *Physiological Optics* was about space perception, and that was something else. There the great mechanist was finally obliged to confront psychological questions because space perception appeared to depend on learning. And, alas, now that we have Helmholtz facing the quandary of psychology, standing there on the psychological brink, we must abandon him in that precarious position while we turn to other matters. But we will be back in chapter 5 to rescue him.

Summary

DESCARTES STOOD on the threshhold. Behind him lay the ancient medical tradition of Galen (animal spirits, and so on), while ahead of him stretched physiological research. Behind him lay the philosophy of Aristotle; ahead stood a mechanistic point of view. Back there was the world of religion; in front of him was science. Descartes' particular physiological speculations did not endure very well, but that is not important; what matters is that other researchers were inspired to test his speculations and come up with better alternatives.

One of Descartes' concepts that did endure was the idea of reflexive movement. Psychology might have begun with the study of reflexes, but that research tradition had a rather irregular and uncertain course and did not contribute directly to psychological thought until many years later. Similarly, Descartes' work on emotion and instinct had little direct effect on the development of psychology. So although he had a more psychological view of many topics than any of his predecessors, he was not directly connected with the eventual development of experimental psychology.

And in spite of some remarkable discoveries about the localization of function in the nervous system in the 19th century, those discoveries also did not lead directly into psychology.

Considerably more relevant to our story was the work of Professor Müller and some of his students, which began to clear up some of the mystery of the nervous system. They, and particularly du Bois-Reymond, vigorously promoted a mechanistic view of physiology. They, again led by du Bois-Reymond, demonstrated the electrical nature of the nerve impulse. Helmholtz measured the speed of neural transmission. Müller's doctrine of specific nerve energies suggested something of how the brain decodes sensory information. Helmholtz extended Müller's doctrine to color vision and to a number of auditory phenomena. And we can see that the focus was shifting to sensory physiology. We can anticipate that experimental psychology would grow out of this kind of physiological research. Physiological work on vision, audition, and especially touch would become an important part of the story of psychology.

Notes

1. Descartes's first book was *The World*, which he wrote in 1633 but withheld from publication because it was Copernican in orientation and he had discovered the troubles Galileo was having with the Inquisition for defending and promoting the Copernican world view. The book, which gives his theory of vortices, was not published until after his death. Certainly Descartes' greatest work was the *Discourse on Method*, which came out in 1637. In 1937 the French postal authorities quite appropriately issued a stamp to commemorate the great book; the stamp shows Descartes and the title page of the book. Unfortunately, they misspelled the title! They brought out a corrected stamp right away, but then realized that the error would soon become a collector's item, so they were obliged to print millions more of the error. Thus we have *two* fairly common French stamps to commemorate his greatest book. He wrote *Meditations* in 1641 and *Principles of Philosophy* in 1644. *Passions of the Soul*, which deals with emotion and instinct, appeared in 1649. *Treatise on Man* in 1662 and *The World* in 1664 were his major posthumous works. The standard collection of English translations is Haldane and Ross (1955).

The standard biography of Descartes is Haldane (1905). More readable and more recent is Vrooman (1970). A good one-chapter account is found in Fancher's charming book (1990). Fancher is high on Descartes, ready to consider him something like the grandfather of modern psychology, and that is not a bad judgment. All biographical accounts of the great thinker confront serious difficulties because Descartes was such an extraordinarily private and secretive person. He had almost no friends apart from Marin Mersenne in Paris, whom he rarely saw but did write to. He never married. He spent the last 20 years of his life, very productive years, wandering in Holland, and no one except Mersenne knew where he was.

2. Some commentators have suggested that Descartes was concerned about how the Church might react to a portrayal of man with no soul. This was a reasonable concern, and actually his works were all put on the Index, that is, forbidden to Catholics, shortly after *The World* appeared. A more interesting possibility has also been suggested: Perhaps because he was a good Catholic he was distressed by where his thought had led him. He could handle his non-Aristotelian view of the world, because that was not really central to the Church's philosophy. Nor was how the body functions a central part of it. But the Church's position on the soul was right at the heart of things, and that was something Descartes could not bring himself to doubt.

3. All of this material on reflexes comes from Fearing (1930).

4. The incident of 1853, which came about because Lotze reviewed Pflüger's monograph, is also mentioned by Fearing (1930), but he attached little importance to it. I go with Boring (1950), page 38, who thought it was important.

5. The wondrous world of the phrenologists and the localization problem generally are briefly described by Fancher (1990) and Krech (1962).

6. The battery story is told by Conant (1947).

7. Du Bois-Reymond's story about the robot was told to me many years ago by M. R. Rosenzweig, but he no longer remembers where he encountered it.

8. The pledge to defend the mechanistic philosophy was very important historically because, as we will see in chapter 4, German scientists at that time were generally not very mechanistic. The story of the pledge is well known because Boring (1950) talks about it. I have given Boring's account of it, plus I have added the beer to resurrect the participants, as it were, and make it a story about people. Boring cites Bernfeld (1944) as his source, but Bernfeld actually tells a somewhat different story. According to Bernfeld, what happened in 1845 was that some of Müller's young associates formed a small private group that they called the Berlin Physical Society, in which they and a few additional right-minded scholars discussed these matters at some length. The only pledging Bernfeld mentions is described in 1842 by du Bois-Reymond himself, and it was a pledge just between him and Brücke. Bernfeld translates du Bois-Reymond's statement of that pledge: "No other forces than common physical chemical ones are active within the organism," and these words are repeated by Boring. Boring had the spirit of the thing right, though, because the four men were indeed very close, life-long friends, they were all about the same age, and they were all vigorous crusaders for the mechanistic faith.

9. Helmholtz wrote extensively on all sorts of topics. The three volumes of the great *Handbook of Physiological Optics* came out in 1856, 1860, and 1866. Then it was revised in 1885–94. A further German edition was brought out in 1911, long after his death. Then, much to our benefit, there was an English edition in 1925 that contain notes and additions by various editors. *On the Sensations of Tone* first appeared in 1863, and it was frequently revised. It too is in English. The standard biography of Helmholtz is by Königsberger, which has been translated by Welby (1906).

10. Although the main lines of the Young–Helmholtz color theory still hold good, there has been a great mass of research on color vision over the years, and as might be expected quite a number of details have been changed. And there have been a number of alternative color theories that have come along to challenge Helmholtz's analysis. One of the most troublesome of these was one of the first, the theory proposed in 1874 by Ewald Hering (1834–1918). But Helmholtz was even more troubled by Hering's earlier (1864) theory of space perception, because it carried on the tradition of Goethe and Purkinje, which we will discuss in chapter 4.

11. Two of Helmholtz's physics students at Berlin, Hertz and Pupin, essentially gave us radio and modern broadcasting. Hertz discovered radio-frequency radiation, and Pupin supported a student at Columbia University named Howard Armstrong who invented virtually all of our important radio circuits.

Chapter Three

Philosophical Themes

FOUR THEMES RUN all through the history of psychology. One of them is associationism, the linking of psychological events. Not all psychologists believe in it, but over the years so many psychologists have endorsed it that it has become a sort of unifying or defining principle. Empiricism, the doctrine that knowledge comes only from experience, is another theme that remains very popular year after year. So too, a mechanistic orientation, such as Descartes demonstrated, is often apparent in those who think about psychological matters, and this has been apparent from his time to our own. Atomism, the belief that a phenomenon is best explained by analyzing it into its basic parts, is another perennial idea in the history of psychology. In later chapters we will see how these themes have become interwoven and intertwined so that they hold together the story of psychology. We will note some other important themes as well, but these four are the major ones. In this chapter we will see where these conceptual themes came from. We will see that they were all well known to the early Greek philosophers, but that they were lost over the years and had to be rediscovered in modern times.

Prelude

INTELLECTUALLY, GALILEO and Descartes, who were so important in the beginning of modern science and philosophy, were much more closely related to the early Greek philosophers than they were to their immediate predecessors. There was a discontinuity in there, a curious lack of progress in both science and philosophy, that we must look at before going on with our story.

The Greek philosophers considered and debated many issues, including our four themes, but perhaps more than anything else the Greeks were rationalists. They glorified the human mind. They believed that we can better appreciate ourselves and the world we live in by thinking about ourselves and

Aristotle

our world. A number of provocative schemes were proposed to make sense of it all. Many of these philosophical schemes dealt with the obvious duality of human experience, the fact that we have both a mental and a physical existence. Aristotle (384–322 B.C.), the greatest of philosophers, was certainly a rationalist who believed in the powers of the mind, but he was also a scientist who believed in the physical reality. But whereas later philosophers might see the two worlds in conflict or as incompatible, Aristotle wove them together into a wonderful, complex system.[1]

He said that plants and animals have nutritive souls, the power to grow and reproduce. In addition, animals have sensitive souls, the power to sense events in the environment. In addition, the human has a rational soul, the ability to reason. For Aristotle, therefore, *soul* is not a spiritual concept but more like the way something functions. It is not something separate from the physical entity, but rather the power of the physical entity to do what it does. The soul is to the body as vision is to the eye, he said. Aristotle criticized many of his predecessors for being crude mechanists; he said they only understood one kind of causation, the mechanical kind. He, on the other hand, recognized four varieties of causation that generally worked together to provide a full explanation of natural phenomena. The *efficient* cause is what the mechanist relies on; it is the force—the push or impetus—that makes the event happen. There is also the *material* cause, the hand or tool or whatever that delivers the force. Then there is the *formal* cause, which is the form or shape that the event or object takes, as when a statue begins to take shape. Finally, there is a *final* cause, which is the reason or purpose realized, as when a boy grows up to be a man. We cannot deal with the boy growing up without looking at all of these aspects of the process.

Aristotle dealt with all of our four major themes. He was comfortable with mechanical systems (we have already seen his heavenly spheres) but he rejected the atomism of his predecessor Democritus because it was nothing

48

but mechanical. He also anticipated empiricism, which we will discuss here shortly. Thus, he said that we come to understand things by reasoning, but we can also learn through experience, directly through our senses. All it takes is sense and memory. And in discussing memory Aristotle anticipated associationism. There were a lot of pieces of what could have been an Aristotelian psychology.[2]

Aristotle died in 322 B.C., just a year after Alexander the Great died. Curiously, Aristotle had been his tutor when Alexander was a boy, and Aristotle's father had been the doctor of Alexander's father, King Philip. The great days of Athens were pretty well over by the time of Alexander's conquest, and Greece rapidly lost its glory when Alexander's short-lived empire began to disintegrate. People moved all over, east and west, and took their philosophies and their religions with them. Athens lost its place as an intellectual center, and the happy rationalistic spirit that had made it a very special center was gone. It was replaced by a negative, skeptical attitude. Aristotle had taught that the human being should be understood in the same terms and explained in the same way as we understand any other natural entity. We grow and reproduce just like everything else, he said. This attitude, which we call **naturalism**, was also lost; it was replaced by various kinds of spiritualism. *Soul* became what it is today, a spiritual concept, something that is not to be bound by the laws that apply to the rest of the world. Science disappeared, except for a few remarkable systemists such as Galen the physiologist, Euclid the mathematician, and Ptolemy the astronomer (all about A.D. 200).

The Churchmen

There might have been a reaction to this spiritualism to restore reasonable values, but that did not happen. The Romans were in charge, and art, literature, science, and philosophy were all in trouble. As the Roman Empire began to crumble, all that survived was skepticism, spiritualism, and mysticism. And for many centuries it only got worse. Saint Augustine (354–430) marked the end of rationalism. He said that we only play games with ourselves by thinking about things. Meaningful and valuable knowledge and understanding can come only through faith. Augustine's passionate message was totally compelling. Or at least it was totally dominant; perhaps there was nothing else to read (almost nothing of the classic Greek work had survived the intervening seven centuries). Rationality was dead. Science was dead. There was no hope for anything like psychology. The only survivor was faith. One wonders if anyone at the time noticed how intellectually grim it looked.

What little scholarship and science could be found in the next centuries were found in the Arabic world. Arab scholars kept the word of the Greeks alive, and added to it some of their own thinking. Then, in the 1200s, things began to turn around. Amazingly, Aristotle's works began to trickle back into the Western world. Many of his writings, generally in Arabic or Latin translation, were collected at the University of Paris. In 1245 a young man named Thomas Aquinas (1225–74) went to Paris to begin his life-long study of Aristotle. In connection with something else, Aristotle once said that some souls are immortal. By emphasizing such points, and by de-emphasizing other points, Aquinas was able to reconcile the word of the great philosopher with the word of God. But, of course, as a believer, he *had* to find a reconciliation. And being the great theologian that he was, he did. In time and after some debate, his analysis was accepted by parts of the Church. The Dominican order, to which Aquinas belonged, came first. Only a few years after his death Thomas Aquinas was sainted, and in due course Aristotle became the Church's official philosopher. After 15 centuries he was back—sort of back. There is not much Aristotle to be found in the catechism.

While Aquinas was working out his remarkable reconciliation, he was taking what looks like a dangerous step. He was reintroducing reason. Augustine had excluded reason, but Aquinas brought it back. In the Thomistic approach faith and reason stood side by side; they were never contradictory, but always supported each other. Faith and reason were the two sources of human knowledge. What you know through faith comes from revelation—what your priest tells you. What you know through reason, philosophical understanding, comes largely from what St. Thomas tells you. But there was room for discussion and debate because the Church had also taken a dangerous step. It had encouraged its scholars to think about things. And to facilitate scholarly activity it had sponsored and supported what would become great universities. By 1300 there were universities at Paris, Oxford, Padua (later the home of Galileo), and other places. The era was called, for good reason, the scholastic period.

The Recovery

There was a gradual return of the rationalistic spirit, and a slowly growing concern for art, literature, medicine, and science. The Renaissance (literally, a rebirth) ushered in a new era of human culture and activity. A lot of attention was focused on the lost glories of antiquity. A lot of effort was put to the practical day-to-day matters of politics, trade, and making money. People began thinking about themselves again. It was discovered that people have many problems, problems other than how to get to heaven. Early in the 1600s we began to enter a new era, the modern era. There is the curious irony, though, that by this time the philosophy and science of Aristotle, which had been lost for so long, had come to assume a position of authority; it had become dogma. The emergence of the modern era was largely based on the overthrow of this relatively new Aristotelian dogma.[3]

Gassendi and Atomism

IN CHAPTER 2 I mentioned a friend of Descartes named Mersenne. He was Martin Mersenne (1588–1648), a friar of the Minimite order and a mathematician who taught philosophy in Paris. He is now known mainly for his contributions to number theory and for his translation of Euclid's *Geometry*, but he also wrote about the physical basis of sound, musical instruments, and voice (Mersenne, 1646). Mersenne's real importance, however, lay not in his own intellectual contributions but in the fact that he gathered around him a circle of friends, and he corresponded with his friends. Mathematicians, astronomers, and philosophers were all included in his circle, and through him kept in touch with one another. He was in contact with Galileo, and we saw that he was virtually the only contact Descartes had with the rest of the world. Gassendi was another member of Mersenne's circle.

Pierre Gassendi (1592–1655) had come upon the ancient work of Epicurus, and devoted much of his life to promoting and popularizing Epicurus's ideas. Such ideas were needed in the new, emerging era of science, he thought, especially since confidence was collapsing in the Aristotelian system. The wisdom of Epicurus was destined to fill the need for a new scientific framework, Gassendi believed, and he was there to make it known to the world. Although Mersenne's friends differed among themselves on how to interpret some of the details, they all endorsed Epicurus's basic notion that matter consists of atoms—nothing else—only atoms. A particular kind of substance has to have a particular kind of atom that gives it its own physical properties. Thus, the atoms of a liquid are round and smooth so they can slide over one another easily. And so a liquid is fluid. A solid substance contains rough, bumpy, jagged atoms, and maybe they have little hooks on them to help them stick together to make a rigid object.

Atoms and Properties

In Aristotle's system, different substances possessed different powers and properties. When Priestley and the old chemists spoke of phlogiston they were in the Aristotelian mode, because they were talking about having the power to burn. Lavoisier was the atomist, because he attributed burning to the kind of stuff oxygen was, to the kind of atoms it had. Lavoisier's revolution was a replay of the ancient contest, about 300 B.C., between Aristotle and Epicurus.[4]

Epicurus believed that atoms are very small, so small they could not be seen. Therefore it was possible for atoms to be quite different from a visible mass of stuff. It seems that nothing is quite the way it appears (which is the essential truth of philosophy). Epicurus thought of atoms differing in size, shape, and roughness. Some of Mersenne's friends introduced a new dimension. Atoms *move* in different ways. Galileo supposed that liquids are made up of atoms in motion. Gases contain still more mobile atoms, while a flame contains the most rapidly moving ones. They are active little rascals that dart back and forth and penetrate other substances, heating them up or melting them. If one mixed such high energy atoms with ordinary matter, one could change the state of the matter. Descartes's view of atoms made them of different sizes and shapes, but all of the same sort of material. All the old atomistic ideas were revived, explored, and debated.

The atomism issue has always been an important one in psychology. Later on we will witness the prolonged debate between psychological atomists, who hold that any large perception is made up of a number of very small sensory pieces, and wholistic psychologists, who believe that a large perception, such as the perception of an object, is direct and immediate and not made up of its parts. The same kind of question arises in the study of behavior. Should we concentrate on small motor units, a contraction here and a twitch there, or rather on large, coordinated acts? The atomism issue never seems to go away.

Hedonism

Gassendi's presentation of Epicurus also called attention to another old Greek idea, the notion of **hedonism**. In its original form, the argument of the hedonists was that pleasure was good and hence ought to be sought. The "ought" part of this makes it an ethical or moral question. The Epicureans argued that pleasure is good not just because it feels good, but because it is ethically and morally good; pleasure ought to be sought because it is the right thing. The other side of it is that pain is bad, not only unpleasant, but philosophically wrong. It is bad, wrong, and evil. Gassendi maintained that even after centuries of moralistic theorizing, hedonism was still a good doctrine. It was surely not as bad as the moralists, the churchmen and the like had made it out to be. Epicurus had emphasized that pleasure was to be measured over the long haul, after all was said and done. The wise man, he said, is one who foresees the consequences of his actions and acts so as to maximize his long-term pleasure. The ethical hedonist is by no means an impulsive pleasure-seeker, as the pious have often argued. On the contrary, the hedonist is a wise person who plans a meaningful life of work and friendship. Thus, friendship among people is good because it produces long-term pleasure. Enduring friendship is far better than a fleeting indulgence.

No sooner was the old ethical hedonism revived by Gassendi than he began to change it. Everyone had understood that people *often* seek pleasure and try to avoid pain; that was what the centuries of moralizing had been about. We should concentrate, it was argued, on acting so as to be honorable, dutiful, righteous, and so on. But is it possible that we are *always* seeking pleasure and avoiding pain? Do we have a universal principle here? Gassendi and his friend Thomas Hobbes (whom we will meet next) argued yes, we invariably behave hedonistically. What this means, if it is true, is that the moral and ethical question is no longer important. If we always act hedonistically then it makes no difference if that is good or bad, it is just how we act. The age-old question of ethical hedonism was suddenly replaced with something much more interesting, at least to us—the possibility of a psychological hedonism, a psychological law that promised to explain behavior.

Those years around 1630, when Gassendi was busy with his life's work, must have been wonderfully challenging. The Aristotelian grip on science was loosening. The Copernican revolution was becoming resolved, and astronomy was becoming a new kind of science. Under the leadership of Galileo physics was taking off and becoming a quantitative science. The medical sciences were also beginning to move forward: William Harvey had just demonstrated how blood flows through the body. Other scholars, such as Francis Bacon, were looking critically at the whole enterprise of science. It was a time of intellectual turmoil. And Gassendi was right: The new success and promise of the sciences called for a new and different philosophy, one that was much more mechanistic than what had prevailed. Aristotle's grip on philosophy was loosening, too.

Hobbes and Mechanism

MECHANISM IS the philosophical view that everything will ultimately be explained mechanically, in terms of machinery. We have always been accustomed to thinking about physical systems, rocks and planets, wheels and engines, in terms of mechanical principles. But the mechanist wants much more—the mechanist also wants people and animals and everything else to follow mechanistic principles. It is rather like the opposite of animism, in which all sorts of natural and physical events are given mentalistic explanations. The mechanist wants to do away with mentalistic interpretations and reduce everything, including the mind, to physical factors. We saw Descartes suggest this point of view but then back away from the possibility and settle for a traditional dualistic position that had both mechanical and mental explanatory factors. A braver, bolder soul, perhaps the first thoroughgoing mechanist, was Thomas Hobbes (1588–1679); he went all the way. His major work, *Leviathan*, was published in 1651. Taken literally, "leviathan" means giant, but the giant Hobbes was referring to was government. The bulk of the book was addressed to social issues and political science, but the first chapter was pure psychology.

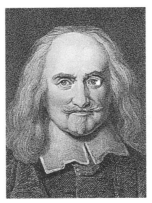

Thomas Hobbes

Leviathan is a charming book; even after three centuries it is a delight to read and provocative to think about. Hobbes does not play around; he tells us simply and directly how things are. There is nothing but atoms, he says, atoms in motion. What we take to be mental activity is really just atoms bumping into each other in the brain. It is nothing but mechanical events occurring in the brain. And when there are vibrations in the area of the heart, then we have a different experience, one of emotion. This agitation around the heart gets communicated to the brain so that we become aware of the emotional feeling. And that, Hobbes tells us, is all there is to our mental life. Clearly, he wanted to do away with the mind and reduce it to a mechanical system. Because he was the first to attempt such a translation, he was not very sophisticated about it. Today we are much more clever in eliminating mentalistic language. But Hobbes did not have our advantage; sometimes he referred to awareness of emotion and sometimes he spoke of awareness as being no more than atoms rattling around in the head. But his intention was clear: It was to make everything mechanical without any place being left for what he took to be imaginary intellectual or rational powers of the mind.

[margin note: MENTAL ACTIVITY]

Mechanistic Heresies

The conventional way to account for behavior was in terms of volition, by reference to free will. We desire to execute a certain action, so we elect to do it, and then we do it. But in Hobbes's view what really happens is that we think of an act, and if that thought is associated with the idea of pleasure, then the blood thins out and becomes more volatile, and the response occurs. On the other hand, if we think of some act that results in a negative consequence, some pain, then the negative emotion thickens the blood, congeals it, and the action is inhibited. Here we see Hobbes going for a deterministic sort of

[margin note: FREE WILL]

hedonism. The ideas of pleasure and pain act directly, because of the mechanics of the body, to control our behavior. So for Hobbes there was no free choice. He acknowledged that sometimes we seem to be "making up our mind," and it may feel to us as though that were the case. But what is happening there is merely that we think of one action and then of another action. And our thoughts, that is, the atoms moving in the brain, move back and forth. Then the last thought we have just prior to actually acting we tend to think of as our volition. But it is not that, Hobbes says; volition is not something extra we add on that controls our actions, it is merely the last thing we think of before we act. So there is no free will.

There is no rationality either, according to Hobbes. What appears to us to be thinking is no more than one set of atoms moving about in the head and bumping into another. If that series of events, that movement of atoms, has happened in the past then it will happen again. He attributed thinking to what would later be called the association of ideas:

> Of our conceptions of the past we make a future. . . . After a man hath been accustomed to see antecedents followed by like consequences, when he sees [it comes about again], he looks there should follow it the same as followed then.
>
> Hobbes (1650), ch. 4, p. 7

He thus provided a totally new view of human behavior, a dramatic break with the Aristotelian tradition. There was no longer any moral judgment involved in human behavior. What appear to be moral decisions occur simply through ideas becoming associated, and that happens for purely mechanical reasons. Hobbes had created a new kind of psychology based on the mechanical view of the world developed by Gassendi, Galileo, and Descartes.

Hobbes did not work out the details of his psychology; we have little more than an outline. His main purpose in *Leviathan* was to deal with social phenomena. For example, he considered why, if people are basically hedonistic, they commit themselves to a social system and accept citizenship in the state when the state makes them subservient and requires them to pay taxes, serve in the army, and so on. Hobbes's answer is that it is advantageous in the long run for the citizen to have a sort of understood contract with the government. Yes, the citizen may be obliged to pay taxes, but on the other hand the government is obliged to protect and defend the citizen. From a long-term Epicurean point of view, it is better all around to have such a contract. Further analysis led Hobbes to the conclusion that it is politically best when an autocratic monarch exercises absolute power. This is not because of any "divine right of kings," but because it works out better for everyone that way.[5]

An unusual feature of Hobbes's writing is that most of it was in English. Nearly all scholars up to that time wrote in Latin, but Hobbes presented his work in English and hence it was widely read and appreciated (and criticized).

Hobbes also violates the rule that revolutionaries and innovators tend to be young people. Hobbes may have been new as a philosopher, but he was 63 when *Leviathan* came out. He stands as something of an inspiration to those who are approaching senior citizenship, because his example suggests it may never be too late to do something important. One complaint his reader might lodge against him is that he did not pursue any topic in sufficient detail to satisfy the reader. He did not write enough about social contracts, or mechanisms of the mind, or anything else, but what he did write was bold and startling. And what he wrote had a great impact. His position in the history of ideas has been much underrated.

Boyle, the Transition Man

A KEY FIGURE in the early advance of mechanistic thinking was Robert Boyle, who was one of the founders of the **Royal Society** in England in 1662. By then Descartes and Galileo were gone, and Hobbes was retired. But the mechanistic movement had infused much of the intellectual world, particularly in England and France. Boyle was primarily a physicist who did experiments to examine the properties of gases. Descartes had defended the idea that there was no such thing as empty space. Matter existed everywhere, he argued. What looked like empty space was actually made up of very small, vacuous atoms. And that was what Boyle wanted to investigate. He perfected the airpump, which made it possible to demonstrate a vacuum; if all the air was removed from a metal vessel it might collapse under the pressure of the air surrounding it. Air could then be regarded as a finely divided substance made up of atoms spaced far apart (which is the modern way of thinking of it). In testing out these ideas Boyle gathered a lot of support for an Epicurean atomism, and he spent the rest of his days defending it.

Boyle was also interested in vision, and that interest was to have considerable impact on later developments. He wondered whether a substance of a particular color might have atoms with some distinctive property. Perhaps if the atoms of an object had a certain size, then the object would be red, and atoms a little smaller might produce yellow. If that could be demonstrated experimentally, Boyle supposed, it would provide complete confirmation of the Epicurean doctrine. Boyle started his good friend Isaac Newton working on the problem. The brilliant young mathematician worked on it for some time, but got nowhere with it.

Boyle had another friend who is central to our story, and that was John Locke. The two of them were together at Oxford. Locke, who was a doctor, once helped him medically, and they remained very good friends. It seems clear that Locke had complete confidence in Boyle's judgment about physical

John Locke

matters. Although Locke had been trained as a doctor, he had little interest in mechanical or physical systems (he said he did not intend to meddle in such matters). Even so, there are places in Locke's writings, a footnote here, a paragraph there, where he seems to endorse the atomistic world view that Boyle had spoken for so effectively. Locke also endorsed other features of the Epicurean philosophy, such as hedonism. But Locke takes us around a conceptual corner, because while he shared with the mechanists many of their beliefs in atomism, hedonism, and determinism, he was not a mechanist. He did not share Descartes's passion for physical machinery or Hobbes's desire to mechanize the mind. But let us look at Locke's position more systematically.

Locke and Empiricism

JOHN LOCKE (1632–1704) was an Englishman, a doctor, a politician, and a scientist. He became a Fellow of the Royal Society in 1668. His occupation was secretary, but he did much more than sit at a little desk. He worked for the Lord of Shaftesbury, a very important man in politics, as advisor, counsel, doctor, and spokesman, all of which made Locke himself a very important man. In addition, he was an impressive philosopher; he was much more thorough, logical, and elegant than Hobbes. His major philosophical work, *Essay Concerning Human Understanding* (1690), presents a powerful, compelling message. He says that our understanding of things, our world, and ourselves comes from experience. *All* of our knowledge and understanding comes from experience. There is a name for this position; it is called empiricism.

57

Opposition to Innate Ideas

Locke presented his empiricism in opposition to the ancient doctrine of innate ideas that had been articulated by Plato and that had somehow survived all the intervening years. Locke said, for example, very much as a psychologist would be likely to say today, that we get our idea of a triangle through having seen a lot of triangles. After seeing innumerable figures with three sides and three corners, we acquire the concept, the *idea*, of a triangle. Plato maintained that there is an idea of triangularity that has reality and existence whether you and I appreciate it or not. The innate idea has its own life quite independently of you and me. I might think I learned about it in kindergarten, but Plato would say, no, that was when I cleared away my ignorance and confusion and was able to appreciate it. The idea had been there all the time, waiting for me to get to it. Locke rejected all this. He said that in the beginning there is nothing in the mind; it is a *tabula rasa*, a clear slate. There is nothing there prior to experience. He observed that primitive people and toddlers have no idea of triangle, or God, or any of the other abstractions so important to Plato and his followers.

Locke saw the old doctrine of innate ideas as being very conservative and as serving conservative interests. And he was a liberal. His empiricism and, indeed, almost everything in his *Essay*, reflected his liberalism. He argued that it is wrong to believe something simply because someone in authority, or your society in general, believes in it. If your society holds to a particular belief and requires you to believe it too, if it tells you that you must believe it because it is an innate idea, then that is a restraint on your personal liberty and a kind of tyranny upon your mind. True understanding comes from either having experienced it or having thought about it and come to your own conclusion. Anything else is intellectual gangsterism. If, for example, we believe in the goodness of God by reflecting on our situation and the logical necessity of His goodness, then we are free and that belief is really our own. But if we are obliged to believe in God's goodness because our society requires it, then we are not free; we are intellectual slaves of the society. So Locke's empiricism arose largely from his distrust of authority. He said that one could not believe what the priests said about religion, what the professors said about philosophy, or what the king said about the country. We must learn from experience.

The Importance of Experience

According to Locke, there are two kinds of experience, one that arrives from the senses, our eyes and ears, and the other that we sense when we look inside, what he called reflection, and see the mind in operation. We can see ourselves sensing, thinking, remembering, and willing. However, Locke paid little attention to reflection because he was not very interested in the actual functioning of the mind, what it does, or how it works. His attention was mainly focused on how our ideas are built up with experience. Ultimately, all of our ideas come from the senses; they depend on what we have experienced. Locke challenged his reader to think of a smell that has never been smelled before.

Our ideas correspond to our sensory experiences. If I see an apple I have a sensation of red. I will also have sensations of round, and shiny, and a number of such elemental sensations. Then with experience I will have a number of corresponding ideas, the ideas of red, of round, and so on. These are all elemental ideas, what Locke called *simple ideas*. With experience these simple ideas will coalesce to form a *complex idea*—the idea of apple. It is only after this synthesis has occurred that I will see the apple as an object and understand it to be what it is. Thus, our ideas of things are constructed from the simple ideas corresponding to their simple sensory properties.

Locke's Psychological Atomism

Locke's conviction that complex ideas are built up of simple ones reveals the atomism inherent in his system. If we are to understand all of our interesting, subtle, abstract ideas, then we have to analyze them into their basic sensory elements. We do not at first see the object; we see its color, shape, and size; we smell the different dimensions of its odor; hear the different qualities of noise it makes. It is only when these sensory qualities have been merged by experience that we can perceive the object, or think of it. Just as the atoms comprising a thing in the physical world do not look like the thing itself, so in the mental world: The simple sensations leading to the complex idea do not look much like the object. A round, red, shiny sensation does not really look like an apple, but that does not matter as long as it arouses the idea of apple. The atomist assumes that appearances are deceiving. It is interesting that while Locke probably believed in the atomic physical world of Hobbes and Boyle, he made no reference to it and there was nothing mechanistic in his philosophy. The atomism is obvious, but it was a new mentalistic atomism, not the old, familiar physical variety.

Locke also shared with the mechanistic atomists their reliance on hedonism as an explanatory principle. He argued that our actions are always governed by our anticipations of pleasure and pain. At one point when Locke was considering the problem of virtue, he noted that a man might be at a bar, see a drink in front of him, anticipate the pleasure of intoxication, and gulp it down. There might be a second man sitting right next to him at the bar who also sees a drink in front of him and who also anticipates the pleasure of intoxication. But this other man also thinks of the disagreeableness of a hangover, and he abstains. The first man might be a drunkard, while the second might be regarded as a man of virtue. Locke insists, however, that virtue has nothing whatever to do with it. Both men are hedonists, trying to maximize forthcoming pleasure; they differ only in the pleasures and pains they foresee. The so-called man of virtue has no particular virtue, but he does have a longer-range view of things. Epicurus would no doubt have been delighted with Locke's illustration of the hedonistic principle, as well as his further observation that if the hangover preceded the intoxication, then no one would drink.

More than anything else, Locke was a social reformer. He was a liberal and an outspoken advocate of various liberal causes, and his philosophy has to be regarded in that context. He had lived through some trying times. Just before the *Essay* was published, he deemed it prudent to flee England and retire to Holland. He wanted to build a better world, and he would build it through education. If our understanding depends upon experience, if our ideas come from what we have seen and heard, then education is crucial. Education can liberate us from the social bonds and shackles into which we are born. That was, in effect, what he said, and what he said was very widely heard, heralded by some and scorned by others.

Some Problems for Locke

As thorough and convincing as he was, there were some problems with Locke's analysis that were apparent to both friend and foe. If our ideas come from experience, do we *receive* our ideas from experience, or do we *create* them out of experience? Are we the authors of our ideas, or do they just arise and present themselves to us? Are we active or passive as our ideas come and go in our experience? Locke was inclined to the active position, to the position that we create our ideas from experience, but he was never explicit about where he stood. The human mind seems to be rather active because it is said to be engaged in remembering, comparing, and so on, but Locke gave us no assurance that the mind can select what idea it wants to work on.

A further problem is that if complex ideas are just combinations of simple ideas, and if the perception of an object is just the combination of its various sensory qualities—and even if we agree that this sort of psychological atomism is valid—then we must wonder about the combining principle. What kind of glue holds the atoms together? Epicurus gave us some physical hooks so that physical atoms could hold on to each other. But Locke gave us no psychological hooks to hold complex ideas together. He could have used a concept of association, but he chose not to do that. Hobbes had such a thing some years earlier (as we saw earlier in the chapter), but Locke rejected that possibility. Nor did he offer an alternative mechanism. Locke simply was not an associationist, even though from our perspective he looks as though he should have been one. He understood that events could become connected through association, but he only used that word to refer to anomalies of learning. For example, he tells of a person who saw a friend die, and who ever since had emotional reactions whenever he entered the room where his friend had died. He saw learning by association as a failure of the ordinary learning processes. Like Hobbes, Locke believed that the main mechanism in behavior was the combination of some idea with the idea of pleasure or pain, but he would not tell us what the combination process was. But these were minor problems for Locke's system. He gave life and spirit to English philosophy, and to psychology he gave empiricism, a magnificent gift.

Berkeley and the Metaphysical Problem

GEORGE BERKELEY (1685–1753) was an Irishman, a deacon, and ultimately a bishop in the Anglican church. Like Newton, but unlike Hobbes and Locke, his major intellectual achievements came when he was quite young. Berkeley saw a threat to his faith in the new mechanistic science of Boyle and Newton and the deterministic philosophy of Locke. He therefore undertook to deny the very existence of the material world, and to provide a new proof for the existence of God.[6]

Berkeley accepted Locke's premise that the mind can know only its own ideas; that was his starting point. But he rejected Locke's next step of assuming that the mind could work actively upon simple ideas to construct new complex ideas. All we ever have, he said, is the perceptions themselves, and they are always concrete and particular, and never abstract. For example, suppose I try to formulate the abstract idea *woman*. I cannot do it; I always think of some particular woman having her own age, size, color, features, and so on. There is no *woman* in the abstract, it is only a word.

Berkeley's Skepticism

Berkeley's argument can be extended to the existence of all material objects. If my mind can know only its own ideas, and these are always concrete and correspond to my perceptions of objects, then my knowledge must be limited to my own perceptions. I see this piece of paper, but what can I know about it? I can only know that I have certain sensations of size and shape and color. I can only know my perceptions. I might try to check its reality by moving my head around to see how its shape appears to change. But that does not help at all; what that experiment shows is that my perception of movement and my visual impressions of the paper are coordinated. I still cannot be sure there is a real piece of paper there. Writing on it does not help either, that just adds new movement–visual coordinations.

At this point Berkeley was on the brink of the philosophical position called solipsism, the position that only my thoughts have any reality—your thoughts do not exist, nor does anything else. It is a logically defensible position, but not a very interesting one. Berkeley had much more constructive plans, however. What happens to the piece of paper when I leave the room and can no longer see it? Does it vanish? Not at all, Berkeley assures us, because God can still see it. Thus, sensory sensations do have permanence, they do not depend on me alone. And the ideas of things that I have do have a claim for reality status, if only because of God's blessing.*

Berkeley's real contribution, however, was not this ploy to solve the metaphysical problem. It was something else that was much more important for the history of psychology. He emphasized the importance of the kind of movement–visual coordinations that occur when we move around and look at things at the same time. Indeed, he supposed that that was how our ideas of space, our "spatial sense," arise. He noted the puzzle that we see the world in three dimensions even though the eye gives us only a two-dimensional retinal picture. When light comes from a particular direction, there is no problem in determining its direction, but how can we tell how far it is coming from? The ambiguity can only be resolved by locating the light source in space. The puzzle can only be solved with experience, and that experience must necessarily be based on movement. We have to learn about converging the eyes, and focusing them, and so on. We must also learn to locomote in space so that we come to know that this object is three steps away, that object is eight steps away, and so on.

Locke had used something like a principle of association to blend together the different sensory qualities to form perceptual objects. Here Berkeley was using something like a principle of association to blend together disparate perceptions of objects to form a schema of space. Our ideas of movement give meaning to what would otherwise be just scattered visual impressions. And it works the other way, too: Seeing objects in space motivates and coordinates our movement through space. Like Locke a few years earlier, Berkeley was a wholehearted empiricist. All of the perceptual coordinations that he stressed, all the correlations of vision and movement, depended on experience. Where Berkeley went beyond Locke was in his detailed analysis of the phenomenon of space perception. His was a major contribution to the development of empiricistic thought.

---

*Alas, even God's grace does not solve the metaphysical problem. Berkeley's ploy gives us an eternal perceiver and an eternal holder of ideas, but that does not tell us that there is anything out there that corresponds with our perceptions and ideas. Hence, Berkeley was forced to the conclusion that there is no reality out there, it is an illusion. He said that our ideas are the only reality.

The Metaphysical Problem

Berkeley's contribution to the metaphysical problem was not significant for psychology, but we must stop here to consider metaphysics generally. It is the question of ultimate reality: What is real and what is illusion? A few notable philosophers, such as Plato and Berkeley, believed that the only reality is the world of ideas and that the world of external things is constructed from our ideas, and is, in short, an illusion. Such philosophers are called **idealists.** On the other side, a large number of philosophers take for granted the external world, and accept its reality. We can call them **realists.** There is a broad spectrum of realists, however, because of the different ways they treat the other realm, the world of ideas. Some realists, like Hobbes, reject the mental world or else try to explain it away with various sorts of mechanisms. Whether they be philosophers or psychologists, I call these people mechanists. (In this history I do not distinguish between mechanists and materialists.) Then there are realists, such as Descartes, who believe in both mind and body. We call them **dualists.**

So an idealist believes in one reality, ideas. A mechanist believes in one reality, machinery. A dualist believes in both worlds. A great number of psychologists are either dualists or mechanists, so it all works out nicely, except for the problem that a lot of philosophers and psychologists do not fit into this outline at all. We have already seen that Aristotle, who stressed function, does not fit, and that the church philosophers, who stressed the immortal soul, do not fit. Now we will observe that Hume does not fit this outline either. Indeed, he fits it so badly that we will be obliged to stop and think about the whole matter again.

Hume and Associationism

DAVID HUME (1711–76) was from Edinburgh, Scotland. As a young man he was, like Locke, a secretary (to General St. Clair), and had the opportunity to travel extensively in Europe. Then he settled down as a librarian at the university in Edinburgh. When he was still relatively young he produced a major work, the *Treatise of Human Nature* (1739). Years later Hume observed in a brief autobiographical note that no one seemed to have read it (it is not easy to read). But in short order Hume greatly improved his writing skills and produced a short, spirited, and entertaining account of many of the ideas that had been presented earlier. This work, *An Enquiry Concerning Human Understanding* (1748), was a great triumph that soon established Hume as (in the opinion of many) the greatest of British philosophers. In contrast with

David Hume

many philosophical writings, it is very comfortable for psychologists and seems to make a lot of sense to us.[7]

Hume's Skepticism

Hume began with Berkeley's uncertainty about the physical world, whereby all one can be sure of is one's own sensory impressions. Locke had assumed that when he looked at, let us say, a table, that there was a real table out there. When Hume looked at a table, he wondered how he could really know anything for sure about it. How could he tell he was not the victim of some sort of illusion? He could be sure of his sensory impression of the table, but how could he be sure of the table? Berkeley resolved his doubts by calling on an Eternal Observer, but Hume's solution had a totally different character. His solution was remarkably simple and direct—he said we cannot know reality. We do know our sensory impressions, we know that it looks like a table, but whether there is a real table out there to produce our sensory impressions we can never know. Reality is simply unknowable.

While Locke needed an associationistic principle but was reluctant to accept one, Hume had no such hesitancy. Locke had all those sensory qualities that needed to be glued together to produce a perception, and all those simple ideas that had to be stuck together to make complex ideas. But that was no problem for Hume because he did not endorse that sort of atomism. For Hume, a perceived object was perceived in its totality and our idea of it, too, was a total configuration. Hume was much more deeply concerned with the sequence of ideas, the fact that one idea follows another in the mind. He observed, for example, that when he hears the voice of his friend in the next room, it suggests to him the idea of his friend's face. The sequencing of ideas is based on association, he assumed. Because the voice and the face have occurred together as sensations, they are associated as ideas. Ideas are simply faint copies, fading impressions, of the original sensations. And just as the original sensations occur together, so the ideas become linked so that one sensation can arouse the idea of the other. In effect, an idea is the aroused memory of an impression.

Laws of Association

Hume had three laws of association. One law, contiguity, was just illustrated. Events that occur together tend to get associated. But while this is what Locke needed, Hume credited it little importance because, he said, events could become associated although they had only occurred together by chance. The second law was resemblance: We tend to associate events that are similar. Thus, a portrait makes us think of the person portrayed. The third law was Hume's favorite. If one event invariably follows another, Hume said, then they will be seen as having a cause-and-effect relationship. All the important events in our lives are those for which we seek their causes and effects. Whether we deal with practical matters, comprehension of the physical world, or psychology or politics, we are generally seeking causal relationships. Cause and effect lie at the bottom of all matters of fact, Hume maintained.

We know that a candle flame can burn, and we seek a physical explanation. We know that a kind word can elicit one in return, and we look for a psychological explanation. There are many ways to deal with such matters, but Hume is bent on asking a deeper question: How do we know these things about flames and kind words? By what line of reasoning do we know the flame will burn? Could we have predicted such a thing if we had never seen it or something like it before? Turning to a more precise art, billiards, Hume (a gentleman of leisure, likely adept at the game) asked: If brilliant philosophers were to inspect the balls, could they determine how to strike the cue ball if they had never before seen such smooth balls rolling around on such a flat table? Are there any a priori laws, any lines of reasoning before the fact, that could disclose the secret of how to hit the ball? Hume saw no hope of there being such a law. Therefore, he concluded, cause and effect lie totally, completely in our own experience. It is only through playing billiards that we can learn how to do it. And we know the flame will burn a piece of paper because we have seen it happen before. More accurately, we have previously had a sequence of sensory impressions where a flickering flame was immediately followed by a smoldering piece of paper. And that, according to Hume, is all we can say about cause and effect. The physical reality eludes us. The mechanism is invisible.

But there is a further interesting aspect of cause-effect relationships. If I observe a candle flame brought over to a piece of paper, then the idea of smoldering paper comes into my mind. But there is something else: I will not only *remember* the paper burning before, I will also *expect* it to burn this time. Hume said:

> We make the remembrance of the thing to be the pre-vision or expectation of things to come in the future.
>
> Hume (1748), p. 53.

And that is all that causation is, Hume said, the expectation that the same sequence of events (perceptual events) will occur again. How gravity can operate over empty space, or what is really happening on the billiard table, or how kind words work may never be known to us in terms of mechanisms; they may forever be no more than predictable events.

Voluntary Action, and Other Niceties

Hume went on to consider Descartes's problem, the problem arising from Descartes's dualism. How can the mind, a nonphysical thing, have any effect upon the body, which is a physical thing? Hobbes had reduced the mind to atoms bouncing around, so in his view there was no causality problem. But Descartes the rationalist could not do it mechanically; he had deliberately given the human voluntary control of behavior. Descartes actually had further problems because he had included God in his system, and God could intervene in both our minds and our actions. But Descartes's most pressing problem was how to account for voluntary action.

This was a puzzle philosophers had devoted some attention to, and there was no shortage of proposed solutions. I will cite just a few of the alternatives. The idealists could argue that the only reality was the mental world, so the physical world was no problem. The French mechanist La Mettrie took a Hobbes-like position and argued that everything was mechanical, and so the mind was no problem. A bit earlier the mystic Baruch Spinoza contended that God in all his goodness transcended both the mental and the physical worlds, and thus united them. Other philosophers, the occasionalists, proposed that there was no interaction between mind and body. A mental event only sets the occasion for an appropriate bodily event to occur. There was no causation, only opportunity. Aristotle and others had argued that moving the body was just one of the things the mind could do; it was one of the *powers* of the mind.

Hume rejected all of this as philosophical foolishness. He noted that invoking a "power" to unravel the mystery did nothing to explain it—it only stated the problem in a new way. Hume's solution to the problem of voluntary action was to step away from all the traditional philosophies and look at it from the point of view of the person who has the volition and makes the movement. The question then is how people know that their volitions cause their movements. The answer should be foreseeable. They know they have voluntary control in the same way they know everything else: They have experienced it before. They have seen their volitions followed by action. Volitions are no different in principle or any more mysterious than flames or billiard balls. Psychologically, the phenomenon is very simple, just another case of expectation.

Psychologists today like to remind each other that correlation does not mean causation. If you have nice data showing how this varies with that, it is merely nice data and does not justify the idea that this is causing that. That was what Hume was saying. And that is what Newton was saying about gravity. We know the effects of gravity, but not how it works. We do not really know what keeps the planets in place, we know only that they have very orderly orbits. This link between Hume and Newton is not a coincidence. Hume subtitled his *Treatise* "An attempt to introduce the experimental method of reasoning into moral subjects." And the method he meant was Newton's (see Smith, 1941). So whether we are examining our own mind, or playing billiards, or tracking the planets, all we can know for sure is that our perceptions follow one another in an orderly manner.

A final comment on Hume is that he viewed the human mind as being quite passive. Locke had seen it as much more active, and full of "powers." For him the mind was busy perceiving, remembering, and comparing, as well as making judgments and decisions. Hume does not mention such activities, but rather lets them happen as a result of association. It appears that as the laws of association are used more and more to order our experience, the mind appears to become increasingly passive. Hume solved Locke's problem of mental powers simply by denying that there are any powers. For Hume the mind just treasures up experience and stores it away to be released later when triggered by new impressions. My being conscious is rather like being at a theater where my impressions and ideas are up there on the stage. I am obliged to sit quietly and watch while they come and go.

Summary

THE MAJOR THEMES we have discussed have now all become so well embedded in psychology that we tend to take them for granted, like the air we breathe. But that is all the more reason why we should stop and look at them carefully. We saw that all four major themes were familiar to the early Greek philosophers, but they then fell out of sight during the long interval between Aristotle and Descartes.

Atomism is the idea that one can best explain visible phenomena by breaking them down into very small, invisible pieces. For Hobbes the visible phenomenon was an idea, while the underlying reality that explained it was minute particles moving around in the head. For Locke the basic explanatory units were small, simple sensory elements, a little color here and a little shape there. But the memory of combinations of such sensory elements gives us all of our complex ideas of objects in the world.

Mechanism is the idea that everything is ultimately to be explained with physical principles. Not only mechanical phenomena but mental phenomena as well follow from, or can be reduced to, physical principles. Hobbes was a mechanist, but Locke and Hume were not. Mechanism is sometimes confused with determinism, the idea that phenomena are orderly, lawful, and predictable. Hume lets us see the difference because he was a determinist but not a mechanist.

Empiricism is the idea that our knowledge of ourselves and our world comes exclusively through our experience. This idea was central to Locke's position, but it was also a part of many of these philosophers' positions. Hobbes, Locke, Berkeley, and Hume are sometimes lumped together and designated the British Empiricists. Both Locke and Hume were very serious about their political liberalism, and their empiricist commitment was an important part of it. For them, education was seen as the road to personal freedom.

Associationism is the idea that after two events have been experienced together, one of them will evoke the idea of the other one. Aristotle entertained the concept, but did not make it important. Hobbes used it to account for human rationality. Locke had something like it, but he was uncomfortable with it. Berkeley and Hume began to make associationism a more central part of psychological thinking, but a full-fledged associationism still lay in the future.

Notes

1. As a young man, Aristotle studied for many years with Plato, who was about 40 years his elder. Democritus was about 40 years older again, but he lived to be an old man and was still alive when Aristotle was a young man. So, around 370 B.C. they all overlapped. The lives and times and the work of these early thinkers have been analyzed in extraordinary detail. Watson and Evans (1991) provide a good summary.

2. Over many years Aristotle wrote a great deal about many topics, but unfortunately he never gathered together his psychological thoughts. They remain scattered throughout his writings, and pulling them together in a systematic way is a tremendous task. Robinson (1989) has recently done a remarkably good job of it.

3. Some other books on the history of psychology provide much fuller accounts of the developments I have merely mentioned in this section. For

example, Brett (1912) and Watson and Evans (1991) make a lot of additional points and provide a lot of documentation. And they look at many more of the early scholars than I have. Right here at the end of this section I must mention an important transitional figure, Francis Bacon (1561–1626), politician–scientist. In his later years he was, in effect, the prime minister of England, definitely a politician. He also had very strong views about how science should conduct itself: Rather than deduce its conclusions from first principles (the philosopher's approach), it should seek generalities only after it has a large quantity of good data (the empirical approach). It should proceed inductively rather than deductively, he argued. Most memorable in Bacon's writing is his warning about the *idols*. An idol is an appearance, or an illusion, that the scientist has to guard against. There are *idols of the tribe* where we misperceive things because we are human, and *idols of the cave* where we make errors because of our own particular circumstances. *Idols of the marketplace* deceive us because of our overreliance on words. And *idols of the theatre* find us blinded by our traditions. Such entertaining insights were to be found in Bacon's *Novum Organum* (*New Method*) (1620), which was written in English in spite of the Latin title.

4. Democritus was the atomist that Aristotle most discussed and most disagreed with, and we know him mainly from Aristotle's comments because almost nothing he wrote has survived. He died in 370 B.C. Then, about a century later, Epicurus began a school in Athens to promote the cause of atomism and hedonism. It was a popular school, and much of its work has survived, although it was unknown until the time of Gassendi. Epicurus taught that we bring much of our pain upon ourselves. It happens because of our greed, avarice, and pettiness. It happens, too, because of our fear of what the gods might do to us. The cure is to lead a modest life devoted to our friends and our work. Lucretius was a Roman poet who wrote *Of the Nature of Things* about 55 B.C. Lucretius stressed the fear of the gods theme; by all reports the Roman gods were fearful indeed. Stones (1928) argues that all through the dark ages when scholarly prospects looked most bleak, there was a thin line of scholars who debated the virtues of atomism. Perhaps, but if so, it was an extremely thin line, because there were at any one time only a couple of Lucretius's manuscripts in existence. Moreover Lucretius's narrow focus on religious problems overlooked many of what are, to us, the more interesting psychological issues discussed by Epicurus. For example, the Roman poet never mentioned hedonism. Finally, by Stones's own account there was an explosion of interest in these matters during Gassendi's lifetime.

5. Hobbes made his living as a tutor, first to a young man who became the Earl of Devonshire; as a tutor he was traveling companion, advisor, teacher, and friend. It sounds like a nice job. Later he was tutor to a young man who would become Charles II of England. One wonders if his conclusion about the power of the sovereign had anything to do with his closeness to the royal family. Be that as it may, there was a problem that required Hobbes to be in Europe, or at least not in England, and that was the civil war going on there. It was the time of Oliver Cromwell, the time (1649) when Charles's father, Charles I, was removed from his throne and beheaded. It was not a good time to be speaking in favor of the king. Hobbes wrote *Human Nature* in 1640 but delayed its publication until 1650. Then in 1651 *Leviathan* was brought out. The two books convey essentially the same message.

Hobbes had some literary skills. Early on he had worked as a sort of secretary for Bacon. He translated some of his work into Latin. He also translated Greek works into English, he translated Gassendi's work into English, and his 1672 autobiography (one of two he wrote) was in Latin verse. In his biography of Hobbes, Peters (1956) emphasizes that Hobbes had become fascinated by the deductive method of Euclid's geometry; he was going to use a similar formalism to systematize the social and political sciences. Thus, he started with very simple psychological principles, and eventually "deduced" how society ought to be organized. Mersenne had translated Euclid, and Hobbes met him about 1636. Was that how it all started? Did Hobbes happen to be at the right place at the right time to conceive his new method?

6. Berkeley's most important works, both written when he was only 24, were *Essay Towards a New Theory of Vision* (1709) and *Treatise Concerning the Principles of Human Understanding* (1710). Later he spoke out on his philosophy of science in *De Motu* (1721) and with an attack on the deist approach to religion in *Alciphron* (1732).

7. Hume's masterpiece was originally published in 1748 with the title *Philosophical Essays Concerning Human Understanding*. Later that year there was a revised second edition carrying the title by which it is now generally known, *An Enquiry Concerning Human Understanding*. In his own time Hume was best known for his *Political Discourses* (1752) and *History of England* (1754). One of his most interesting works is the posthumous *Discourses Concerning Natural Religion* (1779).

Chapter Four

Loss of the Themes

W E HAVE SEEN that Hume looked very much like a psychologist. Perhaps he was the first of us. He had a psychological rule, hedonism, to explain behavior. He had a psychological principle, associationism, to explain at least some of our thoughts. He asked psychological kinds of questions, such as why we think we have voluntary control over our own behavior. He deliberately tried to apply what he took to be the experimental method of reasoning to the "moral" sciences such as politics, economics, and psychology. Should we consider Hume to have been the first psychologist? Real historians do not like such questions, probably because they have no real answers. But we are free to wonder about such things because we are not real historians; we are just psychologists trying to understand our heritage.

And I believe that there is a real answer on the question of Hume's priority as a psychologist. The answer is no. He may have looked much like a psychologist, but he was not the father of our discipline. There are two reasons for this negative conclusion. One is that our discipline is experimental; it seeks to answer questions by collecting data and measuring things. On that score Hume was a philosopher. The main reason, however, that we cannot accept Hume as a psychologist is the lack of continuity between him and us. There was a break during which his views were largely lost. We can look back and see him as an anticipator, but as much as we might like to claim him as an ancestor, he was too remote, and there is no direct connection. *It is connectedness that counts most in historical causation,* I would contend. We could speculate what would have happened if there had been a line of Hume followers, scholars that followed his approach and led directly to more recent times. But our history shows that, on the contrary, Hume was cut off from us by a variety of negative reactions to his ideas. We will first see how he became disconnected from us in England.

Reactions in England

IN THE PHILOSOPHY DEPARTMENTS of the great English universities, both of them, there was total disinterest in Hume's ideas. Cambridge and Oxford philosophers were not impressed. They had been mostly neo-Platonic in Locke's time, and they remained neo-Platonic. Indeed, they remained of that persuasion for a long time. There was a little criticism of Hume's ideas from academia, but most of it came from the clergy who largely regarded the new empiricism and associationism as threats to the established religious order. Those who represented the establishment in philosophy saw little threat, and so just went on about their business. Those learned scholars just mumbled and nodded and puttered. Their names are now all forgotten—and Hume lives on.

About this time, however, one Englishman, a nonacademic, did take associationism seriously.

Hartley the Associationist

David Hartley (1705–57) was a singular individual: He was not a philosopher but a physician with an active practice. Like Hume, he had studied Newton and had been much impressed. But while Hume had been intrigued by Newton's method, Hartley was fascinated by the physical aspects of his theory. He liked the idea of little particles vibrating and moving about. He believed that it was these little vibrations that made vision possible, gave us our sense of color, and ultimately gave us our knowledge about the external world. If it was through vibrations that we come to understand the external world, then they must also provide the key to our own, psychological world. Hartley was a physician, so he knew about nerves. Actually, at that time no one had a very clear idea of what nerves were or how they worked. But that did not matter much, because the nerves had to be the medium. So let there be little vibrations in the nerves, Hartley proposed. Minute motions in those slender little structures would be the physical basis for human experience, he believed.[1]

Scholars generally agree that Hartley was not familiar with Hume's work. That seems likely, because, we recall, Hume's 1740 book was not read by anyone, and his major work of 1748 had appeared only a year before Hartley's opus *Observations on Man* (1749). The two men appear to have arrived at a strong associationist point of view quite independently of each other, which provides us with an interesting case of separate and nearly simultaneous innovation. The history of psychology provides several similar cases of simultaneous discovery. Hume had expanded on Berkeley's associationism, something that he had no doubt felt had been missing from Locke's analysis.

Hartley, on the other hand, proceeded directly from Locke, simply supplying the associationistic machinery, along with the nervous machinery that was needed so that it would make sense to a mechanist.

Hartley was an atomist, like Locke. He was a mechanist, like Hobbes. And he was an associationist, like Hume. In short, he put it all together. He made it coherent. But more than that, we see in Hartley for the first time complete reliance on associations. For Hartley, associations were the whole story. Hume had regarded associations as "gentle forces" that guide or suggest this or that idea to the mind. Hearing the voice of his friend suggested to Hume the sight of his face. Hartley's system had no such gentleness; associations work mechanistically and inevitably. They are powerful forces, and they are the only forces operating in the human mind. Thus, they are all-determining. Hartley, therefore, emerges as a thorough, complete, 100 percent associationist. And he was the first of those.

Hartley had another important first: He was the first to apply associationistic principles wholeheartedly to behavior. His predecessors had linked sensations associatively to form large perceptions, and they had combined ideas associatively, so that a collection of simple ideas could yield a complex one, but they had all left behavior peculiarly out of the picture. Part of the problem was no doubt the recognition that while some of our behavior is automatically controlled by our sensations, much of it is controlled by our thoughts and ideas; in other words, it is voluntary. Making room for voluntary behavior meant that no behavior was explained very systematically. There was the hedonistic principle, which made behavior rather predictable, once the circumstances were known (as with Locke's two men at the bar), but there were no behavioral mechanisms. There was no conceptual machinery to determine what action would occur.

But Hartley was able to go directly to behavior. He saw vibrations coming through our sense organs into the brain, where they might interact associatively, and where they might generate ideas. But then they proceeded out the motor nerves to cause behavior. It was all continuous, and it was all caused by vibrations in neural tissue, nerves, or brain. Then associations played a huge role, because sensations could be linked to yield complex perceptions. Ideas could be linked to form more complex ones. Responses could be linked to make large motor coordinations. Sometimes, Hartley said, a response will flow directly from sensory input; *automatic* was the word he used. But sometimes, after ideas have been formed from sensations, responses will flow from the ideas. That is all we mean by voluntary behavior, Hartley said. And of course, hedonism was there, because the ideas that tend to control our voluntary responses are those that refer to pleasure and pain. The nature of behavior changes with experience, he suggested, because as we learn and start forming ideas, our behavior shifts from automatic to voluntary, that is, from clumsy, chancy, and uncoordinated to well-controlled. Then with further learning it becomes automatic again because we do not have to think about carrying out a well-practiced action. Hartley had a very appealing outline of how behavior worked.

Hartley's Lack of Influence

So by 1749 we had the possibility of a full-fledged, nothing-but associationism. Hartley started from the basic concept that ideas are formed from experience, and that they are but small, subtle vibrations that remain in the brain after the original sensation is gone. Like Hobbes, he tried to make the mind into a purely mechanical device. Then he linked these ideas to each other, to sensations, to responses, and that was that. The job was done, or so he might have thought. The historical fact was that no one paid much attention to Hartley. In later times one could reasonably say he was the first associationist. But he stood all alone out there; he seems to have had few if any intellectual descendants. Interestingly, his book was brought out in several editions, but there was almost no change in content. The second edition was edited by Priestley the chemist, of all people, and the third by Hartley's son, who basically restored the moralistic parts that Priestley had taken out. Then there were further editions up to the sixth, which was brought out in 1834, almost a century after the original opus! Presumably those who revised all these editions were devotees or followers or believers, but were any of them important figures in the history of psychology? It does not appear so.

Hartley seems to have had one follower, and that was James Mill. Mill was the next English-speaking nothing-but associationist. It would appear that Mill was indeed much influenced by the earlier man, and that what he did, essentially, was to keep Hartley's thorough-going associationism, while throwing out Hartley's theology and moralizing along with his vibrational mechanical system. Mill reduced everything to bare-bones associationism. But Mill's major psychological work was not published until 1829. And when it was published, *it* attracted very little attention. It only evoked substantial reaction when it was revised and presented anew by Mill's son, John Stuart Mill, in 1865.[2] And by then there were associationists all over the place. But they had come from elsewhere, from other influences. Thus, it seems implausible to attribute much of a contributing role to Hartley and his follower James Mill, who had changed his message greatly. Hartley's work stood as testimony to the fact that one could do almost everything one might want to do in psychology with associationism. But while this might have appeared as a curious intellectual possibility, there seems to have been little serious pursuit of such a possibility until many years later. Thus, in the English-speaking intellectual world there was a clear break in continuity between Hume and Hartley—the great associationists of the mid-18th century—and those who came along a hundred years later.

The Literary Tradition

By the mid-1700s literacy had expanded greatly. People were reading for entertainment and for enlightenment. The new ideas about the human mind, about our knowledge, our understanding, and even about our behavior were making themselves known not only in select intellectual circles but among a much wider reading public as well. One popular theme dealt with the concept of free will, a concept that had been discussed for a long time, but at this time the old question was being dealt with in new ways. The Catholic Church had always taken the position that there was freedom of the will, and that the exercise of this freedom was a vital moral issue for the individual. It is, the Church said, through our deliberate choice of virtuous acts that we achieve redemption, and ultimately save our souls. Devout protestants began to come to other conclusions, however. Jonathan Edwards (1754), for example, maintained that any exercise of human freedom would be an infringement of the Almighty's powers. If He is all-powerful, then we must be powerless, and our sense of freedom must be an illusion. We might think we are acting morally when we elect to act properly, but our actions are already preordained, and we act at all only through His grace.[3]

One might also conclude that the human will is not free, not because of divine considerations, but for much more mundane psychological reasons, namely, because we always act hedonistically. This view was also discussed and debated rather widely. Locke and Hume were hedonists, as we have seen, and so were Hartley and some of his contemporaries. Hartley had tried to put the morality question on a new footing by first rejecting any idea of personal freedom, and then distinguishing between ideas of pleasure that referred to the present and those that referred to the future. It was an elaborate scheme, and it was not very convincing. Hartley's morality concept seems to have attracted few followers. Even Priestley, who liked Hartley's work enough to render a second edition of it, deleted the business on morality.

Some of the poets of the time and of the next generation are relevant to our story. The English poet Samuel Coleridge (1772–1834) was a well-educated man; he had done his time at Cambridge and had studied medicine in Germany, and he was acutely aware of the gradually emerging new psychological way of thinking. He did not like its mechanistic overtones; thus, he did not like Hartley's approach. But he was fascinated by the idea that we do not generally control our own fate; fate is something that happens to us because of the way we are, perhaps because of our experience. Coleridge was torn between wanting to believe in the glory of the human spirit, and wanting to believe in some sort of deterministic account of human actions. He said we are much like plants, just another part of the biological world of living things. What sets us apart is not our immortal soul, nor the freedom of our will, nor even our intellect. It is that we have imagination; vegetables lack imagination.

The poet William Wordsworth (1770–1850), contemporary and close friend of Coleridge, also struggled with the task of creating a new perception of the human condition. He was on the one hand fascinated by the recent advance of the sciences, and confident that our understanding of ourselves would advance as well. But on the other hand he had to believe that there was a special nobility of the human spirit. He contended that the analytic, logical sort of analysis that was beginning to be applied to human behavior was quite inappropriate, and yet he understood that these were the tools of science. It was through analysis and logic, and yes, even through applying mechanistic principles, that science progressed. It was a dilemma that tormented many of the English romantic poets. The result in literary circles was a retreat of sorts from the psychology of the person, and a move to other matters.[4]

But the problem did not go away. When John Stuart Mill was writing his *Logic* (1843) he could not bring himself to publish it, to put it all on record. So the publication of this, perhaps his best-known work in his own lifetime, was considerably delayed. And ultimately, it probably only appeared at all because he had the assistance of Alexander Bain in the final writing and editing of the work. Mill's problem was that he was at the same time both the foremost psychologist of his day, and also a leading literary figure, and he shared Wordsworth's disdain for logical analysis. Thus, Locke and Hume caused a lot of grief for their literary countrymen many years down the road.

Deism

We can turn back to Locke for another source of intellectual trouble. Recall that he rejected authority as a source of knowledge. His chief example of corrupt knowledge (corrupt because it was based on authority rather than one's own experience) was religious doctrine. Interestingly, having come to doubt the validity of the wisdom received from the Church, he continued to be a believer. He would have to be called a devout Christian. He certainly believed in God, but the God in which he had faith was a somewhat different one than the one the Church extolled. Locke had a rather personal relationship with his deity. His idea of God was derived from his own experience, and from his own thinking about things. Thus, we had a new kind of religion, a religion that came ready-tailored for the individual, suited for the person's own needs and understanding, rather than from the institution of the Church. This new religion came to be called **deism.** It is a funny religion in that it builds no cathedrals and it has no bishops; it has no ministry at all. But it is a religion, nonetheless. Typically (I think I am speaking for most deists), it believes in a creator. We look around and see a wondrous world, all the living things prospering, with the rain falling and the rivers flowing to provide sustenance for all living things. It seems so well-organized, and everything seems so well-suited to its place. Everything we see seems to have a purpose. There must have been a creator to have planned it all. It could not have arisen by chance. Chance alone would have produced chaos, but we see order instead.

So, Locke's God was a creator. Does He still intervene to make sure everything is still in order? There are several possible interesting answers to that question. One variant is that He put things together so perfectly, as one might expect a God to do, that it still runs according to His plan; no further intervention is necessary. Probably He could intervene if He wished to do so, but the creation was perfectly planned, so no further intervention would seem to be necessary. Thus, Locke's God is nothing but a creator.

Interestingly, Locke was not the first deist, although he greatly promoted the concept. Newton, a few years ahead of Locke, had seen the need for a creator. But, he said, once the planets are in place and in motion, and once God has given us a universal law of gravity, everything will work out just as we observe it. Actually, Newton supposed, it might occasionally be necessary to fine-tune the system once in a while because large comets might throw the delicate balance of things out of line.*

Hume, too, was a deist. He developed what he called *natural religion.* But remember, Hume was somewhat dubious about whether the creator had actually created anything—we recall his admonition that we cannot know anything about the external world, we can only know our own sense impressions. Hume also wrote about miracles. He did not actually denounce claims of miracles, but he did observe that we see a lot fewer of them in modern times than we hear about in ancient stories. We see fewer of them, too, as we know more about science. We have to suspect that Hume was a closet atheist.

The Baron d'Holbach lived in Paris about 1770, and the baron is important because he was definitely not in the closet. He was perhaps the first scholar to stand up and announce that he was a free thinker. When Hume visited him in Paris around 1770, the baron threw a party and introduced the English philosopher to his other friends as the great English philosopher and atheist. Hume is reported to have shrunk a bit from accepting that honor. Recall that Hume's natural religion book was not published until after his death. As outspoken as he was, Hume was apparently cautious in some matters. He stayed in the closet.[5]

So intellectual circles in England and France were watching **British empiricism** closely. But they were not particularly interested in the new

---

*How could Newton's creator be surprised by the appearance of a comet? Some ancient jokester noted that such an idea implies that God the Creator is rather fallible and limited in knowledge—of course He does not intervene anymore because He constructed everything so well that nothing needs to be fixed. Actually, there were three phenomena that caught Newton's attention in seeming to call for special creative effort: (1) From where comes all the order and beauty we see in nature? (2) How come everything seems so perfectly adapted, such as instinct in animals? and (3) How is it that our will can cause our limbs to move?

psychological conception of the human mind that Locke and Hume had given us, or the thoroughgoing associationism of Hartley. They were much more interested in the liberal political implications of empiricism. If our knowledge is merely derived from experience, then it is not as much our breeding that matters as it is our education. It is what we learn that counts. Education is important. This idea was picked up and developed by Voltaire, and through him and others it became an important part of the French Enlightenment. That was perhaps the most important immediate repercussion of what Locke and Hume had started. But let us turn to other developments in France.

Developments in France

WE HAVE SEEN that the mechanistic tradition, popularized in France by Descartes, was still alive and well a century later, at the time of La Mettrie (1748). Actually, this was a very healthy tradition. Real historical scholars, who can crowd their pages with obscure names, have noted that even in his own time Descartes was only one of several French thinkers who worried about the mind and the body and the relationship between the two realms.[6] History is always much denser and more complicated than we make it out to be. We simplify it a lot so that we can make sense of it and hang onto some semblance of order. Thus, we remember Descartes and make him a hero and we forget all his contemporaries with whom he shared many ideas. So while we will mark Descartes a hero once again, we will try to remember as we go on that no one is great enough to stand alone against the tide. Descartes had some help from his friends.

French Associationists

There were also associationists in France, a line of them that runs from Malebranche through Helvetius to Bonnet and Condillac, and through to Cabanis. Nicolas Malebranche (1638–1715), the first of the line, was in the next generation after Descartes, and was very much influenced by him. He struggled with Descartes's paradox of how mind and body could interact, and eventually concluded that they could not. He argued for the doctrine of occasionalism, the idea that when something comes to the mind, say, a volition, that event does not cause the body to move; rather, it "sets the occasion" for God to intervene and cause the body to move. Subsequent French philosophers were much more mechanistic, and also in the tradition of Descartes. Charles Bonnet, who was actually Swiss, worried about how the machinery of the body worked, and about how experience builds up a body of associations.[7]

The most noteworthy of these philosophers was Condillac (1715–80) (his name was Etienne Bonnot, but he came from Condillac). He was the most thoroughgoing and consistent associationist of all these French scholars. In his most famous book, *Treatise on the Sensations* (1754), he invites us to think about a statue that stands in the village square. Like any good statue it does not move at all, and does not have much in the way of intellectual ability. But let us imagine, Condillac suggests, that it has just one very humble psychological ability, the ability to associate ideas. And let us imagine that it is endowed with smell, the least significant of the sensory channels. It will then gradually, ever so slowly, begin to build up ideas of the world around it. It can smell the seasons, the flowers in the spring, and so on, and will gradually form the concept of the succession of the seasons. Different times of day might smell subtly different too. Then it will begin to distinguish in this time frame the coming and going of different animals. Thus, gradually the statue would gain many ideas. It would come to know what is happening in the village. If we imagine the statue endowed with additional sensory input, we can suppose it would form many more ideas, including some rather complex ones. If we think of it having all the sensations that people have available, we might expect it to build up the full array of ideas we find in the normal human mind, Condillac suggests. And it is all accomplished with nothing more than the laws of association. He proceeded to derive all sorts of cognitive activities, including the emotions, from associative operations on sensory input. So we find that in France there was a very healthy associationism at almost the same time that Hume and Hartley were promoting it in England.

It would appear that psychology was ready to prosper in France, much as it appeared to be in England. But it did not prosper; it stumbled and stopped. The mechanists who followed in the tradition of Descartes and La Mettrie seemed to turn away from psychological questions. They show up abundantly in the other sciences, especially in all the medical disciplines, all through the 19th century, but we cannot find anyone who looks like a psychologist during this period. Nor do we see anyone following in the associationistic footsteps of Condillac. Later on in the story we will see growing interest in psychology in Germany, Great Britain, and America, but there was no comparable development in France. For some reason, psychology never got incorporated into the French university system as it did in the other three countries. When the great experimental psychologist Alfred Binet began to make his mark around 1900, it turned out that he had no formal background in psychology. Even today, when there are many outstanding French clinicians and physiologists, areas that are included in American psychology, we find that they invariably come from the medical tradition and not from psychology departments. In short, as promising and imminent as a French psychology appeared to be at the time of Hume, it was another dead end.

Developments in Scotland

HUME HAD BEEN a Scotsman; he was born in Edinburgh, and had attended the great university there. We have to note that there is something special about that university. A disproportionate number of pioneer psychologists, people who turned out to be important in developing the discipline, were associated in one way or another with the University of Edinburgh. Hume was also a librarian there for a while, but did not need the work because he had an inheritance and was free to travel. One place he traveled to was La Flêche, a town in northern France. Why there? A century before Hume's sojourn, Descartes had been in school there. Hume believed, and I do too, that the geography of a place has something to do with the kind of ideas that emanate from it. That was evidently true of La Flêche. That was where Descartes learned to write (he was a marvelous writer), and that is where Hume transcribed his unreadable first book into his wonderful second book. What Hume himself could not know, but what provides rather good evidence to support his silly geopsychological hypothesis, is that he would be just the first of a great number of Edinburgh students to make important contributions to psychology.

Reid and Common Sense

Thomas Reid (1710–96) was also a librarian at Edinburgh, just a few years after Hume. His most important work was his first big book, *Inquiry into the Human Mind* (1764). It was directly inspired by Hume's *Enquiry*, but the inspiration was not of the positive sort. Indeed, Reid was very negative toward almost everything Hume had asserted. He began by telling us that philosophers had recently become hopelessly sophisticated and subtle. In fact, he said, some of them (he did not name any names) had even begun to doubt their own existence! Let's settle down and pull ourselves together, Reid said, let's use our common sense. Let's not get carried away with intellectual tricks and rationalistic games about what we can and cannot know. Let's be sensible. And quite appropriately, one of the names of the movement Reid started is **common sense psychology**.

If I look out the window and see a tree over yonder, how do I know that there is a real tree out there that corresponds with my impression of it? According to the philosophical skeptics, such as Berkeley and Hume, I do not know, and cannot know, anything about the real tree because I can only know my sensory impression, which might be a very poor representation of the real thing out there. That is just the sort of philosophical foolishness that Reid wanted to avoid. He said that the *belief* is what matters. If I look out there and I believe I see a tree, then that is all that counts. Common sense solves the

Thomas Reid

skeptic's dilemma. If I believe I see a tree, then that is sufficient for most purposes.

In the *Inquiry*, Reid considered many questions of perception. Indeed he was perhaps the first to make a sharp distinction, and essentially the one we make today, between **sensation** (information coming in from the receptors) and **perception** (how things look to us). He asked, for example, whether the two eyes move together innately, or whether it is a learned skill. He asked, Why do we see things turned the right way around, even though the projection of images is inverted on the retina? The answer in both cases is that although much of perception is innately organized, what we see is also dependent on experience. So it is fair to say that we learn to see things right side up. Notice that this is the same answer that Locke or Hume, the great empiricists, would have given, but there is a major difference. Locke started with the mind being a tabula rasa, we recall; he assumed at the outset that everything depends on experience. Reid regarded it as an empirical question—is it or isn't it? he asked. And he surveyed what evidence he could to arrive at an answer. The answer is not a foregone conclusion, but one yet to be determined. Thus, while he frequently came to empiricistic conclusions, he was also ready to accept nativistic conclusions (the idea that the mind has some sort of innate structure or understanding of things). For example, he talked about instincts, a concept that was most distasteful to Locke.

Another point of difference between Reid and the hard-line empiricists is that while Hume, for example, regarded the mind as mainly passive, being little more than a receptacle for sensory impressions, Reid thought of it in much more active terms. He thought of it as being able to sense, believe, remember, compare, make judgments, evaluate, and so on. For Hartley these mental activities were all derived from associationistic principles—they were powers that were themselves learned through experience, and based on different sorts of learned associations. For Reid each of these activities was just something that the mind does. We do not have to learn to remember, it is just something we can do if we wish to. That is common sense. These **active powers of the mind,** or *faculties,* as Reid called them, are not themselves built up through experience. They are independent of the associative content of the mind. And because of the importance of these faculties in Reid's understanding of the mind, the kind of psychology that he started is sometimes quite appropriately called **faculty psychology.**

Reid's common sense or faculty psychology differed in a couple of other ways from Hume's psychology. Hume was mostly interested in human understanding. He was fascinated by epistomological problems, such as what can we know, and where our knowledge comes from. Hume approached such questions psychologically, or at least in ways that seem quite comfortable to present-day psychologists. Reid also strikes us as being psychological in his thinking, even though he is interested in questions that were quite different from Hume's. Perhaps what that means is that the times had changed. We recall that Locke had arrived at his empiricistic faith because of his distrust of authority as a source of knowledge. Hume was not concerned about that. He wanted to know how trustworthy this new experience-based knowledge was. But Reid was not concerned about that; if he believed there was a tree outside the window, then he saw the tree, and that is all there was to it. He had gotten us back to common sense. But he had a lot of curiosity about why things looked the way they did, which is the central problem of perception. This was a new problem for the psychologically inclined to worry about; no one had really worried about it before.

Stewart: Disciple of Reid

Reid was important academically. For one thing, he was a professor. Almost none of the philosophers we have encountered thus far held university appointments. The professors at the great tradition-bound universities to the south, Oxford and Cambridge, are of no concern to the history of psychology, and those who do concern us were never seriously connected with an institution of higher learning. And this rule holds until we come to Professor Reid, who taught mostly at Glasgow (he replaced Adam Smith as the professor of moral philosophy there). Glasgow is just as cool, wet, and gray as Edinburgh, but in spite of the weather, Reid prospered there. His most important disciple was Dugald Stewart (1753–1828), who ended up as a professor teaching moral philosophy back at Edinburgh. Stewart's view of things was almost indistinguishable from Reid's.[8] Central importance was given to the problem of perception. Little was ever said about the nervous system (none of these people was at all interested in the mechanistic philosophy). Common sense applies to all issues of importance. The mind is active because it is endowed with a lot of faculties. There are some associationistic principles, but they are toned down and mixed up with a lot of other principles so they turn out to be not very important. There is some empiricism—we do in fact learn from experience—but there are instincts and other innate, unlearned tendencies in addition, so experience, too, turns out not to be very important. It was a rather eclectic, loose sort of psychology.

While we see little in Stewart's major works that could be called innovative, we have to note that he was a very popular and influential lecturer, and that he was able to promote his ideas rather successfully. Moreover, he was able to maintain interest in the new common sense or faculty psychology at that critical period in time around 1800 when other psychological viewpoints were in danger of becoming extinct. We have already noted the dearth of mechanists, associationists, and empiricists at this crucial time in both England and France. And there were not yet any of these sorts of people in North America. Psychology was in danger of dying. It was the likes of Reid and Stewart that kept some of Hume's ideas alive, sometimes by mixing them with other ideas, and sometimes by directly criticizing them.

Brown, Mill, and Hamilton

Stewart the charismatic teacher had a couple of important students. One was Thomas Brown (1778–1820), who would soon replace Stewart in the chair at Edinburgh when the older man was forced by his poor health to retire early. Brown was pretty much a disciple of Stewart, and through him, of Reid. They all looked very much alike. The other notable student of Stewart's was James Mill (1773–1836), who was fascinated by psychological matters but dedicated himself to overthrowing the common-sense approach of his teacher. We will come back to Mill in chapter 8, but here I have to say something further about Brown. He represented something of a transition, because he, like Mill, appears to have rebelled a bit against his teacher's ideas. Thus, he did not like to use the word *association*, preferring instead to speak of *suggestion*. One idea "suggests" another. We recall that Hume himself had talked about such gentle forces as suggestions. Brown revived that approach. *Association* apparently implied something mechanistic, which he wanted at all costs to avoid. Like all the Scottish psychologists, Brown was dead-set against a mechanistic or physiological psychology. The mind is not a mechanical thing; common sense tells us that. He also did not like the faculty concept; he thought it had little explanatory value, and so he tried to replace it with a variety of more tangible mechanisms.

Brown also tempered the basic mechanism of association by adding a set of nine *secondary* laws of association. From the time of Aristotle philosophers had tried to summarize with a handful of principles what the laws of association were. Aristotle had proposed similarity, contrast (the opposite of similarity), and contiguity (occurring together in space or time). Some writers over the centuries had abridged Aristotle's handful by making contrast a variety of similarity, or by throwing out both, or by something else. We saw that Hume had cause and effect as his own special law of association. For Brown, similarity and contrast were both gone, and contiguity became proximity. But then there were all the secondary laws, which noted that the strength of an association could depend not only on the proximity of the connected ideas, but also on their vividness, their duration, and the frequency with which they occurred together, as well as such considerations as the current emotion and body state of the individual. None of these schemes, including Brown's, was very convincing or was destined to last very long. Brown's analysis was also of historical interest in that while he was focused mainly on the problems of perception, as his predecessors had been, he was also much more interested than they had been in the problem of habit; that is, behavior, as well as emotion.[9]

In due course, Brown's chair at Edinburgh went to William Hamilton (1788–1856). Everyone who has read Hamilton says that he was a very learned scholar, by far the most scholarly of the whole line. But they also say that, unfortunately, he had nothing to say. For example, he gathered together in one large book the works of Reid and then added a number of his own essays on this and that. One essay looked at the whole long history of the associationism idea, citing everyone even remotely connected with it.[10]

The Emigration of Scottish Psychology

Hamilton's major contributions were published in 1852 and 1859. Thus, we have followed the Scottish story for a century after the time of Hume. And we have come very close to the current era, the era of experimental psychology. The Scottish school does indeed touch modern times. It produced so many common sense psychologists that the Scottish universities at Edinburgh, Aberdeen, and Glasgow could not hold them all. Besides, in the 1800s a lot of Scots emigrated to this country and Canada, and some of them brought the Scottish psychology with them. Thus, in time, Scottish psychology began showing up in American colleges and universities. By the 1880s it was well-established here. At Princeton there was James McCosh. At Yale there was Noah Porter. Both of these gentlemen had come from Edinburgh and both were formidable forces in the intellectual life of the new world. To understand why Scottish-style psychology came to loom up in importance, even while psychology as we know it now had not even been born yet, we have to look at the university system as it existed then.

When colleges were first established in this country, they were all very small and very simple. Harvard and William and Mary were the first to be established, around 1690 (the time of John Locke). Neither was in any sense a center of intellectual activity. Quite the contrary, both had been chartered for a very practical purpose, to train ministers. In the beginning, most colleges were affiliated with some church, and their mission was to produce preachers of the appropriate faith. That might be why so few of the great early philosophers and scientists we have met were affiliated with universities. Italy broke the religious tradition first, which might seem odd because Italy is a very Catholic country and might be expected to be quite conservative in that regard. However, Italian universities were training businessmen, accountants, merchants and the like centuries before anyone else was doing so. There were also some scientists and mathematicians (such as Galileo) at Italian universities long before you could find one at an English-speaking university.

Then gradually, a bit at a time, universities started training medical people. You certainly did not want to be treated by one of those ill-trained doctors; you might have been better off with a minister. The curriculum slowly started expanding to include some physiology and some other sciences in addition to all the classical philosophical material. But the curriculum was still, through most of the 1800s, very restricted. It was nothing at all by today's standards. Then, around the middle of the last century, philosophy departments began offering courses in psychology in addition to the usual fare, which was the classics, rhetoric, and logic. This transition must have happened somewhere around the time that Thomas Reid went to work for the university in Edinburgh, because he is the first professor we have seen who looked and sounded as though he might be a psychologist.

The development of medical programs started in Germany early in the 1800s, but it took quite some time for the idea to catch on in the United States. Thus, it should not be too surprising to learn that even as late as the 1880s most American universities—and all of the wealthy, old, well-established ones such as those that comprise the **Ivy League**—were still in their original business of training ministers. Scottish scholars emigrating to this country had the credentials to rise to the top of the academic world. They were, for the most part, clergymen themselves, because the Church of Scotland had a peculiarly strong hold on what went on in the Scottish universities (they were bound by the same traditions that American schools were). When they came over here they left the Church of Scotland and became Presbyterians. And so in a typical college or university one might find that the president of the institution was a Presbyterian minister, that he taught a course that was taken by all the senior class, and that it was a class called "moral philosophy," in which he taught the psychology of Reid and Stewart and Brown. His special students might even get introduced to Hamilton.

Evaluating the Scottish School

Most historians of psychology look upon the Scottish school as a pretty bad thing, an ugly phase that we were fortunate to survive. Mark Baldwin (1913) says of this phase, "Luckily, it ended." Interestingly, Baldwin probably knew what he was talking about, because he had attended Princeton, where he had studied with McCosh, the last of the Scots. So we have a curious dilemma. As experimental psychologists, they were worthless; in more than 100 years of eminence and intellectual domination, they produced not one experiment. Nothing. Their major lines of thought never changed between the time of Reid and McCosh. How can a new discipline just stand still for 100 years? The whole enterprise was obviously sterile.

But on the positive side, because they were such a large and important group, they produced quite a number of rebels who would ultimately wrest psychology away from them and make it into something very new and different. We have already met one rebel, James Mill, and we will see that he played an important part in our story. Mill's son, J. S. Mill, and his friend Alexander Bain also came from the Scottish tradition, and in rebelling against it they contributed enormously to modern experimental psychology. Also on the positive side, the Scots kept alive all the basic philosophical doctrines that would in time come to define psychology—atomism, mechanism, empiricism, associationism. They did it not by espousing these doctrines, but, ironically, by opposing them. Had they not done so, these doctrines could quite possibly have been lost while other disciplines, other ways of thinking about things and science in general, charged forward in the 1800s. There is an intriguing essay by Fay (1966) arguing that the Scots were good guys; they were our real ancestors. We will return to the Scots and consider this possibility in chapter 8. But for the moment, the jury is still out on the Scottish school of common sense or faculty psychology. We do not yet understand whether it was all a waste of time and energy or whether it provided a critical link connecting us with our philosophical roots.

Events in Germany

THE PROSPECTS FOR an experimental psychology looked pretty bleak after the time of Hume, and when we look at the reaction to Hume in Germany, we will see that the prospects really looked hopeless. We have heard very little from Germany so far; most of our heroes have been English- or French-speaking. German scholars were slumbering. But they were about to awaken, and when they did, they began to take charge. The central character in the German part of our story is a philosopher, unquestionably the greatest of German philosophers. According to his own report, he was a stuffy old professor at the university at Königsberg until he read Hume's *Enquiry*. Immanuel Kant (1724–1804) said that Hume woke him from his dogmatic slumbers. He did not like what he had read of Hume, and so he was challenged to answer him. And in time he did, but apparently Kant really was sleepy, because he took more than 30 years to come up with his rebuttal.

Immanuel Kant

Kant and Nativism

Kant's reply to Hume appears in his greatest work, the *Critique of Pure Reason*, which was published in 1781. Kant begins by accepting much of what Hume had said. Yes, he agrees, our knowledge comes to us through experience. And yes, he admits, we cannot know what the external reality is all about because we are limited by our sensory impressions of things. Our sensory impressions are certain, but things in themselves, what is out there, must always remain uncertain and conjectural. But Hume is wrong, he says, when he contends that all of our knowledge must come from our sensory impressions and our experience with how these impressions relate to one another. Other sorts of knowledge are possible, Kant argues.

Consider the following: Hume tells us we think in terms of cause and effect, we see one thing follow another often enough and we are bound to think of the first as causing the second. Kant agrees with all of this, but then he does a clever trick. He asks: Why do we inevitably think in terms of cause and effect? There is nothing in our experience that teaches us to think in such terms, so why do we do it? It appears that we have no choice; there is something about the human intellect that demands at the outset that we think of things in terms of one thing causing another. And there we are. Kant has lead us to discover something about ourselves and the way we think that is not itself based on experience. We do not learn through experience to think in terms of cause and effect, but we think that way nonetheless. We have discovered something important about the human mind, and we have discovered it (the necessity to think of things as causes and effects) not through experience, but just by thinking about it, through pure reason.

It is an elaborate and complicated analysis, but when he is done with it, Kant has us pretty well convinced that there are several conceptual categories that are like cause and effect, in that we are obliged to think in such terms.

For example, we see things located in space. One thing necessarily lies either in front of or behind the other. We have no options; we are obliged to see things located spatially. We are also obliged to organize our thoughts temporally: This happens first and then that happens next. We have to think like that, Kant argues. He identifies several such categories, and because his argument is so carefully wrought and so complex, we are inclined to agree. One clear conclusion is that not all of our knowledge comes from experience, there is something else. We start with an innate organization, with certain a priori categories. It is like putting information on a floppy disk; you can put any kind of information you want on the disk, but first you have to format it and get it divided up into sectors and zones. The disk must be properly structured ahead of time to receive information from your particular computer or you will not be able to put anything useful on it. And that is the way the human mind works, according to Kant: *The mind is already formatted.*

Kant is important in our story because he articulated a consistent, convincing alternative to the empiricist's position. He did this by making a concession—he allows the empiricist that we do indeed learn from experience, but then he draws a line and insists that there is something else; namely, the innate structure and the a priori categories. Psychologists have always been most comfortable with empiricistic thinking. That is probably the main reason we tend even today to look on Locke and Hume as friends. But it is good to have an alternative, an opposing way of thinking, so that we have a clear polarity. There is a handy name for this antiempiricist, un-Lockean position. It is called **nativism.** The empiricism–nativism issue is one of the great polarities that runs all through the history of psychology. Fundamentally, psychology has always been very empiricistic, but at times it becomes more so or less so. To anticipate a later chapter, and to hint at where we are today, at the present time we seem to be moving away from an extreme empiricism and toward a more nativistic view of things. Thus, Kant's ideas do not seem as foreign to us today as they used to be.[11]

Kant's Impact

In Kant's arguments he often used what he called the *transcendental* method (that word means other things in his system, too). There was nothing really new about the method, but at least Kant was explicit about it. In principle, a philosopher is supposed to start with basic assumptions and then follow them through with a logical analysis to discover what conclusions they lead to. But Kant does it just the other way around: He knows already what conclusion he wants to reach and then he searches for whatever analysis will get him there from his basic principles. What gets "transcended" is the logic. For example, he raises the question of the immortality of the human soul. Science generally comes out one way and religion the other on the question. But Kant the philosopher can settle it. He says we all know scoundrels, people who are no good, who are mean and ugly, who lie and cheat and steal. Sometimes they are made to suffer as they have made others suffer, but all too often they seem to get away with damaging others. These people spend their entire lives without pain while they have been hurting others. And some people spend their entire lives with little joy even though they have given much joy to others. It appears that sometimes justice fails. But, Kant says, it is unthinkable that justice should fail (this is the point at which his logic fails). Thus, there must be a long stretch of time after death in which justice can be served; there must be immortality of the soul.

Kant maintained that it is impossible to have a science of psychology because there is no way one could do experiments on the human spirit. There is no way to intervene experimentally. What one can do is discover something about an individual's culture and religion and language, and so on, and find out something about their social behavior. One can use such observational methods, which Kant call **anthropology,** to discover how a *people* think and act, but there is nothing one can do scientifically to study the mind of a *person*.

Kant was followed by quite a number of German philosophers, but none of them created a psychological tradition. Kant is interesting because he was so very interested in our friend Hume (he says that the whole *Critique* came about because it was "unthinkable" that Hume could be right). But the next generation of philosophers was consumed by all sorts of other matters. One of them, Friedrich Beneke, was actually an associationist similar to Condillac. Another saw life as a series of battles between ideas and opposing ideas. As soon as one conflict is resolved, the new synthesis in turn finds opposition, and the struggle goes on. Another, equally despairing philosopher put it another way: Life does not lead anywhere because it is like a spiral so that we keep coming back to where we have been before but at some higher plane. This, as it turned out, was not the kind of stuff from which psychology could be made. It was far better suited for making poetry. Alas, that is just what happened: The poets took over.

German Romanticism

In 1774 an idealistic young poet named Johann Wolfgang von Goethe (1749–1832) wrote a story about a young man named Werther, who was more or less himself. Werther fell hopelessly in love with a woman he could not have because she was married to a good friend of his. It is a sad story indeed; he loves her because she is a perfect woman, and part of her perfection is her faithfulness and devotion to her husband. Werther keeps in close contact with the couple, however, and worships her up close from afar, as it were. This goes on for some time until the luckless fellow, unable to endure the inner turmoil and unable to do anything constructive with his life, gets a gun. Although Werther took his own tormented life, Goethe skipped that part and went on to write the story and thereby become an unbelievably famous writer. For

89

Johann Wolfgang von Goethe

years young German would-be lovers shot themselves. Guys wore Werther-like clothes. They wrote stories about the story. They wrote songs and even wrote whole operas about it. The German spirit had been set on fire!

The fire spread. Goethe's contemporary Ludwig von Beethoven was close by in Vienna while all this was going on, and we can hear it happening in his music. His first symphony was a lovely thing in the classical idiom he had learned from Haydn and Mozart. The third symphony was heroic, it was dedicated to Napoleon, and sure enough we can hear the roar of cannons and the struggling of people as they rearrange the world. Then in Beethoven's last symphony we have the raging forces of good and evil, and we have the mighty human spirit standing against it all. It concludes with a soaring chorus to announce that in the end man's spirit prevails. How could anyone do science, or philosophy, or anything sensible with all that poetry and music going on all around?

The unhappy truth is that science and philosophy did *not* advance very far in Germany for a number of years. The poets did in fact take over. And Goethe was not done with his mischief. The theory of vision that Newton had bequeathed to us was the dominant source of ideas on vision for a century, up to the time of Goethe. But Goethe did not like it. It was too mechanistic, it made color something out there, it made color merely a part of the physical world, a matter of physical vibrations. Anyone can see, said Goethe, that color is in the eye of the beholder, not out there in the external world. It is a very subjective thing, a spiritual thing, and should be treated as such. He wrote a book, *Theory of Color* (1810), in which he expanded at great length, and with much conviction, on the subjective nature of color. Much of what he had to say is of considerable value in appreciating afterimages, contrast effects, and a variety of color illusions. If you close your eyes and point your face toward a bright sky and then wave your hand rapidly in front of your face, you will experience some vivid flashing colors, maybe brilliant reds and greens. There is surely nothing "out there" in the physical world to explain what you perceive in such a situation. So, Goethe had something interesting to say, but it was more like poetry than science. And in the overwhelming mood of German romanticism, which he had done so much to create, he carried the day. The German intellectual world would be led by Goethe and not by mechanists or scientists. That is why Du Bois-Reymond's pledge to explain everything in physical or chemical terms (see chapter 2) was so important; it marked a turnaround.

Purkinje and Phenomenology

To dispel the conclusion that Goethe was a totally bad influence, I will note one person who was very much influenced by Goethe, and who made important contributions to a number of disciplines, including psychology. He was the Czech physiologist J. E. Purkinje. Purkinje was an observer who seems to have made a habit of seeing things no one had seen before. Peering into his microscope one day he noticed large, distinctive cells in cerebellar brain tissue. They were what we now call Purkinje cells. It is true that he had far better microscopes than any of his predecessors, and that might be part of it, but nonetheless, it is awfully hard to see anything meaningful in unstained brain tissue, so his identification of these things was some accomplishment. Purkinje also introduced the stethoscope into the medical profession. He didn't invent it, but he was rather hung up on using the pulse to diagnose fever and other problems, so he insisted that the doctors in his hospital always carry one with them. It became universally a part of the doctor's uniform. The doctor became the white-coated person with that thing hanging from the neck or stuffed into a pocket.

He discovered that the far periphery of the visual field is colorblind. He was the first to observe, and recognize as such, the blood vessels in his own eyeball. He discovered the **Purkinje shift,** which is the subtle shift in what color we are most sensitive to as the sky gets darker. In daylight we are most sensitive to yellow, while after sunset, before it is too dark to see any color, we are most sensitive to green. Thus, the relative balance of complex, unsaturated colors shifts a little to the short wavelength end of the spectrum as it gets dark. Most of the time we do not notice any change in the apparent color of things, but once in a while we get caught by surprise. Not far from where I live is a small house that usually looks pastel pink. But at just the right time of evening it appears distinctly purple. It is a remarkable transformation, which I would attribute to it being a strange house. But Purkinje apparently saw something like that, made a number of other observations, and then could see what was happening. It is not that he figured it out; he *saw* the shift somehow. He was a truly remarkable observer, in the tradition of Goethe. It was a sort of naive introspection, what we call **phenomenology.** He looked at things and noted, not what he knew about them, but what he naively saw.

He looked with the innocent eyes of a child, rather than with his sophisticated brain. This is an interesting concept, which we will explore later.

Summary

THE MAIN PHILOSOPHICAL THEMES were in place by 1750, at the time of Hume. The momentum of these relatively new ideas carried them along for a while. Thus, La Mettrie developed a fully mechanistic philosophy. And Hartley greatly expanded Hume's associationism, and mixed it with his own kind of mechanism. In France several scholars, most notably Condillac, were developing associationism. The new empiricism looked healthy, and surely played an important part in the French Enlightenment. Thus by the 1750s all the themes (atomism, mechanism, empiricism, and associationism) seemed to be gathering power and influence. The philosophical groundwork for psychology as we know it seemed to have been well laid. But then it started unraveling.

The French soon got involved with a revolution and an emperor, so they were too busy to think much about psychological matters. Besides, there seemed to be some quirk in the French university system that prevented them from getting anything like psychology established.

In Scotland Thomas Reid led an attack, primarily on Hume, because he wanted psychology to be more intuitive and common-sensical. Reid and his many descendants had everything their way for a century or so. This Scottish school served several important functions. It brought something like psychology into the university, both in Scotland and in the United States. It kept psychology alive, and more positively, introduced new ways of thinking about perception and behavior. The Scottish school also kept our themes from disappearing altogether, because they continued discussing association-ism and empiricism. In their hands psychology was certainly not an experimental science, but it was still alive.

Kant attacked Hume because he wanted psychology to be more reasonable, more like in the good old days when God, human nature, and patriotism were important values. And Kant was extremely influential. German scholars had their own philosophical tradition, so they did not participate in the developments we have discussed so far. They would, in time, develop their own brands of mechanism and associationism and so on, but these developments did not flow from Descartes or Hartley or Hume. It was a different culture, and they would have to find these themes anew. They would in time, however, build a superior university system, one that would dazzle the rest of the world. But before that could happen, they had to do something about all those poets and musicians. They had to get romanticism under control.

By about 1830, the future of experimental psychology lay in the hands of German poets and Scottish ministers. Its prospects did not look very good.

Notes

1. David Hartley was educated at Cambridge, first in theology, which he did not like, and then in medicine, which he did. He was a practicing physician, and in his spare time, over a number of years, he wrote the important monument *Observations on Man* (1749). It is a monument to both associationism and the mechanistic philosophy.

2. James Mill (1773–1836), the father, was for a short time a Presbyterian minister, but soon became involved in political reform. Around 1808 he became a close friend of Bentham, the troublemaker, and Ricardo, the economist. Much of his life was spent in promoting the causes of these friends. He became politically involved with *Elements of Political Economy* (1821). He was best known in his own time for his massive *History of British India*, which appeared between 1818 and 1830. In recognition of this work he was made an executive of the East India Co., which became the India House, until the politics of India were rearranged in 1858.

Jeremy Bentham (1748–1832) is important to the history of psychology because he was obsessed with the concept of hedonism. At the psychological level, he took the pleasure–pain principle for granted; it is the source of all our actions. But Bentham's main concern was to extend the principle to the social–economic–political level, where it became the battle cry of utilitarianism, the doctrine that the just society is one that provides the greatest pleasure for the greatest number of people. To put the doctrine in contemporary American terms, it maintains that we should not impose a tariff on Japanese cars, because there are many more people who would gain by being able to buy good, cheap Toyotas and Nissans than there are who would gain by getting paid to make expensive cars in Detroit. Protective tariffs are generally unutilitarian. Bentham was a very poor, disorganized writer (see Bentham, 1789), and James Mill took it as his task to popularize Bentham's ideas. They were very close friends.

Even while James Mill was fighting fiercely for these social ideas, he was also doing his psychological thing: *Analysis of the Phenomena of the Human Mind* (1829) presented a tightly reasoned, full-fledged associationistic psychology in the tradition of Hartley, but without the mechanistic philosophy that had been so important to Hartley. There is a good biography of Mill by Bain (1882).

3. Jonathan Edwards (1703–58) was an American theologian and a Presbyterian minister, who wrote rather extensively about theological

matters, and who was one of the intellectual leaders of what was called the Great Awakening, a revival of religious spirit around 1740. He was for a short time president of what would become Princeton University. His major works include *Treatise on Religious Affections* (1746) and *Freedom of the Will* (1754).

4. This conflict that some of the romantic poets felt between a scientific, psychological point of view, with which some of them were quite sympathetic, and their greater devotion to their literary art is discussed by Abrams (1953). The conflict was particularly painful to John Stuart Mill (1806–73), the son. As a boy he had been meticulously taught and trained by his father to think along certain logical and political lines. He reports in his autobiography (Mill, 1873) that his recovery from a serious emotional breakdown depended on his discovery of things his father had never dreamed of, things like art, music, and poetry. The arts became his first love, and yet there remained his friendship with Bain and his involvement with the new developments in psychology. We will encounter the younger Mill again in chapter 8.

5. Paul Henri Thiry d'Holbach (1723–89) was a wealthy baron, and he entertained himself by writing quite a number of books that were very hostile to the Church, all churches. At first, books like *Christianity Unmasked* (1761) were surrounded by much secrecy and anonymity, but by the time he got to *System of Nature* (1770), everyone knew who he was.

6. History is always much denser and more complex than it is portrayed. And good historians delight in the complexity of its texture. Thus Brett (1912) documents that there were a host of early French mechanistic philosophers who worried about the relationship of mind and body. We tend to forget them and remember only our hero Descartes. La Mettrie was the first all-out, nothing-but mechanist; he took the step that Descartes could not take (see chapter 2). La Mettrie was too much a humorist for anyone to take his *Man a Machine* (1748) very seriously, but it was translated by the early American psychologist Mary Calkins, who evidently thought it was worth something.

7. I will list some of the French associationists and their major works. Nicolas de Malebranche, 1638–1715, *The Search for Truth* (1675). Etienne Bonnot de Condillac, 1715–80, *Essay on the Origin of Human Knowledge* (1748), and *Treatise on the Sensations* (1754). Helvetius, 1715–71, *On the Mind* (1758). Pierre Cabanis, 1757–1808, *Relations of the Physical and the Moral in Man* (1799).

8. Thomas Reid was the first of many Scottish minister–scholars who worried about psychological matters. He wrote three important works. The first, *Inquiry into the Human Mind* (1764), marks the beginning of the "Scottish school." He also wrote *Essays on the Intellectual Powers of Man* (1785), and *Essays on the Active Powers of the Human Mind* (1788). This later pair of books established a pattern followed by a number of Scottish philosophers.

The *Intellectual Powers* are largely based on associationistic principles, and the subject matter is largely perceptual. On the other hand, the *Active Powers* have to do with choice, a little behavior, morals, and religious values.

Dugald Stewart wrote *Elements of the Philosophy of the Human Mind* (1792–1827). The three volumes are divided into the same dichotomy of intellectual and active powers. He stressed the active powers in his later works, such as *The Philosophy of the Active and Moral Powers of Man* (1828).

9. Thomas Brown wrote *Lectures on the Philosophy of the Human Mind* (1820). One thing that was accomplished by the Scottish school's continued discussion of the active powers of the mind was to focus some attention on behavior. They talked about will, choice, and motivational principles that they supposed supplemented the hedonistic pleasure–pain principle. In general, some kinds of motivational factors were assumed to intervene between the intellectual matrix, learned associations, and what people actually do. We will see later an interesting parallel in the history of behaviorism, where the earliest behaviorist (John Watson) tied behavior directly to what was learned, just as Hartley had, while later behaviorists (for example, Edward Tolman), by introducing motivational ideas, began to free behavior from the direct control of what is learned.

10. Sir William Hamilton (1788–1856) is the last of the Scottish minister–psychologists to concern us. His only major work was the large, nonpsychological *Lectures on Metaphysics* (1859). His contribution to psychology is found in his additional notes and essays in *The Psychology of Thomas Reid* (1852). Included in there is his detailed history of associationism. Warren (1921) wrote a very friendly, readable history of the associationistic doctrine, based largely on Hamilton's work. Hamilton's view of things was severely criticized by J. S. Mill in *An Examination of Sir William Hamilton's Philosophy* (1865). For all practical purposes, that marked the beginning of the end of the Scottish tradition.

11. We have noted that Thomas Reid was something of a nativist, who referred to instincts, and something he called *common sense*, which was a sort of intuitive knowledge about what we can believe in. In Hamilton's notes on Reid's philosophy he discusses the special meaning Reid attached to the term *common sense* (Hamilton, 1852). Several scholars have wondered whether Kant paid much attention to Reid. He might have; they were both of a conservative turn of mind, and the timing was just about right because Kant's *Critique* followed Reid's *Inquiry* by 17 years. So there was motive and opportunity.

Chapter Five

Sensory Physiology and Perceptual Problems

B Y ABOUT 1860 German physiologists had reversed the earlier phase of the poets—we should call them the nature-philosophers—and were making rapid advances, particularly in sensory physiology. Helmholtz, probably the greatest of sensory physiologists, was by that time making remarkable progress in the fields of vision and audition. The hope, the plan, the dream, was to be able to explain all sorts of perceptual phenomena in terms of how the eye and the ear worked. It was to be, as much as possible, a peripheral account. Thus, if things look fuzzy, it is because the lens is out of focus. If this color looks brighter than that one, it is because the retina is more sensitive to it. It was all supposed to be due to the peripheral machinery.

But a new problem was emerging, a problem that threatened to spoil the gains that had been so dramatically won by the mechanists. The problem was that a lot of perceptual phenomena appeared to be rather psychological in character, and of central rather than peripheral origin. Some of the problems of perception had yielded to a mechanistic approach, but a growing number of others would not yield. Indeed, the psychology of perception became such a major problem that a new academic discipline, something called psychology, had to be organized to deal with it. As we look at some of these perceptual problems in this chapter we will see how psychology got started.

Early Reaction-Time Experiments

A SEEMINGLY UNIMPORTANT event occurred back in 1795 that was to have remarkable implications for the development of psychology. The minor incident was that Maskelyne, who was in charge, fired Kinnebrook because he did not seem to be doing his job adequately. Kinnebrook was making consistent errors. These gentlemen were not allowed to make errors because they were in what was supposed to be the most precise of all the sciences, astronomy. Maskelyne was the Royal Astronomer at Greenwich Observatory in London. He fired his assistant Kinnebrook, and noted in the official published record of the observatory that whole series of observations were somewhat in error. Further observations were no doubt made, and in time everything was straightened out. Tough on Mr. Kinnebrook, but otherwise no harm done. So why were Kinnebrook's errors important? Because Maskelyne's report of systematic errors ultimately came to the attention of the great German mathematician and astronomer Friedrich Bessel who, about 1820, got to work seriously studying observational errors.*

Kinnebrook had been timing the transit of certain stars. He used a telescope that was aligned to the south and was fixed with a fine wire (or strand from a spider web) running up and down in the eyepiece. As the star appears to pass behind the obstacle—its *transit*—the star blinks out for an instant. Kinnebrook, and a lot of astronomers, would time such observations with a clock that had just been read to the nearest minute, and that was ticking out the seconds. Getting the nearest second was easy, but unfortunately, that was not accurate enough. The observer was supposed to time the event to within one-tenth of a second, and that is where the errors start occurring. Notice that there was no standard of time in 1795 because there was no electrical communication. Time itself was pretty uncertain in those days. Nobody in downtown London had much sense of time because the church bells themselves, the ancient time standard, were so undependable. But time was of great importance to the accurate work of the observatory, so each observatory had to work from its own time standard. And the only way they could know what time it was at Greenwich was to set their clock from the transit time of some standard star. So the integrity of their whole enterprise depended on the accuracy with which Kinnebrook could do his job. The trouble was that Kinnebrook's times were consistently 0.75 second or so later than Maskelyne's own times. A small enough error it might seem, but actually quite intolerable at the current state of the art. All of the work at Greenwich was in jeopardy, and so Kinnebrook was dismissed.

Twenty-five years later, Bessel systematically compared a number of different observers, and found that often there were consistent differences.

---

*Bessel (1784–1846) is best known for his study of this problem, for his measuring for the first time the actual distance of a nearby star, and for his work on what are called Bessel functions. What is a Bessel function? If you hold one end of a length of chain so that it is hanging from your fist, and you start moving your fist in a circle, you will see the thing wobble around for a bit and then start to rotate smoothly. When it is rotating thus, it will be bent in a graceful curve and the lower end will be swinging around in a large circle. The shape of the chain can then be described by a Bessel function of zero order. If you then try to speed it up by rotating faster and more forcefully, the chain will wobble around quite a bit, but finally settle down with *two* humps and the lower end will again move out in a big circle. Now you have a Bessel function of the first order. Engineers use them for solving a variety of problems.

One observer would always be a fraction of a second too fast, another, like Kinnebrook, would be a little too slow. No one knew for sure just who was right because of the impossibility of comparing results from different observatories. The problem took all of Bessel's data-analyzing skill. He was greatly aided by recent work of Karl Gauss. (Many stories have been told about the legendary Gauss, by some accounts the greatest mathematician of all time.) Gauss had recently worked out a mathematical function for errors of measurement. He had discovered that if there is a large number of possible sources of error, and if they all occur randomly and unpredictably, then there is a neat equation that describes the distribution of measurements. It is, unfortunately, an integral equation that cannot be integrated directly, but its different values can be tabulated, and they have indeed been tabulated countless times. It is the bell-shaped normal distribution. Statisticians owe a good deal to Gauss.[1]

The Personal Equation

Bessel assumed that different observers would have different characteristic time errors. All that had to be done for astronomical purposes was to determine each observer's characteristic error and add or subtract that amount from their observations. Every observer would have a **personal equation,** and that is the name given to the whole business started by the unfortunate Mr. Kinnebrook. Ironically, he had been fired too soon, according to Bessel, because he would be perfectly okay once we knew how large his average error was. A further benefit from Bessel's work was a better sense of how accurate transit timings could actually be, because he was calculating variances as well as means for the different observers he was working with.

Bessel is important to our story not only because he was obtaining data on the personal equation, thereby working out the astronomers' problems, he was also thinking about what it could be about sensory systems that could cause such errors. The customary assumption at that time, the assumption made by no less an authority than Johannes Müller, was that nerve impulses are instantaneous. In effect, no time is lost when a nerve impulse goes from here to there. It was also generally supposed that the mind (awareness) followed immediately from sensory input with no delay. Where, then, could errors of as much as a second be coming from? Something seemed to be wrong in the assumptions. Bessel started suggesting possibilities as early as 1822. The eye and the ear cannot compare input directly, he proposed at first; it takes time to shift from one to the other. In a couple of decades there would be all sorts of hypotheses, most of them advanced by astronomers, to whom it was very important to find some sort of solution to the problem. It was suggested that some observers were doing the task visually and that when the star disappeared they had to go back and reconstruct the sound of the ticks, and that was somehow a different kind of process from what the other observers were doing who went at the task with their ears and then had to reconstruct the visual disappearance of the star from memory. It was suggested that the optic nerve might be slower than the auditory nerve. Although both had been assumed to be infinitely fast, the accumulating data were suggesting that perhaps that was wrong and that, somehow, that was where the errors, the personal equation, was coming from. Helmholtz's discovery that neural transmission was by no means instantaneous but actually rather slow made some such hypothesis rather attractive, but the darned nerves involved were much too short for this to make much sense either.

Indeed, none of the various physiological approaches to the problem looked very promising, and so it gradually began to occur to a few venturesome souls that the problem might ultimately be psychological. So much of the evidence indicated that it had something to do with what the observer was attending to, or how the observer switched attention from one sensory mode to the other, or some such factor, that it was beginning to look like a psychological question. One person who held that view was Wilhelm Wundt, whom we will meet up close in the next chapter. Here we will just note Wundt's interest in the personal equation problem. He wanted to get it out of the astronomical observatory and into the physiology laboratory. To that end, about 1860 he devised an interesting apparatus that consisted of a pendulum that swung down along a sort of protractor, with a prominent number scale on it. The device was constructed so that at some point in the swing a click would occur, and the observer's task was to judge when, that is, at what point on the number scale, the click had occurred. From the observer's point of view the task was very like the task of timing star transits. There was visual information and auditory information, and these disparate sensory events had to be correlated and related in some way.[2]

It was the surprising failure of experienced observers to relate the two inputs appropriately, of course, that had given us the personal equation problem in the first place. But while most of the work on the problem, starting with Bessel's pioneering studies, had seen the personal equation as an observational difficulty that had to be overcome, Wundt had a new perspective that was quite different. He saw the troublesome observational errors as providing a handle on how the mind works. For Wundt these observational errors provided a window on the mind itself, through which one might get a glimpse of human attentional processes.

It is interesting how slowly Wundt's approach had developed. He started on the problem with his pendulum in 1860 or 1861, and described some experimental findings in 1863. That made it almost 70 years after Kinnebrook's original misadventure, a good 50 years after Gauss had worked out the mathematics of random errors, and more than 40 years after Bessel reported the first systematic experimental data. Much of the delay can be attributed to the fact that there was no psychology at the time, and that this was precisely the time when physiologists were getting going on such problems. This was just at that time when Müller's students were beginning to flourish. It is interesting, too, that even though Wundt continued to work on the problem for many years he was never really able to solve it; he was never able to see very much through his window.

The personal equation story illustrates a most important shift in thinking about the problem. It started in as a very practical matter, almost a political issue: How do they save the reputation and integrity of Greenwich Observatory? This is the way the astronomers went at it, or at least that was Maskelyne's approach. Then Bessel wanted a more principled attack on the problem, one that would solve the practical problem, certainly, but one that would also provide a dependable and more scientific solution to the problem. But the hard-science approach was not very fruitful for the good reason that the problem was basically psychological and not neural or physiological. It had something to do with attention. Wundt was the first to see this, and in looking at the personal equation from a new, psychological viewpoint, and by doing what was essentially psychological research on it, he became, in effect, one of the first to do experimental psychology. Not the first; that honor clearly goes to Fechner, whom we will meet shortly. And maybe not the second, who could very well be Helmholtz. It is rather tricky trying to sort out the order here because all of these men influenced each other, and all of them were, in one way or another, discovering psychology. Moreover, these events were happening over several years, all during the 1850s and 1860s. But it was beginning to happen! Psychology was beginning to emerge from physiology; it was emerging and becoming something different.

The Complication Experiment

I will take this opportunity to cite a fourth physiologist who during this same time period began to think like a psychologist. He was clearly influenced by Wundt's work on the personal equation, and he would in turn soon inspire Wundt to follow through on what he was doing. He was the Dutchman F. C. Donders, who was the professor of physiology at Utrecht for many years. His early work in 1846 on visual localization was also rather psychological in orientation, but he is best remembered for his research on **reaction time.** His subjects were supposed to respond as quickly as possible to some stimulus given by the experimenter. In the initial research (published in 1868) Donders used auditory stimuli because he had speech-activated timers. Under one condition the experimenter would from time to time utter one syllable that the subject would repeat. Under another condition the experimenter would utter one of several possible syllables and the subject would repeat the same one. He found that the second procedure lead to consistently longer reaction times than the first procedure. Apparently it took his subject nearly one-tenth of a second longer to select the appropriate syllable out of the set of possible ones than it did to respond when there was only one possible response. This complication experiment indicated that if one could believe that the perception of the stimulus and the initiation of the response required the same time under both conditions, then one could infer that the more psychological thing, the selection process itself, required about one-tenth of a second to carry out. This was precisely the sort of thing that Wundt had been hoping to find in his own work. In some ways Donders's procedure was simpler and more direct than Wundt's pendulum procedure, so it is no wonder he was excited about the Dutchman's research. In the ensuing years they both expanded upon the procedure, using lights and sounds and touches, and offering different kinds of choices and decisions for the subject to make.[3]

With Wundt's and Donders's research of the 1860s, we are very close to the beginning of psychology as an experimental discipline, very close indeed. Perhaps their research (together with Wundt's own unusual personal qualities) would have been sufficient to get experimental psychology started, even if Fechner had not come along just when he did to get it started his way. In any case, Fechner is important, and we will get to his story toward the end of this chapter. First, we have to look at the problem of perception.

The Problem of Perception

WE NOTED IN chapter 2 that Helmholtz was a mechanist; he was never happier than when he was being a physicist. He was undoubtedly fondest of the first volume of his *Physiological Optics* where he could regard the eye as an optical instrument, with the lens focusing light at a retinal point, and so on. For him, as for all those who had taken the apocryphal pledge, the physiology of vision was also basically a physical thing. The second volume was largely devoted to his analysis of color vision. It was all a matter of three kinds of color receptors being tuned to the basic primaries. Our appreciation of color was much like our perception in general in that it depended ultimately on what was going on in the periphery. The perception of shape depended on the focusing of light rays on the retinal cells, and the perception of color depended on different wavelengths of light falling on the color receptors. All such perceptual phenomena depended on readily understandable physical events that occur in the eye. A psychological, mental, central event such as the sensation of color is explained by mechanical, physical, peripheral events going on in the eye. It was the best of all worlds for the mechanists, a realization of their dream.[4]

But in the third volume of the *Physiological Optics*, written in 1866, Helmholtz had to come to grips with the problem of space perception. And this was something he could not handle as he would like, because he had convinced himself that space perception is basically a psychological matter.

In spite of the great authority of Kant maintaining that our appreciation of space is innate, Helmholtz was determined to the contrary that it is all learned.

Unconscious Inference

To prepare the groundwork for his analysis of spatial perception, he faced the psychological music with a discussion of perception in general. He began with a remarkable statement:

> The sensations aroused by light in the nervous mechanisms of vision enable us to form conceptions as to the existence, form and position of external objects.

Here we have a dichotomy; on the one hand sensations arise because of light reflected from stimulus objects that happens to fall on the retina. Sensations are generally little patches of color scattered here and there. But what we see, what we are aware of, is external objects, a tree here and a house there. And we do not see the actual objects as such, but rather our idea or conception of them. What we are aware of is our idea of the tree and our idea of the house. How do we pass from the one realm to the other, from the world of sensations to the world of ideas? They are not in direct correspondence, Helmholtz admits reluctantly. Rather, the sensations *enable* the ideas to occur. That is the word he used. The actual process of transformation is obscure for the very good reason that it is a psychological process, and hence difficult to get at experimentally.

Helmholtz's position here is curiously very close to that of Thomas Reid, who said we see the tree because we *believe* there is really a tree out there. But Helmholtz expressed it somewhat differently. He said that the act of perception is like a conclusion or an inference. If the sensations that stimulate the visual system are sufficiently like our idea of the object, then we infer that the object is really there. There is rarely enough information in the sensations to justify such a conclusion, but we make it anyway. A glimpse of the fuzzy green stuff, just a flash of sensory input, and we infer that there is a tree there; we will experience a clear idea of the tree. Helmholtz stressed that this inferential process is quite unlike ordinary conscious thought. First of all, *it is immediate*; it takes almost no time to arrive at the conclusion, and we are totally unaware of any deliberation. It is not that we ponder over whether or not those green sensations represent a tree. The first thing we are aware of is that there is a tree over there. A second aspect of the inference is that *it is irresistible*. It doesn't matter if we understand that someone has painted a picture of a tree in our line of sight, the thing is still going to be seen as a tree. That is why illusions are illusions; no matter how frequently and carefully we measure it and determine that this line is just as long as that line, when we look at the darned thing it looks shorter (see figure 5.1). The psychological process that transforms sensations into ideas is something that Helmholtz did not pretend to understand, but he had a name for it. He called it **unconscious inference.** This name embodied the notions that it was immediate, that it was irresistible and not subject to cognitive control, and, most importantly, that it was based on *prior experience.* If you have no prior idea of a tree, then you are not going to see a tree when you encounter that bunch of fuzzy green sensations.

Different Kinds of Perception

The German language has a few more words to describe perception than English does. There is *Vorstellung*, which is an idea pure and simple, some image pulled out of memory without any support from sensory input. If you can conjure up an image of Arthur's crazy mustache, that is a *Vorstellung*. We would call it an idea or a pictorial memory. Then there is *Perzeption*, which is when you have no memory or recognition of what you see, but there it is. You meet Arthur one day without his mustache, and you cannot keep your eyes off that unfamiliar lip. Because you cannot figure out what it is, it is pure sensation, a *Perzeption*. We call that *sensation*, that is, perception without any meaning. But then there is the more typical perception that lies somewhere in between, having some meaning and also some sensory support. Such a thing we call *perception*. There's Arthur again; we saw him, yes, but we also recognized him by his crazy mustache. In German such a customary perception is an *Anschauungen*, which we can translate as **apperception,** a perception that is supported both by sensory input and by our prior experience. If we attempt to strip away the meaning part of an apperception, so that we are looking only at the sensory part of it, that is a *Wahrnehmung*. The painter is dealing with *Wahrnehmungs* when representing a tree with little splotches of color. In this array of words, it is clear that *Perzeption* is purely sensory, of primary interest to the sensory physiologist. But the other three words require us to include in the formula prior experience, meaning, and verbal labels or symbols of the object. In short, they all get us into psychological considerations.

FIGURE 5.1
The Müller–Lyre illusion.

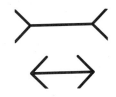

Color was no problem for Helmholtz; he treated it as a *Perzeption*. But space perception was something else. He was convinced that it was an *Anschauungen*, in large part psychological. Our spatial sense is learned, he maintained. Part of the reason for this empiricistic viewpoint was that Helmholtz had carried out an experiment in which subjects wore prism glasses that displaced everything in the visual field. When his subjects were required to handle objects, they made errors in locating things at first, but soon, in a few minutes, they adjusted to the distortion and were able to handle objects without error. Then when first returned to normal vision without the prisms, for a short time they made errors in the other direction. Spatial perceptions are clearly of the *Anschauungen*, or apperception, variety, in that they depend on both sensory stimulation from what is out there and from our prior experience, Helmholtz contended. Both factors are important. Sometimes, he says, we see something that does not make sense, but then we reconceptualize the scene. For example, we will see that this object is not really in front of that one, and then the whole scene snaps into place and makes sense to us. The correct picture comes in part from cognitive factors, and in part from sensory input. Both factors are insistent enough that we cannot dismiss them. He notes that it is easy to read meanings into everything, and rather difficult to divorce meanings and look at the raw sensations themselves. Thus, the whole matter is biased in the psychological direction.

Part of the reason Helmholtz was so firmly convinced that spatial perceptions are heavily based on learning is that such perceptions have to be correlated with voluntary movements. If I move my eyes over a large object, then the sensory excitation changes in complex ways. The sensory pattern shifts this way and that, but my apperception, what I *see*, becomes clearer. And if I move around in space, then not only will the sensory patterns excited by different objects shift systematically, but the relationships among the different patterns will be altered in very complex ways. And yet what I see is a clear picture of how everything is located in space.

Helmholtz had a further reason for stressing the learned part of perception. He tells us repeatedly that the human eye is a poor optical instrument—it is badly constructed and full of distortion. At one point he says that it is such a bad optical instrument that he would not pay two cents to buy one. But, he says, if you get two of them and hook them up to a human brain, then you have a marvelous observing system! Basically, we see much more accurately what is out there than we have any right to see. The whole visual system working together manages to correct for all the distortions and to present us with views of the world that are far finer than we deserve to see. What a dilemma for the great physiologist who wanted so much to reduce all perceptual phenomena to physical events going on in the periphery. What we see was supposed to be determined by the physiology of the eyeball. Yet he was forced by his own understanding of perception to concede that a very large part of it was psychological, cognitive, learned, and organized by prior experience.

Helmholtz was not the first to get caught in the dilemma presented by the problem of perception, that we see the world more accurately than we have any right to see it. But he was the most distinguished, and the problem reached a sort of culmination and crisis with him. And perhaps, too, he was the most torn and conflicted by it. In the next section we will note some interesting anticipations of the problem.

Perceptual Anomalies

ONE OF THE EARLIEST known anomalies, and yet one of the most remarkable, was discovered by a French scientist who was at the time in the court of Louis the 14th. His name was Edme Mariotte, and the story goes that in 1668 he discovered the **blind spot.**

Mariotte and the Blind Spot

When Mariotte told King Louis about the blind spot His Majesty was delighted, especially when he devised his own version of the game. The way the king played the game, he would line up a bunch of court people or noblemen and stare at one face, and then he would close one eye and observe whose head disappeared (see figure 5.2). The phenomenon is obvious—once you have removed a mark on a piece of paper, or someone's head. But left to their own devices, no one would ever discover the phenomenon. No one suspects they have a blind spot in each eye until they get to Psychology 100. People using two eyes cannot see the blind spot because each eye can see what lies in the other eye's blind spot. If a two-eyed person closes one eye the person still cannot see what is missing. One reason is that the blind spot lies well away from the fovea; it is off in the periphery where we generally pay little attention.

But there is something else, another reason why we do not see anything missing in a monocular field. We tend to "paint in" anything that is missing. If you test for the spot with a piece of white paper, the hole gets painted in

FIGURE 5.2
Play the King's game. Close your left eye while you fixate the X.
Then move the page in and out until your friend's head is gone.

white. If you test with a blue piece of paper, the hole will be painted in blue. Then if you test with a printed page, the hole will appear filled with fuzzy printing, too fuzzy to read out there in the periphery, but it certainly looks like printed material. I once did a small unpublished study with subjects who watched a fixation point while I flashed briefly the message "H – T" centered around the blind spot. Subjects knew it was a blind spot study, but even so they were helpless. Everyone reported that the message had been *hat* or *hot* or *hit* and they were generally quite confident in their reports. In short, if observers expect there to be a word out there in the periphery, they will paint in whatever is needed to make it a word, and then that is what they see!

Certainly we have here a major anomaly, a clear case where the perception is not controlled by sensations generated by the eye but arise, somehow, from the mind itself. What appears in the blind spot depends on some sort of contextual effect, because it is controlled by the other things that can be seen in the visual field. Most of the time the filled-in blind spot will provide a perception that is more accurate than we could expect from the sensations coming from the eye, because the sensation is silent but the outside world is most likely to present objects very like those that can be seen in the peripheral context. Thus, perception will usually be a better reflection of what is out there than it should be. All of these anomalies are like that.

One further puzzle: How did Mariotte ever discover it? *Nobody* can "see" it there. We suspect that even the great observer Purkinje could not "see" the hole in his visual field, so how was Mariotte able to do so? The answer is that he did not discover it in the sense of one day seeing it there. According to Helmholtz, the ultimate authority on everything visual, Mariotte knew from the anatomy of the eyeball that all the visual neurons gather together at one point somewhat off center, and exit the eyeball from there. He reasoned that at that point the eye has to be nonfunctional, so he went looking for it. He probably started his research by making a couple of marks on a piece of paper. And what he discovered was an anomaly: How we perceive things in the world does not necessarily reflect the information coming in from our sense organs.[5]

Dalton and Daltonism

A second major anomaly was reported in 1794 by John Dalton, our friend the chemist, when he discovered that he was colorblind. This affliction, which used to be called **Daltonism** after the discoverer, is not rare; it falls on 5 percent or so of people, and it is much more common in men and in certain highly inbred subcultures. Dalton was a Quaker, and they have a high incidence of colorblindness. It is a great nuisance for those who suffer from it. A psychologist I know enjoys hiking in the mountains with his wife in the springtime. She is constantly raving about the wildflowers, which to him are a great effort to see. To him everything out on the hillside is more or less green, and what she calls a wildflower is a very subtle pattern of petals, cute little circular patterns of petal-shaped things. He can only discriminate the petal patterns up close, and the vast hillside of color is totally lost on him. And the ones up close are hardly worth the perceptual effort; he cannot understand why she gets so excited about wildflowers.

Presumably Dalton's friends were laughing at him one day because he had a red sock on one foot and a green sock on the other. And because he was a remarkably intelligent and perceptive person, he was ultimately able to figure out what was wrong with his vision. He probably had some help from his wife. Many colorblind men rely on their wives a good deal in sorting out their clothes. The remarkable thing about all this is that the not-uncommon malady of colorblindness escaped everyone's attention until just 200 years ago. No one noticed because colorblind people labeled grass green and apples red and oranges orange, just as everyone else did. Their sensations were faulty, but because they were able to adjust their language, their cognitions, and their perceptions, no one seemed to notice the gap between sensation and perception.

Fraunhofer and Luminosity

The German chemist Joseph Fraunhofer was fascinated by the world of light and color. He developed the spectroscope, which proved to be an invaluable bridge between the chemical realm and the world of color, because when a given chemical substance burns it emits distinctive colors of light. In pursuing these matters, Fraunhofer discovered in 1815 that the human eye is greatly more sensitive to yellow and green light that falls in the middle of the spectrum than it is to red at one end of the rainbow and blue and violet at the other end. This difference in sensitivity is not trivial; it is on the order of 50 to 1. By all rights, we should see very little except yellow and green; the ends of the spectrum should be lost on us just as the colors outside the visible spectrum, infrared and ultraviolet, are lost. The modern world provides many illustrations of this premise that were not available in Fraunhofer's time. Thus, we now have "tungsten" camera film to be used indoors with incandescent lighting and "daylight" film to be used outdoors in sunlight. Woe unto those who get the films mixed up: Indoor film used outdoors gives insanely blue pictures, while outdoor film used indoors gives nothing but yellow and brown tones. And yet when you or I take familiar objects indoors or outdoors they do not change apparent color.

The explanation, which was only dimly understood by Fraunhofer, is that candles and tungsten lights are extremely yellow and provide almost no blue. Moreover, we have very little sensitivity to what little blue there is. And yet we are perfectly capable of seeing the whole range of hues even by candlelight or with a 40-watt bulb. We see a blue object as blue even though the object is reflecting almost no blue light and our eyes are very poorly sensitive to it. Even so we see it as blue, its true color. This is another anomaly. Another way to say it is that what we see is more closely related to the **distal stimulus** (the object at a distance) than to the **proximal stimulus** (the close-by physical activity in the eye). Indoor film is constructed to greatly exaggerate reds and blues, so used in good sunlight it will make everything look blue and purple. But the human observer is usually totally unaware of the distortion. Once in a while you get deceived. You may have bought what you thought was a green sweater only to discover that it looks blue when you go outside. But those kinds of deceptions are unusual, which is why we find them startling. Most of the time, colors remain true as the illumination changes. And—Fraunhofer's point—most of the time colors remain true even though our sensitivity to them varies greatly.

We have no good explanation of the anomaly, but we have a name for it. We call it *color constancy*. This is merely a label for Fraunhofer's initial observation that *colors are usually judged correctly, even though the sensory information that would seem to be necessary for making the judgment is lacking.*

Wheatstone and Binocular Disparity

Another curiosity was first noted by the physicist Charles Wheatstone, who is today remembered by his invention of an electrical "bridge" that enables one to measure the resistance of an electrical component without passing any current through it. The component is actually functioning, but the current flowing in it is balanced by an equal current that is induced to flow in the opposite direction. Thus he gave us the fascinating concept of measuring a physical system without the measurement process intruding into the system. In psychology we have only just recently arrived at similar noninvasive procedures. It is interesting that all these anomalies were found not by physiologists or anyone who was primarily concerned with perception, but by other kinds of scientists, mainly ones we would classify as physical scientists.

About 1838 Wheatstone described a curious phenomenon. If we look at an object close at hand, then the left eye is going to see a slightly different view of it than the right eye. If you are standing right in front of me, my left eye will be able to see somewhat more of the right side of your face, sort of around the corner, than my right eye can see. With one eye I can see a little less than 180 degrees of your face, but with both eyes I can see a bit more than 180 degrees. The two eyes will have a lot of corresponding sensations. The front of your nose will look the same to both eyes. By all rights, the front of your nose should appear sharp and clear. But the parts of your face that present slightly different views to my two eyes should appear fuzzy and obscure. But that does not happen. Instead, a remarkable transformation takes place. Your whole face looks pretty much in focus, but it is seen in three dimensions. The front of your nose sticks out in front, your cheekbones lie just behind, and your ears lie still farther back. The noncorresponding parts of the images in the two eyes should produce fuzziness, but no, they locate you in space. Your nose is 12 inches away, and your ears 16 inches.

Disparate views to the two eyes, what we call **binocular disparity,** call forth not a fuzzy perception but depth perception. It can be studied systematically. If you present two points of light to the left eye separated by 30 millimeters (mm), and two points to the right eye separated by 32 mm, when those images merge you will see two spots of light in space with the one on the right about 10 percent farther away than the one on the left. If you take two photographs from the Brooklyn Bridge with the camera moved a few inches between shots and present the pictures separately to your two eyes through an appropriate arrangement of lenses or mirrors. Wow! You'll be there standing on the bridge. Suitable instruments were designed by a man named David Brewster beginning about 1846, and by Oliver Wendell Holmes (not the judge but his father the physician) about 1861. These *stereoscopes* became very popular, as did pairs of photographs that would take you to the pyramids, the Roman Coliseum, or almost anywhere you wanted to go (see figure 5.3).

Maxwell and the Wheel

We should look at one further anomaly. The great physicist Clerk Maxwell had a great interest in color, particularly "artificial" colors, which were those that were created without using the actual seen color. One way to do this is to spin a wheel that is painted with black and white spirals. The simplest demonstration is to spin a wheel that is half green and half red. It looks yellow. There is no yellow in the excitation, which is alternatively green and red, but

FIGURE 5.3
Example of a stereoscope image.

the result unquestionably looks yellow. Maxwell reported these and a number of related effects in 1855. It was, again, a failure of our perceptions to match our sensory input. Maxwell's wheel was going to cause all sorts of trouble for later perception theorists. The next perceptual curiosity was going to start all sorts of adventures for perception experimentalists.

Weber and the Sense of Touch

The great majority of the research on sensory physiology during the period we have reviewed was in vision. Some work was also done in audition. The study of the chemical senses, odor and taste, lagged seriously behind, and would not become active areas until the 1870s. But the sense of touch had attracted considerable interest, thanks mainly to the early pioneering work of Ernst Weber (1795–1878). Weber was the professor of physiology at the University of Leipzig, beginning in 1818, when he was a young man. (He was six years older than Johannes Müller, and off to a somewhat faster start.) His major work on touch is the book *On Touch*, which was published in 1834, the year after Müller published the first volume of his *Physiology*. The book contained accounts of Weber's own extensive research, and it described methods and test instruments that are still used today in the study of touch.

You start with a pair of compass points, and touch your subject with one or with both points. Can the subject tell how many points are touching? You have to run a series of test trials randomizing one and both points, and randomizing the separation distance. After running thousands of such trials Weber found that on the most sensitive parts of the body surface, the fingertips and the lips, the two points can be detected as two points even if they are separated by as little as $\frac{1}{16}$th of an inch. On the least sensitive parts of the body, such as the middle of the back, the points need to be separated 3 or 4 inches or they will be sensed as just one. Weber worked it all out in great detail. He also developed a standard set of fine bristles mounted on little sticks. A given bristle was calibrated by pressing it against a chemical balance and noting its force (weight) when it suddenly bends. Armed with such a set of bristles, Weber could run around the body again and determine where the most and least sensitive areas were in terms of detection of touch. The results came out very highly correlated with the previous set of results. He concluded, correctly, that some areas of the body are served by a much richer supply of sensory nerves than other areas.

Weber and Weight-Lifting

We tend to think of touch in literal terms, that is, as touch. But Kant had introduced the confusing concept of common sensibility, which sensory physiologists then had to live with. Any sensation arising from the body

Ernst Weber

or from its surface was included in common sensibility. The sensations of hunger and thirst were included. The sense of effort or fatigue of the muscles was included. Pain was part of it. And everything sensed on the surface of the body was included, even dimensions that had little to do with touch, such as hot and cold. Weber tried to sort out these different dimensions. Thus, *On Touch* was pretty well restricted to what was detected by the skin; that is, pressure detection, temperature sensitivity, and bodily localization. He later wrote an expansion that covered a greater array of dimensions, *The Sense of Touch and Common Sensibility*, in 1846. It is of great historical importance, however, that Weber did not restrict his earlier research just to an analysis of sensory events on the skin. *On Touch* describes a whole series of studies in which subjects were picking up small weights. On a typical trial, the subject would sit comfortably at a table, and in a standardized manner lift off the table a small metal box filled with something so that it weighed 2.5 ounces. Then he would pick up another little box that weighed 2.7 ounces. Can the subject tell that the second one is a trifle heavier than the first? Yes, according to Weber's findings, this small difference would be detected on most trials.

Weber thought of this as touch, but we understand it now as kinesthesis, or muscle sense. The sensory information comes from tension receptors in the muscle tendons and muscle tissue, rather than from the skin. But in his time it was part of the broadly defined touch sense. It does not make very much difference, however, because the important thing in his work was not the discovery of mechanisms but the empirical generalization he was able to arrive at from his extensive research. Weber discovered that a difference in weight of 1 part in 30 was just detectable. This 1:30 ratio was found no matter what the actual weights were. The difference between 30 and 31 grams (about 1 oz) was just discernable. So was the difference between 30 and 31 ounces. And so, just discriminable, was the difference between the more athletic weights of 30 and 31 pounds. This generalization, which we now call Weber's Law, is sort of neat and interesting, but it hardly looks very basic. But it was indeed basic, vitally important, in the history of experimental psychology. It was important because one remarkable man thought it was important. Weber himself did not attach particular importance to his 1:30 generalization, but he had a strange colleague at Leipzig who did.

Fechner and Psychophysics

GUSTAV FECHNER (1801–87) had been a student at Leipzig and had studied physiology with Weber. But then he became disenchanted with the medical profession and turned to mathematics and physics. In 1834 he became the professor of physics at Leipzig.

Interestingly, Fechner had always led a sort of double life. When he was not being a physicist he was a poet, a literary type. Most of his literary work was published under the pseudonym Dr. Mises, and it was rather mystical, philosophical, and strange. He tells us that angels are spherical. He says that all matter, living and otherwise, has consciousness. He suggests that the earth is the mother of us all. He wrote this stuff off and on over most of his life; there was evidently something he was desperately trying to say.[6]

When he was still in his 30s, Fechner became fascinated by a perceptual phenomenon, after-images. He soon discovered that the brighter the light he stared at, the more impressive his after-images were. Soon he was staring at the sun, and soon he was essentially blind. He convalesced for a few years and got his sight back, but he still had a variety of psychological problems, and did not function very well. It was during this reclusive convalescent period of his life that Dr. Mises wrote some of his best-known poetry. And like Descartes 200 years earlier, he had virtually dropped out of society and was spending a lot of time in bed.

According to his own story, one day when he was in bed thinking poetic thoughts, he had an important insight. He knew at the time that it would be important, so he made a note of it. Thus, we know the day when Fechner got himself pulled together and turned around and back on track. It was October 22, 1850. We all tend to anchor our perspective of complex matters with very concrete and specific events and settings. The more concrete the better. So Fechner's memo is nice; it tempts us with a concrete image. Fechner is there in bed on that chilly October day in Leipzig doing something important. What happened, of course, is that psychology was conceived!

Gustav Fechner

The Idea of Psychophysics

Fechner's poetic works had dealt with Descartes's dilemma of how mind and body are related. He was also well aware of Kant's dictum that a science of psychology was impossible because one cannot do experiments on the mind. Suddenly he saw a solution to both problems. His great insight indicated how to do experiments. He was also sensitive to what I labeled the mechanistic curse, which is the peculiarity that it is easy to measure mechanical things and very challenging to measure anything psychological. But he now understood how to measure psychological events. He suddenly saw how to build a bridge that would link the mental and the physical worlds so intimately that all these problems would disappear. He had a new mission: To tie the physical and mental worlds together. He would measure perception, and show how psychological experiments could be done. He was out of bed and into the laboratory, and he never retreated to his bed again.

Fechner started with Weber's generalization that a threshold of difference from a given stimulus was proportional to the intensity of the stimulus. If we designate the threshold difference as ΔS, then Weber's finding indicated that $\Delta S = a \cdot S$, where a is some constant. We have seen that Weber found that with touch $a = 1:30$, so if the stimulus is 30 units, then the difference in intensity that is just noticeable is 1 unit. Fechner distinguished this fundamental finding, $\Delta S = a \cdot S$, by calling it Weber's Law. That label has stuck; we still call it Weber's Law.

Fechner's great insight was that the right side of this equation, the $a \cdot S$ term, is a physical thing. It is given in terms of $\frac{1}{30}$ ounce, or some fraction of a centimeter, or some fraction of a second—it is always presented in some kind of purely physical terms. The right side of the equation is a measure of something out there in the external world, something that can be scientifically accounted for. But the left side of the equation, the ΔS part, is purely psychological! It measures a psychological judgment. It is something cognitive. It usually reflects all the sophistication of the subject because it is ordinarily a difficult discrimination. When you are doing a Weber-style experiment, you have to wait for the subject to make an educated guess because you are typically working close to the discrimination threshold. There is little information to be gained from asking your subject to make a very easy discrimination. Thus, the left side of the equation describing Weber's Law is a psychological matter. And because the two sides of the equation are equal, Fechner said, we have a bridge between the psychological world and some measurable thing in the physical world. And Fechner gave us a name for this kind of bridge: He called it **psychophysics.**

Measuring Sensation

Fechner devoted most of the next 10 years to conducting experiments and working out various details. He studied difference thresholds: How much bigger than some standard must a stimulus be to be just discriminably bigger? He also studied absolute thresholds: What is the faintest stimulus that is just discriminable from no stimulus at all? In both cases there is a "just noticeable difference," the famous **j.n.d.,** between one perceived stimulus intensity and another. The first j.n.d., the first one beyond no intensity at all, gives an experimental value for the absolute threshold. Then the next j.n.d. in intensity will also be quite faint, but it should be pretty easily discriminable from no stimulus at all. Thus, a j.n.d. can be thought of as some sort of a perceptual unit. It ought to be possible to stack up j.n.d.s and build a whole scale of subjective magnitudes.

It was Fechner's plan to build such scales, but to do so he had to conduct a lot of experiments. He introduced three different varieties of psychophysical methods. Interestingly, his three methods are still being used by those who study these things. They have been supplemented by a few other methods, but the original methods he developed are pretty much intact. They are now called: (1) *the method of limits,* in which a comparison stimulus is moved up in small steps from a fixed standard stimulus until the difference can be reliably detected; (2) *the method of constant stimuli,* in which a large set of random differences between comparison and standard is presented; and (3) *the method of adjustment,* in which the comparison can be changed by the subject until it appears to match the standard. With each of these methods the subject is engaged in a sort of guessing game, because all the comparisons are tough to judge. So a lot of data has to be generated and then treated statistically to find means and variances. Overall means reflect some sort of response bias, and it is the variances that are most important because they indicate the discriminability of the stimuli. In spite of the technical details, the different methods appeared to yield similar results.

When all his efforts were gathered together and presented in the vast *Elements of Psychophysics* (1860), they were indeed convincing. No longer was he a crazy poet, he was instead some kind of new scientist. He was generating lots of data with new methods, analyzing it carefully, testing hypotheses, and checking out all the details. He had abundant data, he had a theory, and he was doing what no one had believed was possible—measuring events in the human mind. He was an experimental psychologist.

Fechner's way of measuring human perception and his building of perceptual intensity scales involved an assumption, however, that had to be recognized and considered. Fechner argued that one j.n.d. was psychologically just like another. If you are picking up weights of 30 and 31 grams, you will be just making what seem to be lucky guesses as to which is heavier, because you are working right at the threshold. As a subject you will experience a lot of uncertainty. On the other hand, both the 30 and the 31 will be sensed as far lighter than a new pair that are 60 and 62 grams because there are many j.n.d.s between the two pairs. But the key point for Fechner was that the degree of uncertainty between the new 60 and 62 is psychologically just like the uncertainty between the old 30 and 31. In absolute terms the two pairs are very different, but in comparisons within a pair, the two pairs are essentially alike. After making that assumption, Fechner was ready to forge ahead.

Fechner's Law

Now, there are a couple of ways to go in actually creating a useful scale of perceptual intensity. One is empirical, it involves the tedious business of measuring one j.n.d. after another until the whole scale of physical intensities has been incorporated. Fechner did some of that. But more important historically is a conceptual shortcut he proposed. We go back to what he called Weber's law: $\Delta S = a \cdot S$. We can rewrite this as $\Delta S/S = a$.

But this new, rewritten version of Weber's law is very handy because we can integrate it. From an official, mathematical point of view, we can integrate it if the ΔS term is very small. Technically, we have to rewrite it again as $dS/S = a \cdot dP$, where dS is a change in the physical world and dP is the resulting change in the perceptual world, the detection of difference. When we integrate this to get rid of the differentials, we have $P = \log(S)$. The perception is equal to the logarithm of the physical stimulus. That is a truly beautiful conclusion. But it gets better. Those who are into calculus will have noted the absence of the extra term one always gets when carrying out an integration. No problem. The perceptual response starts when the physical stimulus is at the absolute threshold, which we can label S_o. Incorporating this, we get $P = \log(S/S_o)$.

We celebrate this wonderful little equation by calling it **Fechner's Law.** It says that perceptual magnitude, loudness or brightness or weight, is determined by the logarithm of the physical intensity of the stimulus. It says that perceptual magnitude adds up when physical intensity multiplies. Fechner was guided a little in arriving at this conclusion by the recent work of John Herschel and others on the apparent magnitude of stars. From classical times the stars had been given magnitudes. The 10 or so brightest stars were called magnitude 0, while the 3,000 or so faintest stars one could see were called magnitude 5, and the others were stuck in between. Herschel figured out that this meant that each magnitude was 2.5 times as bright in physical terms as the next magnitude. Thus, the difference between a 0 and a 2 was about 6 to 1, and the difference between a 0 and a 5 was about 100 to 1. The visual magnitudes add up while the physical differences are multiplying. It is a rather silly and arbitrary scale, but it is still being used.

Modern times give us a neater example. Everybody measures the loudness of sound in decibels, and that is by definition a logarithmic scale. A doubling of physical intensity is defined as an increase of 6 decibels, and that is true all up and down the very long decibel (db) scale. If you cannot really hear anything at 0 db, you can hear almost nothing when it is cranked up to 6 db, but it sounds twice as loud. If you have a big stereo putting out 100 db, that will really wake you up, but it will sound twice as loud at 106 db. The sound intensity dimension is interesting because it is so extremely long, and because Fechner's law seems to be reasonably valid over the enormous range of billions to one in physical intensities, and a range of well over 100 j.n.d.s in the perceptual world. Thus, it appears that Fechner had hit on something. If not all, then surely many important perceptual dimensions are related to the logarithm of the underlying physical intensities.[7]

Fechner's Later Years

Fechner lived a long and academically successful life. The original psychophysical work attracted some interest, some support (by Wundt and others), and some criticism. He subsequently wrote a couple of books and quite a number of research papers to defend his analysis. Just the thing for the mature academic. But he was still restless, and he moved on to other problems. Psychophysics is easy, he said, when there is a well-defined physical dimension against which one can correlate the subjective judgments. But what if the physical dimensions are unknown? What if we start with stimuli that have clear perceptual significance, but where we do not know what the physical correlate is? For example, suppose we ask subjects to make aesthetic judgments of stimuli. Is this face prettier than that one? If so, how can we analyze the physical dimensions of the faces to determine what the physical correlate of prettiness is? It was psychophysics turned inside out. Fechner worked on it for a decade and finally published *Introduction to Aesthetics* in 1876. His methods looked like they might work not only in the "hard" areas of psychology, like perception, but in some "soft" areas like aesthetics as well. Perhaps it was all subject to experimentation. Perhaps psychology would be a science.[8]

Summary

JOHANNES MÜLLER'S STUDENTS were committed to mechanistic explanations of physiological phenomena. The greatest of them, Helmholtz, had been extremely successful in accounting for many perceptual phenomena in purely mechanistic terms. The world of perception could be largely explained by peripheral mechanisms, by the structure of the eye, by the distribution of color receptors, and so on. But Helmholtz was distressed by what he took to be the necessity of introducing psychological considerations into the explanation of space perception. His own exploratory experiments had convinced him that space perception was strongly dependent on learning. He was bothered by his understanding that perception of the external world was generally more accurate, more true to life, than the sensory apparatus made possible.

The problem was that space perception depended on psychological factors in addition to the sensory apparatus. For the mechanist this was an anomaly. And it was found not only in space perception, but in many other visual phenomena as well. There were the great anomalies of the blind spot, color blindness, and all the curious instances of color constancy. There was the mystery of binocular disparity. Again, we perceive the external world much more correctly than can be explained by the sensory apparatus. Helmholtz thought perception was like a sort of inference, an *unconscious inference*, he called it, that reflected both sensory physiology and previously learned associations. Sensory input enables us to conceptualize objects out there.

Other physiological workers had found cases where perception was *less* accurate than it should be. As an observer shifted attention from one sensory dimension to another, time was lost, or gained, depending on the individual subject and depending on what the subject was supposed to be doing. Donders and Wundt found that it took time to choose among possible stimuli. Again, what should have been simple physiological reaction times were revealing other and much more psychological processes at work. Wundt would move on from that observation to build a new science.

While attention was being focused on the interaction of psychological and physiological mechanisms, a strange, mystic, poetic physiologist had an insight about how the two realms were related. Even more important, Fechner saw how to do experiments that would measure the relationship between the physical and psychological worlds. He called his work *psychophysics*, and that work marks the beginning of experimental psychology.

Notes

1. A good picture of the history of statistics is hard to come by, but a recent book by Gigerenzer et al. (1989) helps a great deal. They start around 1650 with Pascal and the gamblers trying to determine how much to bet, and the insurance brokers trying to figure out how much to charge. They go on to Bessel and the scientists who were confronted with errors of measurement. They discuss the great British statisticians, Pearson and Fisher, and their acrimonious relationship. And they explain how modern psychologists became so obsessed with statistical inference testing.

2. The story of Kinnebrook was told repeatedly by Wundt. We will discuss Wundt in more detail in the next chapter.

3. Friedrich C. Donders (1818–89), the Dutch physiologist who was professor for many years at Utrecht, is much underrated in importance. No doubt he was a major influence on both Helmholtz and Lotze (regarding visual localization) and Wundt (regarding reaction time). The best access in English to his localization work is Helmholtz's *Physiological Optics*. The important reaction-time paper has been translated into English (Donders, 1868).

4. All of my references to Helmholtz are from the 1925 English translation of the 3rd edition of his *Physiological Optics* and from the nice collection of translated papers by Warren and Warren (1968).

5. All of the anomalies cited here are discussed by Boring (1950); they were all much more deeply appreciated by Helmholtz.

6. There are three possible interpetations. One is that this literary work was some sort of parody of the nature-philosopher's science, the tradition of the German poet–scientists. It is also possible that he was trying to say something serious. The third possibility is that Fechner was crazy. Some scholars, such as Woodward (1972), take his "panpsychism" seriously. One of Fechner's earlier literary efforts, the work on angels, is discussed by Marshall (1969), who thinks he had something to say. There is no question about his seriousness or sanity, however, when it comes to his two major experimental works, the *Elements of Psychophysics* (1860), part of which has been translated by Adler (1966), and the *Introduction to Aesthetics* (1876). He wrote a couple of lesser books and quite a number of experimental and theoretical papers on physical as well as psychological matters. There is a biography of Fechner in Hall (1912). The most authoritative discussion of problems with his model, such as whether it is legitimate to treat all j.n.d.s as though they were perceptually the same, is probably still the classic analysis of Titchener (1905).

7. Is Fechner's logarithmic law still valid in the modern day and age? The question has been discussed at great length over the years by Fechner himself, and Wundt and Titchener. Relatively recently, but still some years ago, Stevens (1956) offered an alternative; it is not logarithmic but a power function, Stevens said. That was a major heresy, but over the years Stevens made a convincing case for it. It seems that, at worst, Fechner had found an extremely good approximation to the way things are.

8. To get going in aesthetics, the corresponding physical dimensions of which are unknown, Fechner worked on an intermediate problem. He had subjects judge the attractiveness of rectangles that differed in their ratio of height to width. His data, reported in 1865, indicated that there was indeed an optimum shape, and that the most aesthetic ratio was precisely that which had been conjectured since olden times. The ratio is .618, a number that has many remarkable, almost magical, properties. The Greeks understood it and called it the Golden Section. They allegedly built the Parthenon in just those proportions. Fechner went on from this case, where the physical correlate could be defined, to more interesting instances where it could not. A nice introduction to Fechner's ideas is Martin (1906).

Chapter Six

Wundt and Structuralism

HAD PSYCHOLOGY BEEN LEFT in the hands of Fechner, it probably would never have gotten established. However, his work inspired a number of people, one of whom was a remarkable man named Wilhelm Wundt. Wundt was most remarkable for the efficient manner in which he got things done. He was a doer; he wrote, did research, and taught. He got psychology going; he got it into the university system and made it a scientific discipline. A new movement needs a father, a seminal person. And then it needs a caregiving, parental person, someone who will watch over, and care for, and attend to all the details so the new enterprise can thrive. And this second person then becomes the founder, the one who had the energy and the power to make things happen. Psychology is fortunate that at just the right time there appeared a founder, a parental person who would start with Fechner's psychophysical methods and use them to build a new academic discipline.

Wilhelm Maximilian Wundt was born in 1832 and spent his youth in small towns in the southwestern corner of Germany. His family had some local distinction because of the numerous teachers and ministers they had produced over the years. His father was one of those ministers. We know from his autobiography (Wundt, 1920) that young Wilhelm was a lonely, sensitive child, and that he daydreamed a lot. And perhaps that is why he showed so little early promise as a student. But when he got to the university he seems to have settled down. He began the study of medicine first at Tübingen and then, from 1852 to 1855, at Heidelberg. At Heidelberg he did his first research; it was done under the great pioneering chemist Robert Bunsen (for whom the Bunsen burner is named). Wundt deprived himself of salt and then measured the salt excretion in his urine. The study was published in 1853 when young Wundt was 21. And with that a totally new pattern was set; no one would ever again accuse Wundt of daydreaming. The paper on salt was just the first trickle of what would become a great river of publications, an awesome torrent of words that would ultimately appear in print.

Wilhelm Wundt

Wundt the Physiologist

WUNDT GOT HIS medical degree in 1855, practiced medicine a short while, and then resumed further research. He worked a short time at Berlin with the professor, J. Müller, although his main contact there was with du Bois-Reymond. His work, on muscle movement, was written up and became his first book, which came out in 1858, when he was 26. In 1857 he had moved back to the University of Heidelberg, and when the university established a new physiological laboratory and brought Helmholtz in to supervise it in 1858, Wundt became Professor Helmholtz's laboratory assistant. Wundt was evidently preparing himself by working with the very best. But we have to understand what kind of position he had gotten into with Helmholtz. Medical students in those days studied physiology from lectures, but they also had to do laboratory work. They had to cut up cadavers; no doubt they had to study the twitching of frogs' legs when the nerves were stimulated. No doubt they had to study whatever it was that the professor and/or the lab assistant particularly wanted them to study. Helmholtz was lecturing and doing his own research, and Wundt was running the lab. We have to suppose that under Wundt's supervision the students in the lab were doing psychophysical experiments and reaction-time experiments when they were not chopping up cadavers. We can imagine that for a time there were many young German doctors who had never seen frog legs twitch, but did happen to know something about psychophysics.

This situation continued for six years, but unfortunately we know very little about the intellectual relationship between Wundt and Helmholtz. We can only guess to what extent Wundt's psychological ideas might have been shaped by interacting with the great physiologist who had probably worried more about the importance of psychological factors in perception than anyone else had. Some historians have suggested that the young man had very little to do with the older man. Others have suggested that, being very ambitious, Wundt was mainly concerned with increasing his autonomy, and that he wanted his own classes, along with the increased status and salary that such a promotion would involve. And that is what happened. In 1865 Wundt achieved autonomy; he was an "extraordinary" professor, and no longer working for Helmholtz. ("Extraordinary" sounds remarkable, but it amounted only to what would be an associate professor in the American system, and it entailed a very modest salary. See figure 6.1 for a comparison of German and U.S. academic ranks.)

Wundt had been offering his own classes all along. In 1859 he had presented *anthropology*, which had the Kantian meaning of something like cultural psychology. Then he offered "psychology as a natural science." Then, it was called *physiological psychology*. At this point in German intellectual history the adjective *physiological* did not necessarily have anything to do with body parts. It could mean rigorous, or scientific, or experimental. So it was clear that Wundt was losing any commitment he might have had to medicine and physiology, and that he was moving off in a new direction. His classes always involved laboratory work, and we can be sure that those experiments and demonstrations were becoming increasingly psychological.

Wundt's academic duties at Heidelberg by no means interfered with his written productivity. He had written some recent articles on sensory psychology, and in 1862 he gathered them up, added an introduction, and published it all in *Contributions to a Theory of Sensory Perception.**

This book was important historically because in the introductory chapter Wundt set out in concise form his philosophy of science, his belief in the value of experimentation, his faith in psychophysical methods specifically and experimental methods generally, and something of the long-term strategy he planned to pursue to make psychology a science. It is all there, and in all the

---

*Wundt's 1862 book on perception presents a problem. It is one of those books, like Newton's *Principia*, that is generally referred to in the original tongue. It was published as *Beiträge zur Theorie der Sinneswahrnehmung*, but historians of psychology—out of affection, or laziness, or perhaps because having plowed through it in German they feel they have license to call it whatever they wish—render it familiarly as the *Beiträge*. And that does not mean anything to one who knows no German. Worse, it does not mean anything to one who *does* know German, because it means *contributions*, which conveys nothing of what the book is about. Accordingly, I will refer to it as the perception book. It has not been translated in toto, but the important first chapter has been; it is included in Shipley (1961).

We will have the same kind of problem with Wundt's most important work, *Principles of Physiological Psychology* (1874), which the learned among us insist on calling the *Grundzüge (Principles)*. That may have made sense when the relevant scholars all spoke German and they were all familiar with the book, but it makes no sense today.

years that Wundt remained active, he never departed far from the goals, the methods, and the philosophy that he set forth.

The perception book was 1862. The following year there appeared another major book, which we can call *Animal Psychology*, where he further elaborated his systematic views. After a mass of other publications, we were presented with what was the most enduring and important of all his works, which is customarily called the *Grundzüge* (*Principles of Physiological Psychology*, 1874). It was authoritative and it was massive (in later revisions over the years it evolved and grew into two and then three volumes). Everything was in there: It included everything that Wundt had said before about movement, all that was known about sensation, the nervous system, the experimental methods of psychophysics, and all his own recent research. It was all gathered together and treated in a most thorough, scholarly manner. That should have sufficed, but no, six years later the whole thing was revised and updated to include much of Wundt's new data. Seven years after that it had to be revised again and enlarged a bit. And that is the way it went; Wundt proved to be a great reviser of his own work. Altogether there would be six editions, each more compendious than the one before. This mass of physiological psychology books should have been sufficient, and would have been more than a life's work for most scholars, but we will see that it was just a small part of what Wundt would ultimately get down on paper.

Wundt the Philosopher

The same year, 1874, Wundt obtained a professor appointment at the University of Zürich, but within a year he was offered another professorship, which he could not resist. Where? At Leipzig, the land of Weber and Fechner! His appointment was in the philosophy department. This might seem like a step backward in the move to make psychology an independent discipline and an experimental science. Wundt's colleagues, his fellow philosophers, were surely not much interested in experimentation, and they

FIGURE 6-1

Approximate correspondence of academic ranks in Germany and the United States.

German system	American system
Professor	Chair
	Professor
Extraordinary Prof.	Associate Prof.
Habilitation ———————	Tenure
	Assistant Prof.
Dozent	Instructor

would not seem likely to provide a sympathetic setting for such a movement. However, Wundt was in charge—he was the professor—so he did not have to be very concerned with what his colleagues thought about his activities. Then too, a founder has to start with what is available. There were no psychology departments at the time because there were no psychologists; Wundt would be the first. So he necessarily had to start as either a philosopher or a physiologist, and he was happy to be a philosopher. It was much like Christ's dilemma; he couldn't be a Christian because there weren't any yet, so he was a Jew. Founders just have to settle for what is available and go on from there. Another part of the picture is that Wundt really was a philosopher. The introductory part of his perception book had outlined his philosophical position, and in addition to giving a lot of experimental material, *Physiological Psychology* had greatly expanded and elaborated his philosophical views. There was a lot of traditional philosophical work to do to develop his system fully. Apart from his penchant for experimentation, which was a little out of character for a philosopher, he was no doubt perfectly comfortable in his new post.[1]

The Leipzig Laboratory

In 1879 the university at Leipzig provided Wundt with new space, including a lab room, and money for equipment and an assistant. He called it the Institute of Experimental Psychology. This then was the first formal, official, institutionalized psychology laboratory. And 1879 is the year that experimental psychologists traditionally think of the discipline as being founded. However, the actual beginnings of things are often hard to pin down. We encountered the problem with Lavoisier's discovery of oxygen. Did he discover it when he did the famous experiment? The problem is that oxygen was not just suddenly discovered, it was also gradually invented. The factual part of the story (Lavoisier's experiment in 1777) is certainly important, but it surely cannot stand alone because Dalton's conceptualization of chemical compounds is also a vital part of the story. What it comes down to is that chemists generally agree among themselves that 1777 was the beginning. Even though such specificity is not strictly warranted from a historical point of view, it gives chemists something tangible, a real date and the name of a real person, that they can celebrate. It seems we all have to have some sort of zero point, an origin, some frame of reference, that we can hang on to easily. For psychologists the zero point, the birth of experimental psychology, was Wundt's new laboratory in 1879.

The first study from Leipzig was carried out by Max Friedrich, who thus in 1881 became Wundt's first Ph.D. in experimental psychology, and thus the first psychology Ph.D. anywhere. Friedrich, Wundt, and the American G. S. Hall served as subjects in a reaction-time study of the Donders type.

But Wundt the founder was not yet done founding things. He established a new journal, *Philosophical Studies*, in 1881. Why did he call it *philosophical* studies when it soon became obvious that its purpose was to publish experimental psychological work from his own lab? Some writers have proposed that he called it what he did just to torment his philosophical colleagues, who would of course never publish anything of theirs in such a psychological journal. Be that as it may, Wundt eventually renamed it more appropriately, *Psychological Studies*. Meanwhile, it carried numerous reports of the work done by Wundt and his many students.

Wundt the Writer

When did Wundt begin to slow down? The answer is that he never did; if anything, he picked up momentum as he went along. Recall that Kant had admonished that psychology, which he regarded as a branch of philosophy, could never be an experimental science. One cannot experiment on the mind, he had said. Fechner had proved him wrong, and he had done so not rationally but empirically, by doing experiments. That was the thrilling part of Fechner's psychophysics. Wundt followed Fechner as far as the simple sensory-motor part of psychology was concerned, but he went back to Kant when it came to higher mental processes. He agreed with Kant that the study of such things as language, culture, religion, and all of the complex and uniquely human activities, could not be approached experimentally. They had to be gotten at by anthropological techniques— for example, by observing different cultures going about their daily affairs. In 1900, when he was 68, Wundt published a book on the psychology of language, using just such anthropological methods. This was not his research, but his analysis of the work of comparative linguists, who were beginning to flourish in German universities. This book was soon revised and expanded to two volumes. Then there followed more of the same kind of analysis of myths, religion, culture, and so on, until by 1920 Wundt had 10 volumes of *Fölkerpsychologie*, which we might call folk, or social, or cultural psychology.

Now, we have to recognize that while the founder was a psychologist, as evidenced by all his psychological publications, and his many psychology students, at the same time he really was a philosopher. He had a large number of philosophy students with whom he was publishing another large mass of material in philosophy journals. And on top of that, he was writing massive philosophical tomes. *Logic* appeared in 1880, and then went through three editions. *Ethics* came out in 1886, and it went through three editions. In 1889 he gave us *System of Philosophy*, and it was also revised twice.

In addition to these major offerings, Wundt put out a lot of minor works that included a book on hypnosis, one called *Essays* and another called *Outlines of Psychology*, which was a widely read introductory-level book. Now, to be sure, there was a great deal of redundancy here; Wundt said the same things

Edward B. Titchener

over and over in different ways and to different audiences. But even so, his writings represent an incredible mass of words. He was not only the first psychologist, he was also almost certainly the most prolific.[2]

And Wundt was also incredibly well-organized. He no longer taught after he was 85, but he kept right on working and writing. In 1920, when he was 88, he had revised everything; all of his major works had been expanded a bit and brought up to date. He then wrote an autobiography. And then he died.

Wundt's Legacy

WUNDT GAVE PSYCHOLOGY its first experimental laboratory. He gave us a journal (but not the first, as we will see). He got psychology recognized as a separate discipline by wresting it free from philosophy. It was only after Wundt that one could imagine there being departments of psychology at universities. And while Wundt was still middle-aged, such departments did begin springing up, especially in Germany and in the United States. To teach in a university one was, and still is, more or less obliged to have a Ph.D. It was Wundt who supervised the majority of early Ph.D.s in psychology, and those young people then became professors of psychology at universities far and wide. Thus, Wundt's biggest contribution to getting psychology going was his many students.

We will discuss his students shortly, but first we must single out one of them, Edward B. Titchener, to make an important point: There remains considerable ambiguity about Wundt and his ideas. We really do not know the man. We no longer read what he wrote (because there is so much of it and most of it is in German) and we are therefore inclined to draw our conclusions about Wundt from what we are told about him. And Titchener told us more than anyone else about him.

E. B. Titchener was one of Wundt's early students, and also one of his most distinguished. He was an Englishman who earned his degree with Wundt in 1892, and then came to the United States, where he soon came to dominate the department at Cornell University. Titchener spoke for Wundt, translated some of his books, used his methods, and generally followed in his footsteps. But he also changed Wundt's system a good deal; for example, he stripped off most of the philosophical aspects of it that had been so dear to the old man. And that is the problem. When Titchener tells us about Wundt we cannot be sure if he is describing the founder's views or his own.

Our uncertainty has been compounded over the years, however, because today no one reads Titchener either; we are much more inclined to read what his students have said about him. And the student of Titchener's who has told us the most about both him and Wundt is the important historian of psychology E. G. Boring. But when Boring tells us about Wundt, it is clear that we may have a problem. We will take a moment now to look at the problem more carefully.

Should the History of Psychology Be Boring?

Just as Titchener had been perhaps Wundt's most important and influential student, so E. G. Boring was perhaps Titchener's most important and influential. Boring obtained his degree at Cornell in 1914. After he had been at Harvard a while, he wrote *A History of Experimental Psychology* in 1929. In the tradition of his intellectual "grandfather," Boring updated and greatly expanded a second edition, which appeared in 1950. And this book quickly became accepted as the standard history of experimental psychology. It is the book that I studied as a student, and it was studied by everyone else of my generation. And it was studied by everyone of the next generation. Students are still studying it. It is a fine book that deserves study. In the tradition of Wundt, Boring stuffed it with facts. It is all full of dates and German words. It is packed with cross-references and loaded with reference notes. In the Wundtian tradition, it is massive, scholarly, and authoritative. Much of the story that has been described here, such as the causal links from Weber to Fechner to Wundt to Titchener, follows Boring's account.

There is little quarrel with the facts Boring presents. Did Fechner's great insight really come to him on October 22nd? Yes, Fechner himself tells us about that turning point. Was Wundt's perception book actually published in 1862? You bet, you can bank on it. Boring was very close to Titchener, who in turn had been very close to Wundt, so surely we can believe what Boring tells us about the relationship between Wundt and Titchener, how their positions were similar and how they were different. Alas, that is just where the problem is. Perhaps the respective relationships were too close. Perhaps Boring did not see Titchener very clearly, and perhaps the latter had not seen his mentor very clearly. The other part of the picture is that Titchener was clearly concerned with establishing his own turf, creating his own space, and therefore had to rebel against, deny, refute, and be independent of Wundt. And then, in turn, Boring had to assert his individuality and independence from Titchener. It may not be only a coincidence that just a few years after he wrote the first edition of his *History*, Boring wrote another book, *The Dimensions of Consciousness* (1933), which reveals him standing precariously with one foot in the introspection tradition (Titchener's tradition) and the other in the modern behavioristic world. Boring might have been going through a stage where he had to liberate himself from his old professor. His perception of Titchener might have been a bit distorted, just as Titchener's perception of his professor was, because of from where each was coming and to where each was going.

The question about the accuracy of Boring's account arose around 1979. In preparation for the centennial celebration of psychology becoming a science, a handful of scholars took the occasion to look at Wundt's work, not second-hand as Boring had presented it, but as the founder himself had written it. And they saw an image of Wundt that was quite different from the one that had been drawn by Boring. For example, Boring's account makes Wundt out to be an atomist. A reading of his work, however, suggests that he was much more **wholistic.** The traditional picture of Wundt shows him as very analytical, always breaking up the whole into its parts. But the written word reveals constant emphasis on unity, synthesis, and forces that pull things together.[3] According to Blumenthal (1975), the German word *Gebilde*, which appears frequently in Wundt's writings, can be variously translated as "organization," "pattern," or "structure," but in his translations Titchener made it "compound." Similarly, the word *gesamt*, which can mean "whole," "complete," or "united," got rendered into English as "aggregate." If Blumenthal's charge is really justified, then Wundt the wholistic theorist became an atomist when he got translated.

Both Wundt and Titchener believed that the proper method for experimental psychology was introspection, but they held quite different views about what constituted the appropriate introspection method. A translator can therefore blur all the distinctions by referring only to their common faith in introspection. Moreover, when Boring tells us about all this, he does not sufficiently emphasize the important fact that while for Titchener introspection was the *only* valid method for psychology, Wundt regarded it as only one of many methods the psychologist could use.

This relatively recent scholarly review of Wundt's writings has given us a quite different picture of the man and his theoretical position, to which we will turn shortly. We suddenly see him as more eclectic and more open to cognitive and dynamic ideas than we had come to believe.

Some very important points about Wundt, however, have never been and cannot be contested. One class of uncontested contributions includes the official things he did. He did found things—the first experimental laboratory to be funded by a university, for example. The various editions of *Physiological Psychology* were authoritative; in effect, they supplied the data base for the new experimental psychology. They also supplied the methods, such as Fechner's psychophysical methods, for the new enterprise. Thus, Wundt established the paradigm. It was he, at least in the beginning, who decided what psychological problems needed to be worked on, what kinds of methods were appropriate, and what the language of the new science would be. Thus, he introduced and defined terms that we translate as introspection, apperception, and other key terms of that era.

Wundt's Students

Another unquestionable part of the Wundt legacy, and probably the most important part, is his students. He had an awful lot of students. In philosophy alone he directed 70 Ph.D. dissertations. That is twice as many as a lot of very distinguished, productive professors direct in their lifetimes. And none of those 70 projects turn out to figure in our story; to us they are just extra chores that were distracting Wundt from what is to us his more important psychological work. More important to us are the 116 dissertations in psychology that he supervised. His students came predominantly from Germany, but quite a few came from other parts of Europe, especially eastern Europe. (Interestingly, only one woman, Anna Berliner, worked with Wundt. She defended her dissertation in 1913, but she is not listed as a Ph.D. in the official records of the university.)

Of major importance to our story is that nearly a dozen of Wundt's students came to him from the United States. These intrepid voyagers went off to the other side of the ocean, typically with little sense of what it would be like to live in a foreign land and be obliged to learn to write and speak a new language. But they were pulled by the great opportunity. If they went to Germany, they could work with the founder and get a Ph.D. degree with him. Then when they returned home they could pretty well count on stepping into a prestigious position at an important university. These pioneers of American psychology set up psychology departments here, they started labs, they founded journals—they did all the things that had to be done to institutionalize the new discipline and make it a part of American academia. We will discuss all these developments, and the remarkable phenomenon of experimental psychology in the United States as an import from Wundt's Leipzig laboratory, when we get to chapter 9.[4]

Wundt welcomed all these foreign students. It apparently did not matter to him that they did not have great command of the German language. He was apparently not concerned that few of his psychology students took his philosophical views seriously. His students, certainly those who came on to the United States, were not the least interested in his broad system. A few of them used his experimental methods, such as the psychophysical methods, and brought that tradition back home. But the great majority of his students, like all students everywhere, went running off in their own directions to do their own things. Wundt produced at most one disciple, and that was Titchener. And even in Titchener's case, it is doubtful that we want to call him a Wundtian. Wundt's American students brought back from Leipzig their Ph.D.s and little else.

When World War I broke out, everything turned around. Wundt was something of a propagandist, and he said publicly some rather unkind things about English-speaking people. One of his pleasant observations was that England is a nation of shopkeepers. But that was a much later development that was partly conditioned by his advanced age and partly by the state of war that had broken out. Earlier on, Wundt had welcomed American students—indeed, all kinds of students—and from 1886 to 1900, a period of a little more than a dozen years, he produced about one Ph.D. a year who would come to the United States to establish and set up psychology as a new discipline in U.S. universities. He gave us most of our pioneers, and that is a very great inheritance from Wundt.

Wundt's System

WUNDT'S PSYCHOLOGY WAS complex; it cannot be described easily. Part of the problem is the difficulty in separating the underlying philosophy from the experimental psychology. Both were important to the founder. He could not separate them; he could not say this is what the new science is all about and that is what I happen to believe about a fundamental reality. In our own time it is easy to distinguish between psychologists and philosophers, but back then, when psychology was just breaking off from philosophy and becoming an experimental discipline, the line was harder to draw. And while we want to think of Wundt as a psychologist, we have to let him be a philosopher also. He himself did not draw a line; he did not think of himself as schizophrenic, part this and part that, because he saw it all fitting together.

The other part of the problem is that Wundt's psychology really was complicated. Moreover, because Wundt lived so long, we have to expect that his system would have changed over the years. After all, his whole long life was full of theoretical activity, and while it is hard to imagine, the period from when he wrote the early perception book to when he died was nearly 60 years, and the period from his death to today is only another 70 years. Thus, his feverishly active life as a psychologist fills nearly half of our entire history. During his own lifetime psychology changed appreciably, and Wundt's view of psychology certainly changed too.

Wundt's View of the Mind

Here we want to understand the major trends, the main themes of Wundt's thought. We want to grasp the key elements that persisted over the many years that he was sharpening up his views. One such key element was his conviction that psychology was a natural science. It qualifies as a science because it is concerned with phenomena, and it seeks to control phenomena experimentally, to measure them, and ultimately to derive general laws that will explain how observable phenomena arise. The major difference between psychology and other natural sciences, Wundt tells us, is that in the other sciences observations are made via instruments of some sort. You and I and other observers can all watch the clock or the thermometer or whatever, and we can all see how the measurement changes as we vary the conditions of the experiment. We have the advantage that we are all watching a public demonstration of the phenomenon. But our experience of the phenomenon is *mediated* by the measuring instrument; our experience is indirect and dependent on the clock or thermometer. Without those tools we do not see a thing.

Psychology, on the other hand, deals with *immediate* experience. We can turn the mind inward upon itself, and see directly, without any instruments, what is there in our own awareness. Our experience is immediate because it does not require the use of any special measuring instruments. Unfortunately, I can see only what is in my mind and you can see only what is in your mind, but that is not a serious problem because we can correlate our experiences, yours and mine, with stimulus events in the physical world. We can use Fechner's psychophysical methods. We can each look at a round, red stimulus object, whose presentation can be nicely controlled experimentally, and we can each report on our experience. For example, we can each judge whether this round, red stimulus is rounder or redder than that one. We can use these methods to explore the mind experimentally. That was the dream that Wundt shared with Fechner. But whereas Fechner had built a bridge between the outer world of physical things and the inner world of the mind, Wundt's research program would use that bridge to find out how the mind was put together and how it worked.

Analysis and Synthesis

Wundt's program consisted logically of two phases. First, it would be necessary to dissect consciousness to find what its basic elements were. What kind of stuff fills our consciousness? The second stage would involve testing hypotheses about how mental processes work to build up what we experience. The first step is *analysis*, breaking up experience into its basic units. Then the second step is *synthesis*, figuring out how the basic units get combined into the wholistic, meaningful masses of stuff that seem to occupy our experience. Analysis and synthesis, that was the program. Unfortunately, Fechner's psychophysical methods and the other experimental methods that were available to Wundt lent themselves admirably to the analysis part of the program, but they proved of little value in the synthesis part. Synthesis was very important to Wundt, and he really wanted to get into it. He wrote a great deal about what he called the **creative synthesis** of the mind. He believed that the marvel of the mind was the unifying forces that he thought he could see in it. You start with a mass of sensations, spots of different colored light here and there, and the active principle of the mind somehow puts them all together to create a perception of some definite object. That was what Wundt wanted to get at. The unfortunate part of his program is that he and his followers spent their lives working on the analytical part of the program, where they had the methodological tools, and never got started on the synthesis part. And as the years went on, as we got into Titchener and structuralism, the situation for Wundt's program only got worse. Wundt talked a lot about synthesis even though his research was predominantly analytical; Titchener was so busy doing analysis that he had no time even to talk about synthesis.

Wundt said that the strong scientific methodologies, such as psychophysics, were, unhappily, only applicable to perceptual problems, to how we perceive the physical world around us. The more complex and more interesting parts of psychology were not amenable to scientifically rigorous methods, but some insight into things like language, beliefs, religious attitudes, and other important aspects of human life might be studied with other methods. And this is why late in his life Wundt wrote *Völkerpsychologie*. In a perception experiment the experimenter can control the stimulus events the subject is experiencing. In the learning of a language, on the other hand, the learning is governed by a multitude of social factors over which the experimenter has little control. Thus, Wundt concluded that Kant had been basically right when he asserted that psychological experiments cannot be done, at least not on the sort of phenomena one would like to be able to study. Early on, in his 1862 perception book, Wundt deplored the fact that almost nothing was known about all the interesting aspects of psychology, such as the development of the mind in children, the comparative study of different animals, and the social factors that contribute so importantly to our mental life. But as we have noted, the prophet has to begin with what is available and go on from there. Most of what was available to Wundt was the new psychophysical methodology.

The mass of research that Wundt's students worked on over the years was addressed to many different problems. They worked on perception, of course.

They studied illusions and size constancy. They also investigated the chemical senses, taste and odor. And a goodly proportion of the research, perhaps a quarter of it, was reaction-time experiments. This latter work always occupied a special place on Wundt's agenda. He had begun doing reaction-time experiments in 1860, and had understood even then that the *complication experiment* provided a handle on psychological processes, which is what he hoped ultimately to come to grips with. His students also worked on depth perception, eye movements, and thresholds. Wundt wrote extensively on aesthetics, voluntary movement, feelings, and association formation, although relatively little research was done in these central (as opposed to sensory) areas. Wundt's system was designed to include all of psychology. His research was much narrower; it was mainly restricted to sensation–perception and reaction-time experiments.

What he wanted to study & what he could study differed.

Elements of Consciousness

We may note some of the key concepts in Wundt's system. One is that the mind can hold, or we can be aware of, only certain sorts of elements. He maintained that introspection reveals three kinds of elements in consciousness. The most easily observed were *sensations*, which are correlated with external stimulus events. Thus, sensations are relatively easy to control experimentally, and that is why so much of the Leipzig research used psychophysical methods. The second kind of element was *feelings*. Feelings can be thought of as sensations that arise from the body, from our emotions and physiological states. But psychologically we know feelings from the way they feel, and not from where they come from. When we are angry we are aware of the anger, but not usually conscious of the increase in heart rate, the change in respiration, and so on. So feelings are not just internally aroused sensations. The third kind of element is *volitions*, which are tendencies to respond, or a desire to respond, in particular ways. All of our conscious life consists of blended mixtures of sensations, feelings, and volitions; these mixtures are the only possible contents of consciousness. That is the introspective analysis; the synthesis phase of the system is just a bold assertion from Wundt. He tells us that sensations, feelings, and volitions always go together. They cannot stand alone. For the subject in a tedious psychophysical experiment the sensation might be the major and most important part of the triad, but there remains in the background some feeling, and some thought of responding. They always appear together. That is part of what Wundt believed was the creative synthesis. The mind just works that way. One has to think that at this point Wundt the philosopher had traded places with Wundt the experimental psychologist.

Wundt was a systematizer, a classifier, a sort of psychological botanizer. Sensations were sorted out by quality and intensity. Feelings were judged to be pleasant or unpleasant, calm or excited, and effortful or relaxed. (Wundt's three-dimensional analysis of feelings evolved slowly over the years, and always elicited a good deal of criticism.) Volitions were said to be either expressed in behavior or blocked. In Wundt's system, everything had to fall into its assigned place.

Wundt's Voluntarism

Wundt frequently characterized his own system as *voluntaristic*. He said that we combine the elements of consciousness by an act of will. We focus our attention on this or that element by exercising the will. Thus, the will is rather like the mortar that holds the building blocks of consciousness together. Does the will have its own deterministic rules? No, because introspection tells us that we do in fact focus on concepts and attend to stimuli voluntarily. But though Wundt regarded his system as voluntaristic, and liked that label for it, no one else seems to have regarded it that way. Part of the problem is that Wundt's system is full of complexities and conceptual surprises. For example, he says that it is from the unity of sensations, feelings, and volitions that we derive our sense of self.

Wundt talked a good deal about behavior, but he was apparently not really interested in explaining behavior. Let us look at a couple of potentially interesting things Wundt had to say about it. He said that with the muscle sense we attend to the *effect* of the response, not to effort or the response itself, and that special methods are needed to circumvent this problem. He was saying, as James had said a few years earlier, that a movement is controlled by the idea of the consequences of the movement. But rather than accept this as a rule of behavior, as James did, he saw it as a problem to be circumvented, because he wanted to analyze the mind, the elements of consciousness. He was not very interested in finding explanatory principles of behavior.

Wundt also said at one point that associative principles not only combine sensations, so as to give us complex ideas and perceptions, they also serve to connect sensations with movements. But in time, as the response becomes habitual, it can occur before the subject can detect the elements that are associated. Once again we see Wundt focusing on the awareness of mental elements, rather than on the associative principles themselves or on behavior. We should perhaps conclude that Wundt did not stand as far from Titchener's structuralistic position as some recent scholars would have us believe.

Learning and Other Matters

Finally, to get some feel for how Wundt went at things, we can look at how he dealt with a couple of specific theoretical issues. On the inversion of the retinal image, Wundt followed Lotze (1852), who had proposed the theory of *local signs*. The idea is most easily seen in the skin senses rather than vision.

Suppose you suddenly have an itch somewhere near your left elbow. You reflexively move your right hand to the itchy place, or more likely, close to the itchy place. Then a small adjustment will bring your hand right to it, so you can proceed to scratch it appropriately. This adjustment response will be readily learned, so that the initial reflex will become somewhat modified. When this happens, the specific location of the itch will come to serve as a local sign for the appropriate movement. Eventually you will build up a sort of map of the whole body surface, so that you will be able to go immediately to any spot on the skin. The visual field is just the same. If you were guided by inappropriate, inverted reflexes initially, they will become corrected with experience so that you will come to look down at just the right place in the real world so you can attend to something in the upper part of the retinal image. The analysis is very empiricistic, because it basically requires our sense of space (as well as our sense of where we and our parts are) to be all due to experience, just as Berkeley and Helmholtz had said.

On the question of free will, Wundt was so concerned with conscious experience that he could not really address the question. He certainly did not believe that mental events, such as our volitions, were caused by bodily events, such as what was going on in the nervous system, because he was a **parallelist.** Like Fechner, and everyone else in the German tradition, he believed that mind and body followed independent courses of action, which just happened to be highly correlated. But he was terribly interested in the awareness of volition, how it felt when one seemed to exercise one's will. And he was convinced that volitions became associatively linked with the sensations and feelings that always accompanied them, so that a sensation could come to arouse a volition. But whether our volitions were invariably caused by other psychological events he did not discuss directly.

Wundt also discussed attention. In his voluntarist model, we are free to focus our attention here or there as we wish. Or so it seems. But the psychological reality is that these things are all hooked together associatively. Certainly our attention is going to be captured by the brightest color, by the loudest noise, or by whatever is the most salient stimulus before us. Perhaps attention is not free at all, but only a slave of the stimulus situation. Wundt waffles back and forth between these two positions, because both are important in his overall scheme of things. To make matters worse, there was a new concept (new to us but old in German philosophy), **apperception.** When there is a significant bunch of sensations we are attending to, other sensations lying around here and there tend to become assimilated to the central mass of sensory stuff. The focus of attention will tend to pull in and incorporate the other sensory details to the apperceptive mass. And it gets worse because this mass of sensory material is also linked with other sorts of associations, memories and such, that give meaning to what we see.

We have seen all we need to see of Wundt's complicated, abstract system. The small part that we have seen reveals him as still very much a philosopher, interested in broad generalities and abstractions. It shows him as eclectic, variable, and a little unpredictable. It is perhaps inevitable that any scholar who writes as much as Wundt did is going to say a lot of different things, even some contradictory things. If a learned man spills out enough words, then sooner or later he has to say almost everything one is looking for him to say. But while it is true that Wundt held very closely to certain unchanging ideas, it is also true that he leapt all around the place using different methods, approaching things in different ways, and defending different sorts of ideas. He *was* loose and variable. And he was obscure. Perhaps his American students failed to bring home his message because they had not understood it. Or perhaps they had understood it but did not like it. And perhaps they did not like it because it was so complicated and so eclectic. Wundt's was not a simple, pretty system. It cried out to be simplified. So we turn next to Titchener, who did in fact bring a condensed and simplified version of Wundt's system to this country.

Titchener and Structuralism

WE HAVE ALREADY SEEN that Edward Bradford Titchener (1867–1927) was an Englishman (he never gave up his English citizenship) who studied in Germany and then moved to the United States. When he took the important position at Cornell University in 1892, Cornell became something like a Wundtian outpost in America. Titchener was extremely important and influential, in part because of his position at Cornell, and in part because he was a very strong and capable person. He set about simplifying Wundt's vast system. For example, he stripped off most of Wundt's philosophical complexities.

Structuralism: The Structure of Sensory Awareness

Titchener accepted Wundt's dictum that *psychology is the science of immediate experience.* One turns the mind inward and observes directly what is there in awareness. He understood Wundt's concern that our attention tends to focus on external objects or other products of perception rather than on our raw sensations. But, he insisted, we must fight that tendency and report only the sensations themselves. To report introspectively on meaningful objects or other products of perception is to make what he called the **stimulus error.** It is to report on the stimulus object or what it means, rather than the sensations. Wundt was fascinated by the synthesizing processes of the mind; that was ultimately what he wanted to understand. Wundt viewed the analysis of sensations into their elements as a necessary prelude to the all-important

137

synthesis part of the task. For Wundt, analysis was a means to an end; for Titchener analysis was an end in itself.

For Titchener, structuralism consisted of breaking up meaningful perceptions into their elemental sensations. Any other psychological enterprise was a corruption. Some of his young American colleagues wanted to study development in children, or behavior in animals, or disturbed behavior in the clinically ill. They could study such things if they wished to, Titchener said, but their efforts had no place in the discipline of psychology, and certainly had nothing to do with experimental psychology. Experimental psychology had to be pure; it had to use the right method and follow the approved path. Anything else, any application, was out of bounds for experimental psychology.

Wundt had called his own system voluntaristic. And while it remained a little uncertain what he meant by this, or how much he was concerned with behavior, Titchener left no doubt about where he stood. One of Titchener's virtues was that you always knew exactly where he was. Behavior played no part in his system. The only valid question regarding volition was how it was experienced in awareness. What does willing the occurrence of some behavior feel like? What sensations arise? If I will my hand to rise, do I have some special sensations in that arm? Later in his life Titchener handled feelings in the same way, by reducing them to sensations. Wundt had struggled with feeling, and his analysis changed markedly over the years. Titchener also struggled with it, but finally (Titchener, 1921) got it all reduced to sensation. Even the all-important good–bad dimension, the hedonic remnant from earlier associationists, was reduced to nothing but sensations. A bad feeling is nothing but certain hard-to-describe sensations arising from the mouth and throat.

With Titchener we really do have conceptual simplicity. We have parsimony. There is no behavior, no instinct, no feelings or emotions, no motivation. There is no function either, nothing is ever happening. There is nothing but the march of sensory impressions into and out of awareness. We sit there passively like we were back at the Hume Theater watching our sensations rant and rave upon the stage of our consciousness. We cannot participate in the apparitions before us, we have to accept them as they appear. We do not even really understand anything we see because we are supposed to be looking at the raw sensations themselves rather than interpreting and giving meaning to them. The picture we get of Titchener's psychology is rather like a vacation on the moon. It is very clear and clean, and stark and simple, but it is also rather barren, sterile, and uninviting.

It is interesting that Titchener himself gave us the best name for his view of experimental psychology. Curiously, he thought of himself as simply a psychologist, and then he attached labels—functional, behaviorist, or whatever—to everyone else. But in 1899 he wrote a paper attacking the functional approach, and he contrasted it with his own "structural" approach. And that label stuck because it seemed so apt. He wanted to study, and he wanted everyone else to study, the *structure* of the mind. He did not care how it worked, how it functioned, what the synthesizing processes were, where behavior came from, or anything of that practical nature. He was only interested in the *content* of mind. What is in awareness at a given moment, and how does it relate to the stimuli the experimenter is presenting? That is the only thing, he thought, that psychology should concern itself with if it was to be a science.[5]

Titchener's Other Side

Now I have to admit that I may have presented the structuralist position in a way that would make it look unattractive. Perhaps so, but in fact it was an ugly paradigm, or so most Americans have thought. Perhaps I set it up so that the reader would not take it very seriously. That may be, but the truth is that American psychologists in general have not taken it very seriously. However, Titchener did have a number of important students who, at least for some time, endorsed the structuralistic cause. He also wrote a great deal, and his writings were uniformly respected because of his great scholarship and command of the relevant literature, and his broad understanding of the issues. He did not believe broadly, as we have seen, but he understood broadly. He was unquestionably the most important psychological scholar in the United States during much of the early years of psychology here. And like it or not, the structuralist position does have one very real virtue: It is simple and clear. One might not agree with the program it proposed for psychological research, but one could not deny that it provided a very strong anchor point for psychology. If nothing else, it gave everyone a springboard, a place to jump off from.

But let me try to balance things up a little better. Titchener's view of things was very rigid, but it did change gradually over the years, so he was not totally inflexible. Boring (1937) gives a very sensitive and personal account of how some of his concepts changed over time. In this connection, Young (1961), who was one of his later students, indicates how he only gradually abandoned will and emotion and feeling, and only by 1924 had reduced everything psychological to sensation. Titchener was a 100 percent structuralist only at the end. To Titchener's credit, too, is that he worked with women students. Margaret Washburn (who received a degree in 1894) was his first graduate student, but she was not alone. Half of his first dozen or so students were women. That seems a little out of character for such a conservative man, and sure enough, there is ample evidence that the thing was not his doing at all; Cornell had very liberal and advanced ideas about women students, and as the big gun there, Titchener was obliged to work with them.

139

He had other talents; he was musical, and an avid collector of old coins, and he could speak perhaps a dozen languages. In his obituary Boring (1927) made it clear that he had tremendous admiration and respect for his Cornell mentor, but the basis of Boring's warm feelings was the old man's toughness, his ability to hang on to what he believed even when no one else did.

Summary

WUNDT INSTITUTIONALIZED psychology. He wrenched it out of philosophy where it had always been before and made it a separate discipline. He made it autonomous, with its own place in the university, and its own journal. It now had its proper problems to investigate, and its unique methodology for investigating them. With Wundt psychology had an ordered place. It did not occupy an arbitrary location, but rather was stuck in there between philosophy and physiology, where it could overlap a little with both of those older disciplines. But it was not philosophy because it did experiments, and it was not physiology because it studied the mind. In addition to these general accomplishments, there were all the specific things Wundt did—all those books and papers, all that scholarship, all those students. What an impact he had.

One of Wundt's most capable and dedicated students went off to spread the word in the New World. It turned out that the word was not very well received by the natives. They were pretty restless, and Titchener was a little late because the Americans were already putting together their own version of psychology, and it was something quite different from both Wundt's and Titchener's versions.

A number of recent scholars have insisted that Wundt and Titchener were very different, and that whatever unkind things we may say about the younger man, the older one should not be indicted along with him. Wundt looked like a modern, they say, and there is much we can still learn from him. His system was dynamic, functional and cognitive, they say. But his system was also very structuralistic. It put all that emphasis on the analysis of mind. Furthermore, Wundt maintained that the experimental method, which had given birth to the science of psychology, applied only to the sensory input and motor output parts of it, and all the most interesting and important parts of it remained in the hands of the armchair philosophers. He advocated experimental methods but then built a wall around them to restrict their use. The Americans were not going to allow psychology to be confined in such a manner. Once back home with their Leipzig Ph.D. degrees, they would quickly break down the Wundtian wall and begin to apply experimental methods to the whole psychological landscape.

Notes

1. Some of the basic facts of Wundt's life are given by Boring (1950). See also the obituary by Titchener (1921). An independent account is given by Bringmann, Balance, and Evans (1975). Diamond (1980) gives a sensitive and sympathetic account of Wundt's early years. Emphasis on his early daydreaming is found in his own account of his life (Wundt, 1920). Bringmann and Tweney (1980) have edited a remarkable and valuable collection of chapters that look at Wundt's life and work from many different angles.

2. There is no reason to list all the books, or even all the major books, that Wundt wrote. Titchener and Geissler (1908) compiled a bibliography that is quite complete to that date (and it is 15 pages long), and then Titchener updated it several times in the same journal. Students will be more interested in the few of Wundt's major works that have been translated into English. These include *Lectures on Human and Animal Psychology*, 2nd edition of 1892, translated by Creighton and Titchener in 1901; *Outline of Psychology*, translated by Judd in 1902; and the all-important *Physiological Psychology*, 5th edition of 1902–03, which was translated by Titchener in 1904. There is also his *Ethics*, translated by Titchener and Washburn in 1895, which in spite of the philosophical title is very much the work of a psychologist.

3. Some of these centennial scholars are Blumenthal (1975, 1979), Bringmann (1975), Danziger (1980), and Rieber (1980). The flavor of this movement is perhaps best expressed in the book edited by Bringmann and Tweney (1980).

4. Tinker (1932) provides a list of all of Wundt's doctoral students. I will take from that list those who either returned to or else immigrated to this country. James McKeen Cattell was the first and perhaps the most important of these young scientists to return to the States with a degree from Leipzig. He was also Wundt's first laboratory assistant. (I give in parentheses the year of the degree, for Cattell, 1886.) Just as early, but less important, was H. K. Wolfe (1886) who returned home and went to the University of Nebraska. Eduard Pace (1891) came back to Catholic University. Edward Scripture (1891) went to Yale. Frank Angell (1891) went to Cornell and then to Stanford. Lightner Witmer (1893) came back to the University of Pennsylvania. George Stratton (1896) ended up at the University of California, Berkeley. Charles H. Judd (1896) went to the University of Chicago, and then to New York University. Guy A. Tawney (1897) came back home and went to Beloit College. Walter Dill Scott (1900) went to Northwestern.

In addition to these doctoral students, there were other Americans who were greatly influenced by the old man, and spent some time with him. G. Stanley Hall worked briefly in Wundt's lab back at its inception in 1879.

Harvey Warren also visited Wundt for a short time starting in 1891. In addition to all these Americans, Hugo Münsterberg (1885) and E. B. Titchener (1892), who were not Americans, immigrated to the United States to take important positions at Harvard and Cornell, respectively, after taking their degrees with Wundt. In short, more than a dozen of the first American psychologists were products of the laboratory at Leipzig. We will have occasion to meet several of these people later on.

    5. Titchener also wrote voluminously. He kept track of everything happening in Germany, and translated quite a bit of it. He wrote a number of his own books, and about 200 papers that appeared mainly in *American Journal of Psychology*, of which he was editor from 1921 to 1925. His opus magnus was the huge *Experimental Psychology: A Manual of Laboratory Practice*, which was divided into two volumes and then divided again into student's manual and instructor's manual. It came out between 1901 and 1905. At that time it was the ultimate authority on everything Titchener thought to be the science of psychology, and it was highly influential for many years, even among those who did not really follow Titchener. He also wrote some more accessible books, such as *An Outline of Psychology* (1896), which went through three editions, and *A Textbook of Psychology* (1909), which was also revised twice. The latter is quite readable, and provides a very congenial introduction to Titchener's structuralism.

Chapter Seven

The Periphery in Germany

WUNDT TALKED a lot about apperception, which is essentially the center of attention. It includes a body of sensations plus a body of material that is tied associatively and conceptually to the sensory input. This apperceptive mass is the meaningful material that we are aware of at any one time. It occupies center stage in attention. There are always other things, both sensory and associative, going on in the periphery, and some of this peripheral material tends to be drawn into the apperceptive mass. Psychology itself was rather like that during Wundt's early years. He himself was the center of attention. He and his many students stood before the footlights, and everyone watched them and thought about them. But there were a few other psychologists on the periphery who made significant contributions to the discipline, even though they did not enjoy Wundt's unique position at center stage. Indeed, it turns out that some of these people on the periphery were quite remarkably talented in their own right and made great contributions to our story. So let us consider this peripheral context inside of which Wundt and all his students were placed.

We started the story of psychology by gathering together many bits and pieces. We have seen something of how it all seemed to coalesce around the psychophysical experiments, how Fechner and then Wundt got all the philosophy and the problems of perception, and all the physiology pulled together. The first part of our story is like one end of an hourglass; it began large and loose but by the end of the 19th century it got focused down to something that was conceptually very simple, namely, Titchener's structuralism. But now we have to recognize that history is not linear, and that not all attention was actually focused on structuralism. There is always a context, a periphery, which we now have to look at. We also have to start preparing ourselves for the other half of the hourglass: the tremendous proliferation in the 20th century of different sorts of psychological approaches. In this chapter we will look at the German part of the periphery.

Ebbinghaus and Memory

HERMANN EBBINGHAUS WAS BORN in 1850 in a small town in western Germany, near Bonn. He was 18 years younger than Wundt and 17 years older than Titchener; he was right in between. He attended the university at Bonn, but moved to Berlin where he studied with the great historical scholar F. A. Trendelenburg. Following a stint in the army he went back to Bonn, where he got a doctoral degree in philosophy in 1873.*

Then for several years he wandered; he traveled in England and France. Historians suspect that he read the British associationists, perhaps Bain. Historians state as a fact that he read Fechner; they say he bought *Elements of Psychophysics* at a Paris bookstall (but see Watson & Evans, 1991). And evidently Fechner moved Ebbinghaus in much the same way he had moved himself on that fateful day when he leapt out of bed and ran to the lab to do experiments. Fechner had understood that it *was* possible to do psychological experiments, and one *could* measure things that no one believed were measurable. And he had done it. But Fechner's particular methods were applicable only to a limited range of phenomena, namely, the relationships between physical stimuli and psychological perceptions. That was the problem that had obsessed Fechner. What turned Ebbinghaus on was that he saw that the same sort of experimental attitude could also solve other psychological problems. The associationists had talked a lot about memory, but, perhaps because the associationists were philosophers, there had been no experimentation. Ebbinghaus saw that just as perception had yielded to an experimental attack, memory could too. It *was* possible to do experiments on memory, and one *could* measure psychological things, like memory, that no one thought were measurable. And just like Fechner before him, he went to work on the problem all by himself.

---

*Ebbinghaus got his degree when he was 23. From our perspective, 23 years of age seems rather young to be getting a doctorate, particularly if the person has spent some time in the service. The mean age for bright young American veterans getting their Ph.D.s is probably 30. However, the discrepancy is very likely due not to any inadequacy of their system but to the inefficiency of our own. American school kids wiggle around in their chairs for 12 years and learn about 3 years' worth of stuff. Ask a high-school graduate who Napoleon was, and you might hear, "A little short guy who played around with Josephine and got syphilis." What is the relationship between the sine and the cosine of an angle? "Yeah, I learned that in trigonometry." Who was Beowulf? "An English writer, but you can't understand him anymore because he's 800 years old." This is obviously a bright kid who has been in school, but something is not quite right. There might be something wrong with our system.

Hermann Ebbinghaus

The Study of Memory

It seemed to Ebbinghaus that to study memory systematically it would be necessary to control the original learning, so he set about learning bunches of new material. He discovered that meaningful material, such as poetry, was too quickly learned and too easily remembered, so he started learning nonsense material. He sort of invented nonsense syllables, and made up a catalog of them. Then he would randomly select a short list of syllables, and memorize the list. After an interval that might be an hour, or six hours, or one day, or six days, he would test himself to see how many syllables from his list he could remember. From the results of doing such experiments over and over again (always using himself as the subject), Ebbinghaus could draw some general conclusions. After one hour he might remember 85 percent of an average list; after a day only 50 percent, and after six days just 15 percent. Plotting up all the data, he had a retention curve, or turning it upside down, he had a forgetting curve (see figure 7.1). Yes, indeed, it was possible to measure memory!

Over a period of five years or so Ebbinghaus carried out a number of such experiments, varying several variables such as the length of the list and the amount of original learning. He wrote it all up, added just a bit of theory (innocuous stuff such as a distinction between adjacent and remote associations, but all in the associationistic tradition), and published it as a short monograph, *On Memory* (1885). An English translation shows it to be a really beautiful little monograph. Simply but elegantly written, it is nicely thought out, it provides a little innocent theory, the different studies are sensibly developed, and the whole thing is completely convincing. And believe it or not, most of the reported results still stand, 100 years later. It remains a great experimental report today; in its own time it must have been totally stupifying. It was immediately seen as remarkable, groundbreaking, epochal stuff. Everyone was impressed, and within a year Ebbinghaus was awarded the greatest prize German academia had to offer, the chair in philosophy at Berlin.

Ebbinghaus at Berlin

Ebbinghaus did not follow through with more work on the research that had made him famous, however. One can understand that having been his own subject, learning endless lists of nonsense syllables for several years, he did not want to do any more of that. But one would think that he would have had students who wanted to pursue this new work. Ebbinghaus did not follow it up and he had no students who followed it up. Actually, he reported very little research of any kind, and he seems to have had few students of any consequence. It seems that he just fizzled once he got to Berlin. He did accomplish one thing, however. In 1890 he established a new journal whose full name was *Journal of Psychology and the Physiology of the Sense Organs*, but which is usually just called *Zeitschrift*, which means "journal." It contrasted with Wundt's journal in several ways. Wundt's journal died in 1917 when the old man was no longer able to devote sufficient attention to it, but the *Zeitschrift* is still in business. Wundt's journal was very personal; it published only papers from the Leipzig lab, or papers that were sympathetic to his particular view of things, and it was tightly edited by Wundt himself.

FIGURE 7.1

The sort of forgetting curve reported by Ebbinghaus. As time passes, less of the material is remembered.

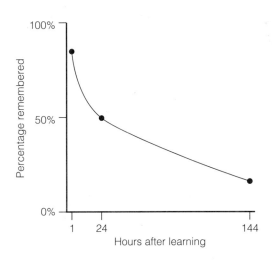

Ebbinghaus's new journal was much more broadly based. It carried all sorts of papers, and it was edited by a diverse group of distinguished psychologists and physiologists.

Ebbinghaus's lack of productivity at Berlin was rewarded by his being replaced as the professor there in 1894 by Carl Stumpf, whom we are going to meet shortly. Ebbinghaus then shifted over to a less prestigious position at Breslau. He did not accomplish very much there, either. But he did do something important, and as we might expect, he did it extremely well. He wrote introductory books. *Principles of Psychology* first appeared in 1897; it summarized the basic experimental approach of Fechner and Wundt, as well as his own work on memory. It captured the exciting spirit of experimentation without burdening the reader with gruesome detail. It is aptly described as a textbook rather than another handbook. (It is referred to as his *Grundzüge*, the same as Wundt's overwhelming work on physiological psychology, which indicates another reason I do not like shortened German titles: They are not descriptive.) The book was extremely popular, and went through several editions. In 1902 he brought out a still shorter and even more popular introductory book, familiarly called the *Abriss*, which we can call *Elementary Psychology*. And it in turn went through many editions, and several translations, even after Ebbinghaus's death in 1909.

Ebbinghaus's career was unusual in that he did almost no research and had few students, only one of any consequence. William Stern studied child development, and was one of the first psychologists to study language in children. He founded the first German journal for applied psychology, carried out a psychological study of Helen Keller, and gave us the concept of the Intelligence Quotient. He was perhaps as inventive as his mentor had been. But otherwise Ebbinghaus took little advantage of his exalted position at Berlin. He did not seem to do much of anything there. But what he did contribute was important: the new journal and all those textbooks, which were to be the standard introductory books for a whole generation of prospective young psychologists. No one had to struggle through Wundt any more. And we cannot forget his one great experiment, the wonderful work on memory, that showed all the world that experimental methods might well be put to work in all areas of psychology, and not just a narrow part of it.[1]

G. E. Müller

GEORG ELIAS MÜLLER (1850–1934) was no relation to Johannes Müller, the physiologist (Müller is a very common German name). He was born the same year as Ebbinghaus but outlived him by 25 years. And he was enormously more productive. He was a very different kind of man from Ebbinghaus, but the two scholars formed an interesting pair and seemed to complement each

147

other. Müller started his university life at Leipzig, but that was before Wundt got there. Then he moved to Berlin (university students seemed to move around a lot in those days), where he studied history with Trendelenburg. Then he seems to have been fascinated by the work of the philosopher–psychologist Lotze. (We met Lotze in connection with the question of whether reflexes reveal intelligence, and again in connection with his theory of local signs.) He spent a year with Lotze at Göttingen, and did his thesis research, on attention, under Lotze's direction (that was in 1873, so he got going just as quickly as Ebbinghaus had).

Then Müller spent some idle years, in part because he was recovering from an illness, and in part because he could not find suitable employment. But during those slow years he was in Leipzig, where he met Fechner and became fascinated with psychophysical methods. And that set him on a new course. In 1878 he published an important monograph, *The Foundations of Psychophysics*, which was a critical but not unfriendly analysis of Fechner's methodology and data treatment. It was a major contribution. At that time, almost 20 years after Fechner's great work had been published, only a handful of investigators had adopted his psychophysical methods to look at perception. Wundt had, of course, and so had J. L. R. Delboeuf in Belgium, but Müller was one of the first to get into psychophysics. *Foundations* was offered as his habilitation research, and he was appointed **Dozent** at Göttingen. (In German universities something comparable to a second dissertation has to be offered and defended to get habilitated, and usually it is only at that point that one can offer courses.) When Lotze moved on to Berlin in 1881, Müller became the professor at Göttingen, a position he held for 40 very productive years, and he continued writing for a number of years after he retired. Only Wundt lived longer or accomplished more. And Wundt never had as elegant and well-equipped a lab as the one Müller was eventually able to create. Noteworthy, too, is that Müller's lab was begun in 1881, only two years after the one in Leipzig; of course Wundt had been doing experiments for 20 years before his lab became official.

Müller the Methodologist

Müller's career can be broken into phases. In the first phase he did psychophysics. In the 1890s he became interested in memory and he pursued that for a decade or so. Then in the last phase he devoted his thoughts primarily to the problem of perception, particularly color perception. In all these phases, Müller was basically a methodologist. He worried about how the stimuli should be presented, how the conditions should be varied, and how the data should be analyzed, and he worked out methods for dealing with such matters. In the psychophysical experiment, for example, it soon becomes clear that because of various response biases the data are not very nicely distributed from a statistical point of view. Müller found that certain data transformations would produce much more nearly normal distributions, and make the subsequent data analysis much easier. A number of his early students collaborated with him in working out such problems.

Later, when Müller got into memory research, he (along with his lab assistant Friedrich Schumann) invented the memory drum, the demonic device that presents verbal material for the subject at a fixed, unrelenting tempo. Methodologists love to have precise control of their stimuli. He was delighted with Mary Calkins's invention of the paired-associate procedure (she had tried to do research with Müller but Göttingen was then not admitting women students). Her procedure allowed one to study associative learning without worrying about which stimuli came at the start and which ones came in the middle, and so on. Subjects could learn pairs of words or nonsense syllables whose order of presentation was scrambled over trials. His early students and collaborators evidently shared his interest in methodological matters, and they include some names that are still familiar to those who work on human memory: F. Schumann, A. Pilzecher, L. Martin, and A. Jost.

But later on, Müller worked with another breed of student. David Katz and Edgar Rubin were basically gestalt psychologists. They were two of the most important people in that movement, and we will encounter their work later on. We tend to think of methodologists as being conservative, and so might be surprised to see the young methodologist grow up to be a rather liberal and cognitive thinker. Müller wrote a book that was critical of the gestalt movement, so how could he have produced a pair of young scholars who were very early instigators of it? We don't understand him very well. Another curiosity is that Müller worked with some of the first women psychologists. We just saw that Mary Calkins collaborated with him, although she was never actually his student. Christine Ladd-Franklin worked with him briefly in 1891. Lillien Martin was not granted a degree, but she worked in the Göttingen lab from 1894 to 1898, and published with Müller. And Eleanor Gamble, an American from Cornell, worked with him in 1896.[2]

The Loyal Opposition

IN POLITICS the party out of power traditionally opposes anything and everything, no matter how neutral or reasonable it might seem to be, if it is proposed by the party in power. In this country we just call these minority troublemakers the party out of power, but in Britain they are called the loyal opposition. They are loyal enough, at least to the flag and the Queen, but they are generally dead-set against anything they think might conceivably give an advantage to the people in power. And if they cannot conceive of any such advantage they vote against it anyway. There are troublemakers like that in science also. For example, when it looked like Helmholtz had the color-vision problem all wrapped up, along came Hering with new data and new theories. Hering was part of the loyal opposition; everyone seemed to be running this way but he had to make trouble by going in the other direction. Now we are going to look at a connected line of psychologists who have been organizing the loyal opposition for a long, long time. Indeed, their descendants are still making trouble. These folks were loyal to psychology but profoundly opposed to the people in power.

We are at the point in our story where Wundt and Müller and Ebbinghaus were just getting experimental psychology organized, and getting everything put in order. They were doing well as a team, and they were certainly the ones in power, but there was trouble brewing out there in the periphery.

Franz Brentano

Franz Brentano (1838–1917) was born just six years later than Wundt; they were virtually contemporaries. From the time he was a boy Franz was headed for the priesthood. In 1855 he began his education at Berlin, and there he soon fell under the spell of Trendelenburg. The great historian–philosopher sold the young man on Aristotle, and Brentano never abandoned that philosophy. Certainly a Catholic scholar does not have to be an Aristotelian, but many are, particularly if they have a Jesuit background. In any case Brentano became an Aristotelian, and that meant he was about to make trouble—he was going the wrong way. Remember that Aristotle was precisely what psychology had been trying to get away from ever since it all began with Mersenne's friends, Hobbes, Gassendi, and Descartes.

In 1864, after a substantial amount of education, he got his degree in philosophy and was also ordained. He was soon appointed *Dozent* at the university in Würzburg, a post he held for several years. At that time the pope was not considered infallible, but the question of infallibility had arisen and it had stirred up considerable discussion among Catholic scholars. There were seemingly good arguments on both sides, so there was extended debate among the scholars. It was in this setting that in 1869 Brentano published a paper arguing for the liberal position; that is, against infallibility. This, together with several papers on Aristotelian matters, resulted in Brentano's promotion to professor at Würzburg. He was doing very well. Then in 1872 the question of infallibility was finally settled and it was proclaimed that at least when the pope spoke *ex cathedra*, from the throne, he was indeed infallible. Brentano was dismayed, and did what he thought he should do, which was resign both his priestly robes and his professorship. He was a remarkable man of principle.

Then with little to do for a time he wrote *Psychology from an Empirical Standpoint*, which appeared in 1874. This was an important work, and the work for which Brentano is best remembered. It is interesting that Wundt's monumental *Physiological Psychology* came out the same year. Both books were about psychology, but they could hardly have been more different. Wundt wanted to do research to understand how the mind works, but Brentano was not interested in the research approach, he wanted to understand how we experience the world around us. Wundt was a philosopher, and while there was a lot of philosophy in his book, it was basically a book about science. Brentano was a philosopher too, and his book contains much that is Aristotelian, but it is basically a book about human experience. The word *empirical* in his title is tricky. It certainly does not mean anything like getting the facts, nor does it mean anything like building associations with experience. It means describing how things look and feel. In effect, Brentano was proposing a new kind of phenomenology.

At the beginning of *de Anima* Aristotle chided his predecessors for presenting one-dimensional views of the mind, taking it like Democritus to be all mechanical, atoms in motion, or taking it like Plato to be all mental, a collection of ideas. In much the same way, Brentano opposed all the other psychologists of his day, from Bain and Mill to Fechner (remember that he did not yet know what was coming from Wundt), on the grounds that they had all made the human individual so passive. It was all cognition (knowing) with no conation (motivation). The soul makes the body work, Aristotle said, and it does so using both its cognitive and motivational faculties. Brentano would have been upset by Titchener's attempt to make our minds nothing more than collections of stimulus inputs. No, said Brentano, we are active, we are the movers. Even a seemingly passive process like perception involves our activity. If you look at a red apple, there is nothing about the apple, nothing intrinsic to it, that makes it red except for some light reflecting properties of the thing. The redness comes from you. It is something you do; it is an *act of yours* that makes it red. When I look at the apple, it is me who reddens it. Indeed, when I look at an apple, I apple it. This approach is sometimes labeled **act psychology** because of its stress on activity.

Brentano never put on his priestly robes again—indeed he renounced his faith—but he did get back into academia. In 1874 he obtained an appointment as professor of philosophy at Vienna. He taught there for 20 years, and became a very popular lecturer. He did not publish much more, a couple of books around 1900, but he was influential, primarily because of his great 1874 book and because of his power at the podium. He retired in 1894 for a variety of personal reasons, including failing eyesight. Brentano will come up again in another chapter because early in his tenure at Vienna he had a bright young medical student who not only sat in on his lectures but did some independent study work with him. That young man was Sigmund Freud.[3]

Rudolph Lotze

Before we forever leave him behind us, we have to mention Rudolph H. Lotze (1817–81) once more. He was an old-timer, 15 years older than Wundt, and he was at Leipzig as a medical student 40 years before Wundt got there as a professor. He then became *Dozent* at Leipzig in both philosophy and medicine in 1837, at the time when both Weber and Fechner were there. So he goes back to the raw beginnings of things. While at Leipzig he published a good deal, but works that are of no interest to us. On the strength of this work he was offered the chair of philosophy at Göttingen in 1844; he held this distinguished position most of his life, until 1881 when he went to Berlin. That was when, as we have seen, G. E. Müller came to Göttingen, replacing him.

Lotze lived rather comfortably in the two worlds of philosophy and medicine (or physiology). He was perhaps the first German scholar to look at the philosophical implications of physiology, what it meant in the world of ideas for there to be a nervous system. In effect, he was discovering psychology—the area in between—all by himself. Wundt himself had tried to stay clear of the physiological realities. The problem was that not much was known about the nervous system at that time. Lotze's views on these matters, including his famous theory of **local signs,** were described in detail in his *Medical Psychology* (1852). This book is a curiosity in that it is, at least according to Boring (1950), the first work with *psychology* in the title, but I believe Herbart was writing about *psychology* way back in 1816.[4]

Lotze is important for our story mainly for political reasons. He was highly placed, and what he said was influential. For example, it was rather important what he said about the merits of this or that young scholar who might be seeking a university position. Certainly he was instrumental in getting Brentano placed at Vienna. Lotze was also important because he had two very important students. One was G. E. Müller, whom we have already met, and about whom there can be no question regarding importance. The other was Carl Stumpf, whose importance is not so obvious, but quite real nonetheless.

Carl Stumpf

Carl Stumpf (1848–1936) was born in northern Bavaria just two years before Müller and Ebbinghaus, so they were all closely contemporaneous. He was quite musical as a child, and he composed and played several instruments; music would be his life-long love. He went to the university at Würzburg but found that there was no music instruction there so his

Carl Stumpf

music had to be set aside for the time being. Stumpf floundered for a while, and then he encountered Brentano. And the young priest–scholar, who was himself just getting started at Würzburg, totally captured him, just as Brentano had been captured by Trendelenburg only a few years earlier. Stumpf had a teacher and Brentano had a disciple. During the year 1867–68 Stumpf left his master and went to Göttingen to do a dissertation with Lotze.*

Equipped with his degree, Stumpf went back to Würzburg for two more years of study with Brentano. And then, equipped with his mastery of the new Christianity, he went back to Göttingen for three more years of association with Lotze. He became a *Dozent* at Göttingen. Thus, thanks in large part to Stumpf's traveling back and forth, the three men were tightly linked together. When Brentano's conscience made him give up his position at Würzburg, it was young Stumpf who replaced him (Lotze no doubt had a lot to do with that also). But on this trip he was a professor. At this point, 1873, he made his first psychological statement, and it was an important statement. He wrote a book on perception that departed sharply from the Helmholtzian empiricistic model and argued strongly for a nativistic view of perception. It was clearly in the tradition of Kant, Goethe, and Hering. That tradition had been alive for the better part of a century; but that was just the start. Stumpf

---

*Stumpf got his degree when he was 20, and that is pretty young even by German standards. Note that the early date, 1868, puts him ahead of any other psychologist, so one might wonder if his was the first degree in psychology. No, it was a strictly philosophical dissertation. Wundt presided over the first psychology Ph.D., Max Friedrich, in 1881.

and his students kept it alive another century and more. The loyal opposition was getting organized.

Another important aspect of perception as Stumpf regarded it was that it was global, what would later be called wholistic. He rejected the analytical approach, the breaking up of a perception into its constituent elements, and argued that our immediate perception is of whole objects and meaningful things. In effect, he was calling for a return to something like the naive phenomenology of Purkinje. There was something curiously prophetic about this message because the real perceptual atomists, mainly Wundt and his followers, were just getting started. Stumpf's call for a different kind of introspection, naive as against analytical, would have been much more timely later, in another 20 years or so.

Stumpf the Musicologist

At this time in his life Stumpf was evidently being torn in different ways. He was moving increasingly into psychological matters, although he was too much a philosopher to do any research himself, or even to think like a psychologist. But he was also too interested in practical matters and the world of science (an interest he had acquired from Brentano, curiously) to thrive as a philosopher. And he still loved music, although he had been neglecting it for some time. Aha—insight—closure—a new organization—he would study music. He would look at it scientifically, psychologically, and philosophically. He set to work, and after a number of years produced the unique work for which he is best known, *Psychology of Tone* (1883–90). And there he integrated his philosophical inclinations, his interest in psychology, and his love of music.

In 1894 Ebbinghaus was deposed from Berlin, as we saw, and that distinguished chair then went to Stumpf. He had wandered around among several universities, but now he had arrived. He was finally settled, and could start on what looks to be the most important phase of his career because at Berlin he had a number of outstanding students, some of whom were destined to battle gallantly for the loyal opposition.

People from most places would have said at that time that Vienna was the most musical city in the world. But in spite of the fact that Vienna was packed with German composers—Johannes Brahms, Gustav Mahler, Richard Strauss, and others—German people would have said that Berlin was the most musical city in the world. That is what Stumpf said. He was enthralled, and he became enormously active and influential. He set up an institute to collect and study the music of traditional peoples. He set up a center to study children. He got involved in all sorts of activities. And he began a massive multivolume musicological work that was published between 1898 and 1924. He also wrote some further theoretical papers on perception. Stumpf retired in 1921 after a long, busy career and then continued to work on music for another 15 years.[5]

Stumpf's Students

I don't know that Stumpf's passion for music turned out in the end to make much difference either to psychologists or to musicians. More likely, Stumpf's major importance comes from his many important students. Only one of them followed his lead into the world of music: E. von Hornbostel became a noted musicologist. Most of them wandered off, as students are inclined to do, to make their marks doing other things. One of his earliest students, from before his days at Berlin, was E. G. Husserl, who promoted rather successfully his own version of phenomenology. It was similar to Purkinje's approach: You open your eyes and what do you see? It can be expanded: You open your heart and what do you feel? It was not a very scientific approach because it did not lend itself to analysis and quantification, so it did not generate much research, but it did become very popular in Germany.

Another student, O. Pfungst, made his mark by solving a puzzle of sorts. There was a famous horse, Clever Hans, who could solve arithmetic problems. Someone in the audience would yell out, "How much is four plus three?" and the scholarly horse would tap its foot—just seven times. There was, as one might imagine, tremendous public clamor about Hans, who seemed to be more intelligent than the average horse. There were believers and scoffers, so Stumpf was asked to examine the situation and report on the animal's intellectual ability. Stumpf the philosopher didn't really know one end of the horse from the other, but Pfungst did. Pfungst discovered that Hans could only do arithmetic when his owner was nearby; take the owner out of the vicinity and Hans became as stupid as any other horse. Then he figured out that Hans was not really stupid, he was reading extremely subtle body-language signals that the owner was giving—a slight movement of the shoulder, a minimal nod of the head would make the horse start and stop tapping its foot. These movements were so subtle that no one in the audience saw them, and the horse's owner did not know he was making them, but Hans, who was pretty clever in his own horsey way, picked them up. It was not a good day for the equine intelligentsia but it was a great day for psychology.

Friedrich Schumann was an early student who became Müller's assistant for several years (he helped him develop the memory drum), and then returned to work in Stumpf's lab. Some of Stumpf's better-known students at Berlin were O. Abraham, A. Gelb, and W. Poppelreuter. Stumpf also had a couple of American students. Max Meyer was at the University of Missouri for many years; he worked on acoustics and aesthetics. H. S. Langfeld (who got his degree at Berlin in 1909) was at Harvard for several years and then moved to Princeton for the rest of his career.*

Around 1910 Stumpf had two other important students: Wolfgang Köhler and Kurt Koffka. We do not know if Stumpf regarded them as special at the time, or if he saw them as the next carriers of the banner, but it turns out that they were. They were two of the main figures in gestalt psychology. They argued for all the unpopular causes, nativism, wholism as against atomism, and phenomenology. Stumpf lived to see Köhler and Koffka leading the loyal opposition into the next generation.

Oswald Külpe

THE ESTABLISHMENT, the people in power, feel danger all around them. They feel endangered by the ignorant, those that just do not know or believe. The establishment has to engage these barbarians in battle so they can be converted to the right way of thinking. There is also the loyal opposition, who constantly defy the correct way of thinking and cause all sorts of trouble. If the establishment is empiricistic, then it always has to be on the lookout for nativists who might be running around out there. The establishment can also get into trouble from within its own ranks. Sometimes the trouble comes about quite innocently. Perhaps a bright young believer discovers a neat methodological advance. That's nice, but perhaps it undermines the credibility of important work that did not have the advantage of that methodology, so that the classic work, a bulwark of the paradigm, now looks a little shabby. That is a rather cruel fate. But perhaps the cruelest fate that can befall the establishment is when one of them, an upright, right-minded soul, rides off to conquer new territory. Determined to expand the paradigm and extend its generality and power, this true believer rides off into new provinces, but then encounters terrible dragons, such awesome problems that the entire enterprise goes to pieces. That can happen; it happened to Külpe.

I knew Langfeld when I was teaching at Princeton, back in 1957. He was retired then, but he was usually around the department and he loved to talk about the old days. And perhaps it was through chatting with Langfeld about how it used to be that I first got interested in the history of psychology. I cannot say for sure, but more than likely the combination of having an office right next to the departmental library and talking with Langfeld is what turned me on to it. He had not supervised a student or done any research for years, but that was all right; that sort of thing was for the ambitious young people (like me) to do. I remember Langfeld as always a gentleman, and always wearing a white suit and a fresh carnation. Experimental psychology is such a new thing that Stumpf's career, and Langfeld's, and mine cover its entire history.

Oswald Külpe

Külpe at Leipzig: Heir Apparent

Oswald Külpe (1862–1915) came from Latvia, but his family was German, and the land was Russian. He had something like an identity crisis. His education did not make his place any clearer. He studied intermittently at Leipzig, where he met Wundt. He went to Berlin, where he studied history. He studied at Göttingen, where he met Müller and started a dissertation in his lab. He studied at Dorpat, where he went back into history. And then he found himself: He was in Leipzig, working for Wundt. (See figure 7.2 for the locations of the universities.) He finished the Müller thesis, with Wundt's blessing, in 1887. That was early enough to make him one of Wundt's first psychology students. He stayed on at Leipzig as *Dozent* and as Wundt's assistant, succeeding Cattell. He was there for several years. Thus, he was the lab assistant when Titchener was there and they became good friends. In 1893 Külpe wrote the important book *Outline of Psychology* that was thoroughly Wundtian in outlook but much neater and simpler than Wundt's presentation. *Outline* was popular, but even more successful was *Introduction to Philosophy*, which first appeared in 1895, and then went through many editions and was translated into English. Again we see Wundt's philosophical ideas and their relation to the experimental psychology, but it was neat and simple instead of the tangled web that Wundt had woven.

More good news: Külpe was elevated to professor at Würzburg in 1894. He had inherited a good lab there, and he made it bigger and better. He had those important books and a number of technical papers, and at the relatively young age of 32 he was the professor at Würzburg, one of the top four or so universities as far as psychology was concerned. He could count on having outstanding students at Würzburg. But the best news was that Külpe now knew who he was—he was a Wundtian. No more identity problem.

I noted earlier that the majority of Wundt's students moved conceptually and methodologically away from him. We have already noted one exception in Titchener, who remained fairly true to the faith although he did simplify it greatly and strip off most of its philosophical ornamentation. And he had gone away to a primitive land. Külpe also clung to the faith. He also simplified the message and presented it in a more attractive manner, but Wundt was quite tolerant and flexible about that sort of thing—in part, I suppose, because he kept rephrasing his own position. And Külpe was quite close at hand in nearby Würzburg. A great future looked assured; he was the heir apparent. But beware! He was in serious danger. He was unaware of Hume's geopsychological hypothesis. Külpe was in the wrong place. Würzburg was the land of Brentano and Stumpf!

Külpe at Würzburg

Around 1900 Külpe did what a believer in the established paradigm is supposed to do, namely, push out the frontiers, extend it to new domains, expand it to include new phenomena. He understood that Ebbinghaus had understood that Fechner had understood that the mind could be measured. Fechner had measured perception, Ebbinghaus had measured memory, so why could he, Külpe, not measure thought? Yes, he would measure thought.

FIGURE 7.2

Germany before World War I, showing where the major psychology departments were and some of the major cities where there was little experimental psychology.

He would do it in a very Wundtian manner, with experimental control of the stimuli and the subjects introspecting on their thoughts. He would give subjects a simple little thing to think about and find out what their thoughts looked like. Wundt, the master, had said that one could not use the methods of experimental psychology on the higher mental processes, but perhaps he was being overly cautious. And wouldn't it be grand if the methods did work!

The first reported study on the project was done in 1901 by Karl Marbe, whose subjects worked on a standard weight-lifting task, but also had to introspect and report what was in mind as they decided which was heavier. Marbe found that his subjects had a lot of imagery of the weights, but could report nothing about the decision process itself. It was just suddenly . . . pop! There it is. The decision itself seemed to come out of nowhere. A. Mayer and J. Orth did the study again using some variations, and got the same failure to introspect on thinking. Henry Watt did it again in 1904, this time using verbal material. Subjects had to decide if one word, "fish," was subordinate or superordinate to another word, "trout." But again, consciousness seemed to contain only the result of the thought process, and not the process itself.

Watt had introduced a new wrinkle in his procedure, emphasizing or not emphasizing the task, or what he called **Aufgabe,** which means something like the purpose or intention of the subjects; we might call it "set." It is manipulated with instructions. *Aufgabe,* it turns out, is very important in determining what sort of results one gets, but it too is essentially invisible to introspection. When you are ready to attack subordinates and superordinates in a particular way, you do so, but that has no effect on what is in consciousness. Narziss Ach (1905) called these motivational effects **determining tendencies.** They were vague, unseen motivational forces that affected thought processes, but that were invisible in the sense that subjects could not introspect on them. Karl Bühler (who was then Külpe's lab assistant) and several very capable students worked on the problem in a multitude of ways. The experimenter presents a 6 and a 7 beneath it, and after the subject has introspected a bit on this, the experimenter suddenly says "add" or "multiply." What is in mind between hearing "add" and imaging "13"? Absolutely nothing. Külpe had an array of excellent students who in time would do very well for themselves, but were certainly not doing him any good. He had one student who would do the Wundtian cause a lot of harm in a few years. Max Wertheimer got his degree in 1904 and went on to lead the gestalt movement.

Külpe with all his good intentions had been overcome by two fearsome dragons. One was the monster called **imageless thought.** The Würzburgers had found, and demonstrated repeatedly, that thought processes are not accompanied by images. In a sense Wundt had been right, the introspection method would not work in this arena. But in a larger sense Wundt was wrong, because he dreamed of finding synthesizing principles, of understanding how the mind puts things together. But now Külpe and his students had shown that Wundt's introspective approach would never be able to do that. The second beast was also rather gruesome. The contents of consciousness are determined not only by stimuli that can be physically presented and experimentally manipulated, they are also determined by mysterious forces, or Aufgabes, or determining tendencies. That "13" certainly is dependent on the 6 and 7 out there, but how in the world can a structuralist explain that the subject sometimes "sees" 13 and sometimes "sees" 42?

Both Wundt and Titchener were furious and outraged. They accused Külpe of using sloppy and inappropriate procedures. But Külpe was trained by Wundt for 10 years and he was nothing if not a diligent student; he surely knew what he was doing. The problem was clearly not with Külpe the experimenter or with his numerous experiments, but rather in the paradigm he believed in. Külpe abandoned this line of research in 1909 when he left Würzburg. Würzburg had ruined him. He died six years later, at 52.[6]

Summary

IN 1879 THERE WAS one lab, which was located at Leipzig. Twenty years later there were four large, well-funded, active labs, at Göttingen, Leipzig, Würzburg, and Berlin (to list them in the approximate order of their excellence). And in addition, other, less important labs had been established at Freiburg, Munich, Bonn, Breslau, Marburg, and Halle. Some of these may have fallen into disuse as their founders moved around in the system, but the pattern is clear: There was an explosive growth of experimental psychology.

In 1879 there were no experimental psychologists; that is, nobody bore the title of psychologist. Wundt was a philosopher, as were Brentano and Lotze, and Ebbinghaus and Müller were essentially unemployed. Most of these men were philosophers in spirit as well as title. Brentano was 100 percent philosopher, who philosophized about psychological matters such as perception and motivation. Although he believed in science, he had little interest in research. Lotze also liked science, and dabbled with research, but only in the musical realm. Wundt, perhaps because of his medical background, liked experimentation. But his research was always embedded in his massive philosophical system. The next generation was much more experimentally oriented. Ebbinghaus was a researcher, although he did not do much of it. Külpe did lots of research, but it, too, was controlled by his philosophy rather than by his data. Of all these German pioneers, only Müller was 100 percent psychologist.

And we can see lines being drawn. Wundt did his sort of research, and none of his students seems to have pursued the study of memory. They talked about it but they did not research it. Müller the methodologist followed up Wundt's work and Ebbinghaus's work. He was the clean-up man. But the three of them made a nice team of experimenters because they shared methods, concepts, and roughly the same view of what psychology should be. And their differences in style let them complement each other and strengthen the team.

Then on the other side of the line, the loyal opposition had a much more wholistic, phenomenological, and motivational view of psychology. If we check out our basic themes, it is easy to see Wundt and his allies as atomistic, empiricistic, and associationistic. The mechanistic theme is unclear, because they were all parallelists. And the loyal opposition took the other side on all issues; they were wholistic, nativistic, and something else besides associationists. Their Aristotelian leaning excludes any simple mechanistic faith. But the two sides took essentially opposite sides on all the basic themes.

One further comment about geopsychology. The four universities where the drama was working itself out all lie quite close together geographically. Leipzig is in the middle, which seems fitting. Berlin is only 100 miles to the north, Göttingen only 80 miles to the west. And Würzburg is only about 120 miles south. Germany is a large country, so why is it that nothing psychological was happening in Hamburg, Munich, or Cologne? Why was the new psychology concentrated just east of the middle of the country? The puzzle gets bigger: Wundt all by himself had dozens of students from northern and eastern Europe, so why didn't psychology take hold in Romania and Sweden and other places his students returned to? What was it about the center of Germany that made it such fertile ground for the new experimental psychology to grow in?

Notes

1. Hermann Ebbinghaus wrote one of the most stunning, important, and nicest research reports ever: *Uber das Gedachtnis* (1885). Fortunately, it has been nicely translated by Ruger and Bussenius as *On Memory* (1913). His most popular and elementary introductory text, the *Abriss*, was translated by M. Meyer in 1908. For biographical material on Ebbinghaus see Shakow (1930).

2. Georg Elias Müller (1850–1934) is second only to Wundt in importance in German experimental psychology, but there is strangely little information on him, and nothing of his seems to have been translated into English. I think that after the psychophysics book in 1878 he never wrote a book or any large work that could have been translated. His publications were usually in the form of short research reports. To understand what he was up to in the early days when he was into psychophysics and memory it is necessary to dig out references to him in Titchener (1901–05). But for some idea of Müller's methodological contributions with Jost, Pilzecher, and others see Woodworth (1938). His outcry against the gestaltists is in his book *Complex Theory and Gestalt Theory* (1923). It was not so much that he was opposed to them as that he thought they had stolen his stuff. For biography all we have on Müller is Boring (1935, 1950).

3. Franz Brentano (1838–1917) was for a century essentially inaccessible to those who don't read German, but now there is a translation of his all-important 1874 book *Psychology from an Empirical Standpoint* by McAlister and others (1973). On his life see Puglisi (1924).

4. Rudolph Hermann Lotze (1817–81) at some point gave up the Rudolph and became Hermann. He did not write anything that we are likely to want to read. His major work was *Medical Psychology, or Physiology of the Mind* (1852). He died almost immediately after arriving at Berlin. Just before he died he gave a series of lectures titled *Outlines of Psychology* that was translated into English by Judd (1886). There is biographical information on Lotze in Hall (1912).

5. Carl Stumpf (1848–1936) is best remembered for his *Psychology of Tone* (1883–90). The huge work *Acoustics and Musicology* appeared in many volumes between 1898 and 1924, but might not have been very important. The story of Clever Hans was told by Pfungst (1907), which is in English; a shorter account of the famous horse, nicely put in historical perspective, is Boakes (1984). It is hard to get a good look at Stumpf on feeling and motivation, but we get a glimmer from Titchener (1917) who vigorously attacked his views. Beginning in 1930, Carl Murchison started a series of volumes called *The History of Psychology in Autobiography*, which is an excellent and valuable collection of autobiographical chapters. The 1930 volume has a (translated) chapter by Stumpf. See also the obituary by Langfeld (1937).

6. Oswald Külpe (1862–1915) wrote a popular *Outlines of Psychology* in 1893 that was translated by Titchener (1895). The two men had been very good friends early on. This book is still perhaps the best summary of what Wundtian experimental psychology looked like. I think Külpe's importance is greatly underestimated. He was a pivotal person between the earlier Wundt and the later gestaltists. Wundt saw him as a defector, but it is not clear that that was so. He had those troublesome data and that Würzburg tradition both working against him. I know of no biographical material in English to indicate whether he got converted to the new cause or was merely the victim of his troubles. Humphrey (1951) gives a detailed account of the imageless-thought research, and cites all the literature.

Chapter Eight

The Periphery in Britain

T HE BRITISH TOOK LITTLE heed of the explosive growth of psychology in Germany and America. There would not be an effective psychology laboratory in England until well into the 20th century. Part of the problem was the extraordinary conservatism of Cambridge and Oxford, the two grand old universities. There was a new university at London that began taking shape early in the 1800s, but it came to life only very gradually. Much of the impetus for psychology's growth in both Germany and the United States was the remodeling of the two university systems. Perhaps it follows that British psychology was retarded because the great universities there would not change. Certainly it cannot be a coincidence that the two important Englishmen we are about to meet never held any kind of university position. The third person we will meet, a Scotsman, ultimately became connected with a university, but his powerful impact had little to do with his university connection. Let us visit England first.

Darwin and Evolution

CHARLES R. DARWIN (1809–82) was a bit younger than Fechner and a little older than both Wundt and Lotze. He grew up in Shrewsbury, which is a town about 60 miles south of Liverpool. The family was affluent; his father was a quite successful physician and his mother was from the Wedgwood chinaware family. Charles had a notable grandfather, Erasmus Darwin, who died before Charles was born, but who was nonetheless an ornamental part of the family. As a boy Charles loved animals—he played with the big ones and collected the little ones. He also collected rocks and shells and plants, and organized all his collections very carefully.

Darwin had a rather uncertain education. He did not care for medicine at Edinburgh, nor for his clerical training at Cambridge. But at Cambridge he was befriended by the botanist John Henslow. Shortly after Darwin

Charles Darwin

graduated in 1831 Henslow recommended him to a certain Captain Robert FitzRoy as a naturalist, an observer and collector who would be an ideal companion on FitzRoy's forthcoming voyage. FitzRoy's primary mission was to survey the coast of South America, but he thought it would be a good thing to look at the flora and fauna along the way. Darwin was just a kid and lacked experience, but he was bright and eager. In retrospect, it sounded like a foolhardy adventure. They were to be at sea for two years, and there was no pay. There was not much to gain from it for the young man, and much to risk, but Darwin was ready for the adventure. At their meeting in London, however, FitzRoy had his doubts.

The Voyage of the Beagle

It has been said that enormous outcomes can come from insignificant causes. For example, it has been said that if Cleopatra's nose had been one-quarter inch longer then our entire history would have unfolded quite differently. If there is anything to that, then it is more than likely that if Darwin's nose had been one-quarter inch shorter we would not now have his theory of evolution. It seems that FitzRoy did not like the lad's nose; it was "weak," he said. But Darwin was a likable young man and eager to go, so the matter of the nose was put aside and the deal was arranged. They set sail on the *Beagle* in December 1831. The two-year plan was a little optimistic; it actually took them five years to return. (See figure 8.1.)

Darwin collected and recorded many marvelous things. He wrote up innumerable notebooks that were full of plant and animal and even human observations. For example, he noted that the natives around Tierra del Fuego fished while standing barefoot in the water. He could not even step in the water it was so cold. Perhaps, he thought, it had something to do with the fact that these people had very heavy ankles and fat feet. He noted that there was no timidity among the birds and animals of the Galápagos Islands; he could walk right up to them. Maybe it was related to the fact that there were no humans on the islands. He noted that on the Galápagos there were lizards that jumped in the water to catch prey, odd behavior for a lizard. But then he observed that there was a lot of food in the water and very little on the land. He liked the little birds that looked like finches except that they had mis-shapen, unfinch-like beaks. Aha—they didn't eat what finches normally eat.

Darwin had notebooks full of such observations; they would keep him occupied for years. One thing seemed clear, however: What seemed at first to be oddities of nature turned out to be very good adaptations to the prevailing circumstances. If you are going to make your living standing in cold water, then it is extremely helpful to have fat feet. It is easy to see plant and animal forms adapted to their environment if you prowl around in the

FIGURE 8.1

(a) H.M.S. Beagle, *shown in the Straits of Magellan. (b) The route of the* Beagle's *five-year voyage around the world.*

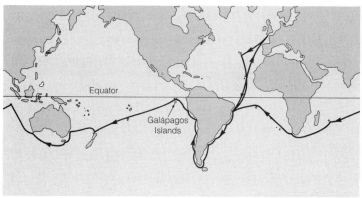

familiar fields of England, but it is much more demanding on the observer to see such connections while wandering all around South America. But Darwin had become a skilled observer, and he was able to make sense of many of his observations. The variety of life forms clearly had something to do with the variety of habitats in which organisms lived. The curiosities of behavior must also be related to the diversity of environments.

What about the environment? There were two theories. Darwin had been studiously reading about geologist Charles Lyell's new idea, called uniformitarianism, which was that the forces that mold the geological world are always the same, and they can only change things by operating over great spans of time. The older view, called catastrophism, held that remarkable and miraculous changes can happen once in a while, like the great rains in Noah's time. Darwin worried about such problems while aboard the *Beagle*, and gradually became a uniformitarian, even though he realized that processes like erosion to round off a mountain top would require enormous amounts of time. In Argentina he discovered fossils of sea creatures up in the mountains, indicating that the ocean had once been up in the mountains or that the mountains had once been down under the sea. Any such displacement would take a very long time, but that seemed to make more sense than to suppose that the mountain had suddenly leapt up there.

Darwin got home in 1836; he went the long way around, across the Pacific and the Indian Oceans, so he observed coral reefs and other exotic things to wonder about. He had been sending specimens home all this time, along with material from his notebooks, and he had kept in touch with Henslow and others. When he got home he found that he was a very famous young man. He was world traveler, geographer, geologist, botanist, you name it. In 1839 he was elected to membership in the Royal Society. At 30 he was one of the youngest members ever. The same year he published a book that made him all the more famous; its lengthy title is invariably shortened to *Voyage of the Beagle* (1839). At 30 he was famous and could have retired (there was money enough in the family that he did not have to work), but he was just getting started.[1]

Natural Selection

Darwin worried about Malthus's assertion that population grows evermore, while resources are ever limited. There has to be competition for the fixed amount of available resources within any given species as its numbers increase. This seemed to mean that there is not only the familiar sort of competition between predator and prey (cats and mice), or between different predators (cats and dogs both look for mice), but within each species (some cats are better mousers than others). Gradually, hesitantly, Darwin began to put it all together. He sorted and reorganized his collections. He got more and more specimens (people all around the world were sending him stuff). He read, talked to his friends, and thought about it. He was finally moved to action by correspondence from Alfred Wallace in 1858. Wallace was somewhere in Malaya dying of some terrible disease, he thought, and sent a short paper to Darwin because he did not know who else to send it to. It seemed that Wallace, a bright young fellow, had Darwin's theory! He had not put it together as patiently and carefully, but there it was. Darwin then did the honorable thing of presenting both Wallace's paper and one of his own (which he had written years before but had never published) to the Linnean Society in 1858. The next year he published his great book. Darwin was fond of long titles, and in this case I will go along with him because the title pretty well tells the story: *On the Origin of Species by Means of Natural Selection, or the Preservation of Favoured Races in the Struggle for Life* (1859).

You start with the idea of there being vast amounts of time. You allow for the world to change slowly, mountains rising, rivers changing their course, or drying up, or becoming lakes. You recognize that as the environment changes a species will be threatened by too much water, too little sunshine, too little vegetation, or something of that sort. But within the species there is variation, and some individuals will have traits that let them survive the change better than others. If the time is long enough, and the change in their world is great enough, then the slight survival advantage of some individuals will accumulate so that the ultimate descendants may bear little resemblance to the original species. You will have a new species. Over on the other side of the mountains perhaps the changes in geology and climate were not so great, so that the original species is still carrying on. So now, after all the eons, there are two species where there used to be one. To say it again: There is a struggle for life, there is something like racial variation, and some races or characteristics are favored as the world changes, then in time natural selection will produce a new species. It is all there in that long title.

The majority of biologists liked the new concept of natural selection, the idea that some survive and some die off. Certainly few biologists subscribed to the biblical notion that Noah had everybody on board. Indeed, various ideas of evolution had emerged in the first half of the 1800s. Grandfather Erasmus had one version. About the same time (1804) Lamarck had another; he thought that an animal's *efforts* could change reproductive cells somehow so that the effect of those efforts would be passed on to the offspring. Thus, if I am a grazing animal and I really try to stretch up to get the upper leaves on a tree, then my young will tend to have longer necks. Eventually, if they all keep trying, they will be giraffes. It was a wonderfully progressive, liberal idea. The Marxists liked it. Another variation was that God is still tending His animal and plant kingdoms, and He gradually improves some of them. It would be a planned evolution; it was headed somewhere. Some people contended that some sort of evolution was applicable to the animals, but we humans are exempt from the process because we are already created in the image of God. By 1859 there was a rich variety of evolutionary schemes, but all of them were couched in some sort of familiar human terms, something like God's plan, individual effort, or improvement of the species. Somebody was in charge of the process. God, or the giraffes, or somebody had it under control. Darwin's concept of natural selection implied a much less pretty picture. No one is in charge, it just happens. There is no plan, no purpose, it just happens. It happens in the same way, at the same speed, and for the same reasons that the mountains rise up, or the water goes away, or the weather gets colder. Some survive but many die when the world changes.

Darwin admitted that he was concerned about how the clergy might react to his kind of evolution. And he had every reason to be concerned, because that is where the bulk of his opposition came from. Accordingly, he talked very little about the human species in the *Origin*, but he gathered up his courage and got to it in *The Descent of Man* (1871). If we are different from other creatures, he said, it is only because we have more intelligence, communicate more, and have more flexible instincts. In other words, Darwin was saying that the difference is only quantitative. In other words, we are part of the animal kingdom, part of the world of living things, even part of the slowly changing planet. In other words, you can forget what your priest or minister told you about how people were created. On the *Beagle* Darwin had seen such a variety of species that he knew they could not have all been stuffed into the ark, and besides that Noah had no way of gathering up the curious creatures that lived on the Galápagos and so many other exotic places. Clearly, new species were coming into existence, but what was their origin? For Darwin that was the mystery of mysteries. It should be clear why so many religious people do not like Darwin.

Darwin and Psychology

We can step aside from the really big, general issues and ask about our own special interests. How did Darwin affect psychology specifically? The answer is, in many ways. Immediately after *Descent* he wrote another book, *The Expression of the Emotions in Man and Animals* (1872). He did not, like the philosophers, worry about what the emotions were, how we know them, or how they feel. He took the existence of emotions for granted and concerned himself with how they are expressed behaviorally. He used a variety of techniques. Remember that Darwin had friends he kept in touch with all around the world who were sending him bugs from Bulgaria and lizards from Liberia. He asked a host of these people to tell him how kids there responded in happy situations and in sad or distressing situations. The results could not have been clearer; all over the world kids smile when they are happy and cry when they are sufficiently unhappy.

A different approach: He had some minor theoretical proposals about how opposite emotions are expressed using opposing muscles groups. For humans, the frown and the smile illustrate his argument. For cats, you have the arched back in the angry cat and a sort of lordosis posture in the happy, sociable cat. Darwin located an old man who was very skinny. The thin skin of his face appeared to just sit on top of his bones and muscles. Darwin was then able to see precisely what facial muscles participated in different human emotional displays. He described a "grief" display, which is characterized by a tight, unexpressive mouth, and eyebrows that slant up in the middle. This is a mixed emotion, a combination, he suggested. Grief arises when one has reason to cry, but crying is voluntarily suppressed. There is, of course, a crying expression, which involves a square mouth and a wrinkled forehead. When we try to suppress crying we have very good voluntary control over the mouth, so it gets tightened up rather than assuming the square, crying shape. But we have little control over the forehead muscles. Therefore, in grief we get the peculiar tilted eyebrows. Darwin went after emotion anatomically, developmentally, comparatively, and cross-culturally. It has been said that it would be 100 years before psychologists made any significant advance over Darwin's analysis of emotion.

Darwin reported one other thing that is immediately relevant to psychology. His first son, William, who was called Doddy, was born in 1839, and the proud father, the incurable observer, kept a diary of the boy's development. He recorded the appearance of different reflexes and different motor skills, along with the appearance of different learning abilities such as being able to learn by association. For unknown reasons, Papa Darwin did not publish the diary record for a long time, not until little Doddy was 37 years old! It was short, but it remains an interesting chronology of an infant's development. Even with the very long delay in getting his observations into print (Darwin, 1877), his diary was easily the first of many similar developmental diaries that would come along. Even Preyer (1882) was not prior.[2]

Darwin's New Perspective

Those are a couple of Darwin's immediate and concrete contributions to psychology. Much more important in the long run, however, have been Darwin's indirect and abstract contributions to the field. Brand-new conceptual issues sprang up as a result of the fact that Darwin thought about life as no one had thought about it before. And it was those new conceptual issues and new perspectives that would affect psychology most profoundly. The idea of natural selection implied first of all that there is *continuity* of species; there is no difference in principle between man and animal, there is no gulf between us and them. For the psychologist, continuity had many implications. For example, it meant that they had some intelligence and we had some instincts.

Second, Darwin's theory of evolution was *naturalistic*. It made us a part of nature. We did not have to worry about the special status granted us by

169

divine creation, which had largely exempted us from all the laws of science. We could regard ourselves as part of it. This would seem, at least logically, a necessary first step that had to be taken before psychology could be a science. Fechner may have been just banging his head against a wall if he believed in the glorious freedom of the human spirit at the same time he was trying to measure something inside there.

A third aspect of the theory was that it required *variation* within a species. It was no longer possible to think of a population of individuals all conforming to some set of standards. There were no prototypes, no essential natures, no types. Within any living population there had to be individual differences.

These three aspects of Darwin's theory, the continuity of species, the naturalistic approach to all species, and the idea of variation within a species were relatively easy to see and were historically the first aspects of his thinking to attract the attention of psychologists. But there were additional nuances of Darwin's view of evolution that were more subtle, and only appreciated after psychology itself had evolved somewhat further. Although the citation of these facets breaks the continuity of our story, it seems less important to hold strictly to the story line than to take the opportunity to celebrate Darwin's extraordinary contribution. One subtle point, even today not well recognized, is that the new evolution gave us a new *mode of explanation*. We have always understood machines: The idea that this part goes up and down when that part goes around, or the idea that muscles swell up when the nerves pump fluid into them. We know that sort of thing from everyday experience. We also know from everyday experience that our own actions are controlled by our plans and purposes. Those are the two familiar modes of explanation. But the natural selection idea was something else. All it says is that within the population some survive but a lot die off. This does not imply any kind of machinery, and there is clearly no plan or purpose—it just happens. It is a new way of explaining things. Such a way of explaining things takes some getting used to, but in time psychologists would get used to it. Indeed, it has gradually become characteristic. Physiologists have their machinery, philosophers have their intentions and purposes, but because psychologists live somewhere in between, they cannot always go either familiar way. And so psychologists propose explanatory principles such as the law of reinforcement. The rule is that a response occurs frequently because it has been reinforced. But this is precisely the same Darwinian mode. Like natural selection, it is not mechanical and it is not purposeful, it is just a hypothesis about observable events.

Darwin's view of things emphasized how the environment exerted pressure on a species to change. Adaptations are adjustments to the *environment* and its gradual changes. The prior concept had been that a given creature has its own inherent character, which, if not God-given, at least

170

expresses the essence of the beast. The new view was
fixed identity because it is always the product of
environment. The species is always in transition. T.
individual reflects its species membership, certainly, but b
the individual and the mean behavior of the species hang
the environment presents.

Philosophers and scientists alike had always taken the pc
know about something, then you know it. Things are wha   ...re. But
Darwin tells us that there is another part of the story; the things we know have
a *history*, and that history is also part of what the thing is. It might be an
evolutionary history, a genetic history, or a developmental history. Things are
never just as they are; they were made, or they evolved, or they grew up.
Everything has a story that we may well need to know before we can
understand the thing itself.

It is also clear that Darwin was fascinated by *behavior*. At the Galápagos
he noted animals (e.g., finches) that looked odd, but just as often he noted
animals (e.g., lizards) that acted strangely. With emotion it was the emotional
expression that intrigued him. In his developmental diary it was Doddy's
behavior that was most often described. Virtually all of the philosophers and
all of the pioneer psychologists we have met up to this point were obsessed
with the mind. They were caught up in what the mind is, how it interacts with
the body, how it can know, what it perceives, what it feels, how it is organized,
and on and on. In Darwin we see for the first time a person who did not worry
much about mind problems, but who was fascinated by behavior. And isn't
that refreshing!

One of these conceptual issues, the matter of variation, captured the
attention of the next person we are about to meet. But it will take us a few
chapters to find psychologists who were turned on by some of Darwin's other,
more subtle conceptual contributions.

Galton and Individual Differences

IN FRANCIS GALTON (1822–1911) we meet an individual who cannot be stuck
in any pigeonhole because he did a little bit of everything; he was an
extraordinarily creative and inventive man who made major contributions to
a number of disciplines. He was born in Birmingham, England, in the house
where his great grandfather, Samuel Galton, had lived. This is to say that the
Galton side of the family was old, well-established, and monied. It looked
pretty good on his mother's side, too; her father was Erasmus Darwin. Thus,
Galton and Darwin were cousins—half-cousins, actually, because Erasmus
had been married twice and our two heroes had different grandmothers. But,

Francis Galton

quite likely because Charles became famous first and because he was 13 years older, Francis frequently referred to him as his cousin.[3]

Galton the Adventurer

The cousins were very different in some ways. Charles had suffered through his university years and made few friends except for Henslow, with whom he prowled around in the fields. In contrast, Francis thrived at Cambridge, competed for prizes, and made numerous friends with whom he would continue to keep in touch. Charles was basically a retiring person, and as he got older he maintained a massive correspondence with many people, but he rarely ever left his home in the country. Francis, on the other hand, had innumerable friends, lived in London where the action was and where he became involved in many activities, and traveled constantly. But there were also some curious parallels. Just out of college, Darwin had gone around the world in a small boat, just for the adventure of it. While still a student, Galton ventured off for six months to such exotic places as Syria, Egypt, and the Sudan. That trip did not bring him fame, but his next trip did. Galton finished Cambridge and then for several years led the life of the wealthy young gentleman: He rode and hunted, sailed the seas, and caroused with his friends.

In 1850 Galton had talked with another cousin, who put him in touch with the Royal Geographical Society, who in turn got him thinking about unexplored areas of Africa. Curiously, that was only 140 years ago, but there were large unexplored areas everywhere. No European had ever been anywhere near the central part of many of the continents. He organized, headed, and paid for an expedition to South West Africa, now Namibia. The British had a thriving colony in Cape Town, but Galton was headed for Walvis Bay, 750 miles up the coast and totally unexplored. Most of the people he encountered there had never seen a European before. It is a dry, miserable place, a land of dry riverbeds, a part of the world where nothing grows because all the soil washed out to sea millions of years ago. It is one of the most desolate places on earth. Galton did not know it, but he could have scrabbled around in the sandy beaches of Walvis Bay and found diamonds there! He and his party pushed inland several hundred miles, surveyed everything, made notes on everything, hung around for nearly two years and then sailed home. Galton had become the great explorer. This was the time of exploration. The 1850s was the era when Stanley found Livingstone, when Perry sailed into Tokyo Harbor, which no Caucasian had ever seen before, when Burton discovered Mecca, which no Christian had ever seen before, and when Speke found the source of the Nile. It was the great era of exploration and discovery, and Galton was there at the outset. He was famous; he was elected into the Royal Geographical Society and other distinguished groups, including the Royal Society in 1856 when he was only 34, almost as young as his cousin had made it. In time Galton would become important in the administration of Britain's various geographical societies, and he remained active in this capacity for many years.

Galton the Measurer

About 1860 Galton became fascinated with weather; he discovered anticyclones, invented devices for measuring and recording weather data, and helped establish the Meteorological Office, something akin to our National Weather Bureau. He was a vital part of the office for 40 years. Interestingly, one of the first people to stir up interest in weather, especially forecasting it for sailors, was our friend who judged a man by his nose and who was now Admiral FitzRoy. He too had done very well after the great voyage of the *Beagle*, although he died poor.

Galton always loved machines and devices, and he invented quite a number of gadgets for doing things in a better way. He devised a sort of adjustable supersonic dog whistle, which enabled him to determine the upper limits of hearing in animals. He wrote a great deal about fingerprints, around 1890, and finally convinced Scotland Yard to use prints for identification purposes rather than the complex and fallible French system, which measured earlobes and other parts. Early on he wrote an experimental report on the efficacy of prayer; it was a nicely designed study with praying people not praying and nonpraying people doing it. Prayer had little discernable effect in getting things done, he reported. He reported an experiment on the freedom of the will. He was the subject, and he merely kept notes about those occasions in his daily activity when he seemed to be making a decision. Then he considered the circumstances surrounding those occasions. The question was whether he could find reasons in his prior experience, his current flow of thought, or his motives that might have governed the apparent decision.

Yes, almost always. At most once a day, he concluded, he might do something "freely."

Galton was fascinated by numbers; he was sort of goofy about data. There was a lottery in London where the contestants guessed the weight of an ox. The prize went to whoever came closest to the animal's actual weight. After the lottery Galton got hold of all the tickets so he could study the distribution of guesses. He noted with much delight that the mean was only a pound or two from the true value, and the standard error was very small. Then he started thinking about the data. When we calculate a mean, it is clear that the outlying scores, the deviant ones, have a major effect on the mean. The implication is that in arriving at the mean of the guesses as an estimate of the true value, one gives the greatest importance to the scores of those who are the poorest judges! What a wonderful argument. It is clear that one should not base estimates on means, but on medians. And henceforth, Galton consistently used medians, percentiles, and rank data in describing everything he measured.

Galton could not get enough data. At an International Exhibition in 1884 he set up an "Anthropometric Lab" for measuring people. For three pence you (and Galton) would get your height, weight, and span, along with such measures as the force of your punch, ability to blow up a balloon, grip strength, and reaction time. When the fair was over he set it up again in London and continued to measure thousands of people. We know, for example and for whatever it is worth, that the median man stood just under 5 foot 8 inches and median woman was just over 5 foot 3 inches. Galton had designed and built most of the apparatus, and he published mountains of people data.

Inherited Traits

So far I have mentioned only some of the odds and ends with which Galton occupied his time, and only a few of them. He also experimented with stereoscopic maps, which were vastly superior, he thought, to ordinary flat-looking maps. He figured out a way to make composite photographs of a number of people, and discovered that the composite of a set of siblings was generally more attractive than any one of them. He had endless novelties like that.

Now we can mention the work that was most important for psychology. He said that upon reading his cousin's *Origin* he became fascinated by the concept of variation. Within any population, including the human population, there are going to be great individual differences, and these differences are going to be largely inheritable. That was the whole point of natural selection, and the mechanism of evolution. Thus, we should expect specific characteristics to show up repeatedly in families. Heritability carries along not only physical characteristics but psychological traits as well. So the genealogy of a family might reveal many individuals who were perhaps long-lived or red-headed, but it should also show many who were perhaps very musical or very accomplished. Intelligence was poorly understood in those days, and it was not clear what the term *genius* meant, but Galton took it to mean something like the ability to accomplish noteworthy things. Both he and Darwin were men of considerable accomplishment, he noted modestly, and the fact that they were cousins should by no means be thought of as a coincidence. Indeed, it was just what one should expect if genius was a heritable personality trait.

As always, Galton collected data, and found that, sure enough, if you sort out lists of eminent men in science, literature, the military world, and politics, you find that they are mainly bunched up in families. An eminent man is almost sure to have a brother, father, uncle, and/or grandfather who is also eminent. Galton's analysis was presented in *Hereditary Genius* (1869), a book that brought him great eminence. Evidently people were at that time ready to believe that genius was inherited.*

If you are not attracted to the message of *Hereditary Genius*, you will probably not like what came next. Around 1900 Galton worried increasingly that the poor, the working class, especially dark-skinned people and foreigners, tended to have large families. The obvious danger was that natural selection was no longer operating; it was not the fittest that survived and reproduced. Quite the contrary; because of misguided social policy that helped the poor and encouraged immigration, it was those least fit who held the reproductive advantage. Galton said that the Anglo-Saxon genes that had made England great were in danger of being swamped by the rising tide of riff-raff genes. He called for political action to begin turning things around.

---

*Alas, Galton was so absorbed in descriptive statistics, correlations, and so on, that he rarely asked questions about mechanisms. In this instance he never asked how a man came to be eminent; he never asked why there were no eminent women. Had he worried about mechanisms he would have found that the road to eminence is paved with money. To be eminent you had to go to Cambridge or Oxford, but to get to Cambridge or Oxford you had to be able to afford it, and you also had to have a brother, father, uncle, or somebody who had been there ahead of you. To be eminent you had to have the right friends and connections, which you found at the university, or at polo fields, fox hunts, and sailing regattas. An extraordinary number of the people Galton knew at Cambridge would eventually be knighted (titled "Sir") and would prove useful to him in one way or another. As he became increasingly eminent his own power increased, so that it became ever easier to meet other eminent men and expand his own importance. Similarly, as his own wealth increased it became ever easier to invest it wisely. In *Hereditary Genius* Galton was documenting something he could not see or comprehend: It is not genius so much as money that runs in families.

To start with, he said, criminals should be castrated, and immigration should be limited. The movement was called **eugenics,** and in his later years Galton was its most prominent and powerful leader.

Stepping aside from Galton's political views, he was quite a remarkable man. He had a passion for measuring things, and for presenting data in novel ways. He thought about correlations and percentiles, and promoted their use as descriptive statistics. He had a protégé, Karl Pearson, who later occupied a chair at the University of London that Galton had endowed. Pearson was a most able statistician, and he pushed onward the cause for ranked data and correlations. More than anything else, however, Galton's name stands for individual differences. He measured them, looked at how they were distributed, and correlated them with other measures. Galton's work might have been much more important in the history of psychology if he had gone at things just a little differently. He was probably less interested in psychology than in several other matters, including the weather and the improvement of the race (his race). He only took the study of individual differences fleetingly into psychology and never seriously addressed questions of personality, where his ideas about individual differences might have been very useful. His restless energies carried him from here to there without setting him on any particular course. He had no research program. Perhaps he loved data so much for their own sake that he could not see that some data are more important than others, or see that some data can build upon others to lead somewhere.[4]

Bain and Psychology

ALEXANDER BAIN (1818–1903) was about a decade younger than Darwin and about a decade older than Wundt. In contrast with the two other featured people in this chapter, Bain came from a poor family, and he grew up in Aberdeen, Scotland. As a boy he liked mathematics, and through his own efforts managed to learn quite a bit of it, through calculus. He struggled along, and then went to Marischal College, which was later connected with the university at Aberdeen. He did well there, sharing top honors in his graduating class. In his last year at Marischal he had studied, as was the custom, moral philosophy in the Scottish tradition, the stuff of Reid and Stewart. That evidently turned him on, because the very little we hear from Bain in the next few years is not mathematical, it is psychological. In those days there were a number of popular magazines that dealt with intellectual matters—Westminster Review, Edinburgh Magazine, Fraser's Magazine, Chamber's Journal, Macmillan's, and many others. In those days these magazines were the medium through which the intelligentsia kept informed and made themselves known. And we see Bain popping up in these magazines starting in 1838. The first article was an interesting analysis of sympathy;

Alexander Bain

another early article was on toys. But these were bad years academically for Bain; he sought a position at one of the major Scottish universities, but to no avail. He ended up teaching geography, and teaching at a "finishing school" for young ladies in London. His academic future did not look good.

Bain the Psychologist

Then in 1855 there suddenly appeared, from out of nowhere, the great book *The Senses and the Intellect.* There was nothing in Bain's undergraduate training to explain such a work, and he had not had any graduate training. There was surely nothing in his handful of magazine articles that anticipated such a book. He had held no notable teaching posts, and had done no research. Where had this great, scholarly book come from? Historians of psychology give no hint. Historians of psychology refer to the different editions of the book rather indiscriminately and tend to cite the fourth edition of 1894, which is easy to find, rather than the first edition of 1855, which is rather scarce. But that 40-year spread is critical. The fourth edition appeared when psychology was clearly established, but the 1855 book was there before psychology had begun! In 1855 Wundt was still a medical student, and Stumpf was just a child. Where did Bain's book come from?*

---

*For several years I worried about this question. It occurred to me that Bain had written an autobiography that might make it all clear. But the autobiography is not very helpful; it is little more than a diary. It contains information such as "On Sept 18 we went to the shore for a few days, hoping to find some sunshine." About the 1855 book all it says is, "The big book finally came out in October." It is a peculiarly unrevealing autobiography. Even so, by poring over it and by pulling in some other bits of information, I believe I have arrived at a reasonable account of how Bain's book came into being.

In the summer of 1842, two years out of college and just 24 years old, Bain ventured out of the north country and went to London. While there he met some of the great men of science, such as Faraday and Wheatstone. And he also met John Stuart Mill. He had written Mill the previous September to introduce himself and to indicate that he wished to meet him. Their meeting was wildly successful. Mill was 12 years older, but he evidently found a kindred soul in the young Scotsman (recall that Mill was Scottish himself). Mill was an up-and-coming literary figure, and at one time or another was editor of several of the intellectual journals.

Bain and Mill were to be good friends for 30 years, and they got together regularly most summers to talk and ponder over their emerging psychological ideas. Mill was at this time working on his *Logic*, and Bain helped him a great deal with it. Recall that Mill's father had been a student of the Scottish psychology, and had rebelled against it (Mill, 1829). The younger Mill and Bain no doubt agreed that rebellion was the proper course. So apparently Mill was an important factor in helping Bain develop his ideas. And perhaps because Bain wrote about their common ideas so effectively, Mill never felt called upon to write down his own psychological thoughts. It was a very close and interesting relationship. When Mill died, Bain wrote his biography.

But there is another part of the story. In order to earn a little extra money Bain did a lot of editing, and because some of this work was on the sensory systems, he studied them extensively. He read and was much influenced by William Carpenter's *Human Physiology* (1844) and Bell's *Anatomy of Expression* (1806). This was Charles Bell, of Bell–Magendie fame. This early book on the anatomy of emotion was very important to Bain, and may have been important in getting him so interested in behavior. Interestingly, Darwin in his *Expression of Emotion* also drew very heavily on Bell. Bain's 1855 book contains frequent citations of both Bell and Carpenter. Thus, Bain stood at a unique intersection; he was well-informed about the Scottish school and about sensory physiology, and he would do what no one in the Scottish tradition had done before, which was to put them together. He would introduce physiological considerations into Scottish philosophy. The Scottish associationism would now have muscles and a nervous system.

I will say something about the book shortly, but first I have to go back and complete the story on Bain because we left him in pretty bad straits. There was a companion volume, as the Scottish convention demanded, *The Emotions and the Will*, that appeared in 1859. Both books began to do well, and Bain was offered the new chair of logic at Aberdeen in 1860. (McCosh was the other candidate for the chair—frustrated at not getting it, he fled to Princeton.) Although frequently suffering from poor health, Bain prospered with the security, distinction, and fame he deserved. When he retired from active teaching, in 1876, he founded the very first psychological journal *Mind*, which appeared five years before Wundt's journal began; his most important student, C. Robertson, was installed as editor. Darwin's developmental diary appeared in the second volume.[5]

The Senses and the Intellect

The overall plan of the book was to first describe the machinery and then gradually overlay the mind, introducing it a bit at a time. The plan is reminiscent of Descartes's approach. Much of his physiology is descriptive and anatomical, because not much was known then about function. The brain is described, and then the muscles. Bain treated muscular activity in a new way, emphasizing the sensory feedback from movement. We know what we are doing because we feel it rather than because we are doing it. We know where *up* is in the visual field because we know the eyes have moved up to see it. Movement is prior to sensation. One proof is that we do not sense much of anything when we first wake up; it is only after we look around and start moving that we know where we are. Another proof is that there is so much spontaneous activity. Aided by factors such as good health, rest, and youth, there is a great deal of activity no matter what stimuli may be present. Spontaneous activity is very important to Bain. He takes us through reflexes and sensations from the body, and notes the importance of pleasure and pain. But he is treating events where the intellect is only minimally involved because at first he wants to stay "in the inferior region of the mind."

Bain begins the ascent to the higher levels by asking how voluntary movements first arise. Their source, he says, is spontaneous activity, which is facilitated by emotion. Suppose an infant is stuck by a pin. "If, at the moment of some acute pain, there should accidentally occur a spontaneous movement, and if that movement sensibly alleviates the pain, then it is that the volitional impulse belonging to the feeling will show itself." (p. 294) The volition takes the form of a learned connection between the idea of pleasure, or relief from pain, and the movement. Here, some 50 years before Thorndike, we have what looks for all the world like a principle of reinforcement—more or less random behavior that is only weakly dependent on stimuli, sudden relief from pain, and then we will have associative learning. That certainly does look like our familiar learning by reinforcement. What is not so familiar is Bain's notion that what gets learned is a *volitional impulse*. It is the same mechanism, but it was used by Bain and Thorndike for very different purposes. Bain wanted to explain how we learn voluntary behavior; Thorndike wanted to get rid of voluntary behavior by reducing it to neural connections. A further interesting difference is that Bain allowed for all kinds of different associations, ideas and movements, stimuli and ideas, while Thorndike allowed only S–R connections. Further, Bain urged the importance of associations between responses and outcomes (especially pleasurable ones), that is, between means and ends, because that is what voluntary behavior is all about. This Bain fellow was a psychologist.

An idea, following Reid, is a revival of a former sensation, but there was a difference because for Bain the sensation may be prior to a movement, or follow it, or refer to the sensations arising from the movement itself. The rules of association are contiguity and similarity. We need similarity to get into the higher intellectual realms, he maintained. There were other laws—of diffusion and adhesion—and countless other hypotheses. Bain was always reasonable and interesting, and always provided his reader with a lot of new things to think about. *The Senses* and the companion volume *The Emotions* were to take a dominate position in psychology all through the rest of the 19th century. There was really nothing comparable in scope or power until William James's *Principles* appeared in 1890.

Actually, there *was* another book. Herbert Spencer wrote *Principles of Psychology* in 1855, the same year as Bain's *The Senses and the Intellect*. And like Bain he thoroughly examined all the relevant machinery. Indeed, Spencer was much more mechanistic than Bain, and he was also much less of a psychologist. Spencer was obsessed by evolution, but it was the Lamarckian variety. His 1855 book attracted little attention, but the 1870 revision was considered important, probably because by then evolutionary concepts had become so popular. By that time he had also outlined his vast, cosmic system of philosophy, of which psychology was only a part. Everything from nerve cells to the mind to society had evolved, according to Spencer, but he could cite almost no data to support his many evolutionary hypotheses. For the psychologist Spencer lost his credibility when his major support began to come from American industrialists. His notion that the fittest survive was taken by business moguls as vindication of their predatory practices. When he came to this country in 1882 he was met by Andrew Carnegie. What kind of psychologist was this? He was enormously popular, but for all the wrong reasons.[6] So, let us return to Bain.

A remarkable feature of Bain's career is that it was mainly played out so very early. He wrote *The Senses* when he was 37, so it was not exactly a youthful work. But in 1855 Fechner had to lift weights another five years before his psychophysics book would appear. Wundt was only getting started and had written no books yet. William James was only 13 years old. So Bain was back there at the beginning of things, and in spite of his early start he wrote like a psychologist. Wundt never did learn to do that; he always sounded like a philosopher. And so did James. Bain was rather like Müller in never being anything but a psychologist. Even when he described brain structures he sounded like a psychologist. He did not get that from his friend Mill, it was something he had brought to their friendship. He really was the first. And then he lived on into the 20th century, long enough to see psychology explode as a discipline in Germany and the United States, and even begin to stir in Britain. One must wonder how much of that was he directly responsible for.

A Historical Heresy

FOR MANY YEARS the standard historical account, at least the one perpetuated by American psychologists, has been the story told by Boring (1950). Fechner was the father, Wundt was the care-giving parent and the founder. A lot of Wundt's students came over here and established labs something like the one in Leipzig. There were others, some anticipators and some other scattered people, and some of these people were surely important. Boring did not exclude from his story anyone who might have been important. And so we read all about Locke, Leibnitz, and Lotze, as well as Hegel, Herbart, and Hering. Here I want to consider the possibility that Boring was wrong about a couple of things. Maybe Locke really was important, but we can ignore Leibnitz, and forget what we know about Lotze. Perhaps Hering is rather interesting as Helmholtz's archenemy, but we need not note anything about Hegel or Herbart. The Germans were perhaps not as important as Boring proposed. And perhaps perception in general was not as central as Boring thought. We note that Boring's own research area was perception, and that he might have overvalued its importance.

Perhaps Boring was wrong about something on a far grander scale. Maybe the genealogy he worked out for American psychology, the line Weber–Fechner–Wundt–Titchener, was in error. In chapter 9 we will meet some of the American pioneers, such as James, Hall, and Cattell. Hall and Cattell studied with Wundt but showed little evidence of their Leipzig background in their subsequent work. Cattell was devoted to individual difference in the same way that Galton was. Hall looked more like Darwin than anyone else, while James was clearly indebted to Bain and explicitly rejected Wundt's approach.

In other words, perhaps the ancestors of American psychology were not German at all, but British! Such a heresy is likely to elicit the response, "What about the grand insight of Fechner and Ebbinghaus that mental events could be measured?" The answer to that might be, "What about Galton, who was measuring everything in sight, plus things like the efficacy of prayer?" We did not need Fechner because we had Galton. We did not need the great organizer Wundt because we had the systemist Bain. We did not need any of the German philosophers because we had Darwin to tell us what our experiments mean. The notion of American independence from German psychology is not entirely new. Cattell (1929) raised the possibility. In chapter

10 we will look at the early American movement called Functional Psychology, and we will see that it was indeed very Darwinian in spirit; there was nothing Germanic about it.

So we should always keep in mind that no matter how plausible a history might seem, alternative histories are always possible. In writing a new version based on this heresy, we would still need to get started with our major themes, so we would still start with Mersenne's friends and let them introduce us to atomism and mechanism. We would still proceed with Locke and Hume so we could find out about empiricism and associationism. But then we would focus much more on the Scottish school and much less on the German sensory work. And then rather than psychology originating from problems that arose when the physiologists worried about perception, we could see it emerging as Darwin and Bain began to pay attention to behavior. These two innovators might be much more important in giving shape to American psychology than anyone has supposed.[7]

Summary

HERE WE ENCOUNTERED three important people, but they were not interrelated in any obvious way. They each went their own way. True, Darwin inspired Galton at one point, and they kept in touch. But Darwin kept in touch with everyone; Bain once visited with him for two weeks. These three individuals did not create anything together. They did not start a "movement," as Wundt and his associates started a movement. Nor did they share obvious common interests. Darwin was a biologist who collected all sorts of things. Galton was a gentleman hobbyist who measured all sorts of things. Bain was nominally a philosopher, but in reality he was a psychologist, remarkably, the first one. Darwin did experiments, but his major impact was theoretical not empirical. Galton did experiments too, but his approach was more that of an engineer than a scientist. And Bain never did research. Again, our three Britishers were very different.

They all, however, were vitally important in the development of American psychology, and in giving it its peculiarly American flavor. Galton invented new things to measure, new ways to measure them, and new ways to look at his data, all of which greatly expanded psychology. Bain kept associationism alive by translating it from Scottish into something Americans could understand. He also introduced the musculature to psychology, and proposed a variety of mechanisms to explain what the nervous system and the muscles were doing. Darwin, too, was very interested in behavior, but his main impact both in psychology and in biology more generally was that he forced us to think about life in entirely new ways. He made us think about ourselves as a part of nature. He made us think about the differences among us. He made us get outside ourselves to think about the environment. He made us think about function. He made us think about ourselves changing over time. He would, in the end, redefine psychology.

Notes

1. There is a lot of biographical material on Darwin. He wrote up notes for an autobiography, but probably never intended to publish them. The notes were edited, abridged, and added to by his son Francis and then published as *Life and Letters of Charles Darwin* (1887). Something much closer to the original has now been edited by his granddaughter N. Barlow (1958). This is the source for the story about his nose and almost everything else in my account. The last 40 years of Darwin's life were marred by a strange illness that kept him a virtual recluse in his country home and that has engendered considerable speculation (see Colp, 1977). There is also a nice, new biography by Bowlby (1990), who also discusses his malady.

The famous *Notebooks* have been written up and published. *Voyage of the Beagle* is a delightful story, and provides further information about young Darwin and his earliest thinking. For fun I will give the full original title, *Journal of the Researches into the Geology and Natural History of the Various Countries Visited during the Voyages of H.M.S. Beagle, under the Command of Captain FitzRoy, R.N., from 1832 to 1836.*

2. In 1959 there was considerable celebration of the *Origin*, and a facsimile of the now rare first edition was brought out. The *Origin* was revised every couple of years for more than a decade, but there is still something special about the 1859 book. A hundred years later there was a lot of scholarship about Darwin and evolution. Eiseley (1958) gives perhaps the classiest picture of the context of earlier evolutionary theories against which the idea of natural selection emerged. Darwin wrote a good deal of work that is not very relevant to psychologists, books on worms, predatory plants, coral reefs, and so on. More pertinent to us are *The Descent of Man* (1871) and *The Expression of the Emotions in Man and Animals* (1872).

3. Francis Galton (1822–1911) wrote an unusually instructive autobiography (Galton, 1908) (most great men seem to be at their worst when writing about themselves). There is also the long, loving, and extravagantly illustrated biography by Pearson (1914–30). Karl Pearson (1911) was foremost among those who viewed science as a search for correlation rather than causation.

4. Galton wrote books on travel, meteorology, fingerprints, and on and on, in addition to several books on the genealogy of distinguished men. The latter include *Hereditary Genius* (1869), *English Men of Science* (1874), *Human Faculty* (1883), and *Natural Inheritance* (1889). The autobiography gives a good list of his publications.

5. Alexander Bain (1818–1903) gave us an autobiography, but as noted in the text, it is not very informative. *The Senses and the Intellect* first appeared in 1855, and was revised in 1864, 1868, and 1894. *The Emotions and the Will* was written about the same time but did not appear until 1859; it was then revised in 1865, 1875, and 1899. *Mind and Body* was a shorter work of 1875. All of these works tell much the same story. Mind and body are intimately connected, so that every little wrinkle in the nervous system will make a little bump in consciousness, and yet we do not know, and may never know, how the two worlds are tied together.

6. Spencer (1820–1903) was a curious character. If the unheralded appearance of Bain's 1855 book was something of a mystery, then Spencer's 1855 book looks like a genuine miracle. He too has an autobiography (Spencer, 1904), and it says he had virtually no formal education, that he read almost nothing, that he was an engineer and an inventor, and that he embarked on the psychology book after reading Hume. He did it all himself. I certainly cannot recommend that even the serious scholar read Spencer. Durant (1953) says of the 1870 book, "To the reader who can pass alive through these 1,400 pages of physiological and psychological analysis . . . " (p. 282) If you want to know about Spencer, then read Durant's charming chapter on him. Usually a person either liked Spencer or they did not. Galton spoke highly of him, but he was one of the few people about whom Darwin could find nothing good to mention.

7. When I teach history of psychology, I sometimes require a paper on whether American psychology would not have ended up exactly as it did if there had never been a Fechner or a Wundt. The student has to argue either for or against the hypothesis of independence. I remind the class that the Germans did research whereas the British did not. And I point out that Wundt was a major source of early American Ph.D.s, and that such credentials are important. I tell them that, on the other hand, Americans brought back from Germany little more than their credentials; we were not going to subscribe to Wundt's view of psychology, or to Titchener's. I remind them of the long-term importance of Darwin to our psychology. I point out the similarities between Bain and James. When the papers come in I usually find that one or another of these points is expanded to defend or reject the independence hypothesis. Over several classes the results have come out about 50:50. I have gained little insight into the matter, and so do not require such a paper anymore. But from this exercise a number of my students have learned something important: Some of the really interesting historical questions do not have any answers.

Chapter Nine

The American Pioneers

WE HAVE SEEN that there appear to have been two separate psychologies, one with a strong experimental orientation that flourished in the great German universities, and the second with a more speculative flavor that was taking root in the British Isles. Now we will see how America, the vigorous young melting-pot society, put these various elements together in new ways, something that probably could not have happened in either of the older, more established societies. We started building our own universities, copying from the German model. Meanwhile, our impatient young intellectuals were going to Germany to get the Ph.D.s that they could not yet get here. And their dissertations were usually experimental; they liked measuring things, and they liked apparatus, methodology, and data. But these students had little use for the way German scholars thought about things, so they rejected both the German view of science and German philosophy.

The British university system was even more archaic than our own, so there was little interest in a British education, at least in the sciences. But American intellectuals liked the way British thinkers thought about things. In particular, we liked Darwin's biology, the way Galton was measuring things, and Bain's psychology. Moreover we understood Bain's predecessors, the Scottish philosophers against whom he was rebelling, because we were rebelling against them here, too. Let us first look at the development of the American university.

The Rise of the American University

UNTIL THE TIME OF the Civil War there was a set, highly predictable pattern. All American colleges looked very much alike. They were small; even the big ones were small. Harvard was a big one, but in 1854, when it was enjoying having been in business for two centuries, it had only 18 faculty members.

After the war of 1860, it had expanded a bit to 27 faculty members. All of the colleges had limited curricula. Essentially the student studied the classics: Greek plays (in Greek, of course), Julius Caesar's life and Cicero's Orations (in Latin of course), some Bible, some math, and a little philosophy such as logic and rhetoric. The concept was that the young man's mind needed discipline, and that was what he was there to get. Although he might end up with some familiarity with the classics, he was not really supposed to learn much of anything. Another feature of these old colleges is that they were generally run by the clergy. Their primary purpose was to train ministers. The system was rigid, and it seemed unlikely to change. There seemed to be too many conservative pressures for there to be any change in the system, but it did change, and rather dramatically.

A Time of Change

One remarkable event occurred in 1862 when Congress passed the Morrill Act, which gave land and other advantages to the states if they would build state universities, and if these universities would provide instruction and do research on agriculture, mining, industry, and so on, to help the divided nation make the most of its resources. A few states jumped right into it, and in just a few years most states were participating in the program, and of course competing with each other. Soon a new breed of university appeared that offered practical instruction and the opportunity to do research. And it was run not by clergymen but by boards and panels of laymen, social activists, and politicians. That was precisely what had happened in Germany some years earlier.

Another thing happened. Colleges for women began to pop up here and there, but most prominently in New England. Vassar, which opened in 1861, claims that it was the first. There were already something called women's colleges, but by modern academic standards they were pretty bad. At a men's college students could at least learn Latin; at a women's college students learned to be "ladies," how to be polite and how to balance a book on the head. Vassar may have led the way in changing all this, and certainly other schools soon followed its example. It was a remarkable transformation.

Another dramatic thing happened. A wealthy businessman decided to give one of the New York State schools a magnificent bequest, but only on the condition that he could run things, such as select who would be the president and set the curriculum. The state legislature accepted the deal, and even decided to name the school after the benefactor. His name was Ezra Cornell, and he had some unusual educational ideas. He chose Andrew White to run things, and White proved to be a remarkably able administrator. White was enthusiastic about Cornell's idea of a curriculum. Cornell's guiding concept was that a university should be a place where *anybody could study anything.* The student should not be constrained to a study of the classics, but should be able to delve into any kind of knowledge, whether it was science, literature, art, history, or whatever. It was a remarkable idea, which soon revolutionized higher education. Cornell, the first liberal arts school, opened its doors in 1865.

One other event has to be noted. In 1869, shortly after Andrew White took charge of Cornell, Charles Eliot was named president of Harvard College. Eliot was only 35, but he was a proper Bostonian, he had been a student there, and he had impressed them with his administrative and organizational skills. He was a chemist. One of his first moves was to do away with the old set of required courses that had typified the traditional curriculum and expand the college's offerings. Moreover, he introduced what he called the *elective system.* Students could take a little of this and some of that, much as they do now. It was an idea similar to Cornell's, and it had the same effect of getting students concentrating on some area of study that interested them. Eliot also began to expand the faculty rapidly. He had to hire new men to teach all the new electives.

This sudden expansion was expensive. Facilities had to be built, people had to be hired, all the new students flooding in had to be dealt with, and so on. It was expensive, but it turned out that Eliot was equal to the task. Indeed, we saw for the first time what is now all too familiar: The chief administrator is largely a financier. He has to go to local businesspeople, alumni, and wealthy people in the community and convince them that it is in their own best interest to make a major contribution to the college to help make it into something different, a university. Eliot was adept at doing that.

The people of the country had shown very little interest in the old college system; there was little concern about how ministers should be educated. College enrollments had been falling even as the population had been expanding. But after the Civil War, the trend slowly turned around. The new state universities—and the local pride that went with them—no doubt had a lot to do with it. Wisconsin had to have a better university than neighboring Illinois, and as long as the Feds were paying for it . . . politics as usual. But the people did get involved and they were concerned, because for the first time the universities promised useful and important results, something the people wanted. It was a remarkable transition.[1]

The Teaching Credential

Accreditation is always very important, and since the new idea of the university was largely predicated on the prestige and status of its faculty, there was pressure to have a properly licensed faculty. The Ph.D. suddenly became very important because it was the appropriate license. As the new universities arose and expanded there developed a critical shortage of Ph.D.s. The degree had been given occasionally in this country as early as 1861, but few of the old colleges were qualified to grant such degrees, so the whole system was in a bind. There was a tremendous need for Ph.D.s to teach in all the new universities, but very few schools (basically only the Ivy League schools) were in a position to grant them. The answer for the ambitious young scholar was to journey over the ocean and get the critical degree in Germany. Thousands of young men, and a handful of young women, did just that. One of the reasons Wundt was so important to American psychology is that he was the major source of psychology Ph.D.s during the time of the crunch, which was the 1890s. In other areas, such as chemistry and history, that were a little more advanced, the crunch probably came a little earlier. And Ph.D. crunch time just happened to coincide with the sudden development of psychology as an independent discipline in this country, so for psychologists the crunch was particularly acute.

Although psychology came to a boil on the academic scene in the early 1890s, it had been quietly brewing for some years before that. And its beginning here was very similar to how it got going in Britain. There it started with Alexander Bain; here it started with William James.

William James

WILLIAM JAMES (1842–1910) was just 10 years younger than Wundt. And like Wundt, James got into psychology rather gradually and uncertainly. For both of them there was a good reason for the slow start: Psychology was an ill-defined area at the time. No one knew for sure what psychology was.

James's early life was unusual because although his father was not rich, he was well-enough endowed that he was not obliged to work. Young William did not have a very good male role model. Another uncommon feature of the James family life was that the father sometimes took the family to Europe for extended periods. So young William grew up with art museums, foreign literature, and European culture rather than having to worry about what he was going to do. That gave him a broad perspective, but seems to have prevented him from knowing what he was looking for. He went to Harvard, wandered around, and then in 1869 got his medical degree at Harvard (he was then 27, so he had not actually wasted much time wandering). Perhaps because he had gone on a biological expedition with Louis Agassiz to the Amazon river and returned from there ill, James always suffered from fragile health. President Eliot appointed James to the Harvard faculty as an instructor in the anatomy and physiology department. Thus, while James was at first a medically trained physiologist, he had a broad cultural background.

William James

The Metaphysical Society

The first thing of note young James did was set up an informal, friendly group who called themselves the Metaphysical Society, which undertook to worry about the philosophical problems of the day. It was an impressive group. The membership varied some from year to year, but generally it included the following members. Chauncey Wright was the eldest, and at that time probably the most able of the faculty in the philosophy department. He was a staunch follower of John Stuart Mill, and was much moved by Mill's critical examination of Hamilton (Mill, 1865). Thus, the society was concerned about the apparent self-destruction of the Scottish school. Wright was the effective leader of the group, and he had a sort of Socratic style that got everyone involved in an issue.

Charles Peirce belonged to the group. He too was a philosopher, an earlier Harvard student, who was never able to hold down a regular teaching position, even though everyone recognized he had enormous ability. He was a brilliant man who had irregular habits and trouble getting things carried through. Everyone seemed to agree that Peirce was the brilliant one in the group. He was a few years older than the others, and pondered the deep issues more than anybody else. He liked to talk about ideas that later would be seen as pragmatism. He was thinking about such things around 1870, but it would be James who would make pragmatism popular 30 years later, because Peirce, with no academic affiliation, had no way of doing so.

Another member of the group was Oliver Wendell Holmes, then in Harvard's law school, but later chief justice of the Supreme Court. Holmes wrote *The Common Law* in 1881, a remarkable book in many respects. It was very strongly behavioristic. Holmes rejected the concept of justice and introduced the idea of social cost. Thus, if a man is found guilty of carrying out a robbery while using a gun, then, Holmes says, he has to be put away. Executing a robbery is dangerous enough, but to carry out a robbery with a gun—even if the robber had no intention of using the gun—is so dangerous that society cannot allow it. He has to be locked up. Holmes said that the robber's intentions were relatively unimportant; it is the menace to society that matters most. One wonders if Holmes brought such behavioristic ideas to the group, or if that was something that came to him after arguing these things out with James and the others. Any way one looks at it, Holmes was an early anticipator of behaviorism.

The Metaphysical Society had some lesser members, both law people and philosophers, who came and went over the years. But the basic set of people that met regularly between 1870 and 1872 was an outstanding group. They worried about all of the preceding concerns. They also worried about what would turn out to be basic psychological issues. There was in the intellectual community of that time an indigenous psychology, Reid's psychology of common sense, which had been imported from Scotland. The club worried about where to go now that Mill had demolished Hamilton, the most scholarly of the line. The club worried about Kant and the revival of interest in Kant's skepticism, such as his assertion that one cannot know anything about what is out there in the real world. The group was not convinced that Kant's attempt to salvage moral values amidst the uncertainty about reality was viable, and they tried to improve upon it.

The Harvard community also had its own religious commitment; it was Unitarian. The Metaphysical Society was concerned with the fact that Unitarianism had collapsed intellectually in the last few years. Another problem had arisen: A scholar had to believe in the advance of science, even Darwinian science, which appeared to be saying that God had lost control of things and that now we were all just evolving. How does one reconcile the world of science with the world of spiritual values? How could one follow a spiritual or religious life and still pay attention to what the new biologists were advancing?[2] For James there was a terrible rift between the world of spirit, values, responsibility, and everything else worthwhile on one side, and science, which he also believed in, but which stood way over yonder on the other side. James struggled with the problem all the rest of his life, and many of his writings reveal his conflict. Some of James's conflict was self-inflicted. Thus, in 1870 he made a personal pledge to himself that he would believe in free will. He understood that if he could continue to defend his stance on free will in the face of new developments in biology and psychology, then that would prove that his will really was free, and that he really could make an arbitrary decision about what he chose to believe.*

Into Psychology and Out Again

In 1875 James started teaching a psychology course in the physiology department. In 1876 he was promoted from instructor to assistant professor. In 1878 he began work on his great psychology book, but it would take him 12 years to get it done and published. In 1880 president Eliot shifted him from physiology to the philosophy department, and he became a full professor there in 1885. (In those days there were no associate professors, only assistant and full levels.) In 1889 he was still in the philosophy department, but he was designated a professor of psychology. In effect, this made psychology a branch of philosophy. He kept this title until 1897, at which point he appeared to have done what he wanted to do for the new discipline, and he became once more a professor of philosophy. His was a rather complicated career. Part of the complexity was due to the fact that Harvard, although liberal in some ways, was rather conservative in others, and Eliot was unwilling to break off the psychologists into a separate administrative entity. He needed those distinguished scholars to be a presence in the university's renowned philosophy department.[3] Actually, this tradition persisted for some time; it was not until 1934 that chairman E. G. Boring broke psychology loose from philosophy and made it an autonomous department at Harvard.

James seems to have had trouble settling down; he had started in medicine, although he was not very interested in physiological matters, and certainly had no desire to do physiological research. He then moved into philosophy, but his interests at that time were largely focused on psychological matters. Then once he had completed the *Principles* he was essentially done with psychology and was ready to move back to philosophical issues. Thus, James was really a psychologist for only about 15 years, between 1875 when he started teaching psychology and 1890 when the *Principles* was published. It was a phase he went through. After that he was only waiting for Münsterberg to arrive and take charge of the psychology division of the department. When Münsterberg arrived permanently in 1897, James immediately went back to being a philosopher. During the 1880s James published a number of papers on psychological questions that anticipated some of what would eventually appear in the *Principles*. But even these psychological papers reveal him to be a philosopher at heart. Some scholars

---

*James used the word *fiat* to describe what he meant. In the legal world, a fiat is an arbitrary law, usually one that never got voted on. It need not make any sense nor serve any particular popular purpose. When the French revolutionaries decided one day that the new republic should adopt the metric system and gave the people a few weeks to switch over to it, that was a fiat. When James decided he would believe in free will, that was a fiat.

191

have recently characterized James as the spoiled child of psychology (e.g., Ross, 1991).

We see that James was really only dallying with psychology. He also had very few graduate students; most of the people one thinks of as being James's students actually turn out to have been supervised by Münsterberg. It should also be said that James was not in the least interested in research, and never carried out any himself. But he was an effective professor, and was able to inspire the young people around him to dig in and get their hands dirty. Not every philosopher can do that. James's place in our history hangs on two things. One is that in his own time he was the most distinguished faculty member of a very distinguished department in a very distinguished university. He held a commanding position. The other thing, which makes James important even today, is his great book *Principles of Psychology* (1890).

James's Principles of Psychology

PSYCHOLOGY IS THE science of mental life, James says at the outset, but he warns his reader there are many ways one can go astray in attempting to pursue it. The psychology of the Scottish philosophers includes the human spirit, but no body. The psychology of Bain and the associationists errs the other way because it is soulless and because it pretends that one can know all about a house by knowing where all the bricks are. And neither of these accounts is any good because neither cares a thing about the brain. On the other hand, we cannot follow the mechanistic direction pointed out by Descartes because the mind *does* play a part in our behavior. James observed that if you put a piece of paper between a magnet and some iron filings, the filings will leap up and cling blindly to the paper to get as close as they can to the magnet. But if you were to build a wall between Romeo and Juliet they would not each cling to their own side of the wall but would think of some way to get through, around, or over it so that they could actually contact each other. The mind does make a difference. In a machine the means is fixed, it works like a machine. When there is a mind the end is set, and the means is adapted to circumstances. The mind chooses and then pursues goals.

Physiological Principles

James said that we must navigate our way carefully between the physiological approach, never losing sight of the brain, and the introspective approach, always looking inward to see how the mind is working. He rejected what he understood to be the narrow views of parallelism, materialism, and idealism, and set his course straight through the rocky waters of dualism. There is a mind and there is a body and they interact.

James devoted almost 200 pages to explaining how the brain is put together, how the sensory organs work, and how the mind relates to the body. There are two highlights in this treatment. One is the chapter on **habit**. Habit comes from repeatedly practicing some voluntary behavior, practicing it enough that we no longer have to think about it. We can carry out the action while thinking about something else. Given enough practice, we can walk and talk and chew gum all while we are thinking about something else. Habit is the great flywheel of society—our most precious conservative agent. Without it we would not be able to get much of anything done. With practice behavior becomes easier, faster, better channeled, and more accurate. Behavior comes to carry itself along. A response in a chain of responses might initially require our voluntary intervention, but with practice it becomes dependent on the feedback from earlier responses in the chain. Thus, the whole chain can become a larger unit. This concept of habit was not new with James; he gave credit for it to William Carpenter and Herbert Spencer.

A second interesting feature of James's discussion is what he called the **psychologist's fallacy.** He said that just because a human subject can carry out instructions and make a certain kind of analysis, such as breaking the perception of an object into a mass of specific sensory elements, that does not mean that the perception actually consists of that mass of elements. No one but a psychologist would ever think such a thing. Our perception of an object is primary and complete in itself; it is not built up from bits of sensory detail. Red is not just a lot of pink, he said. Here James was clearly squaring off against the structuralists, and that was something he enjoyed doing from time to time. On the other hand he discussed psychophysics and Wundt's reaction-time experiments at some length. So he respected their data, but he had little use for their concepts. His psychology was quite independent of anything that had gone on at Leipzig.

Consciousness

Chapter 9 is a marvelous, introspective analysis of what he called the *stream of consciousness.* It shows James at his best. Our awareness is not like a stage on which ideas (or sensations) come and go. At the theater we are a slave of whatever is presented to us. Rather, consciousness is more like a river, a stream, that passes before us. We can attend to the mass of water moving along without looking at anything in particular, and hence be aware that time is passing. Or we can attend to a part of it, perhaps a stick being carried along, and focus for a time on its characteristics. Then it, like everything else, passes away. Our consciousness depends on the context, our other thoughts and other things confronting us. These ideas show James to be a remarkable and shrewd observer, a trait noted by many of his friends. Most of us look and see what we expect to find. Perhaps James saw things more like what they are.

Attention was very important to James. The way we exercise our will, he maintained, is by paying attention to this or that stimulus; with the right stimulus in mind the appropriate response will follow. The big question he struggled with is whether attention is an active thing, something we do, a fiat, a *cause* of what follows. Or is it a *result*, a consequence of prior stimuli, our ongoing behavior, or perhaps the association of ideas? He could not prove it one way or the other, and he was clearly uncomfortable with his own uncertainty on the issue. Nonetheless, he elected to come down strongly on the side that attention was a cause. Wundt had waffled on the same question, but he (and certainly Titchener) had come to the opposite conclusion, that one attends to the clearest stimuli in the field. They reduced the psychic function of attention to the sensory property of clarity. James felt that this was structuralism gone mad. Wundt had recognized that there was something further involved, but even though he called himself a voluntarist, he was not going to call it volition; he called it *a sense of effort*. Volition was an effort, and effort was a sort of sensory thing, and that was the way he was going to regard it. James went to war with Wundt over this (he had Münsterberg's help on this issue because he and Wundt had gotten into a bitter quarrel about it) and contended that there was no sense of effort. James was the real voluntarist after all; he was the one who believed in free will.

All of this material is covered before we finish the first volume of James's book. With the tough basic issues cleared up, James goes on to deal with a variety of subjects, and the remaining chapter headings begin to resemble an introductory psychology text. There are chapters on conception, discrimination, memory, and the perception of time. There is also an important chapter on association. James makes the remarkable proposal that what gets associated is not ideas (Hume) or sensations (Wundt) but objects. If I see an apple tree, then I am likely to think about an apple. This view is no doubt predicated partly on James's wholistic, as opposed to atomistic, view of what is in consciousness: We are aware of objects, not sensations. He took as fact whatever could be observed, and what we observe are things and persons, meaningful stuff, certainly not meaningless bits of sensation. We have to adopt a sophisticated attitude and work very hard at it to see a sensation. Although James used associationism to account for how things are connected in the mind, he did not rely on it very heavily. He regarded the ability to form associations as a physiological mechanism rather than a part of the mental apparatus. Like John Locke 200 years earlier, James was an associationist, but did not seem to know it.

Behavioral Principles

As we approach the end of *Principles*, James turns increasingly to behavior. There is a short chapter on movement in which he clearly describes an idea that was running rampant at the end of the 19th century. The idea was shared by many psychologists and most physiologists. I bring the point up here because we will see it later as a fundamental part of Freud's thinking. The idea is that any kind of sensory stimulation leads to a sort of excited state of the nervous system that has to be taken care of. It was as if a stimulus increased the physical energy level in the nervous system. That excess energy *had* to get out of there, it had to be drained off one way or another. Bain had talked of this and had stated what he called the law of **diffusion.** Any stimulation, he said, that cannot find direct expression, perhaps as reflexive behavior, will be drained from the nervous system by the execution of random and uncoordinated acts, general muscular tension, and a feeling of emotion. The necessity to drain the energy is all the greater, Bain suggested, if the stimulation arouses an emotional reaction. James went along with this concept; thus, he spoke of the *escape* of central excitement through the motor apparatus.

James had an interesting chapter on instinct. He refused to follow the traditional dichotomy between intelligence and instinct. We intelligent beings don't have fewer instincts, he said, we have more of them than other animals. The main difference is that because we are capable of learning so much more, our instincts are very rapidly obscured by the effects of learning. It is really only on the first occurrence of its action that we can see the instinct acting by itself before it is overwhelmed by learning. The second major point is that the instinct manifests itself not so much in some pattern of fixed, reflex-like behavior, but that because of the instinct the animal finds enormous *interest* in the relevant external object. The hen is fascinated by the egg, and if the egg does not look to you like something you want to press your bosom against, well, that is your problem, because that is the way the hen sees it. Instinct is something much more, and something much more interesting, than just a complicated set of S–R reflexes, as the mechanists had proposed.

James's chapter on the will is interesting because like many of the other chapters it presents a novel point of view and introduces a new fundamental concept that has to be taken seriously. He concluded that the will is free; that should come as no surprise. He concluded that we determine our will by focusing attention on particular stimuli, and that should come as no surprise. What is surprising is how simple the basic mechanism is in James's formulation. It is much like Hume's treatment of volition. What we have to do, James said, is have a clear idea of the consequences of our actions. And that is all there is to it. I conceive of my hand rising, and sure enough, up it goes. Action follows the idea of its result. The idea of the consequence causes the response. He called this the **ideo-motor principle.**

Sometimes, like raising my hand, it obviously works. But sometimes it does not seem to work very well. Suppose it is a cold morning and my alarm has just rung. I say, "I have to get up." But then I think, "It's cold out there, and the bed is so comfortable." Again I say, "I have to get up." I go back and forth between my sense of what feels good and my sense of duty. And I can go on like that for some time. Now, according to James, what produces the inaction is not a failure of the ideo-motor principle, but rather that there is no clear, uncontested idea. Instead I have two conflicting ideas that compete for my attention. One has something to do with comfort while the other has something to do with getting to work. Nothing is happening because my mind is not set on any specific outcome. But at some point, usually, I say, "Hey, I'm getting up." It is cold, as I knew it would be, but I am finally up. Once the outcome is clearly in mind so that there is no more conflict, then the action follows.

James went on to observe that the idea that really controls a behavior can change with experience. A person just learning to play tennis thinks about which foot is carrying weight, about follow-through, about watching the ball, indeed, about all the immediate body adjustments the coach keeps stressing—and stands a good chance of missing an easy shot because focusing on such immediate outcomes does not make for good tennis. The more accomplished tennis player has an idea of a more remote outcome, perhaps the ball zinging over to the far corner of the court. And zing, there it goes over to the far corner to win the point. There is an important shift from immediate to remote consequences.

The James–Lange Theory of Emotion

In the mid-1880s, about five years before James finished his book, he and a Danish physiologist named Carl Lange published, quite independently, papers in which they proposed an unusual theory of emotional behavior. Accordingly, even though James was the writer who made it famous, it comes down to us as the **James–Lange theory of emotion.** Remember that James started in with the admonition that one should not forget the body. Remember, too, that he had a concept of habit according to which the mind no longer controls a well-practiced response because it has come to be controlled by stimuli arising from earlier responses. The body was indeed conceptually important to James, he saw it as having its own laws, laws that did not transcend but could bypass what was happening in the mind. Unless we made a particular effort to intervene, the body would generate behavior according to its own rules. And so it was with emotion. According to the James–Lange theory, emotion was a feeling, introspectively something like an inner sensation, that was often a very important part of our experience. That much was granted. But according to the new theory, emotion was not a *cause* of behavior. It was a *result* of our behavior. I am out in the woods and I see a bear. My heart rate goes crazy and I start running. Then I am frightened. The fear arises because of the behavior, the accelerated heart rate and the running-away behavior. It is not the case that I run because I am frightened. No, I start making adaptive behavior in a critical situation, and the emotion follows. It is basically an **epiphenomenon**—inconsequential. James's theory of emotion survives to this day, not universally accepted by any means, but thanks to the efforts of Schachter and others it is still viable.[4]

It is interesting that James talked so much about behavior, and that he had so many different mechanisms to handle it. He could explain voluntary behavior with the ideo-motor mechanism and well-practiced behavior with habit. He also had instinct to explain why some things are so much nicer to do than others, and he had emotion that introduced another kind of behavioral control. Although the body can and does run itself much of the time by following its own physiological rules, the facts of voluntary behavior indicate that the mind can and does intervene from time to time in the affairs of the body. He might have thought that he had found a good middle ground, or a good set of compromises, between what were to him the irreconcilable worlds of science and human spirituality.

Principles is long and complicated; James felt obliged to consider alternative positions at every step of the way. Much of it is presented argumentatively, as though he could only present his own view of an issue after all possible alternatives had been disposed of. But James also had a wonderful way with words, bending them this way and that, and pulling them out of the heavens, apparently, to convey just the right shade of meaning. A century later it is still provocative, and it will always be a joy to read.[5]

Hugo Münsterberg

JAMES WAS HIGHLY instrumental in getting two faculty members into the philosophy department. One was Josiah Royce, who joined the department in 1882 and turned out to be a dazzling philosopher. The second was Hugo Münsterberg, who arrived 10 years later and turned out to be a very important psychologist. Münsterberg first arrived with a temporary appointment, because he could not decide whether he wanted to be in this country or in Germany. Then in 1897 he finally accepted a permanent appointment at Harvard. Whereupon, we noted earlier, James promptly became a professor of philosophy again, certainly a more comfortable label for a man primarily concerned with the world of the spirit. But actually, James had relinquished to Münsterberg all the duties of running the psychological part of the department when he had first arrived. Thus, Münsterberg was put in charge of the laboratory, something that James found distasteful. Münsterberg was also made the immediate supervisor of the psychology graduate students, and it was he who directed and guided their dissertation research. So while James was there, ever ready to influence the lives of the young psychologists to be, he could keep his hands clean and his head in the philosophical clouds by turning everything over to the ambitious and extremely energetic young Münsterberg who just sponged up duties and responsibilities.

Hugo Münsterberg

Münsterberg's Career

Hugo Münsterberg (1863–1916) was one of Wundt's earliest students; he got his Leipzig degree in 1885, went from there to get an M.D., and was making his way up the academic ladder at Freiburg when he got the call to Harvard. When he returned to Germany for two years, E. B. Delabarre was brought in to take things over. He was an American who had gotten his degree with Münsterberg back in Freiburg in 1889 and had been at Brown University since 1891. One of the reasons that James liked Münsterberg was that he had gotten into a bitter battle with Wundt. The difficulty was that in his initial attempt at a Ph.D. dissertation he had argued that Wundt was wrong—our sense of motor effort did not arise from our perception of the motor discharge to the muscles, but rather was comprised of the feedback from the muscles. Effort was the sensation from muscle contraction and movement. Wundt refused to accept the dissertation and Münsterberg was obliged to undertake another study that Wundt would approve. But in a few years Münsterberg published the original study as his habilitation research. Wundt was furious at that, and probably would have stood in the way of Münsterberg's further advancement anywhere in Germany. But James was delighted, not only to see the trouble in Wundt's camp, but also because Münsterberg had come out so strongly for a position so much like his own. So it turned out well for Münsterberg, and, of course, it turned out after all that he was right and Wundt was wrong about effort.

Münsterberg continued to think about the motor side of things, and ultimately developed the concept that our ideas are not so much the result of perception, but rather of our readiness to act in certain ways. We see things that will let our latent behavior be released. Thus, the motor apparatus was at least as important as our sensory equipment in the perception of things. He emphasized motivational aspects of behavior, what we want and what we strive for. He stressed will. It is our will that gives the real world substance, at least for all practical purposes.

He wrote one work that was primarily philosophical, *The Eternal Values*, which appeared in German in 1907 and in English in 1909. An eternal value is something that we value for its own worth rather than because it serves some personal purpose. Truth is that sort of eternal value; we organize our lives around such values. Values operate teleologically in everyday life, whereas facts operate causally in the world of science. It was a large-scale philosophical theory that encompassed a great deal, but it was not worked out very convincingly. Nonetheless, it did again focus attention on the motivational aspects of behavior, looking at them broadly—both mechanistically and teleologically. He helped provide a nice antidote to the structuralist approach that had totally discounted motivation. James had suggested some motivational ideas, but he had not emphasized them. Münsterberg added that emphasis. One of Münsterberg's most important students was Edwin B. Holt, who kept these motivational concepts alive at Harvard for several years when they seemed to have little chance of surviving. And as Münsterberg moved ever more into applied psychology, it was Holt who would become the experimental center of the department.[6]

Münsterberg was extraordinarily energetic, and his duties in the psychology division of the department and his fling at serious philosophy took up only a part of his time and energy. Foremost he had a very strong, practical bent. He wanted to get psychology out into the world where it could have some impact. He became an applied psychologist. Moreover, he became a popularizer who wrote quite a number of books and articles for the general public. He talked with journalists and thereby attracted to himself and to his profession more than a little public attention. Harvard professors are supposed to do that, to get out of the ivory tower and into the world, but it seems that Münsterberg did a little too much of that. His colleagues began to look the other way. A later generation would, however, look to him as the founder of industrial psychology, as a leader in psychotherapy, and as a pioneer in such diverse areas as eyewitness testimony, patriotism, ethnic, gender, and national differences, and the psychology of movies. Much of what he had to say about such matters was reasonable and appealing, but it was largely conjectural because he rarely had any substantiating data. There is curious irony in the fact that Münsterberg had been brought to Harvard in the guise of an experimentalist so that James could go on about his serious philosophical business, but while he was doing what he was supposed to do, he was, without anyone at the time realizing it, also changing psychology in a very fundamental way. Henceforth psychology would not only be something different from philosophy, it would also be something different from an ivory-tower science, the sort of pure science that Titchener wanted. The new discipline would also relate to the larger world and begin to spin off practical applications. It was a most unlikely source for the beginning of applied psychology.[7]

G. Stanley Hall

THE G STANDS FOR Granville, but his friends called him Stanley. In any case, he was one of the earliest American pioneers, second only to James himself. Stanley Hall (1844–1924) was only two years younger than James. He was a Massachusetts farm boy who made his way to Williams College and from there to Union Theological Seminary in New York. It was the custom of the seminaries at that time for the impending graduate to give a sermon as a sort of final exam. The story goes that Hall's trial sermon was so bad that the faculty did not criticize it, they just knelt and prayed for him. He was evidently too scholarly to be a minister, and was advised to go to Germany for further education. Away he went for three years at Bonn and Berlin, where he studied with du Bois-Reymond and Trendelenburg (there he is again).

After that visit to Germany, Hall drifted; he was a minister briefly, a professor of English at Antioch College for a few years, and then a tutor in the English department at Harvard. At Harvard he got to know James, and began his graduate study with him. His dissertation was physiological and was actually carried out under the supervision of the physiologist Henry Bowditch, but the degree was in the philosophy department, their first, and he is generally considered to be James's first student. Hall is also supposed to be the first American Ph.D. in psychology, but the circumstances are so complicated and irregular that the distinction of being first seems a little dubious. The year was 1878, which would put him three years ahead of Wundt's man Dietrich.

Hall then went back to Germany for further study of physiology. He spent a year at Berlin and another year at Leipzig, where he worked in Wundt's brand-new lab. Upon coming home in 1880 he had no position, but hung around Harvard for a year trying to participate in things. Up to this point, nothing had gone very well for Hall. He had earlier trained as a minister but had neither the ability nor the inclination to pursue it. Now he was 37 and had his degree but no job. But just then things changed, and from then on everything would go Hall's way.

A Change of Luck

The Johns Hopkins University was new; it had been established in Baltimore just a few years earlier, in 1876, and it was unique among American universities in that it included no undergraduate college; it was strictly a graduate school. It was designed for nothing but serious scholarship, in the style of the German universities. It would turn out in a few years that such a scheme would not work, mainly because it could not attract a sufficient number of qualified scholars to fill its graduate programs, so it had to

Granville Stanley Hall

introduce a small undergraduate college to provide itself with scholars that were good enough. Hopkins was, however, a distinguished university right from its outset, and it was to play a major role in the history of psychology. Harvard's Charles Peirce had been teaching philosophy there, but he proved to be something of a disaster in executing his duties so he was let go, never to find another academic home. Hall replaced him in 1883. In 1884, when Hall was just 40, he was advanced to professor; he had at last found his place.

When Hall went to Hopkins he found the same situation that prevailed at Harvard: There was a philosophy department, but it had two divisions, philosophy proper (where Peirce had been) and the new thing, psychology (where he belonged). Altogether, there was a most remarkable group of young men there, many of whom went on to become the next generation of pioneers in psychology. This group included John Dewey, J. McK. Cattell, E. C. Sanford, G. T. W. Patrick, Y. Motora, J. Jastrow, W. H. Burnham. Dewey was not closely associated with Hall; he was doing his dissertation work (1884) on Kant with Professor Morris. Patrick and Sanford were Hall's students and got their degrees with him in 1887 and 1888. But it is not clear about the others, and to what extent Hall worked with them or influenced them. Was he responsible for turning any of them toward psychology? Hall established a laboratory at Hopkins in 1883 and his background was strongly physiological. Was it the possibility of doing experimental science that attracted the attention of this remarkable collection of soon-to-be psychologists?

We should notice how very early Hall had gotten into the psychology business. Wundt had not settled into Leipzig until 1874. It was only nine years later that Hall settled into Johns Hopkins, and his lab appeared only four years after Wundt's official, university-funded lab was set up. Hall was not to be at Hopkins very long, however. Another new university was taking shape near Boston. A man named Clark had two ambitions, one was to immortalize himself by building a university, and the other was to intervene in its affairs so that its students could be guided as he thought best. The university was to have profound problems with Mr. Clark over the next decade or so, but it all looked very promising initially. Hall was the new president (I said things were going to go his way). In 1888 Hall and Clark negotiated the character of the new school; it would be quite small with only five departments. It would be a graduate school only, in the manner of Hopkins. The ground rules set, Hall went off to Europe once more to study the structure of universities there. In 1889 Hall moved into little Clark University with two of his young colleagues from Hopkins. Hall himself became ever more active in psychology, even though E. C. Sanford would run the psychology lab and chair the department. W. H. Burnham was put in charge of the educational psychology department. Psychology was destined to be a big part of Clark. And, in turn, Clark University was to play a major role in psychology; it produced a large number of psychology Ph.D.s over the next 20 years or so.

Hall Organizes the Field

Some rare people seem to be natural-born organizers. While most of us stand around and watch, the movers and shakers get things done. Wundt was one of those, and so was G. Stanley Hall. Nothing got dusty when he was around. In 1887 he started the first American psychology journal, the *American Journal of Psychology*. It started just 6 years after Wundt's *Philosophical Studies* and 11 years after Bain's *Mind*, neither of which was really the place to submit the sort of experimental work the young Americans were doing. Psychology needed its own journal, and Hall supplied it. But that was only the beginning. In 1891 he founded the *Pedagogical Seminary*, a rather mysterious title that later got changed to *Journal of Genetic Psychology*, which is still a little mysterious. It was basically developmental psychology. In 1915 there appeared *Journal of Applied Psychology*. In 1904 there was another, short-lived one, *Journal of Religious Psychology*.

One summer day in 1892 Hall was talking with a group of psychologist friends about how they should organize a society of psychologists. They decided to do it, and perhaps because this gathering occurred in Hall's home, they decided to make him president. And that is part of how he came to be the first president of the American Psychological Association. Surprisingly, perhaps, William James would be only the third president.

Hall's style was to work on something furiously for a few years, and then move on to something else. He admitted that he got carried away with his enthusiasms. Initially he had been interested in movement. His research at Harvard had been on movement and space perception and he continued to work on movement when he was at Hopkins. At Clark he turned to developmental psychology, which he approached from an evolutionary and adaptational point of view. Then he moved up the age scale a bit. His

Adolescence (1904) was a popular book, a classic. He got interested in psychoanalysis, and managed to get Freud and Jung over to Clark for a celebration in 1909, so that we and they could get to know each other. It was unquestionably an important step in the gradual acceptance of psychoanalysis in this country. Hall never gave up on religion, and he returned to it in earnest in the 1910s. Moving on up the age scale, he wrote *Senescence* in 1922. Shortly before he died he wrote an autobiography (Hall, 1923). He was 80, and had just been elected president of APA for a second time.

He was not always easy to get along with, but he was widely respected, and this recognition was all the more remarkable because so much of his life had been devoted not to the respectable world of the laboratory, but to the real world, the complicated world of kids growing up, people getting old, and the practical world of applied psychology. His work in these new areas not only helped to make them legitimate parts of psychology, his vigor and enthusiasm caused many others to follow him.

James McKeen Cattell

ONE OF THE GRADUATE students Hall met at Johns Hopkins in 1883 was James McKeen Cattell (1860–1944). He had begun graduate work in 1880 in Germany at Göttingen under Lotze. We recall that Lotze died in 1881, and that his chair was given to Müller, so Cattell just missed Müller, which is something of a coincidence in that for a time they did very similar research. He also studied briefly with Wundt, before returning to the United States. He was a restless fellow, and was only at Hopkins a short time, and so it is not clear whether he was in any way influenced by Hall. It might not be a coincidence that Hall was then absorbed in the study of movement and that when Cattell went to Wundt in 1883 it was to work on movement and reaction time.

Cattell was the first American to do a dissertation with Wundt. The brash young American and the distinguished German professor got along very well. This rapport was quite remarkable because they disagreed about a fundamental point. Wundt was one of those ordinary normative scientists; he wanted to know what effect a particular treatment had on average; in other words, he liked means. Cattell, on the other hand, was fascinated by individual differences, so he liked the variance. It is actually much to Wundt's credit that he accepted this sort of divergence, accommodated Cattell's passion, and began to think about different "styles" of responding. They got along well, and published some important papers. During this time Cattell was also Wundt's lab assistant, his first assistant. The story goes that upon arriving at Leipzig the never-shy Cattell announced that Wundt needed an assistant and that he would be it. And he was.

James McKeen Cattell

After getting his degree in 1886 he poked around for a couple of years. He wanted to work with Galton, who he thought shared his passion for individual differences, but they were not able to work anything out, so that came to nothing and a year at Cambridge accomplished little. Then in 1888 he was appointed professor of psychology at the University of Pennsylvania. He established a laboratory there, which was the earliest, after Hopkins, in the country. His appointment at Penn was also remarkable in that he was the first professor of psychology, before James or Hall or anyone else. But this appointment was followed in 1891 by the major move to Columbia University, where he would remain for many years. He immediately set up a lab at Columbia that proved to be remarkable for the great number of students that would pass through it.

Major Accomplishments

Cattell was another one of those who gets things done—establishing the lab and supervising it, hiring faculty and organizing them (Columbia's department was destined to grow until it became the largest in the country), keeping track of all those students (for several decades it produced more Ph.D.s than any other university), and editing and managing all those journals. Cattell did journals. He and Mark Baldwin (whom we will meet shortly) began the *Psychological Review* in 1894. It has always been psychology's premier journal for theoretical papers. Cattell was the editor until 1903, when Baldwin bought out his interest. (In those days the journals were not only run by a powerful editor, they were also commonly owned by the editor.) But that was just the start. In 1900 he started *Popular Science Monthly*, which was another theory-oriented journal. If the name sounds familiar it is because Cattell sold the name to the current *Popular Science* people years ago, and continued his journal under the banner of *Scientific Monthly*. He edited many editions of his

American Men of Science (later editions contained a lot of women, but that did not affect the title). For decades he was also editor of *American Naturalist* and *Science*.

All by himself Cattell was an institution. His initial work on reaction time was widely recognized as important. It got into attention, different styles of responding, different sorts of errors made under different circumstances, the critical part played by instructions, and the various interactions among these variables. These matters led him into a similar analysis of psychophysical data in general. Again he found different sorts of errors—for example, false positives and false negatives—and he wrote important papers on how to treat some of these problems statistically. In the 1890s he and G. E. Müller were the major methodologists of psychophysics.

But Cattell was moving in another direction and he plunged into developing mental tests, an area he made his own (Cattell, 1890). He and his colleagues and his many students made mental testing an important part of psychology both at Columbia and elsewhere. He left Columbia in 1916, and retired from teaching, but continued working with his journals.

Mark Baldwin

JAMES MARK BALDWIN (1861–1934) usually went by his middle name. He was just a year younger than Cattell, and they overlapped briefly, in 1885, in Wundt's Leipzig lab. The difference was that Cattell was embarked on a productive research program there whereas Baldwin was just visiting. He returned to Princeton, where he had been an undergraduate, and obtained his degree with James McCosh, theologian, moral philosopher, president of the university, and the last of the Scottish common sense psychologists. In 1889 Baldwin got an appointment in philosophy at Toronto, and promptly set up the first Canadian psychology lab. Four years later he was called back to Princeton to build a new psychology department and a lab there. McCosh was still alive, but his era was over. After 10 years Baldwin moved to Johns Hopkins, where he set up another lab. The one founded by Hall almost 20 years earlier had fallen into disuse when he went to Clark, so Baldwin did it all over again. Baldwin was only at Hopkins from 1903 to 1908, however, because he got caught up in personal trouble, in addition to which he was probably losing his zest for psychology. He was an independent man of means, a man of the world, and he traveled a lot. Most of the last 25 years of his life were spent in Mexico City and Paris.

Although he organized those three laboratories, he was not himself a researcher and I don't believe he ever published an important experimental paper. Together with Cattell he founded *Psychological Review*, as we have seen. In the next few years they cooperated in bringing out other journals,

Psychological Index, Psychological Monographs, and *Psychological Bulletin*. He also edited the large, very important, long-lived and much-cited *Dictionary of Philosophy and Psychology*. Baldwin had few students; certainly they were not a big part of his importance, as Cattell's students were for him. He was important because of his books. During the 20 years or so between the time he went to Toronto and when he left Hopkins and, in effect, left psychology, Baldwin put out a surprising number of books. Some were designed for the popular market, some were rather technical, but all of them were wonderfully crafted. His first book was serious; it was in the tradition of Bain, with Bain's two parts, and even with Bain-like titles: *Senses and Intellect* (1889) and *Feeling and Will* (1891). These books would have been much more important if they had not been swamped by the appearance of James's *Principles* at the same time. His last effort was not serious but a delightful autobiography, *Between Two Wars* (1926). Here Baldwin took the opportunity to tell stories about all the important people he had known, not just psychologists, but all sorts of important people around the world.

Where Baldwin paved new ground was in developmental psychology. He wrote *Mental Development in the Child and the Race* (1895), which combined a behavioral orientation, evolutionary thinking, the functional sort of approach that was beginning to spread across the country, and an enthusiasm for a basic experimental outlook. It was a very important book that went through several revisions. It articulated a naturalistic, biological orientation that Baldwin largely shared with Hall, but which he was the first to describe effectively. It played an important part in establishing developmental psychology as a legitimate area for psychologists to study.

Summary

JAMES STARTED WITH the conflict he saw between the importance of human spirit and morality and the inevitable march of science, particularly the science of Darwin, which he saw as posing a clear challenge to traditional human values. James saw that a new discipline, something called psychology, could fit in between. And that makes his thought rather complex because he insisted on having a little of each; much of psychology is mechanical, but much of it is mental. And James missed the point of the whole thing because he placed little faith in experimentation. However, although he himself was not interested in research, he always encouraged others to get into the lab. Perhaps his problem was that he was primarily a philosopher. The next pioneers were a new breed, primarily experimenters and only secondarily philosophers. This distinction is certainly not a dichotomy, however; we have seen that Baldwin was well over on James's side, Cattell stood over on the other side, and Münsterberg was in the middle.

We have seen another dimension brought into the picture. Cattell and Münsterberg started in as experimenters, purists in the Wundtian tradition and trained by the old man himself. But by the turn of the century, both of them were fully committed to applied psychology. Because they were powerful figures and well placed at Columbia and Harvard, they were enormously influential in spreading psychology out and away from its original experimental center.

These American pioneers had seen Wundt the founder at work, and they evidently had learned how to get things founded. Hall, Cattell, and Baldwin started new journals. And they started up labs at major universities. Hall started the APA. No doubt much of the distancing of American psychology from its German roots was due to the ease and rapidity with which we got set up over here to do everything psychological in our own way. Psychology caught on and prospered here as in no other country. Part of that can be explained by the development of our unique university system. Part of it was no doubt due to the presence on the scene of certain unique individuals, such as Hall. Some of it, though, seems to hang on something peculiar in the intellectual life of the country at that time. It is as if a century ago we had a need for our own kind of psychology. The next chapter indicates what kind of psychology that was.

Notes

1. It would be wrong to conclude that all the changes that I have described happened all at once around the time of the Civil War. It is better to think of continuous change, with certain landmark events occurring at that time. For example, there were women's colleges, such as Oberlin, Mt. Holyoke, and Hollins in the South, years before Vassar opened. However, they had little to offer academically. Vassar may well have been the first to take education seriously (Rudolph, 1962). There were also several state universities long before the Morrill Act (the Land Grant Act) was passed. Michigan was already an important one. Iowa and Wisconsin also predated the act, and there were entities called University of Georgia and University of North Carolina before 1800. Moreover the line between state and private schools was not as sharply drawn as it is now. The states have given financial support to nearly all colleges at one time or another.

There were also many new colleges that popped up all over the country before 1860, little ones like Mills out in California and big ones like Pittsburgh back in Pennsylvania. There was a kind of craze that seized communities and religious sects to set up little schools in every new town in the country. Already before the Civil War, hundreds of these new schools folded because they lacked a population base, or money, or both. And even the dramatic events of the 1860s that I have stressed occurred more or less gradually. Thus, it took Harvard's Eliot more than a decade to get the elective system operating effectively. Rudolph (1962) gives an elegant account and a broad view of all these developments. Veysey (1965) gives a detailed account focused on Hopkins and Harvard.

2. Fisch (1964) gives a good account of this group. It is hard to know just what they were up to because they met informally and nothing got written down.

3. In its prime days, the 1890s, the philosophy department consisted of the following. George Parker (1842–1933), a Bostonian, Harvard graduate, and divinity student, who wrote mainly about ethics. He had been a student of Francis Bowen, the original "modern" philosopher at Harvard, and succeeded him as chairman. He taught in the department from 1872 to 1913, and even that long tenure was not enough for him because he hung around there another 20 years. William James (1842–1910) was also a Bostonian and Harvard student. He taught in the philosophy department from 1880 until 1907. In 1882 James went on a year's leave and was able to get an outsider to replace him. This was Josiah Royce (1855–1916) from the Wild West (Grass Valley, California). Royce studied at Berkeley and Johns Hopkins, getting his degree there with Gilman in 1878. His temporary appointment was so successful that he was invited to stay on. Royce was an intellectual giant, perhaps the greatest of American philosophers; he was systematic, logical, thorough, and thoughtful. Thus, he nicely complemented James, who was unsystematic, intuitive, inconsistent, and empirical. His most readable work is perhaps *The Religious Aspects of Philosophy* (1885). He dealt with the sort of things Kant had worried about.

There was also George Santayana (1864–1952), who was Spanish, but moved to Boston, went to Harvard, and taught there from 1889 to 1912. After that he lived mostly in Rome and wrote. He did philosophy, but was by nature a poet, and is now probably best known as a writer. It was he who said that those who do not understand their history may be doomed to relive it. The fifth member of the department was the psychologist Hugo Münsterberg (1863–1916). The history of the Harvard department has been ably described by Kuklick (1977).

4. Most people had thought (most people still do) that emotion *moves* us to action; that is what the dictionary says. But James was looking at it as a behaviorist would; we are moved to action by automatic mechanisms like reflexes and habits, and by our volitions and where we choose to focus attention. How we feel comes later and is not important except perhaps in sustaining our defenses, our aggression, or whatever. Cannon (1915) attacked

the James–Lange theory on several grounds, one of which was that emotional body reactions have too slow a latency to produce appropriate action. Cannon wanted to get emotion back someplace in the body where Descartes had put it, and out of the head where James had moved it. But Cannon should have read James again rather than consulting his dictionary, because James very well knew that action comes first and feeling later. Schachter and Singer (1962) proposed a compromise according to which there has to be a bodily context (such as heightened levels of norepinephrine) for there to be any emotion, but the specific emotion is determined, as James said, by how we label our own actions.

5. William James (1842–1910) had written several important papers in the 1880s, including the one on emotion, which were later made into chapters of the *Principles of Psychology* (1890). James frequently apologized for the immensity of the *Principles*, and to atone for his sins brought out *Psychology: Briefer Course* in 1892, which was an extremely popular introductory text. He wrote *The Will to Believe and other Essays in Popular Philosophy* (1897) and *Varieties of Religious Experience* (1902), both of which were quite popular and influential.

At this stage, James was beginning to find peace from his earlier conflicts. He was also beginning to work out the pragmatic ideas he and Peirce had struggled with 30 years before. He said we should accept a belief if it can be demonstrated as true, or if it is consistent with other things we believe. In the case of a religious belief, demonstration is hard to come by, but there are other criteria, such as whether holding the belief makes us behave differently, and whether it meets our moral needs. If we are better for believing it, if we find it morally helpful, then from a pragmatic point of view the belief is true. Kant, who had started all the trouble 100 years before, might have been pleased with the way James was going. His last major work was *Pragmatism* (1907). The standard biography of James was by his student, friend, and colleague Perry (1935). For an elegant, perceptive, chapter-length summary of the *Principles*, see Heidbreder (1933).

6. Edwin Bissell Holt (1873–1946) was from Massachusetts, attended Harvard, and did graduate work there, getting his dissertation with Münsterberg in 1901. He then served on the faculty until 1918. Holt always thought of himself as a disciple and follower of James, and that is how others tended to regard him. It was expected that he would do a revision of the *Principles*, but he never got to it. He wrote *The Concept of Consciousness* (1914), in which he argued, as James had suggested, that the mind was not a *thing* that could be located in the brain, but rather a *function*. It happens when the brain is working. Holt's best year was 1915. That was when E. C. Tolman, whom we will meet later, got his degree from him (so did the brilliant, eccentric L. T. Troland, who would soon replace Holt in the department). At the same time there appeared his major work *The Freudian Wish* (1915). This seemingly

209

simple work is rather complex. He began by making Freud a great hero, a great student of behavior. Then he began translating Freud into his own terms—and undoing him. He said we know a person's motivation by their actions. The wish is nothing but a readiness to act out certain behaviors. Behaviors all have specific neural causes. So ultimately motivation and ethics are all neurological. James never said anything like that, nor did Freud; Holt was just off on a trip. His last work *Animal Drive and the Learning Process* (1931) was hopelessly mechanistic. On the positive side, Holt did keep alive James's and Münsterberg's motivational ideas, such as that we should define motivation in wholistic ways, and in terms of behavior, and in terms of ends and purposes. He kept those ideas alive long enough that Tolman could put them together.

7. Hugo Münsterberg (1863–1916) wrote a great variety of books, both academic and popular. Some of them were: *On the Witness Stand* (1908), a skeptical view of the reliability of testimony, *Psychology and Industrial Efficiency* (1913a), generally accepted as the beginning of industrial psychology, *American Patriotism* (1913b), a fling at ethnic and social psychology, and *Psychology General and Applied* (1914), which looks at all sorts of applications. Hale (1980) describes Münsterberg's impact on applied psychology, and there is a biography by his daughter M. Münsterberg (1922).

Chapter Ten

American Functionalism

ARLY AMERICAN PSYCHOLOGISTS did not like structuralism; they did not like either Wundt's or Titchener's version of it. Even those pioneers who had gotten their all-important Ph.D.s with Wundt were generally not ready to follow him into the study of reaction time, the organization of apperception, or the scaling of sensory dimensions. And there was certainly no enthusiasm for the philosophical system that was so important to the founder. The pioneering American psychologists had also largely rejected the Scottish common sense approach. So what did these young scholars believe in; what drummer did they follow? The truth seems to be that no one was listening to a drummer; they all wanted to be free to do their own thing. The pioneers we met in the last chapter were all thinking about very different things. James worried about the human spirit, Münsterberg wanted to get into the real world, Hall worked on development, Cattell studied personality, and Baldwin wanted to get all the different theories organized. We see very little overlap. The Americans believed in diversity, and in having the freedom to create one's own niche in some new area of psychology.

This need to be independent, to explore new domains, and to be unconstrained by dogma, was an important part of what it meant to be a functionalist. Thus, it was certainly not a dogmatic school of psychology, and that makes it particularly difficult to say just what the movement was all about. It was an inherently free but fuzzy doctrine. **Functionalism** took shape rather slowly, which again makes it difficult to see just who the early members of the group were. It took them a number of years to become self-conscious enough to see who and what they were. And as with all major movements, there were early anticipations of it.

[handwritten margin note: rejected Wundt]

Anticipations of Functionalism

IMAGINE YOU HAVE FOUND a curious-looking insect. There are a couple of ways you might examine it. One is to put it under the microscope. To do that you have to kill it first so it will not move around, but then you can count its legs and eyes and teeth, and describe all its parts. That is the way Titchener looked at the mind. He went at it as an anatomist might: Kill it first and then dissect it so you can examine its parts. The other approach is to turn the insect loose and follow it around. Then you may discover how it moves, what it eats, how it mates; you may discover something about how it works and how it functions. That was the approach the functionalist took to the mind. The functionalist wanted to see the mind in action, wanted to understand what it was doing.

We have already noted some anticipations of this kind of approach. Remember that back in 1853 Lotze said consciousness arises when the individual encounters a novel problem. That is a functionalistic approach because it says something about what the mind is doing and suggests something about why the mind is active. Remember that Brentano in 1874 emphasized that we have to view the mind in action because even something as passive as perception involves active participation. That is functionalistic in spirit because it says something about the mind in use. The basic issue is how one should regard the mind. Is it a bunch of dead stuff to be described, like an object under the microscope, or does the mind have a life of its own with activities to carry out, functions to perform, and purposes to fulfill?

Darwin: A Concern with Behavior

The functionalists were concerned not only with how and why the mind functions, they were also interested in the function of behavior. That was part of their broad, open perspective. Therefore, we can see Darwin, who was always more interested in behavior than in the mind, as an anticipator. He was vitally interested in those behaviors that paid off in the big survival game, such as eating, predation and defense, and mating. Ultimately all behavior serves the purpose of survival. Reflexes have to be adaptive, and if we cannot understand how a particular reflex is useful, that only means we do not understand our subject very well. Darwin was interested in how plants move and grow, and gradually came to see, for example, how the movements of growing vines facilitated fertilization. He understood the function of emotional expression. Why do we have emotions anyhow? What function do they serve? They are important in social communication. If I am feeling angry, it makes sense for me to communicate that so that you will go away and quit bothering me and not risk getting hurt. If I am feeling friendly, I need to communicate that too so that we can be friends. Darwin was a functionalist through and through, but it took some time for some of his ideas to be assimilated by psychologists. He was an anticipator.

Ladd's Physiological Psychology

George Trumbull Ladd (1842–1921) was born the same year as William James. He went to a theological seminary and then worked as a minister for 10 years. He taught for a short time at Bowdoin College in Maine, as a professor of moral philosophy. In 1881, with only a couple of years teaching experience and virtually no scholarly work to his credit, he moved to Yale. At that time Yale was in transition, trying to be a university, but still suffering from the Noah Porter (Scottish) tradition. Ladd did rather advanced things at Yale, such as teaching his moral philosophy classes about Wundt and the new experimental psychology. He had no real lab, and was little interested in doing research, but he was a real scholar who studied everything coming out of the German labs, and he started writing a book about it. His *Elements of Physiological Psychology* came out in 1887 and was an instant and smashing success. It was a good book—big, well-organized, and easy to read (or at least a lot easier than Wundt's books). It was a welcomed bridge across the Atlantic at a time when American would-be psychologists were getting interested in the possibilities over there. It was also an important bridge between the spiritual world Ladd had known as a minister and the scientific world he was getting to know.

Ladd was an important anticipator of functionalism because of the early appearance and popularity of his 1887 book. His contribution to the functionalistic cause has been so nicely summarized by Boring (1950) that I can do no better than outline his account. Boring's account, which was admittedly derived from Titchener, also helps us begin defining functionalism. There are four points. (1) There is in each of us an *active principle*, something we can call the self. Ladd thought of the mind as both a collection of Wundtian contents, sensations and such, and activities that the self performs. It was sort of a blend of Wundt and Brentano. (2) Consciousness, which is something the self does, has a *purpose*. Its function is to help us solve problems. In a Darwinian sense, the function of the mind is to adapt the individual to its environment. (3) If the mind has a purpose then psychology becomes *teleological*. (4) If the mind is to be useful, then it must give us some benefit in the *business of living*. But living is a very practical matter, so the function of the mind can also be found in the world of practical affairs. Psychology, therefore, needs to expand into applied and practical areas.

Once Ladd began to write books, he could not stop. There were almost a dozen variants of the *Physiological Psychology* in the next decade, some shorter and some longer and some less physiological, but none was as successful or as popular as the original. And it endured; in 1911 Woodworth collaborated with him on a revision, which in turn was widely used for many years. In 1892

Edward Scripture, one of Wundt's early students, was brought to Yale to set up a real lab. Yale had made the transition, at least as far as psychology was concerned. In 1892 Ladd was elected the second president of APA, after Hall and before James. Evidently they really did like that book with its functionalistic tone.[1]

James's Principles of Psychology, Again

William James was another anticipator. He was quite sympathetic to Ladd's point of view. Indeed, his *Principles* is like Ladd's *Physiological Psychology* in many ways, and was quite likely influenced by it. To start with, it is full of physiological mechanisms. Also, one of James's longest chapters deals with the self. James's view of the mind is certainly active: It directs attention and makes decisions. Mind has unquestionably evolved for some purpose, James said. He believed in applied psychology; we remember that James's right-hand man, Münsterberg, was foremost among applied psychologists. In short, Boring's analysis of Ladd's book could have just as aptly been made of James's book, written three years later. James was busy doing too many other things, however, to be properly called a functionalist. He was rescuing the soul from the sciences, and rescuing the sciences from metaphysics, and distracting himself with spiritual matters. All these other activities prevent us from labeling James a functionalist. But he was close to it; perhaps we should think of him as transitional.

John Dewey and Functionalism

AMERICAN FUNCTIONALISM really began with John Dewey, the philosopher. When G. Stanley Hall got to the philosophy department at Johns Hopkins in 1883, John Dewey (1859–1952) was already there doing graduate work in philosophy. Dewey was studying Kant with G. S. Morris. And believe it or not, Morris had been a student of Trendelenburg![2]

Dewey got his degree in 1884 and then followed Morris up to the University of Michigan. In short order he wrote *Psychology* (1886). There were several things about this book that made it nice. It appeared very early, at a time when psychology was just stirring. It was not massive, like Bain's and Spencer's works. It was not in German, like Wundt's work, which had not yet been translated. It was not very physiological in orientation, as the books of Spencer and Wundt were before and those of Ladd and James would be later. It was nice because Dewey's later works were mostly, to say it nicely, a little obscure. *Psychology* was highly readable and it contained a number of interesting, simple ideas. One interesting idea: Dewey said that if it is possible for an act to occur, then it just occurs, but if it is thwarted or blocked in some

John Dewey

way, then an emotion arises. It was an interesting new way to regard emotion. Another idea: Dewey said that an idea was not a memory of some prior perception, but rather an anticipation of an expected perception. Some of Dewey's earliest ideas reveal him to be concerned with the activities of the mind, and with its function rather than its contents. His functionalistic ideas were taking shape. In the next few years Dewey established himself as an up-and-coming young philosopher, and in 1894 he left Michigan to go to the new University of Chicago.

Dewey had not been at Chicago very long when he published a paper in 1896 on the reflex arc, which is his most famous contribution to functional psychology. The paper refers to the well-known hypothetical case of the infant who sees a pretty little candle flame—and pokes it with a finger. The infant quickly withdraws the finger. That is generally regarded as a defensive reflex, but no, Dewey says, that is not the correct way to regard the situation. The finger movement is not just an automatic response to a painful stimulus. It is tempting to regard it that way because it seems so nicely scientific. But to look at it that way is to oversimplify things and pass over all the important aspects of the situation. The stimulus is not a fixed thing, because it changes its value after being touched. The response is not an entity in itself, it is part of the child's adaptation to its environment. It is arbitrary and artificial for psychologists to focus their attention on just the stimulus and the response and to consider only that the one now causes the other. We are tempted to do that because they are easy to record, but, Dewey says, we must look at the whole coordinated situation and think about how the child is changed because of it. Dewey's paper was primarily an attack on the narrowness of an analytic approach, and atomism more generally. He regarded the mind as an instrument that we can use to adapt more adequately to the world around us—a view we call **instrumentalism.**

The Chicago School of Functionalism

AFTER A COUPLE of years of incubation to get it organized, the University of Chicago was opened in 1892. It was done largely with Rockefeller money. At the outset it had beautiful buildings and a strong faculty. The faculty was acquired mainly by raiding other universities, that is, locating good people at other institutions and offering them irresistible salaries. The successful raider has to have money, of course, but Chicago had it. By 1895 it had what would prove to be a wonderful philosophy department (initially it was the department of philosophy, psychology, and education). Dewey, G. H. Mead (also from Michigan), and A. W. Moore were installed, and each of them was destined to make a major mark on American philosophy. Together, but under Dewey's leadership, they began to create what would be called the Chicago school of functionalism.

Dewey believed that philosophy should not be cloistered in an ivory tower, but rather should be put to use in the real world. It should be useful to society. Philosophers should not concern themselves with the problems of philosophers, but should get out there and work on the many problems of the people. This was a new idea, and a new variety of pragmatism—a really pragmatic pragmatism. Dewey was also a liberal. In contrast with the many philosophers who defend traditional values, Dewey wanted to experiment, to innovate, to poke into new ways of thinking. He wanted to reform philosophy by throwing out worn-out metaphysical ideas and pushing on to today's practical problems.

Dewey did not go much further as a psychologist because about 1900 he turned to other things, such as education. He believed that schoolchildren should not be required to learn particular subject matters, but rather should be encouraged to develop skills and interests. They should also learn by doing, rather than by listening to lectures. In 1904 Dewey left Chicago for the newly organized Teacher's College of Columbia University. And there for another half a century he developed his ideas on education and society in general. He wrote extensively, mostly about educational matters. But he retained a strong interest in psychology, and was active in the APA. He was elected president of APA in 1899. Dewey was also, true to his philosophy, a social activist. For example, early in the new century he was a founder of the American Association of University Professors and the American Civil Liberties Union.[3]

James Rowland Angell

Angell illustrates Galton's notion that genius is hereditary; in his family it was being president of a university that got passed on. His grandfather had been president of Brown, his father was president of Michigan, and he became

James Rowland Angell

president of Yale. J. R. Angell (1869–1949) regarded himself as a student and disciple of William James. He had been at Harvard studying with James around 1890, but went to Germany to do doctoral research. He studied with Erdmann at Halle (just west of Leipzig), and was writing his dissertation when he ran out of time. It never got finished because in 1893 he took a teaching job at University of Minnesota. Then in 1894 he was offered the chair of the brand-new psychology department at Chicago. A lab had already been established there in 1892 by C. A. Strong, so Angell was not the founder of the department, but historically he was the most important member of it. So there he was, with no Ph.D. but nonetheless very well placed in the academic world. Perhaps doctoral degrees were not really as important as everyone assumed they were.

Angell first collaborated with his colleague the philosopher Moore on a reaction-time experiment that was in the Cattell tradition of examining different types of responders. They sorted out sensory and motor types of subjects. It was an important experiment, and also transitional in the sense that it introduced a functionalistic interpretation in place of the customary structuralistic interpretation of reaction-time results (Angell and Moore, 1896). Angell published a paper in 1903 in which he stood up more strongly for functionalism. He followed Titchener's earlier papers that had distinguished structure and function, which was essentially the same distinction that was made by biologists between how cells were put together and what it was that a system of cells did. Whereas Titchener had claimed that only the structural part of the analysis was appropriate for the young science of psychology, Angell put function first. Structure means nothing if we do not know the function.

The keynote statement, the definition of functionalism, was Angell's presidential address to the APA in 1906. In it he indicated three dimensions of functionalism. First, functional psychology was the study of mental operations as opposed to mental elements; it is *functional* rather than structural. It sought to discover how a mental process works, in much the same way that a biologist might seek to discover how respiration or locomotion or feeding works. Second, functional psychology was the psychology of the *uses* of the mind. One fundamental use of the mind is to mediate between the needs of the organism and the environment. Mental processes do not operate in isolation; they are but part of the organism adjusting and adapting to its world. Third, functional psychology was concerned with *all* of the relationships between the organism and its world, and with *all* relationships between mind and body. This third principle was intended to be generalized to include behavior, which was a body function, and applied psychology, which was a part of the environment. The little word *all* in there was also intended to mean that functional psychology was wide open and ready to study all aspects and areas of psychology.[4]

It was a permissive and liberal program that encouraged psychologists to do whatever they wanted to do. There was no fixed agenda; there were no obligatory methods and no required concepts. It was the antithesis of Titchener's rigid, tight, and demanding orthodoxy. One complaint one could make about functionalism is that it was nothing but permissive; it did not really assert much of anything. It was not a theory, or a program, or a set of methods, or even much of a point of view. What Angell proclaimed was that the mind has a purpose, and that its purpose is to help us adapt to the environment. Habits function nicely to get us along in familiar situations, he said, but in novel situations it is useful to have consciousness take charge. But this in itself is a poor guide to further research. There is a simple answer to this complaint; it is to say, "Go forth young men and women and devise your own techniques for studying whatever interests you."

And that is what they did. In the next decade or so Chicago produced a number of very able men and women who would push psychology out in new directions. The first of them were Helen Woolley, developmentalist; John Watson, behaviorist; and Harvey Carr, experimentalist, who would in time take the baton from Angell and lead Chicago onward. Other outstanding students were Walter Bingham, applied psychologist, and Walter Hunter, experimental psychologist. The common pattern was one of diversity.

The movement at Chicago was held together largely by the strength of Angell's personality. He gave it direction and kept the spirit alive in much the same way that Cattell was the center of things at Columbia and Titchener was in charge at Cornell. It was a sort of cult of personality. When Angell went off to the presidency of Yale in 1921, the chairmanship passed to Harvey Carr, and so did the leadership of the movement. Carr rose to the occasion. He wrote a popular introductory book in 1925 that represents perhaps the culmination of the movement, and is certainly the most systematic and considered statement of its basic principles.

Boring (1950) said that functional psychology is a name for what a psychologist does when freed of systematic compulsions. It is a name that could be applied to many of the pioneering American psychologists, in part because so many of them were set to do their own thing, and in part because so few of them were hampered by compulsions. Titchener and his people were compulsive, of course. But one could be compulsive in other ways. For example, if there had been an ongoing program of physiological work, it could have created compulsions, an overriding mechanistic philosophy, and so on, but such an orientation had not developed.

Similarly, a systematic Protestant or Catholic psychology would have surely brought along its own set of compulsions, points that had to be believed and defended, but that did not happen, and around 1900 there was very little sectarian psychology. There might have been something inherent in American culture that dictated what shape our psychology would have to take, but that did not happen either. We were surprisingly free of compulsions, and sure enough, a lot of us were functionalists.

Functionalism at Columbia

SIMILAR DEVELOPMENTS WERE occurring elsewhere, but most notably at Columbia University. The story there was not dependent on Dewey being there after 1904. Rather, it depended on the presence there of Cattell and some of his students. Cattell had started his research career with Wundt working on reaction time and psychophysics, but his abiding fascination was with individual differences. At Columbia he pursued this interest by developing personality questionnaires. He was off, like a functionalist, into the real world peopled by real people.

Columbia also had the advantage of being in the right place, with a huge population base. It was a large organization and became in the first few decades of the 1900s the largest producer of psychology Ph.D.s in the country. Columbia was also blessed by their decision to hire a couple of their own first Ph.D.s. Edward L. Thorndike (1874–1949) had spent a year working with William James in 1896, and then moved to Columbia because they provided better financial support. He then completed his dissertation under Cattell's supervision in 1898. It was a great dissertation, on a par with Ebbinghaus's habilitation research. It was the cat-in-the-puzzle-box experiment, the first large, systematic study of animal learning. We will describe this work, and Thorndike's interpretation of it, in chapter 13; here we just note that it was the sort of research nobody but a functionalist would have undertaken.

After being elsewhere for a year, Thorndike was brought back to Columbia, Teacher's College, where he showed many more functionalistic inclinations. He measured personality, he studied measurement, he taught statistics, and more than anything else, he got into educational psychology. His book *Educational Psychology* (1913) really marked the beginning of that area of psychology. In effect, it was Cattell and Thorndike at Columbia that legitimized and institutionalized Galton's aspiration to measure all sorts of practical mental phenomena. After 25 years of working in a variety of applied psychology areas, Thorndike returned to experimental studies of learning, human learning. And for a time he totally dominated that field.

Cattell's other star student was Robert S. Woodworth (1869–1962) who was an undergraduate at Harvard along with Thorndike, then followed Thorndike to Columbia and Cattell. His dissertation was not so famous, but that does not matter. He was strongly into physiological psychology, and went off in 1899 to teach physiology at Harvard. He studied with the great British physiologist Charles Sherrington in 1902, and then was brought back to Columbia. In 1911 he revised and coauthored Ladd's *Physiological Psychology*.

But Woodworth was not just a physiological psychologist, he was active in many areas. He published an early paper on dreams, and another on imageless thought. In 1918 he wrote *Dynamic Psychology*, which was an attempt to introduce motivational concepts into experimental psychology; he was a pioneer in the area of motivation. He wrote an extraordinarily popular *Experimental Psychology* (1938), which was the standard handbook for many years. He wrote an even more popular introductory book in 1921, which was the standard text for decades of psychology students.*

Woodworth wrote an important book on the history of psychology in 1931, and it went through major revisions in 1948 and 1954. Even as Woodworth adjusted to the changing field, it remained an important book and a lovely history. But an even lovelier history was written by Edna

---

*When I took Psych 100, the textbook was Woodworth's fourth edition, and I remember thinking that this new thing called psychology, especially the physiological part of it, looked very exciting. Woodworth had turned me on. I was lucky enough to meet Woodworth at a convention in 1960, when he was 91. He was not very vigorous, but he was quite alert, he was enjoying himself at the meeting, and he seemed interested to meet a young psychologist one-third his age. I was pleased to be able to tell him he had turned me on to psychology.

Boring (1950) raises the interesting question of who, at any given time, is the "dean" of psychologists, the most distinguished living psychologist by virtue of some unknown formula combining contribution and seniority. James was clearly it during the last decade of his life. Perhaps Hall was the next dean. Later, Thorndike could probably claim the title in the 1940s, his last decade. But then there can be no question that it went to Woodworth until we lost him in 1962. Who next? Perhaps Piaget. In the 1980s, perhaps Skinner. Finding the dean is a nice game.

Heidbreder, who got her degree with Woodworth in 1924. I doubt that anyone can read Heidbreder without scribbling down little notes that can be cited later; she is amazingly quotable. In contrasting James's approach to Titchener's, she said, "Whereas Titchener was intent chiefly on making the new psychology a science, James was more concerned that the new science be psychology" (Heidbreder, 1933, p. 152). In summarizing the functionalistic spirit at Columbia she observed that

> the psychological scene at Columbia presents a motley aspect. . . . Animal psychology, the psychology of tests and measurement, the various kinds of applied psychology, the orthodox and unorthodox varieties of experimental psychology, theoretical discussions of learning, of intelligence, of measurement, and of the bearing of psychology generally—all are represented, and all go their separate ways. (p. 298)

Heidbreder was quite right; in the era she was writing about, the 1920s, psychology had branched off in many directions and the different branches were becoming autonomous. The diversification that began under the functionalist influence would continue (see chapter 15). Another point is that the initial centers of functionalism, Chicago and New York, were just the sources of the movement; once it got under way the same spirit spread all over the country.

We have to review the major themes that hold the story of psychology together. We recall that the structuralists endorsed most of the thematic issues. They were certainly atomistic, empiricistic, and associationistic. Titchener's stand on mechanism was complicated because he was not looking for physiological data, at least not late in his career, and he was not a reductionist because he insisted on the importance of mental data, so he occupied a sort of middle ground on mechanism. German parallelists are difficult to locate on the mechanism dimension. But the functionalists are hard to locate on all of the dimensions. They were so permissive! Some of them were looking at the details of behavior, but some of them looked at it on a large scale. Some were clearly empiricistic, but others endorsed fixed patterns of development, instincts, and other concepts of a nativistic sort. The mean was right down the middle of the road, and the variance was enormous. Some of them were associationists, but some of them were not. It seems that our major themes do not do us much good when it comes to categorizing the multifaceted functionalists. They were marked by a freedom from predispositions and methodological commitments. They believed, and I do too, that psychologists should relish good data from wherever they find them. They should not be restricted by any preordained methodology or set of philosophical commitments.[5]

The Emancipation of Psychology

THE DEVELOPMENT OF AMERICAN psychology was in large part a matter of emancipation. First, we had to break away from philosophy. We have seen how James's psychology was compromised by all his philosophical commitments, such as to free will. We saw how Wundt's psychology was bogged down by all his philosophical considerations. To become psychologists we had to free ourselves from the confines of philosophy. In discussing Dewey, Durant (1953) paraphrases him: "Philosophy is in flight today before the sciences, one after another of which have run away from her into the productive world." (p. 395) It started with astronomy and physics, then other physical sciences, then the biological ones broke free, and now the "moral sciences" were breaking loose. Philosophy was left holding very little, hardly enough to survive on. The sciences were becoming productive. The fact that philosophy had been stripped of all its sciences was one reason Dewey thought it should turn to practical matters, such as people's relationship to their world. Philosophy too should become productive. At the same time, Dewey argued, theology should be left to the theologians. Otherworldly problems had not done philosophy much good, and they certainly would not do psychology any good either. Dewey was arguing for emancipation.

The Philosophical Problem

Let us recapitulate. If we look back at our ancestors, we find quite a few philosophers. During the 100 years from 1650 to 1750 we find Hobbes, Locke, and Hume who were great ones. In France, Descartes was a great one. Each of them contributed greatly to what would become psychology. During the next 100 years, up to about 1850, the Scots were philosophers, and the Germans were philosophers or poets or both. And while some of them made important contributions to what we are now, certainly none of them could be called a psychologist. Then a little after 1850 there appeared some philosophers, such as Lotze, Brentano, and Stumpf, who began to look like psychologists, but who were basically philosophers. And there was the curious case of Wundt, who was a philosopher, but an unusual one because he did experiments. Just a little later we find Müller, who was not a philosopher, and who also did experiments. But just doing experiments is not the whole story, because James and Bain never did experiments, and yet they were surely psychologists. The key to being a psychologist was evidently not the absence of philosophical interests, nor the presence of experimental interests.

The problem was not that the early psychological thinkers were philosophers, but that their psychology and their philosophy were forced to fit into their preconceived notions. Thus the Scottish common sense school made psychology subservient to their Presbyterian faith. Christians by and large had fashioned psychology so that it would serve their ideological purposes. This really started in the fourth century with St. Augustine, who taught us how to think of the human mind spiritually, as though it were a God-like entity. That concept would not go away, and it dominated our thoughts about ourselves until just recently. The German poets, and to a large extent the German scientists who followed them, were perhaps not very religious but they were nonetheless all wrapped up in issues of spiritualism. They were enthralled with the glory of the human spirit. It was perhaps just a Teutonic variation of the Christian theme.

To get psychology going it was necessary to get it away from the soul's destiny with eternity and to make humankind once again a part of nature. The old Greeks had looked at the human mind naturalistically, but then we forgot how to do that. We had to wait for Darwin to break the life sciences away from the philosophers and from the ancient religious tradition.

The Metaphysical Problem

We also had to give up worrying about the basic realities, the mind stuff and body stuff and Descartes's problem of how they affect each other. The Germans—Fechner, Wundt, and most of their contemporaries—were parallelists. That was not a bad way to look at Descartes's problem, as it turned out. But there was a much better way, which was merely to ignore it. You take bodily events to be data and you take mental events to be data. The functionalists said that we end up with two kinds of data that we know to be related, and we do not have to worry about the relationship between them. Precisely how the mind makes contact with the body, what the mechanism is, is a metaphysical question that we can leave for philosophers to worry about.

The way of psychology is to look at its own phenomena. When we do that we find that there are mental phenomena and body phenomena and that both sorts of things can be described—and that is all there is to it. That was the way of Bain, who wrote incessantly about neural currents in the brain at the same time he was writing about perceptions and feelings. That was the way of James, and of Dewey, too. It was also the way of Newton when he was summarizing his thoughts about gravity. We recall that he had no hypothesis, no mechanical principles, for how it worked. Perhaps all new sciences assert themselves in the same way: They forget about the underlying realities and start to describe their phenomena. As the great medical researcher Hughlings Jackson put it, "The study of the causes of a thing must be preceded by the study of the thing." That says it.

Curiously, and ironically, we became liberated from philosophy when we came to accept two distinctively American philosophies, James's pragmatism and Dewey's instrumentalism. Both dismissed the metaphysical problems; James worried about the realities when he was being a philosopher, of course, but when he was being a psychologist he stuck to the phenomena. He did not have to worry about epistemology, how we know what we know, because he proceeded from the facts that were known. Everyone is so familiar with what an emotion is, he said, that he did not have to define it. Thus, he sidestepped any possible metaphysical or epistemological problem, and could go on directly with emotion.

In general, functionalism provided a convenient, useful, and neutral platform on which American psychology could stand and do what it wanted to do. Functionalism let psychology be psychology without clinging to any of the traditional philosophies. Like psychology itself, functionalism was fresh, new, and different, and it was ideally suited to nourish and guide the new science. It is interesting that James and Dewey are the last philosophers we will meet as we continue our story. Those two philosophers emancipated us from philosophy.

The Physiological Problem

But our emancipation as an independent intellectual enterprise would also seem to require that psychology free itself from physiology. If philosophy was our father, then physiology was our mother, and maturity requires one to stand apart from both parents. It turns out that Mom has had a peculiarly strong hold on us, much stronger than that of the old man. Breaking away from her is a complicated part of the story. Recall that much of the appeal of Bain's psychology was that he talked about physiological matters, brain currents, sensory fixtures, and the motor apparatus. He was adding some machinery to the traditional Scottish associationism. Recall that James liked machinery too; if one were to read James's *Principles* aloud, approximately the first 12 hours of the tale would be about the nervous system. Ladd's famous and popular book was physiological. The mind was in there too, but the book was all about machinery. Only Dewey's nice little book was not grounded on physiological facts and principles. We have to believe that much of the credibility of what Bain, James, and Ladd had to say about purely psychological matters hung on the fact that it could be seen that these gentlemen knew what was really going on in the body and in the brain. It seemed to be a matter of credibility. We are much more inclined to believe what a physiological psychologist says than what, for example, a social psychologist says. It is a credibility bias. It is a bias rather like the tendency of some to believe more readily a declaration if it is stated by a person with a Bostonian accent than if it is stated by someone with a Southern accent.

It is particularly interesting that what the Bostonian (James) was saying was that we should accept mental data just as readily as we accept body data. We saw James as very wise, but we did not accept this wisdom. Over the next several years psychologists would come even more to overvalue the body data and sell short the mental phenomena. In just a few years psychology would be overwhelmed by a very believable and influential Southerner, John Watson from South Carolina. He was a thorough mechanist and a powerful polemicist for the importance of the body and neglect of the mind. So the credibility bias that made James and Ladd so believable was to grow into an obsession, and make even an extremist like Watson seem believable. In other words, it would be many years before psychology could be emancipated from physiology, and our dependence there would get much worse before it was alleviated. Some might say that there is nothing wrong in such a dependence because, after all, physiology and psychology are closely related sciences, so the situation there should be quite different from our historical relationship with philosophy. Okay, Mom, if you say so.

The Founding of American Psychology

IT IS COMMONLY SAID that William James had the first psychology lab in the country. It is true that there was a lab associated with his first psychology course in the Harvard medical school in 1875. Perhaps the students did work with some equipment and collect some data, but nothing much came of it; there were certainly no published reports from James's lab. The first productive lab was the one Hall set up at Hopkins in 1883. It closed when Hall left in 1887, and then did not open again on a permanent basis until Baldwin got there in 1903. The third lab, and the oldest continuously operating one, was at Pennsylvania, started by Cattell in 1887. The next three labs were begun by people who had been students at Hopkins when Hall was there: William Bryan at Indiana in 1888, Joseph Jastrow at Wisconsin in 1888, and Edmund Sanford at Clark in 1889. All three of these men were important in the early days of psychology, running their departments, organizing APA, writing and doing research. Bryan became president of Indiana in 1902, however, and we then lost sight of him.

There were pioneers establishing labs everywhere: H. K. Wolfe at Nebraska in 1889, J. H. Tufts at Michigan in 1890, G. T. W. Patrick at Iowa in 1890, Frank Angell (cousin of James R. Angell) at Cornell in 1891 and at Stanford in 1893, Scripture at Yale in 1892, and E. A. Pace at Catholic University in 1892. At the same time, Baldwin and Cattell were moving around and setting up labs wherever they went—Baldwin at Toronto in 1889 and at Princeton in 1893, and Cattell at Columbia in 1891. Also, E. B. Delabarre was getting going at Brown in 1891, C. A. Strong at Chicago in 1892, and J. R. Angell at Minnesota in 1893. Altogether, there were about two dozen labs by 1893. Thus, all the Ivy League universities and many of the state universities had them by then. There were even a couple of labs established at smaller colleges. The lab at Trenton (New Jersey) State Normal School was started by Lillie Williams in 1892 and the one at Wellesley was started by Mary Calkins in 1891.[6]

The First APA Convention

Note that back in the early 1890s there were not as yet any functionalists, only a few anticipators. Although American psychologists might have been impressed by Ladd and James, the predominant mood at that time was still structuralistic. Sokal (1973) has resurrected the program of papers presented at the first meetings of APA, and that 1892 program tells the story. Eleven papers were presented by nine people (what a cute little convention). Five of the papers dealt with historical matters or with local events, but six papers reported experiments. The experiments were on psychophysics, sensory phenomena, and reaction time. It was such a puny program that fairly detailed abstracts could be given, so it is possible to' see that the problems and the procedures were all very Wundtian and Titchenerian. Presenting papers were Wundt's students (Cattell, Münsterberg, Pace, and Witmer), Hall himself and three Hall students (Jastrow, Sanford, and Bryan), along with Nichols, an experimentally inclined Harvard philosopher. Thus, the meeting was dominated by Wundt's people and by Hall and his people. Titchener discussed a presentation, so we know he was there, but there is a legend that he never attended another APA meeting. It was obviously a meeting of structuralists.

Looking back at that miniconvention a century ago there was one fascinating hint as to where American psychology would go. The prophesy came, curiously, from Münsterberg, the only one there, apart from Titchener, who was not an American. The German newcomer, who had only just gotten here, saw something that was to forecast a new direction for American psychology. He was also announcing where he would be headed. He said,

> the range of problems for psychological laboratories is still too
> limited; it stands too much under the influence of the more or less
> accidental starting-points. It started several decades ago with the
> psycho-physiological studies of sensation, psycho-physical relations
> and reaction-times; one objects, not wholly without justice, that
> it has really advanced scarcely a step, and that these problems can
> be solved just as well in physiological laboratories. Every one
> becomes impatient with a science which, as if in hypnotic fascina-
> tion, stares constantly at only one single problem out of the
> endlessly great circle of its possibilities. (Sokal, 1973, p. 283)

As soon as he ventured over to this country, Münsterberg was clearly ready for functionalism and for applied psychology.

Early Presidents of APA

Here is a list of the first elected presidents of APA.

Year	President
1892	Stanley Hall
1893	George Ladd
1894	William James
1895	James Cattell
1896	George Fullerton
1897	Mark Baldwin
1898	Hugo Münsterberg
1899	John Dewey
1900	Joseph Jastrow
1901	Josiah Royce
1902	Edmund Sanford
1903	William Bryan
1904	William James (again)
1905	Mary Calkins
1906	James Angell

We have met all of these people except for G. S. Fullerton (1867–1925), who was a philosopher with serious experimental interests. He was at Pennsylvania when Cattell got there, and they collaborated on an important methodological paper on the distribution of errors in psychophysics data (Fullerton and Cattell, 1892). It is interesting that only two of these early presidents were students of Wundt, only Cattell and Münsterberg. Thus, the "flood" of Wundtian Ph.D.s were rather poorly represented among these most prestigious psychologists. Interestingly, Cattell and Münsterberg were both rather rebellious characters and could in no sense be regarded as representatives of Wundtian structuralism; they were both busy doing their own practical and applied things. There are, in fact, no structuralists on the list. Indeed, the mightiest structuralist, Titchener, never was elected president, although in terms of importance, scholarship and distinction, he probably deserved to be. Over the next several years there would be more presidents that had come from Wundt's Leipzig laboratory, and there would be several of Titchener's students. There would even be an occasional structuralist or former structuralist. But the main tendency is clear: The great majority of these first presidents were either anticipators of functionalism, outright functionalists, sympathetic to the cause, or de facto functionalists because they did applied work.

We can make some other interesting summary observations of this list. There are about 5 philosophers among the first 15 presidents. James, Royce,

Fullerton, and Dewey were surely philosophers, and Baldwin got his degree in philosophy, and never did any research, so he looks like a philosopher. Ladd, Calkins, and Angell never actually received Ph.D.s. So less than half of the first 15 presidents had Ph.D.s in psychology! So why had everyone dashed off to Germany?

Another observation: The first 7 all came from Ivy League schools; if we add Chicago to the Ivy League, then the score is 12 out of 15. It cannot be due to chance; there must be another factor in there, and it looks like something we might call prestige. On the other hand, Calkins was a woman, was located at a minor college, never had a graduate student to work with, and was never formally granted a Ph.D., and yet she was regarded so highly by her colleagues that she was elected president in 1905. So it is not just a matter of prestige. Like the cosmos after the big bang, psychology settled down pretty quickly and the APA presidency would become rather predictable. It would be a man or woman who had made an important contribution in some area of psychology favored by the functionalistic point of view, an area such as learning, developmental, measurement, or personality.

We saw in chapter 9 that the American university system came into being during the last decades of the 1800s. It was a tough transition, and it took some time to transform the old colleges, which had been mainly training clergymen, into the big, multidisciplined research universities that we have today. The fact that all those psychology labs were established early in the 1890s suggests that the transition was well under way by that time, and that the system was growing fast enough to include all the new psychology departments. That is partly true, but there were still some problems and some aspects of the system that were failing to keep up with new developments. There was still a strong conservative streak in the system. One of the worst problems in the university system in 1890 is that there were no women in it. During the 1890s, however, a few tough and determined women started breaking down the barriers. In the next section we will look at some of these pioneers.

Pioneer Women Psychologists

IN 1890 WOMEN WERE denied admission to graduate schools. Then even if they managed to squeeze in they were denied Ph.D. degrees. Then even if they managed to get a degree they were denied teaching positions at top-level schools. In spite of all these problems, some women did begin to get into the system, and a few earned for themselves permanent places in the story of psychology.

Christine Ladd-Franklin

The first woman to make a mark on psychology was Christine Ladd, who was born in 1847. She was back in time, a contemporary of James. Even as a young girl she was very intellectual and fiercely independent, and when Vassar announced that it would be a new kind of intellectual opportunity for young women, that is where Ladd wanted to go. She was there in 1866, in the second entering class. After graduating from Vassar she taught school for several years, but that was not intellectual enough to satisfy her. But when she went searching for higher education in her field, mathematics, there was nothing available for a woman. She was able to work out a deal at Johns Hopkins, however, whereby she could sit in on certain lectures but would not be officially admitted as a graduate student. Partly on the strength of her great intellect, and partly because of her dogged determination, she got into other classes, did research, and indeed fulfilled all of the degree requirements. They refused to award her the degree, however. She was at Hopkins from 1876 when it opened until 1882, which indicates that she was just a bit ahead of G. Stanley Hall, who arrived at Hopkins with his new degree the next year.

At Hopkins she met and married another mathematician, Fabian Franklin, and changed her name to Christine Ladd–Franklin. He had a long and productive career in New York, but she did not; she taught occasionally but generally it was night classes or community college sort of duty. She did write quite a number of mathematical papers, but she is known mainly for two things, one of which was her theory of color perception. It was an opponent-process theory, like Hering's and unlike Helmholtz's, and she defended it ably and spiritedly in spite of not being able to do any critical research. The last full statement of her theory was published in 1929 when she was 82. She is also known for being a militant feminist who wrote and spoke whenever she could about the plight of women, particularly their academic disadvantage. She hounded Titchener for years about not allowing women into his personal club, the Society of Experimentalists. By all accounts she was the wrong person to have on the other side of an argument; terribly bright, tough, and determined, she usually got her way. And because of her crusading for the cause of women, those who came along later had it just a little easier.

Lillien Martin

Lillien Martin (1851–1943) was born just four years after Ladd-Franklin, and like her she was a schoolteacher for several years. Teachers needed only a couple of years of preparation in those days. In 1880 Martin went back to college, also at Vassar. After Vassar, and more teaching, she decided one day

229

she would go to Germany and undertake the serious study of experimental psychology. The very next day she bought her tickets and resigned her teaching position.

She went to Müller at Göttingen, and would have gotten her degree with him in 1898 except for the rule that women did not get degrees at Göttingen. However, upon returning to the United States, there was a job waiting for her at Stanford. She did some important research on perception and esthetics, and taught at Stanford for several years. In 1915 she became head of the department. This was far and away the highest academic station of any of these pioneering women. Martin had foreshortened her career by getting into it so late in life. She was 48 when she started at Stanford. But she was not done when she retired in 1916; she started a whole new career, traveling, lecturing, going to meetings, and promoting causes. She also studied aging and kept a private practice. She remained a vigorous, active woman until one evening, when she was 91, she suddenly got dizzy and died.[7]

Mary Calkins

Mary Calkins (1863–1930) graduated from Wellesley and then began teaching there. Wellesley had the tradition of hiring young women teachers who had little or no specialized training because at that time there was no place they could get it. In Calkins's case after three years they wanted her to take off a year and prepare to teach psychology. Calkins was very bright and enterprising, and her father and some friends pushed hard for her acceptance at Harvard. While both James and Royce supported her application as a graduate student, the university balked. After considerable negotiation, Harvard finally permitted her to attend some lectures, specifically James's seminar covering the material in his brand new *Principles*. Calkins studied with James in 1890 and also with Sanford at Clark. Clark did not admit women on a regular basis until 1900, so her study with Sanford again had to be worked out on an individual basis. She then returned to Wellesley for a year. Her first three years of teaching had been in classics, of all things, but now she was teaching psychology and setting up a lab. That was her deal with the college. But then something went wrong with the plan; Calkins wanted more, much more.

The next year she was back at Harvard in the same ambiguous situation, this time working with Münsterberg on matters of associative memory. At the conclusion of her study and research in 1895 she took an informal, unofficial examination to defend her dissertation, and by all reports hers was the finest examination performance that the distinguished philosophy department had ever witnessed. But even after a lot more hassle, there was still no degree. She would eventually receive honorary degrees, but never the Harvard Ph.D. She returned to Wellesley, where she directed undergraduate research, taught, and wrote prolifically for 34 years. The majority of her later work was in

Mary Calkins

philosophy, and it was important enough that she was elected president of the American Philosophical Association in 1918.

Calkins never married, she never left her parents' home in Newton, a suburb of Boston, and she cared for them all her life. Her original family was always her only family. Much of her life was spent riding the streetcar from Newton to Wellesley and back. In considering the pioneer women psychologists Scarborough and Furumoto (1987) stress that they were confronted with a choice of family or career. *Or* is the operative word here. No woman managed to do both. Ladd-Franklin had a husband and children, but no academic career. Her office desk was the kitchen table. Martin never married but had a good career at Stanford. Calkins and Washburn, whom we meet in a moment, never married but had outstanding careers at women's colleges. There were some variations on the theme—for example, Milicent Shinn got her degree and her work was well known, but she had no career. She never married either; she took care of the family household.

Margaret Washburn

Margaret Washburn (1871–1939) was another graduate of Vassar. Like Calkins, she did not wander far geographically. She had come from upper Manhattan, which was then out in the country, and Vassar was nearby. At the time of her senior year, Vassar was still doing psychology in the Scottish manner, but she got excited about it anyway. She spent a year studying with Cattell on the west side of upper Manhattan, but Columbia was not admitting women, so at Cattell's urging she went to Cornell to work with the newly arrived Titchener. They got along well, the pompous, Germanic professor and his first student, the bright and eager young woman.

Washburn was the first woman to receive a Ph.D. in psychology (1894), either here or anywhere else—a great accomplishment. When old Ezra

Cornell said anybody could study anything at his university, the "anybody" was taken seriously. Her dissertation, published in Wundt's journal, was certainly Titchenerian. It investigated the interaction of visual and touch sensations. She continued in structuralist directions for some years, and taught for a few years at Wells, Sage, and Cincinnati. Then in 1903 she was invited back to Vassar where she had a long, productive career. She was elected president of APA in 1921, the second woman, after Calkins, to be so honored. In 1931 she was elected to the National Academy of Sciences, the second woman of any discipline to be a member of that distinguished body (the first was Florence Sabin, M.D.).

Washburn's fame hung on two things, administrative work for various psychological groups including APA, and a long series of experimental papers on animal motivation, an area in which she was a pioneer. Her best known and most important book was *The Animal Mind* (1908), which is still a gem. There was also considerable interest in her motor theory of consciousness, *Movement and Mental Imagery* (1916).[8]

Milicent Shinn

Milicent Shinn (1858–1940) was mentioned earlier. She was a magazine editor in the San Francisco area when her niece was born, and she started a baby diary, much as Darwin had done 50 years before. It was an excellent and exciting diary, and when parts of it came to the attention of psychologists at the University of California at Berkeley, they invited her into the graduate psychology program. With the completed diary as her dissertation, she got her degree there in 1898 and published a popular account of her work in 1900. The record is cloudy, but Shinn appears to be the fourth woman to get a degree in psychology; Titchener had trained Alice Hamlin by 1896, and Scripture had trained Theodate Smith at Yale the same year—Smith worked as Hall's research associate for several years. Shinn was definitely the first woman Ph.D. in psychology at Berkeley, and I don't think there were any men ahead of her. The department had just been organized by George Stratton (a student of Wundt's) in 1896. She may have been the first psychology Ph.D. on the west coast.

Shinn was not very important in the overall story of psychology, and Ladd-Franklin was not a psychologist, although her color theory was important and she did join APA. But the other three women, Martin, Calkins, and Washburn, were certainly very important. They are gathered together for discussion here because they are women, but they also show up here and there in our story because at some point they did important work. Each of these early women was also amazingly tough and determined. They had to be to survive in a world so dominated by men, and with the whole system so set against them. And some of them seem to have suffered from the same sort of obsession that had seized Fechner and Ebbinghaus, the strange notion that one could measure mental phenomena. And they went for it.

Summary

WITH THE EMERGENCE of functionalism in the 1890s American psychology began to take on a distinctive shape. It was quite different from the psychology of Wundt, and it did not look much like the psychology of Bain. There was something definitely American about it. It concerned itself with function rather than structure. What does the mind *do*, it asked, what function does it serve, and what is its purpose?

American psychologists were committed to the collection of data rather than to fitting their psychological thoughts into any larger intellectual framework. They had no old philosophical or religious doctrines to defend, and hence they were free to wander in different directions and collect all sorts of new data. James and Dewey had both advanced philosophical doctrines that had the effect of freeing psychology from all of philosophy. Early American psychologists did not need philosophical guidance as they went about collecting their data.

There remained considerable interest in physiological matters and in neural machinery, but the functionalists were not restricted to those interests nor were they restricted by them. That is, there was no proper way to think about the nervous system. And a psychologist could ignore the machinery and ask questions about personality, or about development, or about how animals learn. Functionalism allowed psychologists to look at any psychological phenomenon, invent all sorts of new concepts, and use all sort of methodological tools. Psychology appeared to be freeing itself from its historical ties with both philosophy and physiology.

And the American functionalists were ranging far afield. Whereas Titchener's structuralism had an extremely narrow scope, our psychology was expanding everywhere. It was particularly interested in studying behavior. Animal psychology was going to become increasingly important. And we were free to study children, and how they develop, and personality, and how it varies among us. The testing of intelligence was about to become a major enterprise. Thorndike would take psychology into the schools, and Münsterberg would take it into the courtroom, and into business and industry. There was something very practical about the new American functional psychology. We were not just going to understand how the mind works, we were going to build a better world with this new knowledge.

Notes

1. Ladd is known mainly for his many textbooks; he did little or no research and had few students. Basically he left us one great text, *Elements of Physiological Psychology* (1887). There is at long last a biography of Ladd by Mills (1969).

2. Friedrich A. Trendelenburg (1802–72) spent the last 39 years of his life as a professor at Berlin. He was an Aristotelian, but not an inflexible follower. He believed in science, especially the emerging sciences of evolution and psychology. He had little use for the prevailing German philosophies. His impact was not in his writings, which are mainly Latin translations of Aristotle's logic, but in his lectures. Rostenstock (1964) tells us something about Trendelenburg and links him intellectually to Dewey, which is not unreasonable. But what about all those other young students who listened to his lectures and then went on to give shape to the new psychology?

3. Dewey was by stages psychologist, philosopher, educator, and social activist, and to really understand him properly his life should be looked at from all of these perspectives. Most of what he wrote taken by itself is incomprehensible, at least to me. I find him tough going. *Psychology* (1886) is nice and understandable, but his later works I find not so nice. *Human Nature and Conduct* (1922) is not too bad.

4. Angell lived longer than any of our pioneers, except for Dewey. His publications marking the development of functionalism have already been cited. There is an autobiographical chapter (Angell, 1936) in Murchison *A History of Psychology in Autobiography*, vol. 3, and there is a sensitive obituary by Hunter (1949). See also Carr (1936).

5. When I teach the history of psychology from a Kuhnian perspective, students are obliged to write a paper to either defend or reject the hypothesis that one of the "schools" of psychology, say functionalism, was a Kuhnian revolution against the established structuralist paradigm. Kuhn's own answer would surely be that psychology is at a preparadigmic stage of development; in effect, there never has been an established paradigm in psychology, so there could not have been a revolution. My students and I discuss this problem and decide to liberalize Kuhn's criteria. We arbitrarily suppose that around 1900 there was a paradigm, and that it was Titchener's structuralism. Given that clarification, the student then has to look for a puzzle, a crisis, a rebellion, and an overthrow. There are other symptoms to look for. Did the old establishment loosen the rules as their troubles mounted? If there was an overthrow, was there a change in world view, a new establishment, new textbooks, and new journal editors? Is there a group of young jubilant winners? Is there a band of old, sore-headed losers? If enough such symptoms can be cited, then it looks like a Kuhnian revolution. Otherwise it does not.

It is a nice exercise. Students read Woodworth and Titchener, and they quote Heidbreder, and usually they decide it was not Kuhnian. Structuralism had its problems (e.g., with imageless thought), but that did not threaten Titchener, they say, he just swept it under the rug. He just retreated to even greater orthodoxy. Those who say it was Kuhnian emphasize the persuasive warfare, the change in world view, and the fallout of winners and losers. All agree that the Kuhnian analysis does not apply very comfortably to the case of functionalism.

6. The data on the establishment of laboratories are taken from Garvey (1929). He counted altogether about 100 at that time, but his data came from questionnaires sent to the schools and might not be entirely reliable.

7. A loving biography of Martin was written by deFord (1948). For biographical material on all of the first generation of women psychologists see Scarborough and Furumoto (1987). Some of their women were not very important historically, however. For a more distinguished group, many of whom came along later, see O'Connell and Russo (1983).

8. The first woman to get a Ph.D. anywhere, in any subject, was Helen Magill, who got her degree in classics at Boston University in 1877. But her training was so poor that she felt obliged to follow it up with an *undergraduate* course of study in England. She did it all, that is, she had both a professional life and marriage and family. However, she made a terrible mess of both. Altschuler (1990) tells her sad story.

Chapter Eleven

Psychoanalysis

HAVING GOTTEN EXPERIMENTAL PSYCHOLOGY safely established in the United States, we can now go back across the ocean to note some further developments in Europe. In this chapter we will return to the German-speaking world, and visit France, to see how Freud's psychoanalysis took shape. We will see that while it arose independently of experimental psychology, the two movements shared some common conceptual and cultural influences. And of course psychoanalysis would in time powerfully impact experimental as well as clinical psychology. It would in time impact all Western thought. Let us start at the beginning.

Of Souls and Spirits

THERE HAVE ALWAYS BEEN psychotherapists, although they have not always been designated as such. In different cultures a psychotherapist may be called medicine man, shaman, magician, priest, or doctor. Let us call them magicians. Because of the magician's special powers or skills or training he is able to heal those with disordered spirits. He can often help the infirm and the insane, or those suffering awful fears, or those with disorganized personalities or maladaptive behaviors. Consider as an example a person who has recently become ineffectual at work, has lost track of friends, often says self-derogatory things, never smiles anymore, cannot be consoled, and suffers from a loss of energy. In our culture we would say that this person suffers from depression, and that a doctor should prescribe little pink pills, which often help people with such disorders return to normal. That is pretty good medicine, but it is not by any means the only sort of medicine that has proven to be effective.

In many parts of the world traditional peoples have entertained a simpler theory about what we call depression, and have often been able to cure it. The theory, believed since time immemorial by tribes in Africa, Australia, the

237

Americas, and various parts of Asia, goes like this. When one sleeps, the soul or spirit can leave the body and travel to visit strange lands, join with departed loved ones, and meet new interesting people. That is what dreams are all about. Ordinarily, the spirit returns and enters the body where it belongs before the person wakes up. But suppose the person suddenly awakens before the spirit has gotten back. That is a serious matter. The person might hallucinate because the spirit, unable to return to the body, is forced to continue its travels. Worse, because the person is deprived of the spirit, the person will act, as we would say, depressed. The magician is called for, and for a consideration he performs an elaborate ceremony, gets the victim totally relaxed and in a state much like sleep, and then with his magical powers coaxes the roving spirit to come home to its rightful person. The cure does not always work, but it works often enough that over the years many millions of intelligent people have believed in it.[1]

Some of these people, and millions of others, have believed in a related phenomenon. Just as it is possible for one to lose one's soul inadvertently, so it is possible to gain an extra soul. One can be invaded and taken over by a foreign spirit. There results a dramatic change in personality, the voice may change, and the person's behavior changes. Some call it madness, others call it possession, everyone calls it a very serious problem that requires the services of a magician. Possession takes different forms in different cultures (which is interesting in itself). In Japan there is an ancient religion, Shinto, that is full of lovely symbols and traditions, and also full of spirits. And from Shinto tradition comes the problem of Kinetsune. Kinetsune is the fox, or the spirit of the fox, who is a clever and devious animal. When things are not going well for the fox, it may invade a person or attach its spirit to them. The person is, in effect, possessed by this no-good spirit and so acts strangely, talks oddly and incoherently, and is usually pretty sick. The magician is called in, and the magician carries out an elaborate ceremony in which he talks to Kinetsune, perhaps in a strange language, and urges him to leave on the grounds that the attached victim is too sick to do him any good. Usually the fox can be seduced into going away with the promise of a hearty meal at noon at the fox shrine. Food is prepared (fried tofu is a favorite) and left at the local fox shrine just before noon. And then, sometimes, comes the magic: Right around noon the victim suddenly becomes normal and is lucid again. The fox is gone. To this day there are little fox shrines all over the islands, and people go there, kids and old folks mostly, to leave a little fried tofu or dumpling or something for Kinetsune.

The Exorcists

Note that there is nothing malicious or evil about the fox. A Shinto fox might have faults but being evil is not one of them. Indeed, he is a rather tragic character who is simply looking for a good place to hide, and if he damages his host he only does so accidentally. In the Christian world of 200 years ago it was very different; Christianity is a very serious religion, and one obsessed with good and evil. The possessed Christian was not invaded by a foolish fox, but by the most earnest and evil of all spirits, Satan himself, or a demon, a henchman of the devil. It could take many forms, but always it was a threat to everything holy. A magician would be called in, and he (it was invariably a man) would carry out an elaborate ceremony with much waving of crosses and chanting in Latin. And sometimes the treatment produced a dramatic cure—the Devil was driven out and the patient returned to normal. Some magicians are better than others at what they do, which is not surprising, and those who were good enough to earn a living chasing demons out of Christians were called exorcists. The devil was evidently quite busy 200 years ago, because there were a lot of exorcists in Europe and in this young country.

The greatest of the exorcists, or at least the most noted of them, was Franz Mesmer. He lived in Vienna in the 1770s, when Maria Teresa was empress and when young Wolfgang Mozart was becoming the center of the musical world. Mesmer was an aristocrat because he had married a very wealthy woman, and their home became a focus of social, artistic, and scientific activity in Vienna. Mesmer himself was musical and had learned to play the glass harmonica, an instrument recently invented by Ben Franklin and for which the Mozarts, father and son, had composed music. After Mesmer's time we do not hear much more about the glass harmonica. What Mesmer sought most was not wealth, or music, or an active social life, but scientific recognition for his great discovery. He had discovered **animal magnetism.** All sorts of magicians had used the laying on of hands to effect their cures, but with Mesmer it was different. He would attach large magnets to the body of his patient and then use his hands to direct the magnetic fluid this way and that until the magnetic fluid was properly channeled. During the procedure the patient would typically fall into a sort of trance, something like a sleepwalking state where they could still talk but were not in control; they were **mesmerized.** Upon returning from this magnetic sleep, the patient would sometimes be much better. Miraculous cures were reported; the blind could see again, the lame could walk again, the catatonic could move again. There are no records of what Mesmer actually accomplished, or what his cure rate was, and we do not even know the details of his methods, but we do know that he rapidly became an enormously popular healer, and that he always insisted that the mechanism was not spiritual but scientific. A cure meant that the magnetic fluid had been set straight in its course.

Part of Mesmer's popularity was no doubt due to his mantle of scientific respectability; to the populace he had that appearance, even though the scientific community itself stoutly rejected his beliefs. Science was beginning to make progress, and people could begin to see its benefits. Certainly animal magnetism made as much sense as all that devil-chasing stuff. Forced to leave Vienna because of legal problems, Mesmer moved to Paris in 1778, where he

Franz Mesmer

again gained great fame as a healer. But because the doctors could not accept him as one of them, there was a great fuss, and eventually, in 1784, an international commission was set up to examine his work and his claims. Interestingly, the commission included Ben Franklin, our chemist friend Lavoisier, and a doctor named Joseph Guillotin, who was so insistent on the virtues of that deadly instrument that it was named after him. Interestingly, and with uncanny insight, they concluded that Mesmer's methods did work, not because of anything to do with magnetism but because of his patients' imagination.[2] Mesmer was ruined, because it was the science part of it that mattered to him, and henceforth we do not hear much about him—he went the way of his curious musical instrument. But in his time he was very important, and attracted many followers and a few disciples. One disciple, the Marquis de Puységur, greatly expanded his master's view of magnetism. Mesmer was important because for him psychopathology was not a spiritual matter, not a competition between this and that spirit, but rather a troublesome magnetic phenomenon that he sought to bring within the bounds of science. He thought he had found the key for doing that, and some people believed him. De Puységur moved away from the magnetism idea, however, and toward something much more psychological that we would come to call **hypnotism.** We had gotten safely out of the spirit world.

Hypnotism

DE PUYSÉGUR AT FIRST used props—not magnets strapped to the body or a tub of water to hold the magnetic fluid as Mesmer had done, but a magnetized tree under which villagers gathered. But then as he became more experienced and successful, his method became more nearly just verbal. That would seem to be the final blow to animal magnetism, but there were several schools of thought, and the magnetic school endured for many years. De Puységur called the trance state *lucid sleep* rather than magnetic sleep, and he understood that this state was the critical part of a cure. It was called lucid because patients who were incoherent in their everyday life would sometimes reveal all kinds of information during the sleep session. De Puységur claimed that during the sleep they could show considerable insight into their disorder, could give a reasonable prognosis, and even prescribe their proper treatment. De Puységur was one of the first to see that these cures depended on some sort of psychological mechanism, so it was no longer a matter of exorcism but a matter of influence. He said that cures were due to the will of the hypnotist and the strength of the hypnotist's belief in his effectiveness.[3]

The Struggle for Legitimacy

A number of hypnotic phenomena were discovered around 1800. Post-hypnotic amnesia was one ("When you return to the wakeful state you will not remember anything about this") and post-hypnotic suggestion was another ("When I clap my hands you will find that you have to howl like a wolf"). The importance of *rapport* was discovered; the more the client respects and likes the hypnotist, the more effective the session will be, and over a series of sessions rapport is sure to increase. Early in the 1800s there was an explosion of interest in hypnotism. The word came from the Englishman James Braid in the 1840s (*hypnos* is the Greek word for sleep). Another Englishman, John Elliotson, reported in 1843 that a well-hypnotized subject could survive surgery with little or no experience of pain. The practical significance of this effect was immediately wiped out, however, because during that decade the anesthetic properties of nitrous oxide, chloroform, and ether were all discovered. Dependable anesthesia was one of mankind's greatest discoveries. There were hypnotists everywhere, all over France and Germany. Some were doctors and some were priests, and a couple were professors; there was a professor of hypnotism at Berlin. They had a number of journals in which all the latest techniques and findings were reported.

Around 1850 the bubble burst. The populace had shown excessive enthusiasm for hypnotism, and it had fallen too much into the hands of entertainers and other people of dubious principles. The doctors in particular had become suspicious of anything hypnotic. They had by then become the major magicians of the Western world, and they had their own methods. Even so, a few doctors continued to explore hypnotic methods. One of these was Auguste Liébeault, who had a large, profitable practice in a village near Nancy in eastern France. At that time, the 1870s, not just city folk but villagers too had rejected hypnotism, probably because the doctors had. But Liébeault wanted to explore it, so he offered his patients a deal: He would treat them with customary methods and charge his customary fees, or he would treat them with hypnotic methods and charge no fee. It is reported that in a few years he had an enormous number of patients—and no income. He wrote a book about his methods, and this book attracted the attention of Hippolyte Bernheim, a doctor who in 1879 had become a professor at the new university at Nancy. Bernheim became a convert to Liébeault's ideas. He wrote a monograph in praise of the new ideas in 1884, and followed it up with a textbook on hypnosis in 1886.

The Nancy School and the Power of Suggestion

This was the beginning of what has come to be called the Nancy school of hypnosis. They called it **suggestion.** According to the Nancy people, when a person is hypnotized they become peculiarly sensitive to the hypnotist's suggestions. It is suggested they are analgesic (actually, they are *told* they feel nothing) and behold, they feel no pain. The Nancy school also developed the concept of **autosuggestion.** We recall that de Puységur had emphasized the importance of the magician's belief in what he was doing. The Nancy school emphasized the importance of the patient's belief in the system. What people believe they can do, they can in fact do. Autosuggestion works like this. You are vacationing in Hawaii and have been out in the sun all afternoon. It seems nice, but you come from Seattle, and you have never before encountered so much solar radiation. You have every reason to believe you are due for a serious case of sunburn. Autosuggestion may be able to save you from such an unhappy outcome. You lie down and go through the relaxation procedure. You say to yourself, "My eyelids are so heavy I cannot keep them open." You say, "My hand is so heavy I cannot move my fingers." When your mood is just right, you give yourself a post-hypnotic suggestion. You tell yourself, "When I am having dinner with my new friends this evening, I will unbutton my shirt and announce that while I should be sunburned, I am perfectly normal." You relax for a few minutes, empty your mind, and then pop back into the real world. Then when you are having dinner with your new friends, you test your faith. You open your shirt and at the moment of truth— sometimes—by golly, there is no sunburn!

In the 1800s we all came to believe that the body follows its own physical laws: Too much sunshine causes sunburn. But the Nancy people said that we actually know no more about how the body works than we know about how the mind can affect it. And for whatever reason, whatever the mechanism, the mind can control the body, and prevent a painful case of sunburn. Perhaps peripheral blood supply is cut back, but we do not have to understand the mechanism, we only need to know that believing in the outcome can make it happen.[4]

Jean Martin Charcot

Charcot and the Salpêtrière School

Jean Martin Charcot (1825–93) spent virtually all his working life as a doctor at the Salpêtrière, which was a huge hospital-like institution in Paris. It was at the same time hospital, poorhouse, jail, nursing home for the aged, and asylum for the insane. It housed a marvelous variety of wretched people; Charcot began the task of sorting them out. He started in 1870 with a large number of women who suffered from convulsions. Charcot understood that some of them were epileptic, with organic (neurological) problems, but that some of them were hysterics, with *dynamic* or functional (psychological) problems. A major breakthrough came around 1880 when Charcot began experimenting with hypnosis because he discovered that a hypnotically induced convulsion looked different from the convulsions of a patient with a "pure" case of neurological disorder. For example, the preceding aura might be missing. And hypnotically induced convulsions looked like hysterical ones. He had begun to sort it out. He went on to make similar analyses of many other disorders.

By the time of his early death in 1893, Charcot was without doubt the most distinguished, most respected, and probably the most able doctor in France. His reputation was based in part on the superb lectures he gave, in part on his many research publications, and in part on the great breadth of his expertise. He was France's best-known pathologist, geriatricist, neurologist, and doctor of psychological problems such as hysteria. In the area of hypnosis, Charcot and his many students and followers constituted what we call the Salpêtrière school. In contrast with the Nancy group, they used it primarily for research purposes and for doing diagnosis, rather than for effecting cures. Charcot was largely responsible for making hypnosis legitimate once again.[5]

The Salpêtrière school viewed hypnosis negatively; the mind can produce serious body problems such as paralysis, convulsions, and blindness. The

Nancy people had a positive view; they saw that the mind can take control over many body processes, and overcome problems such as paralysis, convulsions, and blindness. It can be used to extend the control that the mind has over the body.

Historical Significance

Hypnosis is important in the history of psychoanalysis, but not because it was a pillar of Freud's theory; it was actually a minor theoretical contribution, and Freud never relied on it as a clinical method. The historical importance of hypnosis lies in the fact that by the 1880s, the time of Bernheim and Charcot, there had been a great number of people who had worked with it, entertainers, hoaxers, healers, and doctors, who together had discovered a great variety of ways in which mind and body can interact. In particular, there appeared to be deep levels of mental functioning that could produce all sorts of changes in the body. In Descartes's time it had been very simple: There was the machinery and there was the rational mind, and they interacted at the pineal body. By the 1880s there was still the body and still a rational mind (although it had shrunk somewhat in importance), but the main development was the discovery of the vast, complicated, intriguing area in between and the multitude of ways in which mind and body interact. I have talked mostly about hypnosis, but there was also a host of other peculiar new phenomena. One of these phenomena was sleepwalking, which was found to have some curious similarities to hypnosis. All through the 1800s different mental phenomena were being discovered and experimented with. The fascination with such things was shared by doctors, scientists, and the public at large. Clearly, some sort of unifying theory was needed, and it happened that Freud was there at just the right time to supply it. But before we turn to how he put the puzzle together, let us take a quick look at some of the other pieces.

Intellectual Background of Psychoanalysis

Dreams

People have always been interested in dreams. Dreams seem to let us visit another world. They let us commune again with the departed, they let us journey to far away places and accomplish things we cannot possibly achieve in the everyday world. They can also get us involved in frightening and frustrating situations that we would just as soon avoid. Dreams are where the angels and the demons live. Who has not felt relief waking up from a bad dream, or regret waking from a wonderful one? Dreams are inherently interesting.

The 1860s unleashed a spate of research on dreams. In 1861 R. Scherner published *The Life of the Dream*, which was a systematic analysis of dream content and a scheme for classifying dreams in terms of their hidden meaning; the objects in our dreams are only symbols of their true meaning, he said. At the same time in France, A. Maury reported in *Sleep and Dreams* a series of studies done on himself in which he was stimulated with touch, smell, or noise while sleeping, and he concluded that there was some connection between stimulation and the content of the dream. Maury was also perhaps the first to note that if one practices always promptly writing down one's dreams and making drawings of their content, remembering gets easier and more accurate and more dreams are remembered. The ultimate in learning dreaming skills was attained by the Marquis de St. Denis, who described how he had learned to control his dreaming. He could wake up in the middle of the night to record what he had been dreaming, go back to sleep, and sometimes continue the adventure. He could induce particular dreams, or repeat them, or dream about dreaming. These first reports of dream research in the 1860s triggered a lot of interest in the subject.[6]

Ghosts

Ellenberger (1970) says that spiritism, which is communicating with the spirits of the deceased, started in the United States in 1848, but it is hard to believe it could have had such an instant onset. What happened in 1848 was that a family moved into a haunted house, and when there were tapping sounds from the wall a daughter playfully tapped back, and her taps were answered. Somehow, the story goes, the family and the ghost worked out a code that let them communicate. They learned from the ghost that it had once lived in the house, but had been murdered. The story spread like wildfire, and the family became famous. In no time there were mediums everywhere who organized seances and claimed to be able to put survivors in touch with their dearly departed. Countless Ouija boards were sold. Just at the time when the life sciences were beginning to take hold, and physiology looked so promising, and Fechner was building his bridge between the mental and physical worlds, there was a sort of popular rebound, and we found a new world occupied by minds without bodies. It was, and remains, very popular among the populace, which is perhaps not surprising. But learned men got involved too. The Society for Psychical Research was founded in 1882 by a distinguished group of English scholars. William James, for one, was very interested in their proceedings and kept close track of their work.

Sexual Matters

It is sometimes said that Freud focused attention on sexual matters at a time, the Victorian era, when people sought to ignore such things as much as they could. It is sometimes proposed that such things were not discussed, and problems either did not exist or were swept under the rug. It was supposed to be a sort of prudish, sexless society. Sex was certainly not as open a subject as it is today, but it was surely there, and it was discussed. A substantial literature existed on such subjects as abstinence, masturbation, and inversion (homosexuality). By Freud's time there was a huge literature. The doctors generally took the position that these were abnormalities and that they were caused by neurological problems, maybe little lesions somewhere in the brain.

Richard von Krafft-Ebing was a German doctor who subscribed to this mechanistic concept and collected case histories of people with all sorts of unusual sexual behavior. Some cases were genuine oddities and some were merely departures from the accepted norm. In 1886 his collection of cases, and his neurological explanations of them, were published in a book *Psychopathia Sexualis*. This was revised repeatedly, and enlarged as new cases turned up. It was a wildly popular book; reprinted countless times and translated into dozens of languages, it is probably the most widely read medical book ever written. And interestingly, as successive editions appeared they gradually came to look less like the writings of a neurologist and more like those of a clinical psychologist—he underwent some sort of intellectual transformation, just as Freud did during the same period of time.

Shortly we will meet a friend of Freud's, a doctor from Berlin named Wilhelm Fliess, who had some very imaginative theories about sexuality in men and women. For example, he believed he could determine the condition of a person's genitals by looking inside their nose. We are tempted to laugh at that, but it points to something important: Sex is important not only because it is important in its own right, but because it can affect other things in important ways too. Freud did not laugh at Fliess's ideas. And certainly we can see that Europe was by no means totally repressed sexually in the 1880s. There was a lot of discussion of the possibilities. Charcot had asserted that hysteria arose from early sexual problems. Krafft-Ebing and Fliess, among others, were trying to dig out the neurological basis of sexual disorders. There were many theories, many ideas, many phenomena for Freud to think about.

The Unconscious

The concept of the unconscious was also by no means a new idea with Freud; it had been a part of German philosophy and the German intellectual scene for a long time. Whyte (1960) traces the idea almost back to antiquity. It had shown up, rather vaguely, in German philosophy with Gottfried Leibnitz around 1700. He supposed that there were ideas that did not make contact with anyone. About a century later the influential philosopher Johann Herbart made it a little more concrete. Herbart said that ideas in memory compete for appearance in consciousness. The stronger one shows up in awareness, and the weaker idea does not. Ah ha, the weaker one is subconscious! It is there, somewhere, even though we are not aware of it. It would seem that most of what is in memory is unconscious because we only see a bit of it at a time. Herbart wanted to quantify these things. He believed that two subconscious ideas might interact, and together reach consciousness.

So the unconscious mind was an old idea. But the hypnotists had greatly expanded the realm of material that could be hidden from view. A person could act out a post-hypnotic suggestion and be totally unable to state why they acted as they did. "Why did you howl like a wolf?" Not one subject in a thousand will say, "Because you clapped your hands." The subject will make up a story like, "I thought I heard a wolf off in the distance." Here it is not just a subthreshold idea, it is a reason, a cause, a purpose, something motivational, that is hidden. If you somehow prevent her from howling like a wolf, she will get emotionally upset. It is something she has to do. And she does not know why; she cannot explain it. So not just content can be submerged, powerful psychic forces can lie below the surface. Freud had that to worry about.

Motivation

German philosophy was always peculiarly lacking in motivational concepts, and so was the experimental psychology that emerged there, as we have seen. Fundamentally, everyone was a structuralist. Wundt *talked* about voluntarism, but he did not do anything about it. The loyal opposition, Lotze, Brentano, and Stumpf, *talked* about dynamic principles, but they too did not do anything about it. Only in the 1900s, when Külpe and his students began doing research on determining tendencies, do we find something that looked motivational in German psychology. But there was a remarkable man who stood out as an exception, and that was the interesting philosopher Friedrich Nietzsche. Nietzsche was a brilliant man who at the young age of 25 was installed as professor of philology at Basle. (Philologists compare different advanced cultures, mainly through an analysis of their literature, art, religion, and so on.) His first book, in 1872, was on philology; he looked at the components of Dionysus and Apollo to be seen in the history of Europe. The Greek god Dionysus reigns today mainly in television beer ads, where everyone is noisy, active, adventuresome, competitive, fun-loving, and successful—power people. Apollo was cool, balanced, intellectual, and unemotional. At the outset Nietzsche was interested in human values. His greatest work was *Thus Spake Zarathustra* (1883), which tells of the prophet Zarathustra who conveys the new truth. Before the new truth can rise, however, the old, worn-out truths must be destroyed; Christianity must go (it is too democratic), democracy must go (it makes all men equal), the intellectuals must go (because we need action). He was calling for a Dionysian world. And the book is Dionysian, powerfully written, full of action and drama; everything is overstated. God is dead, the prophet says. The impact is great, but it is emotional rather than intellectual.

Nietzsche was no longer a philologist. Although he continued for a while to teach at Basle, he had become a disciple of Zarathustra. He had already written a book about emotion, *Human All too Human* (1880). He became increasingly negative, angry, and cut off from the world around him. He wrote about a book a year through the 1880s but they, like their message, had become a little strange. His books were not really books, certainly not narratives or even reasoned expositions, they were collections of aphorisms. They were collections of brilliant, intriguing, provocative footnotes without any text. His writing became so disjointed and disorganized that the motivational parts of it are hard to locate. But the themes are there. We deceive ourselves, he said. We do not let ourselves understand causality, or God, or morality, or rationality. We have hidden motives, he said, motives we do not understand or even recognize. A lot of our motivation is therefore unconscious, so we may expect it to be confused, irrational and primitively emotional. In short, we are Dionysian and not Apollonian. And occasionally he mentions very Freudian-like motivational mechanisms. Thus he said that when the noble savage warrior is confined to a civilized society, he will turn his natural aggressive impulses inward, and that gives us our sense of guilt. Elsewhere he suggested that any instinct that cannot find a vent will turn inward, and that is the source of what we have learned to call the soul. Nietzsche was very widely read, and he provided a lot of motivational odds and ends for Freud to think about.[7]

So we have all the pieces of the puzzle. We have hypnosis, which was a powerful method for doing research and for discovering new mental phenomena. Hypnosis also held some promise, at least in Bernheim's hands, of being useful as a method of therapy. A mass of psychic phenomena had apparently been discovered and needed now to be explained. There was a great deal of interest in sexual behavior, especially those behaviors that were unusual. A handful of people had begun to think about motivational matters. The concept that there were unconscious levels of mental activity was ready to be explored. The old, comfortable, Cartesian dichotomy between mind and body had been replaced by a trichotomy with mind over here, body way over there, and a vast fuzzy area in between. We were ready for Freud to clear things up.

Sigmund Freud

FREUD WAS BORN in Pribor, a small town in Czechoslovakia, in 1856. That year is easy to remember because it was just 100 years after Mozart was born. And the date, for those who like to celebrate famous birthdays, is May 6.

Sigmund Freud

When Sigmund was four his family moved to Vienna and he remained there all his life except for his last year. When the Nazis invaded Austria in 1938 Freud slipped away to London, and he died there in 1939.

Our story of psychology has, up to this point, mentioned no Jews. The reason for that is mainly that in the last century there was a lot of antisemitism in Germany and Austria, and quite a bit of it everywhere else. Jews had therefore been pretty well excluded from the system, and very few could be found in German universities. Münsterberg was a Jew, but he repudiated his heritage, and always thought of himself and presented himself as German. In a politically correct world the fact that Freud was Jewish should not make any difference, and should not even be mentioned. But everyone does mention it as if it were an important fact. Perhaps it is not important. Freud was a nonbeliever, and perhaps it doesn't matter what faith he did not believe in. On the other hand, perhaps there is some connection between the father–son relationship in Jewish tradition and the fact that Freud's major insights occurred shortly after his father died. There is also the connection that a large percentage of psychoanalysts have always been Jewish.

There is another connection, which is that Vienna had been a particularly antisemitic city, but in the 1860s there was a liberal restructuring, which included the University of Vienna opening its doors to Jewish students. Young Freud saw the opportunity and went off to its medical school in 1873. He had been at the top of his class in secondary school, and he also did very well in medical school. The medical students were allowed to take elective courses, and Freud elected to study under Brentano—so he started in learning a little off-beat psychology. Students were also supposed to become engaged in research under the direction of this or that famous medical professor. Early on he worked with Claus, the comparative anatomist, and published his first research in 1877. Then he switched over to work with Ernst Brücke, the neuro-histologist, who we remember was one of those who pledged with

Helmholtz and their friends in Berlin to be mechanists. He continued to work under Brücke as a student for five years and then as a lab assistant another year. Under the militant mechanist Brücke, Freud became very well-indoctrinated in the mechanistic faith, and probably repressed everything that Brentano had taught him.

The Ambitious Young Doctor

It was while Freud was working with Brücke that he met Josef Breuer (1842–1925). By all accounts, Breuer was an extremely nice guy who was well-regarded and well-liked by everyone. He was about 40 while Freud was a lad of 25, but they became quite good friends, and the older man was extremely helpful and supportive. He referred patients to Freud, lent him money, and helped him in many ways. Indirectly and unintentionally Breuer was a major contributor to psychoanalysis, as we will see. Freud got his medical degree in 1881, but hung around the university another year. He took a lowly position at the Vienna General Hospital where he could continue doing research. He got involved in several projects there, and worked in many divisions of the hospital. He worked for a short time in Theodor Meynert's lab. He got interested in a new drug, something called cocaine. Freud was probably the discoverer of its local analgesic effects, and he did some research with it. Stick it on the eye and you can do eye surgery. He wrote a paper stating that it was useful for treating morphine addicts because it substituted for morphine without creating an addiction. Very quickly there were a host of cocaine addicts in Vienna and poor Freud took quite a beating. The young scientist had been a bit too eager to publish. But one had to publish, and it had to be hot stuff in order to make it in the medical sciences. Like now, the academic world and the world of medical research were extremely competitive, and that was the world Freud wanted. He had no intention of being just another family doctor.

Up to this point Freud had surveyed a variety of medical disciplines, but his research was mainly in neurology. That changed dramatically when in the winter of 1885–86 he received a small travel grant (probably because of Meynert's recommendation). He went out west to Paris to work with Charcot. He ingratiated himself to the great man by assuring him he wanted to translate his lectures into German, whereupon Charcot became very helpful and supportive. Immediately upon returning to Vienna he presented a classic paper on a Charcot phenomenon, male hysteria. Hysteria had classically been thought of as a disease of women (the word refers to the uterus; initially, the hysteric was a woman whose uterus was supposedly mislocated).

Charcot had been studying men who were filing insurance claims because while they were traveling in these newfangled railroad cars they had suffered trauma from being jostled about. The trouble did not arise immediately; it appeared later. Claimants would argue that because of the accident they subsequently lost all feeling in the right hand, and now they could not work. Charcot had found that in hypnosis a subject told he cannot feel anything in one hand loses sensitivity right up to the wrist, and the analgesia runs right around the wrist. He called it *glove analgesia.* But Charcot the neurologist knew that the nerves to the hand run up and down, and not around in neat circles. In the case of real neurological damage, the analgesia runs in up-and-down patterns. The insurance claimant who has glove analgesia rather than the up-and-down variety must be a hysteric. Interestingly, it was often seen in men, indicating that hysteria was not just a disease of women. Did Charcot affect Freud? Apparently so: He named his first son Jean Martin! He referred to him once as always stimulating, instructive, and splendid.

Freud was transformed: He was no longer a Brückean mechanist, he was impelled to move over to some unknown territory, some new kind of psychology. It would not be a quick or easy transition. Indeed, it would take about 10 years and extraordinary effort on his part, but Freud would become a totally new kind of doctor.

Upon returning to Vienna from Paris, Freud settled down. He got married, moved into a house (he had been living at the hospital), and started a private practice specializing in nervous diseases. Freud had some concern for building up a remunerative clientele, and he understood that there were a lot more neurotics out there than there were people suffering from organic problems. For similar practical reasons he soon abandoned hydrotherapy, electrotherapy, and dietary cures, and started working with hypnosis. In 1889 he was off for a brief visit to Nancy, and became impressed with Bernheim's ability to help hysterics with hypnosis. Freud was slipping out of neurology.

The Connection with Breuer

Freud was greatly impressed by Breuer's account of his treatment back in 1880 of a very famous young woman, Anna O. Anna's father was slowly dying, and she attended him during these difficult times. But before he died Anna herself became totally disabled by a variety of hysterical problems. Her vision failed, her arms and legs became bent into useless distorted positions, she became unable to speak intelligibly, and she got to the point where she would not eat. And she kept getting worse. It is not clear how Breuer even kept her alive, but he did; he committed a tremendous amount of time to her treatment.

Anna would cycle spontaneously back and forth between normal consciousness and something like hypnotic sleep. One hot summer afternoon she wanted something to drink, but when Breuer brought her a glass of water, she appeared to find it disgusting, and would not drink. She then lapsed into her hypnotic state, in which Breuer could communicate with her, and when he talked about water she acted out an emotional incident from her past. She had once seen a dog, an ugly, dirty dog, lapping water out of a glass. She described it very emotionally. Then when she bounced back into her normal state, Breuer offered her a glass of water again, and this time she drank it eagerly. Breuer saw that if an emotional situation was remembered and acted out in a hypnotic state, that could reduce some sort of hidden emotional block. The block was unknown to the patient herself and could only be discovered in the hypnotic state. The emotional block also expressed itself in apparently inexplicable weird behaviors. But the expression of feeling under hypnosis apparently drained the emotional content of the original traumatic incident from memory, and enabled the patient to remember it unemotionally. Over the next year Breuer dug out, one by one, all Anna's symptoms and was able to relate them all to incidents that occurred while she was caring for her dying father. Anna was cured from her life-threatening problems, and indeed went on to be a very successful woman. The bottom line is that Breuer had discovered that the expression of emotion under hypnosis can reduce the emotion that lies below the surface, which is invisible to the client but which gives the client great distress in terms of hysterical symptoms. He called it the *talking cure*. Freud began calling it by the old Greek word **catharsis.**

It is curious that this case, really the first psychoanalytic treatment, involved nothing sexual. Anna O.'s symptom-causing emotional traumas involved fear and guilt linked to events that occurred when she was caring for her father. In seeking to apply similar treatment to a few of his own hysteric patients, Freud gradually discovered that the method did not matter. Sometimes hypnosis was helpful, but sometimes he could find the source of trouble just by questioning the patient: "What were the circumstances, what had happened, when did you first experience this symptom?" What did matter was the catharsis, reliving the traumatic emotion. He and Breuer wrote a short paper on hysteria in 1893, and then they went their separate ways. Breuer was, however, persuaded to collaborate on a book *Studies of Hysteria* (1895), which was obviously written by Freud, and which discussed Anna at length. Two unanswered questions intrigued him. One was why the strength and persistence of the symptom were so wholly out of proportion to the seriousness of the precipitating incident, as if the person had been permanently changed by it. The second puzzle was why the patient could not recall the precipitating incident on their own without the therapist's coaxing. It was as if the incident had been *repressed*, or somehow swept from consciousness. That was the beginning.

Freud's Transformation

To this point, Freud had been active professionally as a neurologist. He had written a good deal about cerebral palsy, paralysis, anatomical matters, and had made some comments on Charcot's work. He had also, as promised, translated Charcot's lectures, as well as Bernheim's major book on suggestion. But he was basically a neurologist. In 1895 he wrote a monograph, tentatively titled *The Project*, on psychological phenomena as seen from the neurologist's point of view. In the spirit of Brücke, it was thoroughly mechanistic. If you stimulate a neuron it will regain equilibrium by discharging, if it can. If it cannot immediately discharge, then a tension will be set up—that sort of thing. But the *Project* was never published. Apparently Freud set it aside because he had begun a great intellectual transition that would take him out of neurology and into psychology. At one point Freud said that the transition began with a silly dream about a woman he called Irma who had a bloody nose. From that dream one summer day in 1895 he began to see the importance of symbols in dreams, and how the symbols prevent the dreamer from seeing what the dream is really about. He began to see the great importance of sex in motivating dreams. Freud brooded about these things, and when his father died the next year, he brooded all the more, because he and his father had not had a good relationship. We know about his brooding because he wrote many passionate letters in which he confided in his one close friend Wilhelm Fliess (1858–1928), the Berlin docter he had met in 1887. Fortunately Fliess kept his letters, and luckily they still exist. They tell about Freud's attempts to analyze his own dreams and his own minor neurotic hang-ups. Freud struggled bitterly with himself for about four years.

Freud was done with his struggle and described the resolution right at the turn of the century (the book was out by November 1899, but it was dated 1900, which is a deception publishers still practice because it makes a book look more up to date). We find Freud's resolution of the conflict, and the new Freud himself, in *Die Traumdeutung* (1900). The book we call *The Interpretation of Dreams* has all the major themes. It is full of sex and violence. Mighty battles go on between conscious and unconscious forces. Unpleasant thoughts and impulses are repressed, only to pop up repeatedly in disguised form in dreams. Nothing is ever quite what it seems, first because everyday objects become translated into symbols, and second because the reasons, purposes and causes of them are hidden. The interpretation of dreams can bring them out of hiding. Freud revealed a lot about his own dreams, and hence much about himself. He always regarded the book as the most important single statement of psychoanalytic principles, and indeed it is. The movement was under way.

Psychoanalysis

Freud was at his best when writing popular works, and *The Psychopathology of Everyday Life* (1901) remains a masterpiece. All behavior has a cause, he said, even trivial and silly behaviors such as dreams, slips of the tongue, and forgetting things. You forgot a guy's name? Of course, you owe him money. You forgot to mail that letter for your wife? Of course, you do not want to be your wife's servant. You say you forgot your dental appointment? You said one thing when you meant to say just the opposite? So it seems, but in reality the slip of the tongue reveals the unconscious desire to have it the other way. You have deceived yourself once again. Dreams are further obvious cases of self-deception.

The Psychopathology of Everyday Life suggests that there is no sharp line to be drawn between you, me, and other normal folks and the people who are crazy, because the same mechanisms are at work in us all. It suggests, too, that our psychological life is deterministic. If the odds and ends, the mental debris, have motivational causes, then all mental events have motivational causes. There is no error variance; everything has a psychological cause. We can see here evidence of Brücke's training, and Freud's early mechanistic background, but we can also see that during his great transition he learned to translate the sort of mechanical causation that characterized his early work into something quite new and powerful, something we can call psychological determinism. The mechanical kind was familiar, but the psychological kind was new. Locke and Hume had perhaps glimpsed such a thing, but after his struggles Freud saw it clearly. All psychological events have causes, and if the cause of a particular event is not available to consciousness, then we can probe the unconscious and find it.

Freud was now working furiously; his *Three Essays on the Theory of Sexuality* appeared in 1905. Sex and sexual disorders are hard to get organized and start talking about, but Freud does it masterfully in the first essay. He begins by defining the sex "object" as the *person* that is sexually attractive, and the sexual "aim" as the *behavior* through which the sexual instinct tends to be expressed. Then he refers to the different objects and aims that clinicians find in their clients. Society is judgmental about such things, but Freud is not. He had a neutral platform from which he could discuss the different possibilities. He could talk about same-sex objects and aims, for example, what same-sex couples do when they get in bed. This framework also makes it easy in the second essay to talk about infantile sexuality, and the stages it goes through during development. The third essay discusses briefly how everything gets reorganized at the time of puberty. For example, foreplay is a sort of recapitulation of earlier stages of development, so that kissing takes us back to the baby oral stage. *Three essays* was repeatedly revised and added to. Thus, in 1915 we learn about penis envy, and in 1920 there was a discussion of the all-important Oedipus Complex, although that had actually been part of the system from the beginning.

Freud never stopped adjusting and modifying the theory, mostly making it more complicated. Some of these developments were made when he was getting on in years. The concept of *thanatos*, the death instinct, was developed in 1920, when he was 64. The modern interpretation of the id, ego, and superego came along in 1923, and he worked out a new theory of anxiety in 1926 when he was 70. But although important parts of the theory would come along much later, and the theory would continue to mature, the basic shape of things was pretty clear by 1905. And by then Freud's transformation was certainly complete; he was no longer a neurologist but a psychoanalyst.[8]

The Therapy, the Theory, and the Profession

PSYCHOANALYSIS IS NOT a single thing, it is at least three different things, and probably more than three. It is a therapeutic method, a way to help troubled people; it is a theory, a conception of how the human mind works; it is a profession, a body of specially trained people with similar backgrounds who think alike on certain issues. Let us look at these different faces of it.

Psychoanalytic Treatment

Freud may have dabbled briefly with other approaches with his earliest patients, but he was so impressed with Charcot that he quickly settled on hypnosis as the preferred method. It not only promised to effect some cures, it more importantly promised to provide him with scientific data on how the mind worked. At that time he was somewhat obsessed with the question of the etiology of hysteria—where it came from. And hypnosis seemed to be a promising way to get at that question. Breuer's success with young Anna was surely remarkable. But many people were not hypnotizable, and the ones who were might be faking. Some hypnotized people may be so incredibly suggestible that they will report what they think their therapist wants them to report.[9]

The most important reason Freud soon abandoned hypnosis was that he had discovered a new method, which he called *free association*. Patients were encouraged to ramble, to follow their own chain of associations, and to relate whatever came to mind no matter how silly or trivial or vulgar it seemed to be. If a patient bogs down, then that is important because it suggests resistance, barriers set up by the unconscious. The analyst's task here is to notice resistance, repeated themes, curious connections, and to direct the patient in profitable directions. Judging from his case histories, Freud would come in from time to time with questions like, "What do you think that meant?" "Where was your father at that time?" and "When had you felt like that before?"

The free associations of the patient were clearly not exactly free. As far as we can tell from his reports, Freud was always gently pushing the patient in the right direction. The trouble with any methodology is that in time one becomes a slave to it. The method gradually evolves so that it yields the results one expects. Once one's expectations are confirmed, one comes to value the method and be reluctant to change it. One becomes a slave. Freud stuck by his free-association method faithfully. He believed in the sexual source of neurosis, and that is what he always found. On the other hand, Freud always maintained that his observations were continually forcing him to reinterpret events and modify his hypotheses in exactly the way that a chemist or a botanist or anyone else learns from their observations. He thought of it as an empirical enterprise, a scientific adventure. It is not our place here to judge whether the associative method of psychoanalysis is an acceptable way to dig up facts or whether it illuminates the unconscious. Certainly it did prove to be a fruitful source of hypotheses. Is it an effective tool of therapy; does it work? No, according to many skeptics. According to Eysenck (1952), two-thirds of psychoanalytic patients are benefited, but then two-thirds of disturbed people lose their symptoms spontaneously over the same period of time. See also Eysenck and Wilson (1973).

Psychoanalytic Theory

Psychoanalysis is a theory, as well as a method, and there can be no question that it is a glorious theory. Yes, it is hard to test, but perhaps that is why it lives on. Yes, it is complicated, but it is so rich and powerful. Yes, some of it, such as infantile sexuality, looks shocking and unreasonable, but it makes us stop and think. Certainly it destroys the traditional view of rational, free-willed man, but perhaps that is one of the things we should stop and think about. And yes, it has been somewhat overextended to touch religion and art and literature and all sorts of cultural realms, but what an impact it has had. It is a glorious theory. I personally am saddened that in the last two or three decades psychologists and everyone else have begun to ignore it; before that, everyone was reading Freud and thinking about such things.

Freud liked to portray himself as a solitary fighter for the cause, rejected and despised by his peers, his ideas ridiculed, his theories ignored. Nonsense. Certainly from the time of *The Interpretation of Dreams* he was winning increasing fame and distinction. In 1900, at the age of 44, he was well on his way to tremendous fame and distinction. Not everyone agreed with his theories, to be sure, but everyone knew who he was. In 1909 Clark University was celebrating its 20th birthday, and for the big event Hall invited Freud over to give a lecture series. Hall evidently felt that Freud was the most important and interesting psychologist around. He came over, along with Carl Jung and Sandor Ferenczi, gave his lectures and enjoyed his visit. It was just one of many such honors he received. Gradually, imperceptibly, psychoanalysis began to catch on in this country. By around 1940 it had come to provide the basic set of concepts for clinical psychology and for personality theory. Indeed, it was just about the only theory of personality, and personality problems, that we had. Psychoanalysis swept away alternative views and became the cornerstone of that part of psychology.

The theory, to simplify it a little, is that a person has desires and wishes that are sometimes totally unrealistic. Thus, the infant boy simply cannot make love to his mother, as he desires to do. So he ends up with the **Oedipus** problem. This whole episode in his life is so terrible to think about that it becomes repressed. But the pressure that is built up will be expressed in dreams and in other behaviors. Defenses have to be continually shored up, and in the process neurosis may occur. The situation for young girls is similar: They desire love with the father, and because that is unacceptable, it gets wiped out of consciousness. But this repressed material exerts pressure on the psyche and so symptoms appear. Symptoms can arise from other sources that are not incestual (like Anna O.), but Freud was not very interested in them. And that is the theory. But what captured everyone's imagination was the discrepancy between what people think and what they do. The thinking was nothing because the doing comes from hidden forces and not from the thinking. All of a sudden people could be seen as irrational, emotive, and driven by unseen sorts of motivation. It was a major blow to the rationalism that had dominated Western thought for centuries.

Freud began to feel that psychoanalysis had established itself as the only viable way to treat hysteria and other neurotic problems. And perhaps that is why he moved on to extend his ideas to the world at large. In 1909 he gave us a fascinating view of how psychoanalysis could be applied to the world of art. In 1912 a new journal, *Imago*, was started to handle such cultural analyses. In 1913 he wrote *Totem and Taboo*, which had to do with society's morality. He turned his guns on religion with *Future of an Illusion* (1927). He was conquering the world with his ideas.

One further observation on psychoanalytic theory: Back in 1896, before he had gotten seriously into dreams, Freud noted that behind every neurosis there seemed to be an emotional trauma, often sexual in nature. In analysis his patients would tell him of childhood abuse. He proposed what he called the **seduction theory** (a poor word, since it was generally more like rape than seduction). He went on record suggesting that perhaps all neurosis has its source in such traumatic incidents. Then in 1897 Freud began analyzing his own dreams and he soon encountered a dilemma. The dream appeared to have a positive character, its source seemed to be an unconscious wish; the wish is then expressed in a disguised form. But while the dream has a positive orientation, the neurotic symptom appears to be negative, defensive. To get everything lined up properly, he decided to abandon the seduction theory. He told Fliess of this in September. Henceforth the stories of abuse he heard from his clients would be seen in a new light. Such stories were wishes too, fantasies. It was the Oedipal situation again, and more evidence for it. That September was a critical time for the theory, and we will get back to it shortly.

Psychoanalysis as a Profession

Psychoanalysis is a profession, as well as a theory and a methodology. Freud himself was initially intrigued by the possibility of lay analysts, practitioners who were not M.D.s. But they do not do that anymore. To be a psychoanalyst one has to be first an M.D. and second accredited by one of the several psychiatric institutes. Accreditation requires going through analysis, which can be a long, tedious business. Having gotten there makes one pretty proud; it puts one in a special, select group. It also ensures a degree of uniformity of thought. Just as much of the training of lawyers is to get them all thinking and talking like lawyers, so it is with analysts. One can bicker over details, and their journals are full of that, but one cannot depart very much from the party line. Most of the body of beliefs is solidly set. One can alter one part of the theory (such as stressing ego functions) but only by maintaining the orthodoxy elsewhere. It is interesting that at one point Freud (1940) said that psychoanalysis should properly belong to psychologists because they would do research on it and it would be able to evolve. The doctors will entomb it, he said.

Freud was the first, and he had analyzed himself. Second was a woman named Emma Eckstein, a patient made famous as Irma with the bloody nose in Freud's 1895 dream that started it all. She was not really trained as an analyst, but she started doing it around 1897 (she was one of those who made Freud enthusiastic about the concept of lay analysts). Rudolph Reitler is supposed to be next, around 1902, but then the record becomes cloudy.

Freud took seriously the task of promoting the cause. In 1902 he started his famous Wednesday Evening Meetings. Alfred Adler had just arrived in Vienna, and soon became one of Freud's favorites. Wilhelm Stekel, Max Mahana, and Reitler were the other charter members. This era has been described in some detail by Gay (1988); he says that while the Wednesday evening group started in jovially, there were soon too many members, they were there for the wrong reasons, and they had gotten to know each other too well. To get things straightened out, they reconstituted themselves as the Vienna Psychoanalytic Institute in 1908. Important members, such as Otto Rank, had joined the group by then. They also organized the First International Congress of Psychoanalysts in 1908.

Freud had considerable talent in getting together with friends, and getting them organized, but he was not so good at hanging on to his friends. Many of the people he most liked and respected and owed the most to he sooner or later parted company with unhappily. We have seen that he broke off from Breuer around 1894. He abandoned his dearest friend Fliess in 1902. He had a falling out with Adler in 1911 and with Jung in 1912. In time he broke with Rank and even Ferenczi, with whom he had been close for many years. In some instances the cause of the breakdown seems to have been that the other party did not like some feature, usually a sexual feature, of Freud's theory. Others moved off as a matter of course to establish institutes elsewhere, while maintaining close relationships with the master. The close friends, the orthodox ones, included Max Eitingen and Karl Abraham in Berlin, Sandor Ferenczi in Budapest, and Ernest Jones who went to Toronto, then to New York (where he established the American Psychoanalytic Association with about four members), and then back to London. Interestingly, these men were all within a couple of years of the same age, 30-ish, and all in contact with Freud in Vienna at the same time, between 1907 and 1908. This handful of men were, in effect, the second generation of analysts who got the profession going on a worldwide scale.

Carl Jung was also 30-ish when he met Freud in 1907. He was at the famous Burghölzli hospital in Zurich, Switzerland, working under Bleuler, who was a man Freud's age who had studied under Charcot. Jung's work fit in nicely with Freud's, and at first the two men got along very well. Indeed, Jung occupied a special position in Freud's heart and mind. According to Gay (1988), Freud had a sort of neurotic fear of dying young, and had his eye out for a worthy successor. Jung was it; Freud may have wanted him to inherit it all. One thing that was good about Jung was that he was a Christian. It turns out that everybody in Freud's entire operation (except for Jones and Jung) was Jewish. Freud was concerned that if the movement was to be truly worldwide it should not look so kosher. Jung was it. Alas, although Freud knew all about ambition and ingratiation and using people, he did not seem to understand Jung's ambition. Jung had no intention of being the number two Freudian, he was going to be the number one Jungian. And he was on his way up. We will encounter both Jung and Adler again later in the story.

Anna Freud was a devoted daughter who became a dedicated disciple of the dogma and protector of the profession. She was herself a distinguished analyst (she had been analyzed by her father, which may be a unique situation). She published a lot but is perhaps best known for her work on child psychiatry and on ego defenses (A. Freud, 1936). Anna continued to live in the house in London after her father died. And from there she was active in many worldwide affairs of the association. She kept his things, his personal library, and a lot of his papers and letters. She authorized and sometimes supervised the publication and reprinting of his works. The home became the Freud Archives; it is now the Freud Museum. Anna had also eventually gotten her father's letters to Fliess. She edited them and in 1954 published those she said were of historical interest.

Around 1980, when Anna was about 85 but still very much in charge of things, a young psychiatrist from Canada named Jeffrey Masson appeared. He had risen very suddenly in the international psychiatric arena. He was an energetic man who got involved in many plans to reprint and revise things. For example, he wanted to do the complete letters to Fliess. He was hired as the director of the archives. He was on his way to a distinguished scholarly career.

Masson discovered many treasures among Freud's collected materials, such as notes he had made in books. But he found a letter Freud had written to Fliess dated December 22, 1897, describing a client he was treating, who he *knew* from medical records had been raped by her father when she was two. His letter showed compassion and included a line from Goethe: "Poor child, what have they done to you?" This was only a couple of months after he had decided to take back his seduction theory, so it presented some interesting questions. Why had Freud not reverted back to his earlier theory? He had abundant evidence of child sexual abuse if he cared to look at it. Was it because he liked the new Oedipal interpretation better, even in the face of contrary evidence? Was it because Freud characteristically attached more faith in the internal consistency of the theory than in its external validation? And why had Anna not included it in her collection of letters? It surely looked like it was of historical interest. Did she exclude it because it might upset the theoretical foundation of the profession? Was it because it would make her father, or her, or the whole profession look bad? Anna's response when confronted with these questions was to have Masson fired as the director. He is now essentially out of the profession. He is no longer one of the magicians.[10]

After Freud

WE HAVE SEEN that psychoanalysis took shape between 1895 and 1905, and that while Freud continued for many years to adjust the theory and to expand it into the arts and other areas, the main lines of the theory were in place by 1905. In just a few more years the administrative structure of the institutes, and the journals, and so on, was also in place. The spoils went to the faithful, of course, and Freud was unforgiving to those who dissented from the faith. By 1912 or so psychoanalysis had become an orthodoxy as well as a profession. It seems unfortunate that so many of the bright young believers that had so impressed Freud in the beginning either would be forced out or would pull away on their own. But in some cases, as with Jung, these other people had their own ambitions.

Carl Jung

Carl Jung (1875–1961) got his medical degree in Switzerland in 1901, just after *The Interpretation of Dreams* had come out. He had worked with Pierre Janet in Paris, and had used some of Freud's techniques, such as free association, with his own clients. He and Freud got along well at first, even though they had some very different conceptions. Freud saw conflict between id and superego, with the ego somewhere in between playing the part of the peacemaker. Jung, on the other hand, saw conflict everywhere. The personality is built of many components that are usually in conflict. Maturity, or self-actualization, is when the individual is at peace, and that is accomplished by letting the different factions of the personality express themselves more or less freely. Freud saw dreams as disguised wishes; they

Carl Gustav Jung

reveal the id's impulses sneaking up toward consciousness. Jung saw dreams as symbolic expression of whatever components of the personality were not being expressed in everyday life. Freud saw the therapist's task as making the individual's subconscious fears and wishes known to them. Jung saw it as putting the individual in touch with all the other facets of their personality that were not being expressed.

There are enough parallels here that we should not be surprised that the two men were at first intrigued by each other's ideas. But Freud would not yield and Jung would not bend. Freud believed that a lot of repressed material snuck into awareness through symbols, but Jung was the expert on symbols, and he saw them everywhere, and they were not just sexual, they could represent religious or any other kind of value. Moreover, Jung understood them to be more or less universal; peoples from all over the world share common symbols. That is possible because while each individual has his or her own private subconscious, we all share a common *collective unconscious.*

Superficially, to the uninformed, Freud's ideas look pretty strange. It takes many hours of analytic therapy to convince anyone that, all appearances aside, he or she has an unresolved Oedipal problem. But if Freud sometimes looks like he is in left field, then Jung seems to be somewhere over the fence. A psychologist I know used to have lunch fairly regularly with one of his students. One day the young woman, who was not entirely comfortable with the situation, asked her Jungian therapist about it. He is an older guy, she said, plus he was her professor, and her mother would not approve at all. The therapist told her that she should work on her day-to-day problems, and he would work on her serious problems. And what has she dreamed lately?

Jung was an extremely intelligent and creative person. After a leisurely visit with him, Henry Murray said he was the most learned and intelligent person he had ever met. He gave us a number of concepts that have become assimilated into psychiatry and psychology. There are many Jungian analysts today actively in practice. In terms of numbers of followers or intellectual impact, however, Jung never rivaled Freud. No one has rivaled Freud.

Alfred Adler

Alfred Adler (1870–1937) was also, briefly, one of Freud's favorite associates, but he refused to accept Freud's monolithic view, and in 1911 they parted company. Like Jung, Adler wanted more flexibility in his model of personality, more parts and more complexity, than Freud would allow. That was the focus of their disharmony. For Freud a pathology usually turned out to arise from Oedipal problems, but Adler wanted a variety of mechanisms.

Early on, certainly by 1907, Adler was stressing the notion of inferiority. The infant feels disadvantaged because it is small, unskilled, and without power. It cannot compete with its parent or its older siblings. Often there is some physical inferiority, poor health, poor eyesight, or something of that sort. Often too, the child will *imagine* some inferiority. It will think of itself as handicapped or disadvantaged even when there is little basis for such thoughts. Whatever the source of the particular sense of inferiority, it is nearly universal among us, and it sets the stage for a very basic human motivation, *compensation*. If I am no good at this, then I will learn to excel at that. If I cannot take what I want, then I will learn how to have it given to me. Compensatory motivation explains much of our behavior, Adler insisted.

At some point in life, hopefully, the person may feel self-confidence, and then there emerges a second, offsetting or counterbalancing human motivation, *social interest*. I can serve, help, and love another person. Thus, while Freud had only one basic kind of motivation (because other kinds, such as hunger, can be freely expressed), Adler had two basic motives. We all get cast in roles, too—being a boy, being the eldest child, or being an only child. We are not stuck with such roles, Adler said, but it is easy to fall into them and let them control our lives.

Adler's followers like to note that he could often effect seeming miracles of rapid therapy. Freud wanted to see you for a year or two; Adler might be able to help you in 10 minutes. Sometimes he would invite you to describe some clearly remembered incident from your childhood. What he was looking for was not a traumatic event, but something revealing about an early sense of inferiority, or maybe a glimpse of early social interest. He got such a glimpse with the habitual thief who remembered as a child stealing a gift for his mother on her birthday. Once that was talked out the thief was on the mend. Adler believed that our lives are held together by enduring motivational themes.

In the 1920s Adler visited this country several times, and began writing about his ideas in English. When the Nazi threat arose, he moved to the United States and began to set up institutes of what is called **individual psychology.** Once here he became increasingly interested in working with youngsters, and in the educational process in general. His several books on these topics were widely read. He wrote more for the popular audience than for psychologists. And by this time there was no trace of his earlier life as a Freudian; all those ties had been severed. Among therapists Adler attracted a small band of loyal followers, and some of them can still be found, particularly in New York City. There are two points to be highlighted. One is that at the heart of Adler's system were basic human motives, compensation and social interest. Conceptually, his system enormously expanded on Freud's monolithic concept of whom as youngsters we want to have sex with. Second, the mechanisms of personality were very simple and straightforward. There was no repression, or sublimation, or symbolism. There was no superego, or censor, or death instinct. There was very little magic with this healer.[12]

Summary

WE ALL SUFFER a little when we see someone else suffering. We would like to help but we feel helpless. We therefore call on the gods for help, or else we call on the local magician. We really do not believe in magic, but we know of no good way to handle the suffering, so we call on the magician, and sometimes the magic helps. It is instructive here to see what the different magicians thought it was that they were doing. In olden times some of them were recalling spirits, some of them were chasing away foxes, and some of them were driving off Satan himself. As we get nearer to modern times we find them magnetizing the sufferers.

A little over a century ago we began to get some feeling for what hypnosis was; it appeared to be some sort of heightened suggestability. The hypnotized person might do strange things that make us wonder about human rationality, not to mention the freedom of the will. If you ask the subject why she howled like a wolf, she says something absurd. She really doesn't know. Such phenomena suggest that the parallelists are dead wrong; the mind and the body do not run along parallel tracks, independent of each other. Such phenomena say, too, that the Cartesians are wrong; mind and body do not interact in a simple way. Mind and body are all messed up with each other, and their interactions can be extraordinarily complex. Hysteria, the phenomenon Freud was most interested in, illustrates that a simple fear or guilt can have disastrous effects on the body.

The intellectual background of psychoanalysis included a long tradition of thinking about conflicting ideas and conflicting forces. That would help deal with some of the complexity. There was also a tradition of thinking about an unconscious or subconscious part of the mind, and that would help as well. And contrary to the myth that has grown up around psychoanalysis that Vienna was too "proper" at that time to think about sex, there was a large literature on sexual matters and an abundance of theoretical work on them. These were the pieces of the puzzle that Freud struggled with just before the turn of the century, the puzzle that would show him how neurotic behavior developed. The picture he finally saw was certainly surprising, but it was simple and straightforward. The key was his repudiation of the seduction theory.

Freud said that even as children we have innate sexual desires that are so unrealistic and so frightening that they must be censored and hidden from our view. But this repression has its own price because the repressed impulses are still there in the subconscious and always trying to find expression. We find them expressed symbolically in dreams and in everyday life. In the ensuing war with the id, the ego may be under such stress that it cannot meet the demands of the external world, and then we find neurotic symptoms.

Freud spent the second half of his life confirming the theory with his patients, elaborating it, and explaining it to the world, and extending it through his analysis of art, literature, religion, and society. By the time he was done Freud's ideas had made a very deep and very broad impact on the intellectual world. He also built up a large body of loyal followers, and developed the necessary associations, institutes, and bureaucratic machinery (such as agreements with publishers) to ensure that his work would stand and become an orthodoxy.

Some of his followers did not follow him, however. Some of these defections now do not look very serious, as they involved only small departures from the master's message. But we have seen that Freud was most intolerant of any deviation. Jung's system, which was so much like his own in some ways, was quite intolerable and Jung had to go. He did, and was very successful in building his own band of followers. Adler had started in as one of Freud's first protégés but abandoned it all after a few years. He too attracted many followers. Adler's system ultimately repudiated everything Freudian. It was not sexual impulses that provided the motor for our psychological life, Adler said, it was our sense of inferiority and our need to compensate for it. That complete break with the Freudian model was just what some American therapists wanted to see. But an overwhelming majority of American therapists clung to the Freudian model; for a time psychoanalysis was virtually the only model we had of personality and psychopathology.

Notes

1. I have taken much of this story from Ellenberger's *The Discovery of the Unconscious* (1970). It is an important contribution because it sheds so much light on the origins of dynamic (nonphysiological) psychiatry. But why did he devote chapter 1 to fakirs and shamans and primitive medicine men who were

in no sense scientists, as modern psychiatrists are? There are three possibilities. One is that, being a scholar, he wanted to depict the whole history from the beginning, even though the beginnings were pretty rough and primitive. Another possibility is that, being a modernist, he wanted to show how far we have come: It used to be the spirit world and now it is medicine. It used to be that you lost your spirit, and now it is that you have lost your serotonin. A third possibility is that, being a skeptic, he wanted to show that we had magicians then and we have magicians now.

2. *Imagination* is a technical term, one that had been around for centuries. It appeared in the old literature of Shakespeare, Machiavelli, and Montaigne. The mind can make odd things happen. The mind can affect the body. We do not understand how it is possible, but it happens all the time. We see it every day. The concept deserves its own history.

3. It is a matter of credibility. Part of it is that the hypnotist needs to believe in his system, in what he is doing. The healer has to believe in what he or she is doing. What the patient has to believe in is evidently the power of the therapist. Ellenberger notes that Mesmer was a wealthy man, an aristocrat, and that de Puységur was nobility; he owned the tree around which the villagers gathered. Indeed, he owned the village. When the boss man spoke, they believed, and especially so because these two really believed in what they were doing. So their magic worked. When Freud spoke to his upper-class patients, the ones who could pay his fees, the credibility factor was lost. On top of that, Freud did not believe in the efficacy of hypnosis. So in his hands it was not an effective procedure.

4. The star of the autosuggestion movement was Émile Coué, a retired chemist who took off from Bernheim's work early in this century. Coué urged us to say, "Every day in every way I am getting better and better." The movement is best described by Baudouin (1920).

5. Unfortunately, none of Charcot's work on hypnosis seems to have been translated into English. I have to note here that somewhere after mid-century medical people settled in on a strictly mechanistic view of things. That is largely what made hypnotism fall out of favor. The major trends in medicine were dominated by a few figures, such as the great Claude Bernard and Jean Martin Charcot in France, both of whom were wholehearted mechanists. Charcot could get away with using hypnosis as a diagnostic technique only because he had such a huge reputation as a mechanistic neurologist; he is important in our story because he was on the edge of the mental world, the world of psychological phenomena. In Germany, the dominant style of psychiatry was exemplified by Emil Kraepelin (an early student of Wundt's) and in Vienna the giant was Theodor Meynert (who was the first to talk about Dewey's case of a child sticking a finger in a candle flame, and he had a neurological model for the learning that occurred). Both Kraepelin and Meynert were outspoken mechanists. The doctors maintained a solid front against the unscientific foolishness of hypnosis, and certainly the childish idea that hypnosis could cure a diseased nervous system. They still do.

6. All of this interesting work was cited by Freud (1900), and is discussed by Ellenberger (1970).

7. Nietzsche (1844–1900) was a tragic figure. They had to lock him up the last 11 years of his life. Back when he still had some contact with people, he argued for a Dionysian way of life, but he himself was all intellect and no action. Self-destructive, he put down everything that described his own wonderful self and tried to glorify everything he was not. One of his last books, *The Genealogy of Morals* (1887), is exciting and full of psychological material. There were several philosophers that might have impacted Freud's thinking—Nietzsche, Schopenhauer, Spinoza—but I do not think any of them did. He was not very interested in philosophy. Where did Freud's systematic ideas come from? Freud says repeatedly that they came from his clients, and I think that is probably so. His ideas came from the work he was doing all day long.

8. Any large general library in the Western world will have more index cards on Christ than anybody else. Freud comes in a good second. Probably Marx and Darwin will be way back in third and fourth place. There is an enormous literature on Freud, the man, the source of his ideas, and his theory. There are more books in more languages on Freud than any one person could possibly read. A further problem is that the people who write about Freud don't seem to know how to stop writing. The classic biography by Jones (1953) occupies three volumes. And several books have now been written about the possibility that Jones was too close and too committed to the system to be objective about it. A recent scholarly analysis of the movement rather than the man is Ellenberger (1970), and he goes on for 900 pages. Sulloway (1979) takes a fresh look at Freud, and tries to get behind the myths (e.g., that he was a solitary hero and that his ideas were unprecedented) and that takes 600 pages. Gay (1988) is more up to date, and so has the advantage of more recent scholarship, but he uses 800 pages. Gay also provides an amazingly detailed "bibliographic essay" at the end of his book with thousands of references to Freudian scholars. Fancher (1973) is shorter and fun to read.

Freud was a wonderful writer, and much of his impact on the intellectual world can be attributed to his outstanding writing skills. Moreover, a good writer is easy to translate, and comes across well in the new language. My recommendation is to skip the Freud scholars, forget about where he got his ideas, and just read what he wrote. The beginner might well start with *The Psychopathology of Everyday Life* (1901).

The definitive and "authorized" English source of all Freud's work is the 24-volume *Standard Edition* edited by J. Strachey and others (1953–74). The Government Printing Office has a useful set of abstracts prepared about 1972 by the National Institutes of Mental Health for everything in the *Standard Edition*, with the books abstracted by chapter. Basic Books also has a nice five-volume set of the major short papers. Finally, there are many nicely edited and annotated collections of papers and excerpts from his longer works. A nice collection, because of the valuable notes, is Gay (1989).

9. The Salpêtrière hospital continued to be a great teaching and research facility; Janet was in charge of psychiatric matters after Charcot died in 1893. Just before he died, the value of Charcot's work with hypnotism was called into question by Delboeuf and others. Delboeuf was a Belgian physiologist with many interests. We recall that he was one of the first to check out Fechner's psychophysical methods. He visited Charcot and discovered that his "pure cases" were women who were exhibited again and again, and that these women loved getting away from their dingy wards and out in front of an audience. Charcot had not been selecting easily-hypnotized subjects, he had been selecting actresses! His patients were deceiving him, and he had been unintentionally deceiving everyone else. He was, it seems, more a director than a doctor, because his actresses gave him just what he wanted us to see. Such self-deception could only have happened to a person like Charcot who was so pompous, sure of himself, and set in his ways.

10. Masson wanted to tell his story, so he told it to Janet Malcolm, a writer for *The New Yorker* magazine. She interviewed him for days and presented a long account of his story in a set of articles in the magazine. But Masson was furious because she had not stressed the theoretical importance of his discoveries but had focused instead on his personality. Not only that, his personality had come out not looking too good. One reviewer said that Masson emerged as "a grandiose egotist—mean-spirited, self-serving, . . ." That made him so angry he wrote a book to tell the story his way. Then Malcolm got a book out of it. Then Masson published all the darned letters. And then he got another book out of it. When the dust finally settles, quite likely everybody—Sigmund, Anna, Jeffrey, and Janet—is going to look bad. I did not want to read all those books, so I have cited here his nice little article (Masson, 1984a). It contains a lovely portrait of Anna as a young woman, and the cover shows a picture of Masson that lets everybody judge for themselves at least whether he *looks* arrogant. See Masson (1984b, 1990) and Malcolm (1984).

11. When I teach the history of psychology, some of my students elect to write about whether the Freudian revolution qualifies as a Kuhnian revolution against the prevailing psychological paradigm established by Wundt and Titchener. Usually they say no, it was not a Kuhnian event because psychoanalysis did not arise as a protest against them, and did not come from any crisis in the structuralist camp. The various symptoms of a revolution are also absent. So as revolutionary as it all seems, it was not a revolution.

12. There were a number of important psychoanalysts who came to this country in the 1930s, and some of them broke completely with the Freudian orthodoxy. Karen Horney, for example, developed her own theory that stressed the disturbing effects of social pressures on the individual. Such a view seemed compatible with American psychology in the 1930s, but we have no space to follow up these developments at this point.

Chapter Twelve

Gestalt Psychology

THE GESTALTISTS WERE a small, militant band of psychologists who in their own time constituted the loyal opposition. One might say that they rejected everything that structuralism believed in. They rejected the idea that perceptions should be broken up into little elements of sensation. They rejected the established relationships between mind and body and between sensation and perception, and proposed their own new concepts. They were more nativist than empiricist. And they did not believe in associations as the glue that holds the mind together and makes things meaningful. The gestaltists were obviously going somewhere else. They were so out of step with the rest of experimental psychology that they seemed to have no chance of making any mark on it. Nonetheless, they had a great impact. We will see how that happened.

The Three Musketeers

IN 1910 WUNDT was an old man, 78, but he was still very busy with his horde of students and with revising all his books. He was still very much at the center of experimental psychology. Müller in nearby Göttingen, just off the center, was at the peak of his power and influence. They and their many students scattered around Europe and America were the establishment. So that was the context; against this background comes young Max Wertheimer in 1910 riding a railroad train into Frankfurt, out in western Germany. Max Wertheimer (1880–1943) had grown up in Prague, and had gone to the university there. He did two years of graduate work with Stumpf at Berlin, and then went to Külpe at Würzburg, where he received his degree in 1904. This was just as the imageless thought research was getting going at Würzburg, but Wertheimer played no important part in it. Indeed, in his first few years as a psychologist he did nothing very important as he moved here and there. But when he got off the train in Frankfurt, that was important.

Max Wertheimer

Apparent Movement

There are several versions of the story. According to one version, he was going someplace else and only got off the train to buy a toy, a little stroboscope, to check out an idea. Wertheimer had learned from Stumpf that the structuralists' view of perception was all wrong because they believed that for every perception there had to be something out in the periphery, some sensory quality, that is correlated with it. Perception was nothing but a putting together of sensory elements, so there could be nothing in the perception that did not have its counterpart in the sensory apparatus. Their parallelism required that it be so. But Wertheimer was playing with the stroboscope and thinking about the perception of movement. What about movement, was it an illusion? What about the movies, was that an illusion? In a movie there is one pattern of stimuli and then immediately later another pattern of stimuli, but what you see is movement. There is a failure of correspondence between the sensory and the perceptual. In short, the perception cannot be totally dependent on the sensory material; it must also depend on some other kind of mental processes. That insight marked the beginning of **gestalt psychology.** We have seen that Helmholtz had long before reluctantly concluded that what we see is an apperception, a combination of sensory input and cognitive structures. So Wertheimer's insight was not entirely new. We have also seen, however, that the structuralists were bound and determined to strip away meaning, to look at wahrnehmungs. What Wertheimer had really seen was a way to show that they could not get away with that.

The Frankfurt railroad station story continues. Wertheimer was so excited by his new thoughts that he continued playing with his stroboscope and then went to the university to see if he could start doing research on the perception of motion. Friedrich Schumann (1863–1940) was the new

Wolfgang Köhler

professor at Frankfurt; we recall that Schumann had worked for Müller for several years and had also worked with Stumpf as his laboratory assistant for several years, and Wertheimer had known him there. Schumann was sympathetic with Wertheimer's new enthusiasm, and gave him some lab space and some equipment. Wertheimer got to work at Frankfurt and remained there for six years.

Also recently arrived at Frankfurt were two other young men. One was Wolfgang Köhler (1887–1967), who had studied at Berlin with Stumpf, and did a psycho-acoustic dissertation with him in 1909. Then he went on directly to Frankfurt. The third musketeer was Kurt Koffka (1886–1941), who had gotten his degree with Stumpf in 1908 but then spent a year at Würzburg before heading to Frankfurt. So both Koffka and Köhler were newly there at Frankfurt when Wertheimer showed up, but Wertheimer was slightly older and he knew what he wanted to do, so he took charge. He was the experimenter while Köhler and Koffka were the subjects in the original experiments, the famous experiments that would launch the gestalt movement.

They used a tachistoscope to present briefly an illuminated vertical line, and then an instant later it was programmed to present briefly another vertical line shifted over a little. It turned out to be a quantitative matter of how brightly the lines were lit, their separation, and so on. But settling on a given set of parameters, Wertheimer manipulated the all-important variable, the time interval between the two presentations. He found that if it is too quick, then one sees both lines at once. If it is too slow then one sees this line and then that line, a situation that corresponds with the physical stimulus conditions. But if the interval is just right, then a wonderful new perception emerges: Movement is seen. What was wonderful about the new perception, as Wertheimer had understood at the train station, was that there was nothing in the external world to which the perception of movement corresponds; it

Kurt Koffka

is something that arises from the way in which the observer's head is put together. As Kant had said, we do indeed depend on the external world to gain information about it, but we ourselves also make a vital contribution in terms of how we interpret and organize the information. The gestaltists were going to revive Kant, and even bring him into the laboratory!

They did several variants of the original study, and always got the same sort of results. The appearance of illusory movement was called the **phi phenomenon.** The first publication (Wertheimer, 1912) was offered as a challenge to the structuralist establishment. Wertheimer, Köhler, and Koffka had, if nothing else, galvanized themselves. They knew who they were, and what they believed in. They would continue to work, not so much together as it turned out, but toward the same ends and for the same set of principles. But even though they soon departed Frankfurt and went off in different directions, they would remain close friends, mutual supporters, and defenders of the common faith until the end. Apparently once a gestaltist, always a gestaltist.

Different Routes to the United States

Koffka was the first to leave Frankfurt; he went to Giessen in 1911, and then a number of other destinations before ending up in the United States in 1924. He finally settled at Smith College in 1927. Much of his best work was done there.[1]

Wertheimer left Frankfurt in 1916 when he got the opportunity to go to Berlin. It was a research rather than an academic position, but he had not had an academic appointment at Frankfurt either, only some laboratory space. He did not have a regular academic position until 1929, when Schumann left Frankfurt and he was given the opportunity to replace him. Ley (1990) describes a conversation he once had with Wolfgang Metzger, who had been a student at Berlin and had gotten to know Wertheimer there. Metzger said that Wertheimer's family was wealthy and that he did not need to teach. Metzger said that it was nice to be in a position not to have to depend on a teaching salary, but it was not so nice to have one's work and worth go unrecognized.

When the Nazis came to power in 1933, Germany was no place for an intellectual to be. The German university system, which had dominated the academic world for a century, was virtually wiped out. The country became nothing but a giant military camp. Rather quickly schools, laboratories, journals, everything was gone. And in particular, Jewish intellectuals were quite literally wiped out. Wertheimer was Jewish—he saw what was happening, and he fled. He moved to the New School for Social Research in New York City, which was just being established, and which called itself the University in Exile. It was set up to provide an academic home for scholars like Wertheimer who had been forced to flee their native land. Wertheimer organized its new graduate program in psychology, and then spent the rest of his days there.[2]

Köhler left Frankfurt in 1913 to go to an experimental station on the island of Tenerife, where he did extremely interesting research with animals, which we will mention shortly. Returning to Germany in 1920, he won an appointment at Berlin. Presumably on the strength of the Tenerife work with animals, Köhler succeeded Stumpf as professor at Berlin when Stumpf retired in 1922. Thus, he and Wertheimer were back together at Berlin between 1920 when he arrived and 1929 when Wertheimer left. During the 1920s Berlin was the center of the gestalt world. In 1922 they established their own journal, *Psychologische Forschung*, which ran until 1938 and carried a rich variety of papers as gestalt ideas began to permeate the different areas of psychology. Something like it, called *Psychological Research*, was established in this country after the war. Köhler left Berlin shortly after Wertheimer, in 1934. He came to the United States and in 1935 landed in the safe haven of Swarthmore College near Philadelphia. Notice that while none of the three had moved to a major research university in the United States, certainly nothing comparable to Berlin, they had all obtained decent places at good schools. Köhler had actually visited Harvard and flirted with an appointment there, but he ended up being very comfortable at Swarthmore, and he was able to get a good deal of research done at that remarkable small college.

In short, the three musketeers thrived in their new environment. They had started working together in 1910, and they continued to work in union for the gestalt cause as long as they lived. And while they were able to recruit a number of new believers, they were always the main players in the gestalt movement. Wertheimer was initially the leader, but as time slipped by the leadership of the movement passed over to Köhler. There were several reasons for this transition; one was the depth and breadth of his scholarship, and another was that he outlived the others. In 1959 Köhler was elected president of APA. He was the only gestaltist so honored.[3]

Organizing Principles

PERHAPS THE MOST pointed and central question posed by the gestaltists was this: Why do things look as they do? There are several logical possibilities, most of which can be readily ruled out. (1) It cannot be because things are what they are, because there are too many illusions and distortions. We cannot really trust our senses. (2) It cannot be because, as the empiricists maintain, we learn to compensate for the distortions we encounter, because perception is too immediate, compelling, and universal to depend much on learning. It does not look like learning. (3) It cannot be, as the structuralists argue, that we assemble masses of sensory input, because the phi phenomenon shows that perception is something other than a correlate of sensory input. And so, (4) it must be that things look the way they do because the human mind has organizing principles that enable us to overcome the constraints of what the stimulus situation provides by way of information. Perception is a sort of compromise between the restraining forces (i.e., sensory input) and the organizing forces that are inherent in the human mind.

The Perception of Gestalt

The German word *Gestalt* means something like shape or form or configuration. What we see is not a collection of elements that get put together, what we see is the whole thing, the gestalt. It is not a sorting out of inputs: what we see is the pattern or organization. To understand this principle of organization we need to look at something concrete, like figure 12.1.

Figure 12.1

This configuration is inherently ambiguous; we can see it in various ways. It can be four columns. It can be four rows. Those are easy organizations. So is two fat columns or two fat rows. How about seven diagonals? That does not leap out at the viewer. How about a big square with a little square inside? Or four little squares? Those are not hard to see. But four spots surrounding a fat cross is hard to make out. So is 16 separate spots. Sometimes asymmetrical figures can be seen, such as a square of nine with a border partway around it. Although the pattern is ambiguous, it is always seen as some sort of organization. The reason we usually see squares and lines is that those are what gestaltists call **good figures.** Good figures are easy to organize, they take less cognitive or perceptual work, and they are the natural outcome of perception most of the time. If the observer tries to perceive a "not good" figure, then organizing forces will usually prevail so that squares or lines or something else "good" will be seen instead.

These forces are not just spatial. Suppose that a random half or so of the spots were little *x*s and the rest little *o*s. Then the whole thing would be seen as a mess of *o*s and a mess of *x*s. Identity takes priority over spatiality. Suppose a random half or so were painted red. Then we would see that color takes priority over the other dimensions. Color is so powerful an organizing factor that it would be difficult to see a big square with a little one inside. Common motion is even more powerful. Suppose that a bunch of the spots were not printed on the page but were actually printed on a plastic overlay. If you slowly start to move the overlay, immediately the sloppy bunch of spots that move together would be seen as belonging together. There you have a real organizing force.

Perhaps the figure that is most *good* is the circle. If you see something that is anything like a circle, your organizing forces will make a circle of it, and that is what you will see. Draw a 2-inch circle and leave a gap of ⅛ inch in it, so that it is an incomplete circle, the observer will see a circle. Certainly if the professor draws such a broken circle on the blackboard, every student in the class will see it as a circle. They will say that the professor is no artist, but that thing is obviously a circle. They do not *assume* it is, they *see* it is. This tendency to close up a good figure, so as to make it *more good*, is called **closure.** Closure is a powerful organizing force. If the gap is big, the closure tendency still expresses itself because what is seen is a circle with a funny place, or a circle with a defect. To see organizing forces really take charge we have to weaken the restraining forces (the sensory input). One way to do that is to remove the restraining forces by putting the perception in memory. Show observers a broken circle, remove it, wait for an interval, and then ask them to draw what they have seen. You are likely to get closure. Very often the break in the circle disappears over the interval; organizing forces have made it a good figure, and the forgetful observer remembers a bona fide circle. And we see that the principles of organization apply not only to immediate perception, but to memory as well. As gestalt psychology gradually expanded to other areas of psychology, the original perceptual laws expanded as well.

Perception of Relationships

These simple demonstrations show again that perception does not depend so much on the sensory input as on the pattern. Part of a circle over there influences what we see over here; we tend to see the rest of the circle, if that is possible. Everything depends on **context.** Köhler said that if you stand with your back to a sunny window and hold up a piece of gray cardboard, it will look gray. You then glance up at the opposite wall of the room, which is white but in the shade; it will look white. The gray looks gray and the white looks white even though the gray surface reflects a great deal more light to the eye than the white surface does. We can test the latter point by looking through a **reduction screen,** which is a small hole in a piece of paper that lets us see only a small piece of an object. It removes the surrounding context. With the context gone, we see the wall over there as very dark and the cardboard right here as quite bright. But supply the context, the surround, the whole field, and the relationship immediately reverses. Thus, the localized stimulus devoid of context tells us nothing. Our perception is not just a bundle of localized sensations (he called this the structuralists' *bundle hypothesis*), perception depends on seeing the whole field of objects and the relationships between different objects. The correct perception of the gray and the white (brightness constancy) depends on seeing these elements along with all the other objects and shadows and noting the relationships among these diverse things in the field. The organizing forces will make the field look meaningful, and all the objects will be seen in their true colors and brightnesses.

The relationships in perception were everything to Köhler. While at Tenerife he carried out a number of experiments on what he called the **transposition effect.** Animals are trained to go to a dark gray stimulus (that was where the food was), and avoid the near-black stimulus (no food there). After the animals have learned the discrimination, they are given some test trials in which they have to choose between the same dark gray and a new stimulus, which is pale gray. Now if the animal has learned a specific S–R connection, it should return to the same dark gray that was reinforced before. But it seems that when they are tested most animals go to the pale gray. Thus, it seemed clear that the animals had not learned much about approaching the *specific* stimulus that had been associated with food. Rather, they had learned to approach the paler of the two stimuli—they had learned the *relative* brightness relationship. Again we see that a particular perception does not depend on the input of a corresponding sensory input. The information is there, but it is processed in terms of the observer's tendency to see things relationally.

Denial of Experience as a Factor

One might suppose that while we tend to see stimuli in relative rather than absolute terms, such tendencies are learned. That is, the appreciation of relative brightness is characteristic of the adult observer, and is due to prior experience. In the practical world, relative brightness is more important than absolute levels of light reaching the eye, and one might suppose that we have learned to pay attention to relative values and to ignore absolute values. Not so, the gestaltists say. They developed several "proofs" that organizing principles were innate. Perhaps the most appealing proof was that offered by Gottschaldt (1926). He showed subjects an initial figure, what he called an *a* figure. See figure 12.2.

The *a* figure was always a well-organized, distinctive configuration. Then he would present the *b* figure, which contains the original *a* figure, but in a way such that it was masked by a new and more compelling organization. Can subjects look at *b* and see the embedded *a*? No, it is gone. Gottschaldt ran various conditions, one in which subjects just glanced briefly at *a* and one in which subjects stared at *a* hundreds of times before proceeding to *b*. The prior experience had no effect; even with all that learning opportunity subjects could still not see it. So learning does not matter, and thus the organizing principles must be inborn, innate. That was a fundamental part of the gestaltist's view of things.

One might suppose that circles and squares are seen as good figures because we are so used to them in our modern, mechanized world. Most of us live in a civilized environment full of wheels and rectangular houses with rectangular rooms with rectangular windows and doors. The empiricist asserts that these shapes look good to us because they are so familiar. The gestaltist answers that that is silly. To be sure, there are mechanical reasons for wheels being round, but why are dining room tables and coffee cups so

Figure 12.2

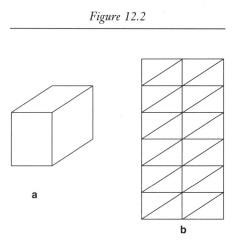

a

b

often round? They are round because they look better that way. You *could* sit at a pentagonal table and drink out of a triangular cup, but you would be uncomfortable in such an environment. We make things round because the circle is such a good figure. You *could* live in a hexagonal house with triangular rooms, but you would hate it. That is why we build the house and everything in it rectangular.

It is not clear who is likely to win such a debate between empiricist and nativist, or how the victory would be decided. Perhaps we have to step outside, perhaps to a primitive land with uncarpeted houses, and do some perceptual good-figure studies. Segall et al. (1966) did a study of illusions such as the Müller–Lyer in several primitive lands, and did find substantial cultural effects, but they did not really settle the debate.

A Word About Becoming a Legend

An interesting characteristic of the gestaltists is that they reinforced their cohesiveness, and strengthened the movement, by constantly citing each other. Credit for any particular idea might go to Wertheimer, the original leader, even though the idea might have been greatly expanded or even initiated from data by Koffka or Köhler. And they were peculiarly unwilling to admit anyone else into their privileged group. If you liked their viewpoint and did something constructive for it, they might use your contribution, but they would not let you join their party, and they would probably say your idea had come from Wertheimer. For example, the three musketeers had all worked with Stumpf, yet his views on, say, phenomenology, were rarely ever cited. They tended to view the gestalt movement as beginning from one gamete: Wertheimer's insight at the train station. But we know that things just do not start that way. There is always a pool of intellectual genes.

There are always some anticipators, people who preceded and unquestionably pushed the movers of the movement, even if they are not acknowledged. Perhaps the most noted anticipator was Christian von Ehrenfels (1890) who did not just mention but emphasized the importance of what he called gestalt qualities, that is, patterns. For example, we recognize a little tune. We hear it again, this time transposed to a new key and played on a different instrument, but we immediately recognize the same tune. All of the stimuli are changed; only the gestalt of the melody stays the same, and that is what we perceive, von Ehrenfels said.

There are always the earlier professors. Are we really to believe that it was only a coincidence that all the musketeers, as well as Schumann (who had to be sympathetic to the original study or he would not have endorsed it), just happened to have studied with Stumpf? Is it mere chance that Stumpf as well as the musketeers was intellectually opposed to everything that Wundt and the establishment believed in?[4]

Phenomenology

The gestaltists believed in phenomenology. It was not quite the naive phenomenology of Purkinje, but it was close to it. The difference is the new dependence on demonstration, the kind of game we played with figure 12.2. That sort of phenomenological game was essential for much of the data the gestaltists relied on. If I say it is easy to see two fat columns in figure 12.1, and you say, yes it is easy, then we are building a data base from which we can go on. The gestaltists were gambling; they were betting that if I said it is easy to see two fat columns in the figure you will not say, nonsense, I see a 4-by-4 matrix. I say, how about four skinny columns, and you reply again, it is a square matrix. The gestaltists needed your cooperation, your willingness to play phenomenological games, your assertion that, yes, you can see it that way. The remarkable thing is that their bet paid off.

One of the greatest phenomenologists, who wrote one of the greatest Ph.D. dissertations (under G. E. Müller), and introduced some of the finest phenomenological games, was Edgar Rubin (1886–1951). He was concerned with organizing forces, and certainly with phenomenology, and with why things look as they do, and yet the gestaltists did not accept him as one of them. Rubin (1915) found a new Kantian category, a new way in which the mind was organized that Kant and everyone else had missed. He called it **figure–ground.** Whenever we see something, that something is the *figure* and we see it against a *ground*, a background, a context. Figure and ground have very distinctive functional properties. Let us look at figure 12.3.

It is easy to see the gray disk sitting on the page. The disk is the figure and the page is the ground. Rubin said that the disk looks like a thing, it has substance, while the ground looks more like empty space. You could touch the disk, poke it, but the empty space of the ground does not look like it is touchable—your finger would just keep going. If you wanted to, you could pick up the disk—it looks like you could spread your thumb and fingers the

Figure 12.3

right distance and grab it. Notice that the boundary always belongs to the figure; that is why it looks pick-up-able. The way to appreciate these attributes is to reverse them. It is easy to see a gray disk sitting on the page. But it is also possible to switch things around. Now you are looking at the book, but someone has drilled a hole in it! The gray area is the background, which lies off yonder somewhere. Now you cannot grab the hole. But you can poke the page, and stick your finger in the hole. With this reversed perspective it looks as though you could put your finger in there and feel that the edge of the paper belongs to the figure and is not a part of the ground, in much the same way that you could pick up the gray thing by its edge when it was the figure. One remembers the figure but not the ground. The ground appears to lie behind the figure, and if you were to punch another hole in the figure you would find the ground lying back there too. Rubin had more than a dozen such generalizations about the differences.

David Katz, another Müller Ph.D., published the wonderful book *The World of Colour* in 1911, where he pushed the new phenomenology about as far as it could go. Among other interesting points, Katz argued that there are three kinds of color. Surface color—the color of typical objects—appears located in space, spread out in two dimensions, and hard, as though you could poke it. Volume color can be seen in white wine in a bottle; it seems to occupy space, but it lacks solidity. The third variety is film color, which is seen by staring into a bright-colored light; it lacks spatial location and solidity. Katz found, however, that these phenomenal differences all disappear and everything looks like film color when seen through a reduction screen. Thus, they appear to depend on context effects of one kind or another. For example, the solid appearance of surface color seems to depend on texture cues, tiny details of the surface. The fundamental discoveries of Rubin and Katz, especially considering how early they were made, would seem to qualify them as gestalt psychologists, but they were never part of the team.

Field Theory

FROM THE BEGINNING, an important part of the gestalt position was the idea that we should think of *fields*, the overall arrangement of things, rather than thinking of things as a collection of elements. Köhler was always fascinated by physics and physical models (for a short time he had studied physics with Max Planck). Early on, in 1920, he wrote a book in which he sought to show the relevance of gestalt principles to a number of sciences, such as physics and biology. He insisted that the old 1800 physics of Laplace, where the universe was accounted for by noting where all the different atoms were located and where they were all going (a structuralistic view), had been replaced by

Maxwell, Einstein, and others with the concept of field (the gestaltist's view). The field concept suggests observations such as that the force was stronger here than it was there. The motion, the voltage, or the heat is greater there than it is here. Thus, psychology, too, should replace ideas like the bundle hypothesis with gestalt field concepts (Köhler, 1967).

More specifically, psychology had inherited a punctate concept of the nervous system—a sensory neuron here and a motor neuron there are all bundled together to explain behavior. No, says Köhler, the brain is not a great bundler; it too works on field principles. There is an **isomorphism** (literally, the same shape) between perception and brain events. If you have a good figure in perception, like a circle, then there has to be something circular going on in the brain tissue. Connections are ignored. It is not a matter of how the brain is hooked up, it is the shape of things that counts. The notion of isomorphism was outlined vaguely in Wertheimer's 1912 paper, but the concept was driven home over the years by Köhler.*

In 1944 Köhler and Wallach reported a series of experiments on what they called *figural after-effects*. The subject stares at a fixation point for half a minute or so, while a big, heavy figure is presented near the fovea. Then immediately a test figure is presented, which contains a fixation point and two little spots. The heavy figure is gone, but one of the spots is near where it had been. The theory was that the long exposure to the heavy figure had stimulated the visual part of brain at some specific point, saturating it in some sense, and thereby distorting the field all around that area. When tested with the two little spots, the one near where the heavy figure had been should appear to be pushed somewhat away from the saturated area, and thus displaced. Then when the subject is asked to judge whether it is lined up with the other spot, it appears a little displaced. Therefore, they concluded, the brain operates not so much through its connections, how the neurons are connected, but according to field principles.

The neural connectionists were not seriously threatened by Köhler's research (see Osgood and Heyer, 1952), but nonetheless it made a good case for Köhler's way of looking at the nervous system. The idea of isomorphism implies that if we see a good figure, such as a circle, then there must be a similarly good figure, a circle, on the cortex. In Köhler's time it was already known from neuroanatomical studies that if one fixates the center of a circle, the circle will be represented on the visual cortex as something like a pair of horseshoes, which is not a very good figure. If one fixates a point on the

---

*About 1960 I heard Köhler give an invited talk at a convention (perhaps it was his APA presidential address). By then the isomorphism idea was about 50 years old. He gave a good talk; the audience liked it and I did too. It was fun to hear him holding forth in such good style. But he told the same old story about Laplace and Einstein and how psychology should be thinking about fields. Köhler was one of psychology's great polemicists.

perimeter, the representation on the cortex is a distorted, unsymmetrical pair of horseshoes, which is a pretty poor figure. Something was fundamentally wrong with isomorphism, but that should not have hurt the gestalt movement, because isomorphism did not appear to be a critical part of it. It was, however, important to Köhler, perhaps because he had been arguing for it since 1920. Perhaps isomorphism was fundamental in his mind because he saw it as a way of making psychology a real science.

Insight Learning

Köhler had another line of work that was greeted much more cordially, and that was his research on problem solving with chimpanzees, which began in 1913 on Tenerife Island, the largest of the Canary Islands. One thing we know about perception is that stimulus configurations are often ambiguous; as in figure 12.1, we can see it this way or that way. Problem solving can be regarded the same way. Now you do not see the solution, but suddenly there is a restructuring, a new organization, and there is the solution. Köhler attaches a banana to the ceiling, above the chimpanzee's reach. There is a big box lying around. The chimp hauls the box over so it is under the banana, he jumps up on the box, and grabs his prize (see figure 12.4). The problem can be made tougher: You start with two smaller boxes that have to be stacked to be tall enough. Sometimes that works, in the sense that the chimp can organize the different objects into a "fruitful" pattern. Köhler reported a lot of different experiments of this sort. He describes the time the chimp did not stack boxes but rather took Köhler by the hand and led him under the banana—and then jumped on his shoulders. He describes Sultan, a very smart (and well-trained) primate, who was in a cage while the banana lay outside beyond reach. Sultan grabbed a short stick and reached for it, but it was beyond reach. Sultan then used the short stick to haul in a long stick, with which he could get the banana. Sultan was ultimately able to connect two short sticks together to do the job.

Köhler's critics have argued that all his animals had extensive prior experience, and ample opportunity to learn all their tricks by trial and error, or by ordinary associative learning. They had sufficient experience that one would expect a lot of generalization, enough for them to solve the new problems easily. But Köhler discarded that approach and offered various new ways of looking at the problem solving. He called it **insight** when his animals got the perception-like reorganization, the sudden seeing of how to structure the environment. It looked like closure when the stick, the fruit, and the animal were all connected. Presumably it looked that way to the animals also, which is why they put it together. What is learned, Köhler said, is something perceptual, and when that is in place the behavior flows directly and easily. Animals do not learn responses per se, they learn to see their world differently, and when they do the behavior just naturally occurs as the fall-out of the new perception. These were remarkable ideas indeed in 1917, the year his research was published.

About 15 years ago psychologist Ronald Ley visited Tenerife Island just to see what remained of the old research station there. In his wanderings he met an 87-year-old man named Manuel, who had been in charge of caring for Köhler's chimpanzees. He was their keeper, handler, and trainer. The old man remembered all about the German scientist, and after he learned that Köhler had died he began to disclose things to Ley that he had kept to himself for many years. It appears that Köhler was doing espionage for the German military during World War I. From the cliffs overlooking the sea Köhler could see if the British navy was around, and if it was not, then he could send radio messages to the German submarines to come up and take on coal from a fuel ship hiding nearby. Manuel remembered all sorts of things that fit together to tell the story, and much of it was corroborated by various old

FIGURE 12.4
Köhler's chimpanzees.

documents Ley was able to dig up. If the story is true, and Ley (1990) claims to have the documentation, then it explains why Köhler was off in such an unlikely, desolate place all during the war.

Lewin and Motivation

KURT LEWIN (1890–1947) received his doctorate at Berlin in 1914; he was yet another protégé of Stumpf who was destined to alter the face of psychology. He remained at Berlin, and worked his way up the academic ladder at a reasonable speed. He was at Berlin all during the critical years between 1920 and 1933 when gestalt psychology was taking shape there. He was in a good position to follow Köhler as professor of the department, but he left in 1933. The Nazis had risen to power and were beginning to destroy the university system, and it was no place for a Jewish scholar to be. His future, like that of the other gestaltists, lay in the United States. He came to Cornell, but was only there for two years. Lewin's most productive decade was spent at the University of Iowa between 1935 and 1945.

Motivational Realities

All his life Lewin was fascinated by the concept of motivation, but his view of it varied considerably over the years. He looked at it this way and that, but throughout all the changes in exposition and explanatory principles he adhered to the idea that human behavior has to be explained in terms of the forces and tensions that move us to action. To begin with I must note that the three musketeers started from perception and then attempted to make the difficult transition to behavior. That transition was generally not very graceful, and their accounts of behavior were generally not very convincing. D'Artagnan (Lewin) started with behavior and what produces it, and then moved on to the problem of how people perceived their own behavior. It was a much easier transition.

Lewin wrote an important paper in 1917 in which he examined the determining tendencies that Ach and Watt had discovered a decade earlier. Whereas the Würzburg studies had demonstrated that a determining tendency (Aufgabe, or set, or what the subject is trying to do) can affect the expression of learned associations, Lewin saw it all as conflict between competing determining tendencies. He was arguing that all mental processes, even those that we understand to be associative, are really caused by psychic energy or tension. These motivational forces control the subject's behavior, and in comparison with these forces the associative connections are relatively unimportant. In both the laboratory and the everyday world, a person's

Kurt Lewin

behavior is always oriented toward some goal; there is always something the person is trying to do, and it is that determining tendency or intention to do something that matters most.

Intentions

We see that Lewin gave little credit to, and saw little explanatory value in, associations. He admitted that there were associations, but he said that they are only important in *controlled* behaviors, where a stimulus has a direct, causal connection with a particular, almost reflexive response. But there is another and much more important class of behaviors, which Lewin called *intentional* actions, and these lack the punctate quality of controlled actions. Instead they follow field principles. When someone wills to do this or that, we cannot account for their action by finding a stimulus here or a reinforcer there, we have to look for psychological forces and tensions that arise from their motives, and from their goals, and how they perceive the particular situation.

For example, suppose you are sitting down writing a letter to your friend Sam. There are things you want to share with him. You write the letter, do the envelope, and then go out and drop it in a mailbox. Lewin says that according to the customary association, reinforcement view of behavior, when you have gotten the letter in the mail you should feel so good, those behaviors should be so reinforced, that when you get back home you should sit right down and write Sam another letter. But, of course, that does not happen. The set or the intention to communicate with Sam sets up a *tension* that persists until the job is done. When the job is done that tension is gone, so you give it no more thought and go on about other things. Or suppose that when you are sitting down writing your letter the phone rings and there's

Sam! "Hey Sam," you say, "I was just writing to you." You talk with him for a while, convey your news, and then say goodbye. Do you then go on writing your letter? Probably not, because the tension involved in communicating with Sam was discharged when you talked on the phone. That was a substitute activity. You are now likely to crumple up the letter you started, throw it away, and smile.

Tensions

Lewin attributed a number of behavioral properties to tension, and he and his students were able to demonstrate some of them experimentally. For example, Zeigarnik (1927) had children working at different tasks, such as building things with blocks. Zeigarnik let some tasks get finished, but interrupted others before they could be completed. Later, when quizzed about what they had been doing, the children remembered more of the interrupted than the completed tasks. If the tension associated with the task is not discharged by completion, then it persists and activates memory. The interrupted task is also more apt to be resumed if there is an opportunity to continue it (Ovsiankina, 1928). Tensions can also diffuse to other unrelated activities, and they can produce confusion and general intellectual deterioration if they are strong enough.

Tension was just one of several motivational concepts that for some years Lewin tried to organize. Tensions can arise from needs, such as hunger, or from quasi-needs, such as when a child needs to finish building something. Any behavioral episode is going to generate tension, and an episode can get started because of physiological conditions, or simply because the individual undertakes to do something. By and large, a behavioral episode is aimed at some specific outcome, it has a *goal*. Goals and outcomes are another major part of Lewin's system. A goal or an outcome has a particular value, a specific worth, that will vary from time to time and from person to person. Lewin calls the value of the goal object its *valence*. Thus, valence is a property of the goal object, which is seen as out there in the environment. At the same time, there is an inner thing, something we perceive as aroused in us, which is how much we want the goal. Lewin called this factor the motivating *force*, and he thought of it as akin to a physical force, which also has both direction and magnitude. You want a particular thing, and you have a certain degree of desire for it. So he tried to represent a force as a vector, an arrow that points in a particular direction and has a particular length. He played with the possibility that faced with conflicting motives a person might resolve the conflict as one would resolve conflicting physical forces, by adding the vectors and going off in some compromise direction. That specific hypothesis did not go anywhere, but it illustrates the richness of the new motivational concepts and phenomena that Lewin worried about.[5]

Social Psychology

Lewin's major impact came not through his writings, but mainly through his personal influence. By all accounts, he had a charismatic charm that made his notions irresistible to his students, and others who knew him. In the last few years of his life Lewin became increasingly wrapped up in social psychology, a field that was just beginning to take shape. Some of Lewin's students came in on the ground floor and became the leaders of the field. I will note just a few of his outstanding students. Leon Festinger got his degree with Lewin at Iowa in 1942. Lewin spent the last two years of his life at the Research Center for Group Dynamics at MIT, where he mentored Stanley Schachter, Dorwin Cartwright, and Harold Kelley. His students did not generally come out looking like gestalt psychologists, but they did not look like the behaviorists of the time either. They talked about things like motivation, conflict, level of aspiration, attribution, and *balance*, a concept that would evolve into cognitive dissonance. They were independent souls who went their own way, studying social phenomena without regard to how they might fit it into any systematic position. They were the people who gave social psychology pretty much the look it has today. There was a little social psychology before Lewin, but it was either behavioristic or devoted to the study of attitudes. Modern social psychology came largely from the gestaltists, particularly from Lewin and the young people that he impacted. We now have to look more generally at the impact of the gestaltists.

Influence of Gestalt Psychology

WHEN THE GESTALTISTS first appeared in 1912 their opposition was clearly Wundt's structuralism. They were opposed to its analytical orientation, and so they sought synthesizing principles, such as their organizing forces. They did not like the empiricistic orientation, and so they emphasized nativistic principles. But they were flogging a dead horse. Wundt himself was off into folk psychology, and German psychology in general was wandering from the way of science into various kinds of phenomenology, humanism, and other diversions. Although Wundt was at the center of things, his kind of psychology was not all that popular by the time he died in 1920. And then in a few years, in the early 1930s, when the gestaltists and their friends fled the German world and arrived in the United States, there was no more structuralism here either. It had pretty well died with Titchener in 1927. Even Titchener's most loyal students, such as Boring (1933), were straying from the path. It was the era of behaviorism. So the gestaltists had to shift gears and take off after a new behavioristic enemy. In some ways behaviorism was a familiar enemy because it was atomistic, associationistic, empiricistic, and built on the wrong kind of mechanism. So it was easy for them to repeat their old arguments against the new enemy; they could still attack the bundle hypothesis, and still argue for the innateness of organizing principles. On the other hand, although there was a battle to be won here and there, there was no way they could win the war. There was only a handful of gestaltists and there were thousands of behaviorists and their number was growing every day; the odds were overwhelmingly against the gestaltists. Even so, they did pretty well. If nothing else, they created an exciting time of intellectual turmoil. And the reason for their success was that they had something to say. In the 1940s, when behaviorism was king of the hill, the gestaltists caught a few ears, but a generation later when behaviorism began to falter, a lot of cognitive ears began to listen to the gestaltists again.

The Gestaltists' Network

Mary Henle was an early convert to the new, antibehavioristic cause, and has written about the spread of the gestalt movement in this country. Henle (1983) describes some of the excitement of those early days, and how the gestaltists and their followers were interrelated. She was an undergraduate at Smith College (graduating in 1934). Koffka was there, and she was dazzled by him and did research with him. Koffka's fellow countryman Fritz Heider was also there, and he was always very sympathetic to the movement. Young Eleanor and James Gibson were also there. Presumably on Koffka's recommendation, Henle went off to do her graduate work at Bryn Mawr, just west of Philadelphia. There she encountered Harry Helson, a Harvard Ph.D. (1924), who was perhaps the first American proponent of gestalt psychology, and Donald MacKinnon, who had studied with Köhler and Lewin in Berlin. Just down the highway from Bryn Mawr was Swarthmore, and Henle was in close contact with the gestaltists there. Her first teaching job was at Swarthmore. Köhler was the dominant personality there, and Köhler's Berlin companion Wallach was also there, along with Karl Duncker, another German refugee who thought like a gestaltist. R. B. MacLeod was the chairman, and he was sympathetic to the gestalt cause (he had brought in the refugees). Richard Crutchfield was on the faculty, too, so it was a very gestaltist, liberal department.

Henle then moved on to the New School in New York, the land of Wertheimer, where she remained for many years. When Wertheimer died his position was filled for a few years by the social psychologist Solomon Asch, who then moved on to Swarthmore. Asch, too, was greatly influenced by these people, and his pioneering work in social psychology showed that influence. What we had here was a sort of gestaltist network within which it was relatively easy for people to move around, as Henle did. There were also special ways into and out of the network; a nonrandom fraction of these people had come from or went to Harvard and Berkeley. Another aspect of this network is that it included quite a number of social psychologists; counting Lewin's people, we have to conclude that the gestaltists were extraordinarily productive of social psychologists. They also produced quite a number of psychologists interested in personality dynamics, cognitive processes, and thought processes. Notice that all these areas lie somewhere in between purely applied psychology and the traditional, hard experimental parts of psychology. They did not train many further perception people, even though that was where the gestalt movement had maintained its largest success. And they did not turn many young people loose in animal learning, even though Köhler and others had stirred up the learning area. Learning fell inevitably into the hands of the behaviorists. It was inevitable because the behaviorists were empiricists so they inherited learning, while the gestaltists were nativists among whom learning is not of central interest. The gestaltists were always fascinated by organization; they flourished when it came to the organization of perception, personality, or social systems.

Further Repercussions

Gestalt ideas were influential and they kept popping up here and there, sometimes in surprising places. Frederic C. Bartlett (1886–1969) was the professor at Cambridge for many years, enough years, in fact, that in the end he unquestionably became the dean of British psychologists. In 1932 Bartlett reported an important series of studies on memory. In one study subjects read a one-paragraph story, and then later tried to recall it. Invariably the recollection was smoothed and polished and reorganized so that it looked like a good figure. The most famous of these, as I had remembered it after a number of years, was something like this: A group of Indian warriors took off in their canoe and attacked a nearby settlement. In the scuffle someone got killed. Frightened, the warriors went back home. In checking out the story I found that my memory showed a great deal of leveling and smoothing, and I had forgotten the whole point of the story. The original story was told from the Indian point of view with many distinctive names and symbols that had little meaning to me. Some of it didn't make much sense. All those features are usually lost from memory. The plot gets reorganized and simplified, so that one remembers something "good." Bartlett said we remember *schemata*. His work was a wonderful demonstration of gestalt principles operating in memory.

A powerful organizing principle in gestalt psychology is good continuation (a bunch of elements will appear organized if they are lined up). Thus, we should expect the gestaltists' efforts to move off into profitable directions that would create conceptually good figures. But that is not exactly what happened. The final word on perceptual phenomena was Koffka (1935), and that was all the closure we got in that arena. There was a lot of discussion and debate, but the gestalt view of perception did not move forward. After a while there were a number of reactions to the gestaltists' idea of organizing principles. I will indicate a couple of these reactions.

J. J. Gibson was very familiar with the gestalt view of perception because he had been a youthful colleague of Koffka's at Smith College. He accepted Koffka's idea that one does not learn to perceive things in space, the principles of perception have to be innate. He also accepted the wholistic approach; we do in fact perceive things in space, he said. But Gibson did not see the organizing forces as lying in the brain. He argued that the organization lies in the information from the environment. When we see an object off in space, we are seeing it in a context, and the context provides texture and perspective information that tells us how far the object is and how big it is relative to other objects in the field. Helmholtz would have said that we learn to use spatial information to correct for different apparent sizes of objects. Gibson said that an object twice as close that projects to the eye an image twice as big will be seen as the same size. That is how the system is organized—it is organized around the stimulus information about perspective (Gibson, 1950). To understand perception, why things look as they do, we should look to the environment to discover how it is represented in the available stimulus information. Gibson's views have continued to attract attention, in spite of the fact that they defy both the traditional empiricist and the newer gestalt ideas by lying somewhere in between.

Köhler had tried to make a case for the concept of isomorphism. It was terribly important to him that the organizing principles in perception be mirrored by the shape of electrical fields in the brain. The hard-core mechanists never for a moment accepted such an idea, because they were committed to neurons firing off other neurons; they believed in circuitry and networks. Köhler's problem was that there really are neurons up there; in fact, there is nothing but neurons up there. Köhler was always caught in that impasse. The way out of the dilemma was discovered by visual physiologists, who found that there are several different kinds of neurons that have quite different functions. First, lateral inhibition was discovered. When a point on the retina is stimulated, excitation goes upward to the visual cortex, but at the same time inhibitory impulses go sideways to other retinal points to cut off any excitation that they might send to the cortex. One result is that everything around the point of maximum stimulation gets blotted out. Thus, a homogeneous area is seen as homogeneous. Boundaries obviously become important because they are going to enclose areas and because there will be contrast effects to accentuate any boundary. A host of figure–ground effects, what look like organization effects, begin to take shape conceptually simply by the discovery of inhibition—a new variety of neural function.

And then *receptive fields* were discovered. At first they were seen as just second-order neurons to which a number of primary receptors were connected. They enabled summation and various sorts of area effects to occur. Then the remarkable work of Hubel and Wiesel showed that in the visual cortex there were units that seemed to be particularly responsive to different sorts of lines. Some responded to verticals, others to horizontals, and still others responded to tilted lines. Some responded to corners, others to little curls. All sorts of visual features seem to be picked up by different sorts of specialized *feature detectors*. Subsequent work gradually indicated something of the wonderful and subtle ways in which perceptual information is coded. It is now clear that the gestaltists were entirely justified in their criticism of what they called the bundle hypothesis because perception does not work like that. But it is also clear that perception does not work as they maintained either; their field ideas were no good. The truth was somewhere else.[6]

In the next couple of chapters it will be clear that the real inheritors of the gestalt tradition were the cognitive psychologists who came along in ever-increasing numbers. Gestalt psychology had much to offer anyone who was skeptical about the empiricistic bias in psychology, or anyone dubious of atomism, or anyone uncomfortable with associationism. It provided some alternatives.

At the time he died Köhler was preparing an APA address that would have described some of the history of the gestalt movement. The unfinished manuscript (Köhler, 1967) ends with the observation that a half-century before, when gestalt psychology was just getting started, it was a great challenge, a wonderful adventure. He had found it so exciting. What we need more than anything else, the old gestaltist said, is people who get excited.

Summary

THE GESTALT MOVEMENT began with a series of studies on apparent motion (the phi phenomenon) that Wertheimer, Koffka, and Köhler carried out at Frankfurt. This work suggested that perception is organized in a variety of ways that have little or nothing to do with experience, and that cannot be understood in terms of combinations of elements. Perception has its own set of rules, one of which is that we see configurations, the gestalt, and not just a collection of pieces. Other rules involved figure–ground relationships, the importance of contexts, and the organization of the perceptual field.

Soon the movement expanded to the study of memory, problem solving, and motivational phenomena. Lewin was particularly interested in motivation, and went on from there to the social interaction of groups. Thus, although it had started as a protest against the conventional way of regarding perception as collections of sensory inputs and memories, it spread out to encompass other areas of psychology. And while the original protest had been directed at the structuralists' view of perception it evolved into a protest against the behaviorists' view of psychology. This shift was inevitable when the gestaltists and their sympathizers came to the United States in the 1930s, because by then American psychology was dominated by Watson and his followers rather than Titchener and his disciples. Their battle with the structuralists was easily won, but they were not able to overcome the behaviorists. Their ideas and sense of rebellion remained alive, however, and served, as we will see, to nourish later generations of cognitively inclined psychologists.

Notes

1. Kurt Koffka (1886–1941), who was the first of the gestaltists to come to the United States, was also the first to write about the movement in English. His long paper in the *Psychological Bulletin* introduced us to the basic ideas in 1922. From early on Koffka sought to extend gestalt ideas from perception to other areas of psychology. His important *The Growth of the Mind* (1921) went off into developmental psychology. The mind develops, he says, not by the accretion of associations but by the gradual differentiation of cognitive structures. Thus, for example, the sense of self arises when the child learns to discriminate between the ego and everything else that comes to be seen as out there. The concept of my hand developed when I began to link up perceptions of the hand with its movements. When this happened I began to appreciate it as my hand. These were difficult concepts, which were never accepted or even understood as well as the gestaltists' views of perception. Koffka's *Principles of Gestalt Psychology* (1935) continued to extend gestalt thinking to other areas of psychology, such as motivation and behavior, and memory and learning. This book represents the most mature and thoughtful statement of gestalt psychology. In some ways it marks the high point in the gestalt movement; in some ways it is the most ambitious statement, and perhaps if Koffka had been a more felicitous writer or perhaps if he had lived longer, it could have marked the beginning of a totally new kind of psychology. Other early systematic statements of the Gestalt position were written by Helson (1925, 1926) and Hartmann (1935).

2. Max Wertheimer (1880–1943) started things moving with his phi-phenomenon paper (Wertheimer, 1912). But that, according to Carini (1970), is just part of the legend. The parametric work that convincingly demonstrated the phenomenon was done later by others, and Wertheimer himself did not follow it up. He did not write very much, but he did start publishing, in German, on what he called productive thinking as early as 1920. Productive thinking is creative, whereas reproductive thinking is merely responding to a stimulus. His major work in English was *Productive Thinking* (1945). It deals with problem solving, tasks such as how to find the area of a parallelogram, a Tennessee-shaped thing, a poor figure. Most young kids cannot figure it out. Give them scissors, however, and then they might see that they can cut off the Memphis part and stick it over by the Blue Ridge Mountains, and then they have a rectangle, a good figure. Then they get it.

Wertheimer has another claim to fame. Abraham Maslow met him in New York early in the 1940s and was impressed that Wertheimer was just about the nicest and most interesting person he had ever met. Maslow knew only two people who he felt were "self-actualizing," and Wertheimer was one of them. In talking to Ley (1990), Metzger said that there was something holy about Wertheimer, and he had penetrating eyes (see the picture of him). Thus, he contributed, involuntarily, to some of our modern models of human motivation.

3. Wolfgang Köhler (1887–1967) had a long and very productive life. His innovative work with chimpanzees at Tenerife led to *The Mentality of Apes*, which appeared in German in 1917 and in English in 1925. This is perhaps what vaulted him to the professorship at Berlin. In English we have *Gestalt Psychology* (1947), which first appeared in German in 1929, *Dynamics in Psychology* (1942), and *The Task of Gestalt Psychology* (1969), which was an expansion of a chapter he had written 40 years earlier. A valuable collection of some of the early gestaltist papers has been translated and edited by Ellis (1938).

4. We are beginning to see how, if you are an important person and have some followers, you can become a legend. First you and your followers distance yourselves from your anticipators. We saw that in the last chapter: Freud *discovered* sexuality, the unconscious, motivation, and more, all without precedent. The cut-off has to be done gradually and carefully. Thus, when he was a young scholar seeking recognition Freud cited everyone around, and he glorified Charcot. Then in his maturity, describing the history of psychoanalysis, he cites nothing before Freud (1900). Related to this, a second thing you have to do is cut yourself off from your professors. Freud forgot all about Brücke; the gestaltists forgot all about Stumpf. Koffka's big book mentions Stumpf three times, but only briefly and not once to his credit. We will see this again in chapter 13. Who did Thorndike study with, or who did Skinner learn anything from? They never tell us. The third thing you have to do is cut off your fellow travelers, others who think as you do. You can steal or assimilate their ideas, but you never mention their ideas as theirs unless you are prepared to put them down. Koffka was actually pretty good about this, and he did give due credit to Katz, Rubin, and many others. But maybe that is why he never became a legend. Excerpts of papers by Katz, Rubin, and the gestaltists can be found in the excellent collection of readings by Beardslee and Wertheimer (1958). This Wertheimer, Michael, is Max's son.

5. Kurt Lewin (1890–1947) wrote a number of important early papers. I have recounted ideas he wrote about in 1917, 1922, and 1926. A number of his early papers have been edited, translated, and published as Lewin (1935). Marrow (1969) has also outlined a lot of Lewin's early research. Lewin wrote two important and influential books, *Principles of Topological Psychology* (1936) and *The Conceptual Representation and the Measurement of Psychological Forces* (1938). This is where we see Lewin struggling with the problem of how to display motivational forces in a graphical manner. Marrow (1969) also includes a biography of Lewin.

6. All of these matters are discussed in modern perception texts. Was the gestalt movement a Kuhnian revolution against the establishment? If we grant for the sake of the argument that the establishment was structuralism, did the gestalt movement constitute a Kuhnian sort of revolution against it? Certainly they looked like revolutionaries; they were running around together and shooting at the enemy. Certainly they considered themselves to be rebels. But their adventure does not meet the Kuhnian criteria because it did not arise from a "puzzle" that the establishment had encountered, or a "crisis" that had built up. It does not follow Kuhn's formula. There is clearly something wrong with Kuhn's formula.

Chapter Thirteen

Behaviorism

B EHAVIORISM HAD ITS ROOTS in England, but as a systematic movement it was peculiarly suited to grow in American soil. It never took hold on the European continent, nor in England until much later. It caught on and flourished here because of the particular intellectual setting that had taken shape here. This setting had two major components, one of which was an appropriate philosophical background that was supplied by the pragmatism of James and the instrumentalism of Dewey. The other component was a distinctive physiological background. Psychology has always emerged somewhere near the boundary between philosophy and physiology. German psychology grew out of sensory physiology and an idealistic philosophy. The American psychology was to grow out of the physiology of movement plus a pragmatic philosophy. The American psychology was destined to be behaviorism; we will see how it swept away and overwhelmed all prior movements. But first we have to look in on developments in England.

The Continuity of Us and Them

EVERYTHING THAT WENT into the culture of Western civilization had led us to believe that there were fundamental differences between us and them, between humans and animals. The Church made us unique by giving us an immortal soul. The philosophers up into the 19th century made us unique by giving us rationality. When the psychologists came along a century or so ago they used the method of introspection, which required that the subjects be introspective human beings. That made us unique in another way because at first no one but a normal, adult, verbal human being could be a subject in a psychology experiment.

But just about then there appeared the heretic Charles Darwin, who said that we and they shared a great deal. We are all part of the evolutionary story, and we are all just part of nature. If we differ from them, Darwin said, we are

295

not different in kind but only quantitatively different. In the animal kingdom we see specialization; we can find animals that walk on the ceiling—we can't do that. We can find animals that fly—we can't do that either. Nor can we run very fast, or swim very well, or kill big animals by biting them. We cannot make spider webs or bird nests. We cannot compete with other animals in doing what they are specialized to do, but we can do our own special thing, which is to be very intelligent. In that arena they cannot compete with us. We became so intelligent that we could invent language so that we would be able to symbolize a thing with a word, and communicate with one another *about* things. Within a few thousand years language developed to such a point that we could use words to symbolize other words and different relationships between words, and then gradually theology, philosophy, and science came into being. Words gave us tradition and culture and belief systems. And so we gained further advantage over them. Now we are so advantaged that we can drive many of them to extinction. It all came about, Darwin said, because during evolution we specialized and became increasingly intelligent.

The biological scientist had a couple of ways to pursue Darwin's concept of continuity. One was to make us machines, too, just as the animals were supposed to be. That is the direction that behaviorism would ultimately go; indeed, that was what behaviorism was all about. But before that occurred, there was for a while a movement to go the other way, to try to model our animal friends in our image. There were good people who proposed that animals were basically cute little furry people, with minimally developed human faculties. The most noteworthy of these animals-are-us people was the biologist Romanes.

George Romanes

George Romanes (1848–94) had made contact with Darwin around 1880 when he was getting started and Darwin was near his end. Darwin liked him and welcomed him as a junior colleague. Darwin turned over to Romanes a lot of material, including some unpublished manuscripts. Some of this material was to see the light of day in Romanes's important work *Mental Evolution in Animals* (1883). Subsequently he wrote *Mental Evolution in Man* (1888). These were both good, scholarly productions, although neither caused much of a stir.

Unfortunately, Romanes's long-term reputation is based not so much on this good work as on the poor impression he made by an earlier book, *Animal Intelligence* (1882), which was strongly based on the animals-are-us theme. He had placed ads in the *London Times*, one must assume, asking for stories from the owners of pets that showed evidence of higher mental processes. This came to be called the **anecdotal method.** The book presents a number of stories that argue for various human-like motives and intellectual skills. There was the dog that had "the beginnings of mechanical understanding" because it had learned to open the front gate when it wanted to go out on the street. There was the dog that showed "the motive of revenge." The story goes like this: A gentleman leaves his two dogs, a big black one and little white one, at the Village Inn for the innkeeper to care for while he goes down the road for a day or two. When he picks up his dogs he gets the following account of events. The innkeeper relates how the big dog had soon left and gone up the road in the direction of the gentleman's home. The little white dog hung around but then got into a scuffle with a middle-sized gray dog. And I am sorry to tell you, the innkeeper says, that the little fellow got much the worse of it. The little dog made its retreat and went back up the road in the direction of the gentleman's home, but it returned in a few minutes in the company of the big dog—who then proceeded to beat up the gray dog. According to Romanes, we can see from this story that a dog can have the motive of revenge, or retribution, in behalf of an injured buddy. We also see that dogs can communicate with each other about these sorts of serious matters, for how else could the little one have gotten the big one to go back to the inn?

Romanes was not alone; there was a lot of popular interest in such issues in those days when biologists, the clergy, and the public were fighting about whether we and they were much the same or intrinsically different. Scholars were torn, as was clear from our earlier account of William James and his associates. A number of books appeared on the subject, books that wondered about the consciousness of animals and wondered how we might draw conclusions about such things.[1]

Lloyd Morgan

During the 1880s, Romanes's decade, systematic psychology had little interest in the minds of animals. But such an interest developed in the 1890s, thanks mainly to the work of Conwy Lloyd Morgan (always known as Lloyd Morgan, 1852–1936). Morgan had gotten off to a rather shaky start, going here and there, and teaching this and that. Then in 1884 he took a position as professor of geology and zoology at the new university at Bristol, in the west of England. However, in 1896 he was promoted into the top administration of Bristol, and after that he was virtually lost to the field of animal behavior. In 1890 Morgan wrote the landmark book *Animal Life and Intelligence*, in which he began to look at animal learning. Back in 1873 the remarkable student of animal behavior D. A. Spalding had reported experiments with infant chicks, investigating how they learn to peck at food, and how they can get imprinted on a moving object. Morgan greatly expanded this work; he emphasized what he called trial-and-error learning. He looked at it much as Bain had, as reflecting the building up of associations in the nervous system.

In 1894 Morgan wrote his best-known book, *An Introduction to Comparative Psychology*, in which he extended his experiments on the learning of birds. Morgan gave young ducklings a dish of water on a black tray. The birds drank and bathed. After a few days of this, he gave them the dish and the tray but no water. He found that the birds jumped in and made all the same drinking and bathing movements. In a very famous experiment Morgan gave chicks some cinnabar caterpillars. Lots of caterpillars are edible, but not cinnabars. Upon taking the first bite of a cinnabar, the chick gapes, shakes its head, wipes its beak, and hops away. The next day when offered another cinnabar, the little bird does not eat it; it gapes, shakes its head, wipes its beak, and hops away. Morgan had found one-trial learning. To account for this learning, Morgan speculated about the chick's nervous system. He supposed that there was a visual center that was excited by the sight of the caterpillar, and a taste center aroused by its taste, and that these became associated very much as Bain and others before him had proposed. While the original sight–peck connection had considerable innate strength, it was overridden by the very strong taste–reject connection that was mediated by the new sight–taste connection. His was a rather modern view of associative learning.

Morgan was a strong advocate of associative learning. He considered two kinds of cases, one like this where sensory events become associated so that one sensation comes to acquire the motivational properties, such as unpleasantness, of the other (this is much like Pavlovian conditioning). He also considered cases where an association is learned between a sensation and a particular response (this is much like operant conditioning). And he sought to attribute as much as he could of the animals' behavioral flexibility to associative learning. Thus, like Romanes, he had a dog that could open the front gate, but Morgan had watched the dog do it the first time. It seems it had just stuck its head through the space in the gate where the latch was, the latch got in the way and became unlatched. The dog pulled its head loose and went out in the street. After doing this countless times, the dog still did it in the same awkward, stereotyped manner. Morgan was quite unimpressed with his dog's "mechanical understanding." It was, he argued, only another instance of a response being associated with a stimulus. Simple associative learning accounted for most and perhaps even all of what an animal learns. Morgan went to some length in the 1894 book to undo the intellectual damage he believed Romanes had done. And notice that he was doing so as a psychologist would, by doing experiments in place of collecting stories.

In general, Morgan cautioned that we should be very careful about making any inferences about higher-level mental activity in animals, especially since it is so often possible to explain their behavior with lower-level mechanisms such as associative learning. He set forth a general law, which has come to be known as Lloyd Morgan's Canon: *We must not interpret a behavior as due to a higher-level process if it can be interpreted as the result of a psychologically lower process.* The higher and lower here refer to evolutionary development, the associative mechanisms being assumed to be primitive, and the human-like mechanisms having been developed and added on later. Watch out! Here come the mechanists, who would in a short time turn everybody, us and them, into machines.[2]

Reflexes

WE SAW THAT PSYCHOLOGISTS lost interest in reflexes after Lotze proclaimed in 1853 that they were of little interest except to the physiologists. The physiologists did indeed follow them up. Pflüger, by coincidence Lotze's opponent in the debate of 1853, had discovered that stimulation of the vagus nerve did not stimulate the heart to beat faster or the intestine to move faster, but rather had the opposite effects. Evidently neural stimulation could *inhibit* movement as well as excite it.

Ivan Sechenov

One person who saw **inhibition** as terribly important in the overall scheme of things was Ivan Sechenov (1829–1905), the first Russian in our story. One reason for our lack of Russians is that like several Asian countries Russia closed its borders throughout much of the 19th century. But there were occasional windows of opportunity where communication was possible, and in the 1850s young Sechenov grabbed the chance to go to Europe and study physiology. He studied with Müller, du Bois-Reymond, Ludwig, and Helmholtz, and with Bernard in Paris. He was learning from all the best, and from the most mechanistic, with the important consequence that he became a thoroughgoing mechanist.

A mechanist is basically one who wants to be able to translate any psychological phenomenon into its physiological causes. Put another way, the mechanist is a reductionist who wants to reduce the mental to the physical. Sechenov understood that it is not easy to do that with the human organism. It is vastly more challenging to reduce the behavior of a human than that of, say, a flatworm with its limited repertoire of responses, very little response flexibility, and a restricted number of highly predictable reflexes. The human has reflexes too, but understanding them provides little purchase on explaining the richness of human behavior. Sechenov saw inhibition as the answer to the problem of human unpredictability. The highly developed human brain is mainly full of inhibitory reflexes, he thought, and that is why we respond to stimuli so unpredictably. Once we have a fuller understanding of inhibition we will be able to explain scientifically the vast complexity of human behavior. He poured forth these ideas in a remarkable monograph, *Reflexes of the Brain* (1863). This document, along with his subsequent work, set the intellectual tone of Russian physiology forevermore, from his time to the present day, and probably well into the future. Russian physiology turned

299

hard-line mechanistic, and their account of anything behavioral would be in terms of reflexes. Although this orientation was totally dominating in Russia, it did not affect physiologists in other countries because, alas, the window closed, and we were not able to follow what they were doing, and they had no idea what we were doing. Researchers in the west and in Russia were actually doing similar things, but no one knew it.

Ivan Pavlov

Ivan Pavlov (1849–1936) did research on digestive reflexes during the last couple of decades before 1900. He found that the secretion of stomach acid and stomach enzymes was extraordinarily well-suited to whatever food had been put in the stomach. The mouth also secretes digestive juices, which we lump together and call saliva, and these too match what food is in the mouth. Thus, a dilute acid causes massive secretion of watery saliva that has the effect of diluting the acid. On the other hand, protein in the mouth causes the release of saliva that is full of enzymes that begin the digestion process. Saliva can also turn starch into sugar. All this work on digestive reflexes won Pavlov the Nobel Prize in medicine in 1904, which was a fitting recognition for his important pioneering research.[3]

Just before the turn of the century, Pavlov discovered that not only would his dogs salivate when food was put in their mouths, they would also salivate when the keeper, the man who customarily fed them, entered the room! Salivating to food in the mouth implied a physiological reflex, and that is what Pavlov called it. And such a thing was clearly a part of science. But if the animal salivates at the *prospect* of food, to a signal of food, then what in the world does a mechanistic scientist call that? Pavlov called it a *psychic reflex*. He was clearly at a conceptual crisis. Pavlov's way out of this dilemma was to propose that he was studying the brain; he saw the study of conditioning as a way to get at how the brain works. The physical processes that constitute what we call the mind can be revealed, he believed, by studying conditioning. He paid particular attention, involving at least half of what he reported, to inhibitory conditioning.

Pavlov's work early in the new century was not available to American psychologists. No one here could read Russian; we could not translate it, and we could not even transliterate it. The first citations of Pavlov in this country gave his name as Powlow. So no one here knew just what he was doing, what his views were, or what his data looked like. And yet by a curious twist of fate that we will get to shortly, Pavlov would become very important in American psychology at an early time when no one had yet read what he had written! What we understood of Pavlov at that time was that he believed in machinery. He did reflexes, and believed that all behavior resulted from reflex action. That was real science. Some reflexes are innate, as when the dog salivates to food in the mouth, but some are formed through experience, as when the dog

Charles Sherrington

salivates to the appearance of the keeper. He called these latter *conditional reflexes* because their appearance is conditional on appropriate experience (and then *conditional* was mistranslated as *conditioned*). When we could finally read Pavlov in 1927 we would find him saying that all behavior, a musician playing the violin or a pair of birds building a nest or any other behavior we might care to look at, simply shows us complex combinations of learned and unlearned reflexes. That was the Russian heritage.

Charles Sherrington

Meanwhile, back in England Charles Sherrington (1857–1952) was at work on reflexes. If you restrain a cat so that its feet hang free, there are a number of curious things about feet you can discover. If you touch the top of a paw with your finger, the cat will lift that paw and place it on your finger—the placing reflex. If you press upward on the bottom of a paw you soon encounter resistance as the cat counters with an extension movement. Interestingly, the diagonal leg also extends—the crossed-extension reflex. If you pull one paw forward, other paws might move too, depending on their initial position, as though the cat were walking. If you press up on both back paws, the cat flexes both front legs, as though it were jumping. Now playing with the feet of a restrained cat is hazardous business; it is better to remove the cat's personality as much as possible. Better yet is to remove the cat's whole cerebrum. Wondrously, when that is done the feet reflexes do not collapse, they actually become greatly facilitated and amplified. Evidently the upper strata of the brain are mostly sending down inhibitory messages, just as Sechenov had guessed.

Sherrington got many of the cat's reflexes pretty well localized in the spinal chord, and got them pretty well integrated in the sense that he understood when the occurrence of one reflex would inhibit another reflex.

Thus, the mindless cat can generally only display one of these tricks at a time. Sherrington worked out much of the circuitry and he concluded that there must be many places where one nerve fires the next one in line. At such places, which he called *synapses*, there is the opportunity for multiple inputs. One input might facilitate another by summating with it. Other inputs, like those from the cerebrum, could have an opportunity to inhibit action by subtracting from the total excitation at the synapse. All of this remarkable work was beginning to show us how the nervous system was integrated. A lot of the control of behavior was organized locally at a given level of the spinal chord. It was surely not the case that all the details of coordination were orchestrated up at the cortex. And much of behavior could be seen as controlled by stimuli—some of them external, like pressure on a paw, but many of them internal, like information about where the paw is and what it is doing. Sherrington showed us how to start thinking about coordinated behavior in stimulus–response terms.[4]

Thorndike, the Transition Man

EDWARD LEE THORNDIKE (1874–1949) began his graduate work with William James and then moved to Columbia. His dissertation was the famous cat-in-a-box study (Thorndike, 1898). The apparatus was a large box that the cat could see out from but could not get out of unless it pulled the dangling string that was connected to a latch on the door. Food was just outside beyond reach. On the first trial the cat reached outside, pawed and scratched at the box, meowed, and washed its face. Eventually it pulled the string, which opened the door, so the cat could go out and start eating the food. Thorndike then grabbed the cat and put it back in the box for the next trial. There were about 20 trials spread over two days. Some details, such as the character of the string, were changed a little for some animals, but that is basically all there was to it. Some of the greatest experiments look ridiculously simple—after they are described.

The Character of Learned Behavior

Thorndike plotted up the time it took to open the door for each trial for each cat, and he presented these individual learning curves. There is a lot of trial-by-trial variability, but there is also a clear overall trend, Thorndike said, showing a gradual and continuous improvement in performance (see figure 13.1). The smooth, continuous character of this trend suggests that learning is a smooth, continuous process. It looks like a gradual but steady strengthening of an association. It looks like an automatic, machine-like stamping in of the association. (These are the words Thorndike would use again and again over the next five decades to describe learning.)

What is the nature of the learned association? Thorndike said it cannot involve ideas, as the philosophers had contended, because then we would expect to see a sudden jump in performance when the cat suddenly got the idea of pulling the string. There is no such indication of any ideas. It must be a direct, mechanical sort of connection between the stimulus (the puzzle box) and the response (pulling the string). Thus, Thorndike provided the basic S–R framework that would dominate behaviorism. Several people, including Hartley, Mill, Bain, and Morgan, had argued for S–R learning, but these people had also allowed for associations linking stimuli to other stimuli, and other associations linking ideas to stimuli and ideas to responses. In **S–R psychology,** what was learned was an S–R connection, and nothing else. That was the only sort of association Thorndike or the later behaviorists would allow. And that was a major turning point in the story of psychology.[5]

FIGURE 13.1

The sort of learning curve reported by Thorndike.
Does it look gradual, or does it break suddenly?

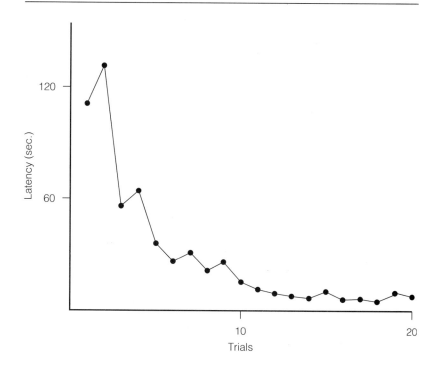

The Law of Effect

In 1911 Thorndike published a book, *Animal Intelligence*, that contained his dissertation work and a theoretical chapter. There he still adhered to a strong S–R position, the nothing-but position, but he added an important new principle that he called the **law of effect** but we just call reinforcement. In the dissertation he had been silent on the question of how an association is formed; he had told us what but not how. He assumed it was the linking up of previously unconnected sensory and motor neurons, but had said nothing about how that happens. Bain (and Spencer) had an explanation, which was that making the correct response results in pleasure, and pleasure causes a sort of emotional surge that somehow connects the neurons. In effect, the association is strengthened or reinforced by the pleasure it produces. But Thorndike could not accept such an account because pleasure is a mentalistic, unscientific term. Let us not speak of pleasure or pain, he said, but rather of the *effect* of the response. If the effect is positive then the connection is strengthened; if the effect is negative then the connection gets weakened. A positive effect he called a *satisfier*, which sounds rather psychological but which really is quite objective and behavioral. A satisfier, such as food for a hungry cat, is something the animal does nothing to avoid but rather responds to so as to procure and prolong it. Similarly, an *annoyer* is avoided, so negative effects are well-defined objective events also. It might appear that Thorndike was just playing with words here, and not really avoiding the old pleasure–pain principle. But his approach had one profound implication. It took the control of behavior out of the head and put it in the environment. Stimuli and responses are out there where they can be manipulated and recorded by the experimenter. And the effect of the response is out there too, being carefully controlled by the experimenter. There is nothing going on in the animal at all except the strengthening of S–R connections.*

Thorndike returned to the learning area in the 1920s, but this time it was human learning that attracted his attention. He wrote several hundred experimental papers (some were applied but a lot of them were theoretical) plus a few books on the subject. He was extraordinarily productive. A couple

---

* Environmentalism, or externalization, had been important to Darwin, because it was the ever-changing environment that shaped the species by making one variant of the species better adapted than another. As the world changes the gene pool gradually drifts so that we always find animals well adapted to where they happen to be. Reinforcement is much like natural selection in that it virtually ensures that we will see behavior that is well-adapted to circumstances, at least in animals like us who depend on learning. But we have also seen that Darwin's emphasis on the importance of the slowly changing environment made it possible to dispose of a creator-type god. Thorndike's emphasis on a rapidly changing environment made it possible to dispose of an executive-type god who intervenes in our affairs. We can even dispose of ourselves as executives. He emptied the head. If you attach sufficient importance to the environment, you lose your mind.

of themes ran through all of his later work. One was that learning always involved the acquisition of new S–R associations. A second was that these associations were acquired by the automatic, stamping-in action of the law of effect. A third was that the thoughts and intentions of the person played virtually no role in learning; he did a lot of work trying to demonstrate what he called *learning without awareness*. As long as a response was reinforced it did not matter whether the subject knew what was happening. The stage was set for behaviorism to appear.

Watson's Behaviorism

JOHN BROADUS WATSON (1878–1958) came from humble circumstances that contrasted with the glory he would attain. He grew up in the farmland of South Carolina, and attended Furman, the nearby Baptist college. After graduating from Furman he taught for a short time at a country school. Then he made the major move to the University of Chicago, the land of Dewey, with whom he began studying. But he soon gave up on philosophy (he said he could not understand Dewey) and turned to more neurological matters. His dissertation was a developmental study; infant rats were found to be impaired in comparison with somewhat older ones in their ability to learn several different problems. Then he studied their brains histologically and found that the development of full learning ability occurred right about the time of full brain myelination (Watson, 1903). Thus he had a nice reductionistic explanation of a psychological phenomenon. Interestingly, while Watson was the first student out of the psychological branch of the department, the capital of the new functionalism, he was clearly in the old-fashioned mechanist tradition.

After getting his degree in 1903, Watson stayed on at Chicago for five years to set up and run the animal laboratory. Among other activities he undertook a series of studies to determine what kind of stimuli controlled the behavior of rats running in mazes. In one study he compared blind rats, deaf rats, and anosmic ones, and found to his probable surprise that they all performed about the same, nor were they different from normal controls. Therefore, he concluded, the maze habit must be controlled by the one sensory modality that cannot be tested, the *kinesthetic* sense. It is feedback from the muscles and joints that controls movement, he said. You cannot deprive an animal of this internal sensory information because if you cut the kinesthetic sensory tracts the animal will fall in a heap; it cannot stand up or do much of anything. But it makes sense for muscles to be controlled by the muscle sense, and it is a huge sensory system (by far the largest). So Watson made a permanent commitment to kinesthetics as being the major source of behavior-controlling stimuli. Running a maze involves a whole chain of

John B. Watson

responses, and we can think of one response producing feedback that then constitutes the stimulus for the next response, and so on. That was the way it worked in Watson's view.

Good news in 1908: Watson was offered a position as professor at Johns Hopkins. And the news got better: Right after Watson got there the chairman Mark Baldwin was obliged to resign for personal reasons. He left to Watson the chairmanship as well as the editorship of the *Psychological Review*. Watson was only 31 and had amazing energy. He also now had amazing opportunity. Soon we would also see in him amazing audacity and ambition.

Watson's Mentors and Friends

Let us backtrack a bit to note some of the people who had helped shape Watson's thinking. There was the German physiologist Jacques Loeb, who had studied at Berlin and Würzburg but went to the brand-new University of Chicago to be one of its pioneering professors. Loeb studied what were called *tropisms*, the movements of animals and plants with regard to light or gravity. Many flowers turn to face the sun, for example. Some insects always crawl up a wall and never down. Some little creatures always approach a source of light. Loeb would paint over one eye of such a creature and find that it now went in circles. The circling looks like complicated behavior, but no, the creature is just doing what it always does, which is to turn in the direction of the eye receiving more light—that is its tropistic way of approaching light. Loeb contended that a great deal of behavior was similarly organized by simple S–R mechanisms.

There was Knight Dunlap, who had gotten his degree with Holt at Harvard and come to Hopkins in 1906. He was a militant mechanist. (Maybe he converted Holt!) He was a capable, forceful man who no doubt encouraged

Watson to think as he did—and then followed him when Watson took the lead. There was also Herbert Jennings, who poked and prodded many of the little animals that live in the water. He would provide a stimulus and then note the reaction. If such work sounds dreary, it is only because it is unfamiliar. Those little animals have some wonderfully complex behaviors. Little hydras that move around by somersaulting definitely somersault quicker and hence travel faster if they are hungry. Once into this adventure, Jennings was no longer poking to see what would happen, but rather mapping out the response repertoire of the animal and cataloging what stimuli it was sensitive to. He was working out the animal's psychology. Jennings was head of the biology department at Hopkins when Watson got there, and they became very good friends.[6]

Watson loved methodology and he wrote an important methodological book with Harvard's Robert Yerkes (in the beginning he and Yerkes had the only experimental animal labs in the country). How do you know if a dog can see color? You give it a number of trials where a green light is followed by food if the dog makes one response, and a red light is followed by food if it makes another response. After a while the dog is getting food most of the time and seems to be discriminating, but you want to make sure, so you continue the training but you systematically vary the brightness of one of the lights, making it brighter and dimmer. At some point, with a dog, the discrimination will break down. Then you know that the dog can discriminate brightness, but not hue. Watson did a lot of research on just this problem. From his friends and colleagues, and from his own research, the message was that behavior is totally dependent on what the stimulus is. The stage was set and the time had come.

The Behaviorist Manifesto

In 1913 Watson published his epochal paper "Psychology as the behaviorist views it." Essentially it says that behavior is everything, behavior is all there is. There is no mind, at least there should be no mind, in psychology. If the philosophers want to ponder the human mind we should let them do so, but the mind does not belong in science. He cited Freud as showing that the mind does not know what it is doing. He cited poor Külpe as showing that the mind cannot even see what it is doing. Let us step aside from the mind, Watson insisted, and get on with the business of science.

In 1914, just a few months later, there came the second blast, *Behavior, An Introduction to Comparative Psychology*. The book is mainly about animal psychology, and a lot of it is methodological. He observed that color perception is interesting, but that our concern with it should be limited to the question of whether it affects behavior. For some species it does and for others it does not. If it does, then we have procedures for studying that, the sort of procedures that were just noted. We do not ask, as Goethe did, how that red patch "feels"; we only want to know how, if at all, that particular spectrum of reflectances can become associated with particular behaviors.

The book accomplished two things beyond describing an experimental methodology. It showed how easy it was to translate all the mentalistic content that psychology was burdened with into simple, easy, pleasing S–R connections. We do not have to worry about feelings and emotions; such things are nothing more than stimuli that arise from within the body. So Watson's behaviorism would minimize everything motivational. Emotions, motives, instinct, and pleasure and pain were all thrown out. There would be no more fire, just cold, hard Ss and Rs.

The other thing the 1914 book did was propose a new theory of learning. It was similar to Thorndike's in that it was all couched in S–R language. But it was very different on one point because while Thorndike was just getting started defending the reinforcement principle he called the law of effect, Watson evidently saw through the subterfuge of effect and satisfiers and suspected that Thorndike was still really thinking about pleasure and pain, and that he had nothing substantially better to propose. Watson had something better: You do not need some special event, like pleasure or a reinforcer or a satisfier, to build up an S–R association, you only need the S and the R to occur together! What matters is that S and R occur in contiguity, and contiguity alone strengthens the S–R connection. If you throw out all the mentalistic baggage and merely couple S and R, they will become associated so that S will regularly elicit R.

This was powerful medicine. First of all it disposed of Thorndike. He shot him down with Lloyd Morgan's canon, just as Thorndike had blown up Morgan himself with it a few years before. We recall from our lesson on how to become a legend that the legend-to-be has to destroy fellow travelers. Thorndike certainly looked and talked like a behaviorist, but no, he was impure. He had to be purified, by killing him off. Watson went to the trouble of publishing a little paper in 1917 that he said settled the matter, because it "showed conclusively" (that is a quote from the paper) that reinforcement does not work. On the other hand, if we bend over to accommodate Thorndike by letting him be another kind of behaviorist, then we will have the problem of having two kinds of behaviorism, and no one will be pure. We will have reinforcement theorists and contiguity theorists. And that is precisely the way it settled out, with two kinds of behaviorism. And there was some warfare between the camps. When Watson was in command, contiguity looked like the winner, but then when Thorndike and his allies took over in the 1930s, reinforcement came out on top. Watson wanted to have it all his way, but later it became clear that we were obliged to live with different kinds of behaviorism. Eventually there would be several varieties of behaviorism.

Watson, the Leader

Both Watson's big theory paper and his book were seen as sensational. Not everyone agreed and not everyone understood what was at stake, but everyone was fascinated. American psychology had no tradition, no real family, and no home. We were looking for a leader. William James could have been a leader but he did not wish to lead. Some wit once said that a leader is a clever person who can see where everybody is going and then runs out in front of them. At this point in the story of psychology we surely needed a leader, someone who could lead us out of the structuralistic mess and our other problems. John B. Watson was right there to lead us, and almost immediately he was elected president of APA.

One problem with instant fame and success is that it is hard to do an encore, but Watson was up to the occasion. He was already interested in making contact with Pavlovian ideas, because while he did not know much about Pavlov he did know that Pavlov was very much a mechanist. There would be lots of Russian immigrants beginning in 1918, but before that no one here spoke Russian. So there was no way to know what Pavlov was doing. But in 1913 a book by Vladimir Bechterev, *Objective Psychology*, was translated into French, and Bechterev too did conditioning experiments and was very much a mechanist. Watson and his graduate students translated the French Bechterev and then proceeded to carry out some conditioning experiments. It was a disaster. They could not get Pavlovian salivary conditioning (Lashley, 1916); they could not get the sort of finger-withdrawal thing Bechterev had reported (Hamel, 1919); they could not get anything. At the last moment they ran a study with a single dog subject where a signal was paired with an electric shock to a paw. They measured two responses, heart rate and foot flexion, and both responses changed over trials. The tradition at APA is that the president is obliged to give a presidential address, and this dog study was to be it. The oral paper was no doubt a huge success, but the published paper (Watson, 1916) left something to be desired. The trifling amount of data he presented obviously misrepresented what they had observed. There are a lot of problems with it as an experimental report, but no matter; Watson's encore had been wonderful. He said that Pavlov had the right method, that he was now a Pavlovian, and that it was all very behavioristic and scientific. Watson was leading us into the future.

Thinking

There are a couple of other facets of Watson's remarkable contribution to psychology. The first is how he treated thinking. We do not think, he said, we only think we are thinking. When children first start to read, he said, they read aloud. As they continue reading they don't speak but they still move their lips, as though they were reading aloud silently. Eventually there is no overt response that we can see, but there are still little twitches and tensions in the muscles of the mouth and throat. And those little, barely perceptible movements have tiny little kinesthetic feedbacks. And it is those minimal little stimuli that determine our behavior, and which we erroneously label as thoughts. They are not mental, however, they are just tiny responses. What you think of as thought is no more than muscle activity in your neck, or perhaps other parts of the body. Thus, if you think about throwing a ball, then the extensor muscles of your throwing arm are probably twitching. Watson was quite serious when he said that everything was a matter of Ss and Rs.

Emotion, Motivation, and Development

Shortly after his APA presidential address, Watson got involved in developmental psychology. He began looking at the reflexes of infants. He confirmed the neat, orderly development of new reflexes, and the neat, orderly dropping out of baby reflexes such as the Babinsky and the grasping reflexes. He noted how infants reacted in different situations. He looked at their emotional displays, and insisted that originally there were only three emotions, fear, anger, and joy. Fear is seen as a number of responses—open mouth, wide eyes, arms up, and a variety of autonomic nervous system responses (which were just being discovered at that time). The way he elicited fear was to hold a baby in his hands—and then drop it (his graduate student Rosalie Rayner was right there to catch the little one). Anger was expressed by reddening of the face, crying, and thrashing around, and it was elicited by pinning down the baby's arms. Joy was known by gurgling and cooing sounds (the smile is not mentioned), and is produced by putting a suitable object in the mouth. Emotion was seen as nothing but certain responses innately made to certain stimuli. Watson did not like the idea of motivation; it was too mentalistic. Accordingly, hunger was a stimulus and eating was a response. There were no instincts, either, only complex chains of reflexes. *Everything* was stimulus and response.

The new *Journal of Experimental Psychology* had installed Watson as the founding editor in 1915. When volume three finally appeared in 1920 it led off with a paper by Watson and Rayner that was destined to be one of the most famous papers that the distinguished journal ever carried. Their paper described the adventures of Little Albert. Albert was a nine-month-old infant who hung around a day care facility at Hopkins. He was a stolid, happy sort of infant. While he was seated on a table he was presented with a CS, which was a white rat. As soon as it was clear that Albert was paying attention to the CS, that is, he reached to touch it, there appeared the US, which was evidently a horrible noise. Above Albert was a four-foot iron rail, which was struck by a heavy hammer. The UR was a great startle reflex, after which little Albert would fall over, cry, and crawl away. Watson gave just a few conditioning trials and then ran a test with CS alone. He found *conditioned fear.* He also discovered, although he did not understand what it was, the context specificity of conditioned fear. In a different room under different conditions, Albert showed little fear of the rat. Watson gave him a couple of reminder trials in the new context, and was then able to demonstrate the conditioning of fear. Watson and Rayner discuss how they might undo any damage they might have done to the little boy. It would be interesting now, they said, to associate the white rat with candy or food and see if they could neutralize the original conditioning. Unfortunately, Albert was taken out of the day care center, so they had no way to do any sort of therapy. But, Watson tells us, should Albert grow up with certain kinds of aversions and phobias such that he felt obliged to seek the services of a psychotherapist, and if that therapist was able to convince Albert that he had unresolved Oedipal problems, then we who are knowledgeable about these things would know that his psychiatrist was dead wrong, because his hangups had all come from classical conditioning.

The Little Albert paper is historically important in several respects. Although it was a minimal study, it was nonetheless the first report of successful classical conditioning in this country, or any country other than Russia. It also prophesied that future classical conditioning research would depend on aversive USs such as a puff of air to the eye or an electric shock to the feet. It also remains one of the great polemical pieces of all time. Presenting little more than suggestive data, the paper came to some far-reaching conclusions: Watson and Rayner said (1) that S–R learning principles explain the development of personality (they had presumably altered Albert's personality), and (2) other approaches to emotional problems (such as psychoanalysis) are useless and wrong. Perhaps the most remarkable thing about this paper is that everyone seemed to believe it; it was widely cited, and, for that matter, it still is. We desperately wanted psychology to be a science, and we were willing to believe that Watson was showing us how it could be.

Watson's Impact

Watson had a wonderful sense of knowing what his colleagues wanted psychology to be, and then promising to deliver just that. If one presents what others want, then it does not have to be presented very convincingly because everyone is already convinced. Around 1920 we wanted a scientific behaviorism; we wanted to believe that everything was just a matter of Rs getting connected to Ss. There was to be nothing else, no mind, no feeling, no emotion, no motivation, nothing but S–R connections. The *zeitgeist* was clear from the number of books that began to expand upon Watson's ideas. A strongly behavioristic approach was advocated by Mateer (1918) for developmental psychology, by Watson (1919) for all of psychology, and by

Burnham (1924) for clinical psychology. There were influential introductory books to promote the cause by Smith and Guthrie (1921) and by Dunlap (1922). The behaviorists went off into social psychology (Dunlap, 1923; Allport, 1924), and they began to influence philosophers and popular writers (Weiss, 1925; Russell, 1927). When Pavlov became available in English (Pavlov, 1927), he fit right in. Holt, James's student who had kept the idea of motivation alive, became a convert and let motivation die (Holt, 1931). Watson had started an avalanche. Benjamin (1986) has indicated the early popular impact of Watson's ideas.

Watson's career ended as dramatically as it began. By 1920 Watson had gotten involved with his student Rosalie Rayner, and the fateful part of that was that he had written some letters to her. Watson was married, not too happily, to a woman whose family was important on the national political scene (the family name was Ickes). The wife managed, somehow, to steal the letters from Rosalie's bedroom; they got to the newspapers and there was a terrible fuss. Johns Hopkins could not tolerate all this, and Watson was obliged to resign. He divorced his wife and married Rosalie, and they were together for many years. But he could not find academic employment ever again. Later on he worked for, and prospered at, a large New York advertising agency. He wrote a number of articles and another book or two, and he worked with Mary Cover Jones on some further fear conditioning studies, such as on how to extinguish fear, but basically he was through.[7]

Varieties of Behaviorism

IT IS USEFUL TO summarize Watson's position in terms of our basic historical themes. First of all, he was clearly an atomist. He had all those little muscle twitches that were supposed to be the physical basis of thought. His approach was analytical; he sought to break up any big piece of behavior, such as building a bird nest, into elemental S–R reflexes. And, like Titchener, he believed that a complicated stimulus had to be broken up into its various stimulus elements. Thus, Watson was in the tradition of Democritus, Locke, Hartley, and Titchener; he was an atomist. Others whom we have to regard as behaviorists might be much less atomistic. We saw that Thorndike took the stimulus of the S–R formula to be the whole experimental situation. That is not a very atomistic approach. When all the behaviorists are counted, we discover some who were just as atomistic as Watson, and at least a few who were more wholistic than Thorndike. But if we arranged all the behaviorists on an atomism scale, we would find most of them well over on the atomistic side.

Watson was a mechanist. He worried about how the brain could be constructed so as to make conditioning possible. He totally rejected the mind; everything was physical. His position gives us the extreme, a sort of anchor, for the mechanistic end of a mechanism–mentalism dimension. He was in the tradition of Hobbes, La Mettrie, Hartley, and du Bois-Reymond. Many of the early behaviorists were probably attracted to Watson's view of things just because it was so mechanistic. They thought that his approach was the only way in which psychology could become a real science. But over the years there have appeared a lot of behaviorists who would spread all over a scale of mechanism versus mentalism. The most interesting and important aspect of this spreading out is that initially they were all mechanists, and as time went by they tended to bunch up in the middle, the neutral zone. Thus, B. F. Skinner, who is so important for contemporary behaviorism, was scrupulously neutral. He did not believe that mechanism had any special explanatory advantage, nor indeed did mentalistic concepts. But behaviorism clearly started in by being extremely mechanistic.

No matter how much the early behaviorists may have differed on the other themes, they were all empiricists who believed in the overwhelming importance of learning. Learning is what makes us what we are. That concept was perhaps Watson's most important and most widely accepted single contribution to psychology. That was his great vision, which he was able to get many others to share. All the early behaviorists believed in the fundamental importance of learning, even though they held somewhat different views of the mechanisms of learning, such as whether learning depended on reinforcement or on contiguity. But the different varieties of behaviorism all agreed that learning was the very heart of psychology.

Watson was an associationist. He argued that everything in psychology could be explained by learned S–R processes. Neither we nor animals ever learned meanings, or valences or values, or anything spatial, or anything else. There were no options; it had to be S–R associations. Almost all behaviorists were associationists, although there was an important exception whom we will meet shortly. The S–R association was the fundamental psychological unit. That was a big idea, and it rapidly spread throughout psychology and persisted from Watson's time in 1920 until quite recently.

Thus, we can see that Watsonian behaviorism embraced all of our basic themes. And although a few of the many people who regarded themselves as behaviorists varied somewhat from Watson's position, by and large they endorsed the same themes. So those old themes were still with us in 1970. This outcome should not be surprising, because, as I indicated in the Preface, the historical themes were discovered by taking a hard look at what psychology looked like in 1970. And at that time it appeared to be firmly based on atomism, mechanism, empiricism, and associationism. But psychology always shows a lot of variance, and sure enough, there were a few independents who did not believe in the themes that defined psychology. After Watson there would be a variety of behaviorisms.[8]

Tolman's Behaviorism

Granting that there was some variance, would it be possible for a behaviorist to emerge around 1930 who was so variant that he was *opposed* to the conceptual themes that defined psychology at that time? Certainly not, you might think, that could not happen. But yes, there was indeed a curious and unique psychologist like that, and his name was Edward C. Tolman (1886–1959). Tolman had come from Harvard, and had gotten his degree with James's man Holt in 1915. In 1918 he got a teaching appointment at the young University of California at Berkeley, and began setting up an animal laboratory much like the one Yerkes had at Harvard for studying learning. For several years he did not do any remarkable research but he did write a few papers on the concept of instinct and on the place of purpose in psychology. In these early papers Tolman argued that behavior is typically focused on a goal, on something of value to the organism. He believed that if one looks at behavior and tries to describe it, it does not look very mechanical or like a collection of reflexes. On the contrary, when we try to describe it, he said, it looks rather teleological. It is probably not teleological in the sense that it is caused by what lies ahead, but it often looks as though it were (Tolman, 1923). It has to be described as *purposive*, which means *as if* it had a purpose. This orientation reminds us of Lewin and the gestaltists, and well it should, because they deeply influenced Tolman's thinking, and he was always happy to acknowledge that influence. He also acknowledged a debt to the British iconoclast William McDougall (1908), who had very similar motivational ideas. Tolman's language, including words such as *purposive*, was deliberately chosen to be provocative and a kind of counterbalance to the mechanistic language that was becoming so popular. In any case, Tolman was vehemently opposed to mechanistic thinking.[9]

He was opposed to atomism. He regarded behavior as occurring in closed episodes. An animal exploring for food will continue to explore until food is found. If an animal is prevented from getting to food by a barrier, it will search for a way to overcome the barrier. This global or **molar** (the opposite of atomistic or **molecular**) view of behavior had been suggested by James and his associates at Harvard, as well as by Köhler and the gestaltists. It focused attention on the motivation that produces a behavior episode and the goal that concludes the episode, rather than on the momentary stimulus conditions that might elicit some little piece of behavior.

Tolman was fascinated by learning, which perhaps makes him an empiricist, but his was a new sort of empiricism because he was most definitely not an associationist. Associations were mechanical linkages of molecular Ss and Rs and Tolman wanted no part of that. He had his own

Edward C. Tolman

distinctive ideas about what was involved in learning, and they were new ideas indeed. Tolman (1932) said that what is learned in some cases is a *sign-gestalt* (the meaning of a cue or signal-stimulus). In other cases animals learn an *expectancy*. And in some cases animals learn *where things are in the environment.* We can illustrate these different sorts of learning with some experiments that were reported from Berkeley in the late 1920s and then summarized in Tolman's 1932 book.

Tolman's Learning Experiments

Williams (1929) trained rats to go by way of a black stimulus to get food, and then tested the animals to see if they would learn to approach the black stimulus. They did. In the first phase of training the black stimulus acquires meaning and value; it comes to mean food and to be valued. In the second phase this sign-gestalt learning is demonstrated by the animal learning to select the stimulus that had acquired value.

Tinklepaugh (1928) investigated the memory span of monkeys. In full view of the monkey, a piece of banana is placed under one of two cups. Then for a brief interval a screen is lowered to cover up the cups (so that the monkey cannot maintain an orienting response, such as pointing toward the food cup). When the screen is lifted the monkey grabs the correct cup, gets its food, and seems to be enjoying itself. The main data of the study involved the deterioration of accuracy with increasing delay intervals, but our concern here is with a wrinkle that was introduced into the procedure. On a few trials Tinklepaugh switched foods when the screen was covering everything up; a piece of lettuce was substituted for the banana. On those trials the monkey would grab the correct cup, stare at the lettuce, stare in the cup, stare at Tinklepaugh, sometimes start throwing cups and lettuce, and sometimes start shrieking and running around. Monkeys like lettuce and will work for it, so why is it a disrupter here rather than a reinforcer? Because the animal really prefers banana, and it *expects* banana. We see that the animal not only expects food, it expects a particular food. And the bottom line is that animals do not learn S–R associations that are reinforced, they learn *expectancies*.

Macfarlane (1930) went on the attack against Watson's emphasis on kinesthetic stimuli in maze learning. He had rats swim through a water maze. Rats are pretty good swimmers, and if the temperature is just right they will paddle along until they get to the goal box where there is a ladder, which they climb to get to their food. When the animals had learned to paddle through the maze, they one day encountered another of Tolman's procedural wrinkles: Water was drained out of the apparatus, so that now they had to walk through it. Notice that all the stimuli are now different, the animal is no longer wet or weightless and the supposedly key kinesthetic cues are changed because it is now walking rather than paddling. So if animals are really learning S–R associations, then Macfarlane's rats should be hopelessly confused, like beginners. But this wrinkle caused very little disruption. So then what were the rats learning? Tolman's brave new answer was that they were learning the layout of the maze, a map of the thing, where the blind alleys and the through path were. They were integrating a lot of spatial information. They were learning something cognitive.

Cog-
maps

Spacial
maps

Tolman had a number of great students by this time. Elliott (1929) showed that rats ran faster and made fewer errors in mazes if they were hungry. Previously he had shown (Elliott, 1928) that they performed better if they were running for a more preferred food. Moreover, if the situation was wrinkled so that they were switched from a more to a less preferred food, then they were seriously disrupted (the Tinklepaugh effect). Thus we can see Lewin's motivation principles in rats, both a need or tension effect and a value or valence effect. The two factors would eventually be labeled **drive** and **incentive.**

Other behaviorists worried about Tolman and his ideas, and how to explain away the cognitive sorts of effects he had discovered. Clark Hull and his followers explained some of them, at least for a time, as we will see next. But Hull also accepted some of them, particularly the two dimensions of motivation. Some other behaviorists just rejected his work out of hand as being too far out. Certainly Tolman greatly enriched and complicated our view of what behaviorism was; Watson had made it all so simple. Some of this enrichment was obviously due to Tolman's incorporation of gestalt ideas. And there seems to be a connection; Boakes (1984) reports that in 1925 Köhler came to this country for an extensive visit and gave a series of lectures. He spent some time at Berkeley, and was particularly interested in what Tinklepaugh was doing. And 1925 was the year Tolman's laboratory began to heat up. Interestingly, Tolman's ideas are much more warmly regarded now than they were in his own time. Then they were regarded as interesting and provocative, but a little strange. They could not be assimilated because

Tolman was fighting a powerful *zeitgeist*. And that *zeitgeist* would be a powerful ally of Professor Hull of Yale, who for a time would find everything going his way.

Hull's Behaviorism

CLARK L. HULL (1884–1952) started with all sorts of disadvantages. As a boy he was poor and was educated at country schools. As a youth he was still poor but worked his way through Alma College. As a young man he was stricken by polio, but eventually got into graduate school at the University of Wisconsin. He got his degree in 1918, but his dissertation research was not published until he was 36 years old, and then it attracted little attention. But he remained at Wisconsin and made a good name for himself in a variety of areas, including concept formation, aptitude measurement, and hypnotism. He had a broad background in many areas of psychology, all of which he had treated in a solid experimental manner.

In 1929 Hull got a big break; he was invited to Yale to head a group of scholars at the Institute of Human Relations. The purpose of the institute was to study how basic learning principles could be applied to an understanding of everyday human behavior. It would have been reasonable for them to focus on human applications, but instead they started building a general theory of learning based mainly on animal studies. Initially Hull was inclined toward a Pavlovian view of learning. He became an authority on recently discovered Pavlov, and did his best to give a Pavlovian account of trial-and-error learning. But there was a turning point in 1935 when Hull wrote a long, thoughtful review of a new book by Thorndike. Hull struggled with the question of whether one should understand and explain behavior in terms of its motives, as Tolman had argued, or in terms of what reinforces it, as Thorndike had proposed. Hull was not certain, but he was inclined to follow Thorndike and go for the reinforcement approach. By 1943 he was totally committed to the reinforcement view of trial-and-error learning, which he called **instrumental learning** (the response is instrumental in obtaining the reinforcer).

Hull's Principles of Behavior

Hull wrote a series of important theoretical papers that culminated in his most important work, *Principles of Behavior* (1943). There we can see that he had retained Pavlov's concept of inhibition and expanded it so that he had two kinds of inhibition. He took over Tolman's drive and incentive concepts. Drive was in the body; it came from bodily needs such as hunger, thirst, or pain. Incentive was out there in the environment; it was the amount of

Clark L. Hull

reinforcement given on a particular trial. The key concept of learning was *habit*, which was the strength of the S–R association. Habit was not directly manifest in behavior because, like all of Hull's concepts, it had to be fitted together with his other concepts. For example, the strength of an observed behavior depended not only on what habit the animal had learned but also on what its motivation was. It was rather like Sechenov's idea that a response does not reflect excitation directly, but is rather a complex function of all the different excitatory and inhibitory things going on in the nervous system.

Hull liked to call his theory a *hypothetico-deductive system;* it started with a set of rather precise and specific hypotheses, and then deduced what the behavioral outcome should be. If experiments confirm the deduced prediction, then that gathers points for the theory. If experiments give unpredicted results, then something has to be fixed, perhaps one of the initial hypotheses. That is the way science works, Hull maintained; that is the way Kepler solved the puzzle of the planets and that is the way Newton solved all those other puzzles of gravity. To make it work the theory has to be quantitative, with equations and constants and all the other mathematical paraphernalia of science. Hull did indeed write hypothetical equations and estimate constants from other sets of data. And he had all those well-defined concepts. Hull's *Principles of Behavior* was an ambitious and noble undertaking. It presented the first quantitative theory of learning—the first theory that honestly confronted the flexibility and complexity of animal behavior, and the first theory stated with sufficient precision that it could be tested. It was, as they said in those days, a *rigorous* theory, meaning that it was strictly empirical. All the terms were clearly defined and could be given numerical values. In other words, the theory was testable. It cried out to be tested.

For two or three decades Hull's theory was intensively tested; it became the great theoretical battleground. Many parts of it certainly did need to be fixed, but other parts, such as the way it handled discrimination learning, held up remarkably well. Amazingly, when Hull was confronted with a serious problem, such as the way he had handled incentive motivation, he was happy to concede the mistake. That was what a good theory was for, he said, not to be correct a priori, but to generate research that would lead to a better model. And Hull's theory generated mountains of research. During the 1950s, more than 50 percent of all the papers published in *Journal of Experimental Psychology* had citations of Hull, mostly his *Principles*. He and his approach to psychology had become the center of things.[10]

The Character of Hull's Theory

Kuhn's critical concept of paradigm refers not only to specific theories (such as the idea that the sun stood at the center of things), but also to a general set of rules determining how scientists go about their business. These rules determine what are accepted as appropriate experimental procedures, how data are supposed to be analyzed, and what sorts of explanatory concepts are acceptable. To maintain discipline in a science the paradigm controls the language of the science. Typically, certain familiar words from everyday language are prohibited. Thus, Titchener's structuralism would allow no reference to the meaning of perceived objects. Under Watsonian behaviorism, there could be no reference to anything mentalistic. And anything that looked like an active principle, such as instinct or emotion or motivation, was forbidden. Hull and his followers began the reintroduction of motivational language, but they had to do it with care. Drive was physiological, borrowed from the hard sciences, so it was acceptable, but incentive was much trickier to put into respectable S–R terms, as we will see shortly.

It was this paradigmic change that went with Hull's theory that made it so exciting at the time. We knew how to proceed. We could argue about this or that detail, but we always knew how to settle such issues: By doing the obvious experiments. Hull's was the right *kind* of theory, according to the new paradigm. Moreover, Hull's theory and the new paradigm (some would say metatheory) promised to provide a firm empirical and theoretical foundation for developmental, social, clinical, and all the other areas of psychology. Everyone could buy into the metatheory. Structuralism did not make it because it was too narrow and restrictive. Functionalism did not make it because it was too permissive and fuzzy. The gestaltists could not do it because they were too far removed from what most psychologists wanted to believe in. Behaviorism was just right; it fitted, it suited, it appealed, and it promised everything we wanted. And so it became the psychological paradigm. Or so it seemed.[11]

The second thing that fueled the takeoff of Hull's behaviorism was that at Yale he was surrounded by a group of extremely capable and devoted young people who were eager to carry the banner forward and make Hull's behaviorism the heart of psychology. We can call these people neo-Hullians.

The Neo-Hullians

Although Hull's behaviorism was founded on animal learning experiments it soon diffused all through psychology. Part of this dispersion can be attributed to the remarkable person of Kenneth Spence, one of Hull's earliest and most capable students at Yale, and for many years his close friend and intellectual sparring partner. Hull and Spence argued about details, but always presented a united front against any other kind of learning theory, that is, any other metatheory. Spence went to the University of Iowa in 1938 and became head of the department there in 1942. He was a powerful head who maintained control of everything in the department for many years. Over the years Spence surrounded himself with other right-thinking behaviorists and they supervised a large number of experimental dissertations (Iowa had one of the largest psychology departments in the country). Everything had to meet with his approval. Sometimes it seemed as though everybody there, including the clinical students, were fighting for the glory of Hullian theory. And they spread out across the great plains, the mountains and all the shores of psychology.

Neal Miller was another extraordinary early student of Hull's. Miller had always been interested in physiological matters such as brain structures, drugs, and hunger. But in the early 1930s he visited Freud in Vienna and returned to do experiments on repression. Neither he nor anyone else found much evidence for repression in rats. According to Sears (1943), another of Hull's young colleagues, Freudian psychology just did not seem to have any verifiable concepts. Clearly, the Freudian analysis had to be replaced with more rigorous learning principles, and ultimately Miller tried to do that (Dollard and Miller, 1950). John Dollard was another of Hull's original inner circle. In the 1940s Miller was also testing animal models of conflict, and enjoying considerable success. The rat can run over there and get food, but it also gets a mild electric shock to its feet. Our lives are full of conflict situations like that. The phenomena were those of Lewin, but their explanation was strictly Hullian.

Another of Hull's brilliant early collaborators was O. Hobart Mowrer. In the late 1930s Mowrer conceived of an animal model of compulsions and other neurotic problems. The model that Mowrer devised involved rats avoiding shock in a shuttlebox. In the lab, why does the rat run from one side to the other when the warning stimulus (WS) signaling shock comes on? In the clinical case, why does Lady Macbeth wash her hands so often? Mowrer (1939) said that the explanation is the same in both cases. There is anxiety or fear, elicited either by the WS or by her sense of guilt. The running response removes the WS, and the hand washing symbolically removes the guilt and the fear. In each case, the learned response is powerfully reinforced by the reduction in fear that it produces. This analysis convinced Mowrer that learning required a reinforcement mechanism, and it no doubt contributed to Hull's conviction on that point, too. But note that in Mowrer's analysis, the reinforcer is a reduction in fear. That is the critical effect of the curious behavior in each case. We can think of fear as a source of drive, something like a disturbance of the body, something like a biological need. Perhaps it is only a special case of a more general rule that reinforcement always involves the reduction of drive. Reduce hunger with food, reduce pain by escaping its source, reduce fear by eliminating the fear signal, and in each case you will strengthen the relevant habit. Yes, that must be it. It was decided. The proposition that reinforcement depends on the reduction of drive became a critical part of Hull's 1943 theory. And we can see how the neo-Hullians, and I have only mentioned the foremost among them, began to spread their new paradigm throughout the diverse fields of psychology.[12]

Hull and his followers were atomistic; they were analyzers, they broke big hunks of behavior up into its explainable parts. A series of behaviors was a chain, to be broken up into links. On the mechanism issue, we see a spectrum, with Miller painted mechanist, Spence appearing quite neutral (a pure behaviorist, one might say), and Hull somewhere in between. It was always machine-like and never mentalistic, even when dealing with cognitive phenomena, but few Hullians were hard-line mechanists. Empiricist, yes, through and through. The Hullians almost never looked at instincts or other sorts of innately organized behavior. And they were all associationists; they all endorsed the S–R habit concept. So they kept the basic historic themes intact. Indeed, they defined our themes as of 1970 or so.

The Problem With Incentive Motivation

To understand what happened to the Hullians who seemed to occupy such a dominant and invincible position, it helps to look at how they handled incentive motivation, which turned out to be a difficult and divisive concept for them. In 1930, when the Hullian enterprise was just getting started, Hull was Pavlovian, and he proposed that the appearance of purpose in behavior, which Tolman had made so much of, could be explained in Pavlovian terms in the following way. When the rat gets to the goal box it makes a distinctive and important goal response: It eats. That particular response, we can label it R_G, cannot occur anywhere else in the apparatus because there is no food anywhere else. But there is a fractional part of it that can occur, and will occur to the extent that R_G has become conditioned to various stimuli in the situation, and that little fractional, conditioned response we can label r_G (pronounced little are gee). In the case of hunger, we might suppose r_G is salivation. Then r_G is going to have stimulus feedback, s_G, and that conceptually new stimulus can serve the very important function of providing a continuous and steady thread of controlling stimulation, which makes the behavior look as though it were directed at the food in the goal. We do not need to refer to purpose or expectancies, as Tolman did. We can reduce it all, Hull said, to simple S–R associations. Subtle, Pavlovian S–R associations, to be sure, but at least the right kind of stuff. It was a great coup by Hull that seriously weakened the threat of what Tolman was trying to do.

The r_G concept then developed slowly, and did not become important until about 1950, at which time the neo-Hullians went in different directions on it; it was a watershed concept. Spence regarded r_G as a motivator; it was the mechanism that explained incentive motivation, which accounted for rats running faster for a preferred food than for a nonpreferred food, or for more food than for less food. Different foods have different r_Gs, and more food has a bigger r_G. Mowrer (1960) made Pavlovian conditioned emotions the mediators of all behavior. There were two kinds of learning, he said, the learning of overt responses by reward and the learning of motivators by classical conditioning. This was the so-called two-factor theory. Miller never did like these little responses, except insofar as he could actually measure them. The trouble was that despite considerable effort, they could not be measured very well. Incapacitating the salivary glands should abolish the sort of behavioral effects that are explained by the r_G mechanism in hungry rats, but alas, the effects are still there.

There were two schools of thought about the dilemma. Miller represented the realistic school, who wanted to find these little rascals somewhere, perhaps in the autonomic nervous system. The relativistic school was not bothered by the physiological problem of measuring r_G as long as the concept worked, as long as it sorted out experimental data consistently (one is reminded of Ptolemy's epicycles). But the problem here was that if r_G is nothing more than a convenient fiction, then there are no grounds for preferring it to Tolman's old ideas of purpose and expectancy. Some said it was consistent with the behavioristic S–R paradigm, which is a reason to prefer it. But the whole point of the S–R paradigm, its value, the only thing it had, was that it was objective; it dealt rigorously with measurable S–R associations and not with fictions. It was an ugly dilemma.

But it was certainly not a new dilemma. Watson had abolished the mind because it was too spooky and not rigorous enough for a scientist to work with. And he gave us a nothing-but S–R psychology. But then to save appearances, to account for the data, he had to introduce some pretty spooky little muscle twitches that could not be observed. Guthrie (1935) had a marvelously simple S–R model that was elegantly parsimonious. But to make it work he had to introduce virtually an infinite number of microscopic stimuli, which was also pretty spooky. The Hullians had this wonderful theory that was so complex and flexible they could go anywhere and do anything with it. But to make it work, even for the simple case of the rat running to get food, they had to introduce those spooky r_Gs. A lot of behaviorists became rather discouraged. It began to occur to some that perhaps the paradigm was no good, perhaps the metatheory should be replaced. We will see in the next chapter that the whole thing would fall apart around 1970. But even before that, Hullian behaviorism was beginning to be replaced by Skinnerian behaviorism.

Skinner's Behaviorism

BURRHUS FREDERIC SKINNER (1904–90) came from a small town in Pennsylvania and went to Hamilton College, where he majored in English. After a year in which he discovered he did not like to write, and having been intrigued by what he had read of Watsonian behaviorism, he went off for graduate study at Harvard. At Harvard Skinner worked primarily in the lab of the physiologist W. J. Crozier, who was a rarity among physiologists in that he was concerned with adaptations of the whole organism to physiological challenges such as hunger. Crozier was not interested in the underlying mechanisms, and neither was Skinner. But he developed his view of the psychological world quite independently of Crozier, the Hullians, and of everyone else, if we can believe his own story (Skinner, 1979).[13] In the theoretical part of his dissertation (Skinner, 1931) he said that when we speak of an S–R reflex we are only referring to the observed fact that S is regularly followed by R (as David Hume might have said). We gain nothing further, at least in accounting for the behavior, by citing intervening neurological events or by looking for something going on in the mind. For the psychologist the reflex should be no more than a predictable response. So at the outset we can see Skinner coming right down the middle of the behavioristic road, avoiding all the mechanistic temptations on the one side and all the mentalisms on the other side. He would later label this neutral type of approach to the explanation of behavior *radical behaviorism.*

Operant Behavior

Skinner always liked orderly data, and in the early days he gradually devised an apparatus that gave him orderly data (Skinner, 1956). He called it an operant chamber; everyone else calls it a Skinner box. It is a very simple box, a little smaller than a breadbox, with nothing in it except for a little cup that food can be dropped into, and a little metal lever that sticks out from the wall about one inch. The experimenter now only has to do three things: (1) put a hungry rat in there; (2) arrange a contingency so that a tiny bit of food is delivered when and only when the rat presses the lever; and (3) sit back and wait. After a while the experimenter has lots of orderly data, a whole stream of lever presses. The data appear even more orderly if they are presented in a cumulative record, which plots the total number of responses that have been counted against how much time the rat has been in the box. One gets a

B. F. Skinner

relatively straight line. Indeed, these data are so orderly that they remind us of a reflex. One might wonder what stimulus is eliciting all these lever presses. But that is the wrong question. We just saw that a reflexive response is not elicited by the stimulus, it is merely highly correlated with it. So we are not looking for the cause of lever pressing but only for a good correlate. And we have that: The response is correlated with its consequence! We can call the food pellets reinforcers because we can embed them in a contingency and control behavior with them (Skinner, 1937). It is not our concern whether they arouse expectancies or whether they facilitate synaptic transmission. The radical behaviorist is concerned only with the fact that making reinforcers contingent on responses generates lots of responses and nice, orderly data. *Control the reinforcer and you can control the behavior.* That is the message of radical behaviorism, or we might call it radical environmentalism.

Skinner found that operant behavior can be brought under the control of an external stimulus. Reinforce the response in the presence of a tone, but not in its absence, and after a while the rat will respond only when the tone is on. The tone becomes a *discriminative stimulus,* one that also does not elicit behavior, or have anything to do with the rat's expectancies or neurons, but that can be used to control the behavior. Importantly, in becoming a discriminative stimulus the tone itself becomes a reinforcer, so that the rat will learn a new response upon which the tone is made contingent (Skinner, 1936). Part of the rigor of the Hullian approach was that it sought to control and predict behavior. With Skinner there is nothing but controlling and predicting. Hull had a whole network of explanatory constructs, but Skinner had only one—the great god reinforcement.

All of this, plus some material on partial reinforcement, was documented and summarized in an early book with the immodest title *The Behavior of Organisms* (1938). Skinner's contribution to learning theory and to systematic behaviorism was essentially complete at this point because over the last fifty years of his active life he was concerned with applications of radical behaviorism and with presenting his ideas to the public. Like Thorndike and Watson before him and like the Hullians who were contemporaries, Skinner believed that the world would be a far better place if only it would pay attention to what he had to say. His first popularization was *Walden Two* (1948), which describes what a radically behavioristic utopia might look like. Like most of his subsequent popularizations, it was widely read but met rather critically by the intellectual and literary worlds.

Spreading the Word

Meanwhile, just before 1950 an unusual series of events was unfolding at Columbia University through the efforts of Fred Keller, who had been a good friend and ally of Skinner's since they were in graduate school at Harvard together. Keller was a strong advocate of Skinner's approach, especially after *The Behavior of Organisms* came out in 1938. One of Keller's graduate students, Nat Schoenfeld, was particularly impressed. After getting his degree during the war, Schoenfeld joined the faculty at Columbia. Then Keller and Schoenfeld together decided to do a very unusual thing: They would become Skinnerian disciples! With the cooperation of the chairman, they turned the department inside out. For example, they taught the introductory course their way, and gave students rats to reinforce. They wrote a suitable introductory textbook and some theoretical papers to make it all clear. They were blessed with a number of outstanding postwar graduate students, and around 1950 the operant movement, as it was called, really began to get moving. By 1960 it was beginning to move into psychological clinics. Systematic desensitization, which first appeared around 1950 with a strong Hullian perspective, became increasing dominated by operant practitioners. They moved into educational psychology. It seemed that reinforcement techniques could be effective with children with special education problems. By the 1960s operant conditioners had also come to dominate whole areas of applied experimental psychology. For example, drug companies had begun massive screening of new compounds, and it was operant conditioners who were doing the behavioral screening.

This flight from the laboratory, as Skinner (1961) called it, was a healthy development because it got what had been a highly academic adventure out into the world of everyday affairs, out there where the problems were. Old John Dewey would surely have approved of it if he had lived just a little longer to see it. Part of the appeal of Skinnerian psychology was unquestionably just this ready applicability to real-life problems. Certainly some of the appeal was purely technological. Data on rats running for food in alleys tend to be variable and limited in scope. The Skinner box generated a lot of data per animal per hour, and there were many new aspects of it to look at. Thus, there were many new schedules of reinforcement to examine and try to understand.

No doubt some psychologists had become disenchanted by the failure of the big theoretical systems, such as Hull's, to yield a very clear picture of behavior. The big theories were too vague, too ambiguous, and too difficult to test against one another. Perhaps there was a retreat from behavioristic theory in general, and the relatively atheoretical operant approach was seen as a good way out. For all these reasons, there was great interest and faith in Skinner's approach to behavior, particularly among the growing number of psychologists who were interested in applied problems.

Skinner gave us a quite different sort of behaviorism. It was not really atomistic, because the units of analysis depend on what holds together empirically. If one stimulus pattern controls a wide class of functionally related responses, then fine, those are the appropriate units. And presumably one could use differential reinforcement to shape up big units or small units or whatever is desired. There is no a priori proper unit. Skinner was certainly not a mechanist any more than he was a mentalist; he was a middle-of-the-road, nothing-but, radical behaviorist. He was not an S–R associationist, nor any kind of associationist. And that is rather refreshing. He said behavior is controlled by the external stimuli with which it is correlated. The correlation might look like a causal link but no, it is only an empirical relationship. And Skinner was an empiricist because of his emphasis on learning; almost all of the behavior he was interested in was learned. His emphasis on the environmental control of behavior, suggesting that the organism brings nothing important to the situation, also implies an empiricist bias. Thus, curiously, Skinner the behaviorist departed from three of the four historic themes that Watson the behaviorist had maintained so strongly.[14]

Summary

BEHAVIORISM REALLY began in England, the home of evolutionary theory and its concern with the question of continuity of human mind with animal mind. But then rather quickly the animal mind started to disappear, and shortly thereafter the human mind disappeared. There was nothing left except neurons and behavior. With Watson and Pavlov the neurons were very important, but then with Tolman and Hull the neurons began to disappear! Tolman did not need them, although he gave us a glimpse of the mind. Hull gave us a glimpse of the neurons, but was scrupulously clean in rejecting the mind. Among the neo-Hullians, Spence rejected both neurons and mind, Miller rejected only the mind, and Mowrer rejected only the neurons.

That elusive behavioral road must be out there someplace. Did Skinner find it? His account is restricted to behavior and the environmental stimuli that are correlated with it; the organism is empty, without a nervous system or a mind, but do we want to follow his purely behavioral road?

Our story has now taken us up to about 1970. At that point we find Watson's behaviorism alive and well in the minds of many physiological psychologists who really depend on neurons to earn a living. But most behaviorists had forgotten it. By 1970 Tolman's behaviorism was dormant, but it was about to stir again. Hull's great theoretical system was in pieces, but some of the pieces still had considerable vitality. The emotional and motivational factors, particularly as developed by Spence, attracted considerable attention. Mowrer's two-factor theory looked healthy. But even while the heart of the Hullian system was falling into disrepair, the people on the fringe of it were moving into the clinic, the school, and other places where there were real problems to solve. Skinner's followers also moved rapidly into these areas and began to take them over. Behaviorism of one variety or another looked very healthy in 1970. It was admittedly still taking shape, but the paradigm was supposed to let such differences work themselves out. We almost had the paradigm that psychology had so long searched for. We almost had the basic core of metatheory, methods, and common assumptions that psychology had been seeking. But our story is not yet finished.

Notes

1. Romanes triggered a lot of discussion about the comparative mentality of animals. After Morgan's response to Romanes, to which we will turn next, there was further discussion by Hobhouse (1901), Washburn (1908), and Holmes (1911). In addition there resulted some research with mice, raccoons, pigs, and other animals not often studied today. Boakes (1984) describes much of this all-but-forgotten work.

2. Lloyd Morgan is now known almost entirely through two of his books, *Animal Life and Intelligence* (1890) and his most important, *An Introduction to Comparative Psychology* (1894). To discover more about Morgan and all these people, see Boakes (1984). Boakes's book is a wonderful history of behaviorism up to about 1930. It is full of interesting details, shrewd observations, and curious photographs. For example, he has photos of Clever Hans and of the gate Morgan's dog opened.

3. Ivan M. Sechenov (1829–1905) was most of his life concerned with metabolic mechanisms, but his biggest contribution was *Reflexes of the Brain* (1863) in which he developed the ideas that started the Russian conditioning tradition, as well as Russian mechanistic thinking. The great man in this tradition was Ivan Petrovich Pavlov (1849–1936). The standard reference on Pavlov is the translation of his lectures by Anrep (Pavlov, 1927). This remains the standard, even though there are other translations of other lectures. The Nobel Prize work is described in Pavlov (1897), and it is still a good account of digestion. The standard biography of Pavlov's interesting life is Babkin (1949).

4. It seems criminal to give such a sketchy account of Sherrington (1857–1952) and his great work. The best account of his work is his book *The Integrative Action of the Nervous System*, which was originally published in 1906 and then revised when the remarkable old gentleman was 90. Unfortunately there is nothing approximating a good history of physiological psychology; Sherrington marked the beginning of the modern era.

5. Thorndike was enormously productive. Everything he touched turned to publications. I will note only a couple of books cited in the text: *Animal Intelligence* (1911) and *Educational Psychology* (1913). His serious entry into human learning was marked by *The Fundamentals of Learning* (1932), which is the book Hull was reviewing when he began thinking about reinforcement. There is a good biography of Thorndike by Joncich (1968).

6. Jacques Loeb (1859–1924) is known mainly for his book on tropisms, which appeared in German in 1889, was revised in English in 1918, and has subsequently been reprinted. He has been frequently and unfairly characterized as some sort of mechanistic villain. Knight Dunlap (1875–1949) was another "villain," and an ally of Watson's at Hopkins. Burnham (1968) argues that Dunlap made a mechanist of Watson. Herbert Spencer Jennings (1886–1947) was named by his father after one of his intellectual heroes; Jennings also had a brother named Darwin. John Broadus Watson (1878–1958) got his middle name from his mother's favorite minister. This and other biographical details of Watson's remarkable life are given by Cohen (1979).

7. Watson's muscle-twitch theory of thought was not so bizarre at the time. A "motor theory of consciousness" had been suggested by Titchener, and such notions were developed by his first student, Margaret Washburn. A considerable literature emerged (see Humphrey, 1951). Watson first wrote three scholarly books, and later two books of more popular appeal: *Animal Education* (1903), *Behavior: An Introduction to Comparative Psychology* (1914), *Psychology from the Standpoint of a Behaviorist* (1919), and then *Behaviorism* (1924), and *The Psychological Care of Infant and Child* (1928) (with R. R. Watson).

8. Students in my history of psychology class have an opportunity to write about whether Watson's behaviorism was really a Kuhnian revolution. They are allowed to make the simplifying assumption that Titchener's structuralism was the earlier paradigm. Most say that it was, it was so remarkable, it involved a new world view, it won converts from the old to the new, and it ended up with totally new journals and textbooks. It surely looked like a revolution. But other students say no, it was not Kuhnian because it did not arise from any crisis within structuralism. Titchener didn't like it, but it did not affect him. One particularly thoughtful student said that if one takes Germanic structuralism and translates it into American pragmatism, behaviorism is what you get. The fundamental principles in both cases are structural rather than dynamic, analytic rather than synthesizing, and taxonomic rather than explanatory, so there was no basic change and no revolution.

In lieu of such a paper students could elect to write a paper about Kuhn's analysis, and explain why it is so hard to apply to the history of psychology, and suggest how a more useful analysis might go. Nothing very interesting came out of these papers, however, until recently when young Mark Mulkerin explained it all. He said that Kuhn was quite right that science is like politics in that it is infused with influence, persuasion, attempts to gain power, and so on. But Kuhn's mistake is that he only recognizes one kind of political influence, the revolution. More realistically, there are many ways to exert political influence. The gestaltists, for example, were not really undertaking a revolution; they were more like guerrillas hiding in the woods always making trouble. The behaviorists were more like an army from a neighboring land that invaded and conquered. Both were politically important, but through political mechanisms other than revolution.

9. Edward Chace Tolman (1886–1959) wrote one of the classics, *Purposive Behavior in Animals and Men* (1932), where he summarized the work of his early students. The important early theory papers cited in the text are dated 1920 and 1923. They are included in his *Collected Papers* (1951). Tolman was always sympathetic to the gestaltists; as a graduate student he spent a few months with them at Frankfurt. In the early 1930s he visited with Karl Bühler, Egon Brunswik, and others in Vienna. There is a short autobiography (Tolman, 1952), which will have to do until Nancy Innis completes her biography.

10. Clark L. Hull (1884–1952) developed a complex and challenging theory, which a whole generation of graduate students was obliged to master. The thing mastered, we all set off to confirm or to repudiate this or that feature of it. It seemed terribly important. Hull wrote a major revision of the theory, *A Behavior System* (1952a), but it never commanded the attention that the *Principles* (1943) had. Once at Yale Hull carried out little further research; he supervised a number of students but he concerned himself mainly with theoretical matters. The early paper on purpose as a habit mechanism, which gave us r_G, was Hull (1930). His tentative shift to reinforcement theory appears in Hull (1935). There is a short autobiography (Hull, 1952b), and there is a sort of diary that was known to his intimates as Hull's *Idea books* (Hull, 1962).

11. In Hull's time there was a rather widely accepted view of what a science should look like. A science includes a number of technical terms, and one should be able to give operational definitions of all of them. Otherwise we can't tell what we are talking about. It turns out that terms like *stimulus* and *response* can be given operational definitions, but terms like *expectancy*, *desire*, and *idea* cannot. That was more or less the view of a number of Germanic philosophers of science who fled here in the early 1930s. There were also P. W. Bridgman and others. So all at once we had most of the Vienna Circle, the logical positivists, and the operationalists all telling us what a science should look like. And by golly, Hull's behaviorism looked pretty scientific. The philosophers had put their stamp of approval on Hull's enterprise. But really, how in the world can a scholar who is basically a logician validate an empirical enterprise? About as meaningfully, I believe, as a fish can teach a bird to fly. The scientist and the bird just do what they do, which is collect data and fly, while the philosopher and the fish can only watch and wonder.

12. Kenneth W. Spence (1907–67) is known to us mainly through his many research publications, although he did pull it all together at one point (Spence, 1956). It was the mass of research he supervised that really fleshed out the original Hullian framework. Spence gave it substance. Spence made it work in the laboratory. He proposed, and usually tested, many alternatives to Hull's hypotheses. He was the main force behind the development of incentive motivation ideas. Although Spence was inclined to abuse people intellectually, almost everyone who knew him felt warmly toward him.

Neal E. Miller (b. 1909) received his degree with Hull. He has always liked things to be simple, and as Hull's theory came together it was much too complex to suit him. Miller and Dollard (1941) produced a sort of blend of Guthrie's and Hull's ideas, which was a neat, simple variety of behaviorism. But it did not attract much attention, perhaps because it was so simple. After 1950 Miller gradually moved away from learning theory and into physiological psychology, where he became a towering figure.

O. Hobart Mowrer (1907–84) was a Missouri boy, a Ph.D. from Johns Hopkins, an instructor at Princeton, and a fellow and faculty member at Yale from 1934 to 1940. Thus, he overlapped with Hull for only a few years, but even so he made a great contribution to avoidance learning, to two-factor theory, and to learning theory generally. From Yale he went to Harvard, and from there to the University of Illinois, where he became increasingly interested in clinical matters. Mowrer's behaviorism was always on the cognitive fringe, and always looking ahead.

My favorite reference on the different varieties of behaviorism, as well as its ultimate decline, is Bolles (1979).

13. Skinner's autobiography (Skinner, 1979) is quite disappointing if one looks to it to understand where his ideas came from or how they took shape. More revealing in this regard is his collection of papers *Cumulative Record* (Skinner, 1972).

Skinner came from Susquehanna, Pennsylvania. In the unborn science of geo-psychology there is one highly significant finding, one really big effect. This fundamental truth is that almost all of the important experimental psychologists came from small towns or the countryside. It started with Wundt, a small town boy. It is confirmed with Müller, Ebbinghaus, and Külpe. Going to Russia we find Sechenov and Pavlov coming from the countryside. In this country the learning theorists, Thorndike, Watson, Hull, Spence, Miller, Mowrer, Skinner—all were from small towns. There is a seeming exception to this rule, but it is borderline. Tolman came from a suburb of Boston (Newton, which is where Mary Calkins lived—which is also interesting). Why are there so few experimentalists from Berlin or London or New York?

14. The failure of Skinner's radical behaviorism to fit the paradigm that prevailed around 1970 no doubt reflects the fact that the paradigm had come from learning theorists, people who shared the vision of psychology becoming a science, while Skinner did not aspire to theory, or share that vision. He had little faith in psychology as a science, and certainly did not like the sort of theory that the learning theorists had constructed. Skinner regarded himself, rightly, as a behavioral engineer, a solver of important problems, rather than a scientist who worries about fruitless abstractions.

And perhaps this same antitheoretical orientation makes believers adverse to looking at their own particular history. Scientists like to examine their history of discovery; they like to celebrate the gradual shaping of their ideas. But engineers do not. Ask a Skinnerian about how the effect being studied was discovered and the disciple is almost sure to cite the prophet (Skinner, 1938). That is a sorry neglect; surely something new must have come up in the last half-century that deserves to be added to the scripture. It would be nice to know the story of the Skinnerian movement.

Chapter Fourteen

Cognitive Psychology

B Y ABOUT 1950, BEHAVIORISM of one form or another controlled the entire psychological landscape. It is hard to believe, but at that time the great majority of all psychologists earnestly believed that all behavior had to be explained by analyzing it into little S–R units, most of which were assumed to have been formed by reinforcement. Not everyone was attracted by such a prospect, however, and there was dissent from a few cognitive psychologists. A cognitive psychologist is basically anyone who believes that there has to be a better model of behavior than that.

This chapter outlines how the cognitive mood gradually came to prevail. To provide continuity with the previous chapter, we will begin with the development of cognitive ideas in animal psychology. Then we will step back a decade or so and take up the development of cognitive ideas in human experimental psychology.

The New Naturalism

SPANIARDS HAVE a wonderful expression, *Viva yo*, which translates as "Long live me," but which really means something like "To hell with you guys." The Spanish-American John Garcia was a graduate student at Berkeley in 1951. He knew about the statistics ordeal for first-year students in the psychology department, but he said *viva yo*. And they flunked him out. Garcia got a job at the Naval Radiation Defense Laboratory (NRDL) in San Francisco and spent several years looking at the effects of atomic radiation and X-rays on animals. In the course of this work Garcia found that if rats drink saccharin in a situation where they are receiving radiation, then they would not drink saccharin when offered it later. A few years later, after NRDL was closed down, Garcia got involved in conversation with a distinguished professor and learning theorist at UCLA. When the professor heard about Garcia's saccharin-avoidance effect he said something like, "Young man, that is

John Garcia

impossible. The animal does not get sick from radiation until half an hour or more after it tastes the saccharin, and you cannot get any learning with such a big delay of the consequence, certainly not in one trial." To which Garcia said something like, "*Viva yo*, rats get food by stealing it from people, and people are constantly trying to poison them, so they *have* to be capable of such learning. If they cannot learn about poisons, then they cannot live like a rat."

Garcia eventually got back into Berkeley, studied statistics, and did a marvelous dissertation that made his case against the UCLA professor. This was the famous "bright, noisy water" study (Garcia and Koelling, 1966). When the rat laps at a drinking tube, tongue contacts are detected, tiny currents are amplified and sent off to activate lights and noises, and it is like a pinball machine. Rats drink bright, noisy water and then receive a foot shock. When tested later, they avoid bright, noisy water. They have evidently associated the pinball-machine accompaniment of drinking with electric shock. Another group drinks tasty water, with saccharin, and then are made sick with X-radiation. When tested later they avoid the tasty water. They have apparently associated the taste with illness. There were two other groups, one that got bright, noisy water and was made sick that showed no avoidance, and one that got tasty water and shock that also showed no avoidance learning.

We seem to have here two separate systems within which learning can occur. One is the *gut* system that is sensitive to gastric events like tastes and illness. These cues and consequences can be linked in this system. The other system deals with the *external* world, the world of lights and sounds and assault of the feet. Such external events can be associated too, but the rules seem to be somewhat different. Thus, contiguity is critical in learning about external events but not in the gut system. And the two systems appear to be relatively isolated from each other, since Garcia's animals showed little learning about drinking saccharin and getting shocked.*

The Importance of Biological Considerations

Garcia had found that animal learning is not homogeneous. Even without accepting the idea of there being two or more systems, it is apparent that some relationships between cues and consequences are learned with amazing facility, whereas others are poorly appreciated by the animal. How are we to understand such large differences in the efficacy of associative mechanisms? By augmenting them with biological principles. Recall Garcia's initial insight: Biologically, rats must be able to avoid poisonous food if they are going to live as opportunistic, generalized feeders, and this is true no matter what the learning theorist has to say. Learning has to fit into the broader context of an animal's relationship with its environment.

One of the first psychologists to understand the potential importance of biological matters in learning was Martin Seligman. He edited a book of papers (Seligman and Hager, 1972) that featured the work of Garcia, some other contemporaneous work, and also some anticipations. Some of these anticipations were frankly cognitive. But they had shown up so many years earlier that no one knew exactly what they meant. Thus, Cogan and Capaldi (1961) found that rats could remember what had happened (food or no food) on the preceding trial, but for several years Capaldi interpreted such memories only as internal stimuli. Petrinovich and Bolles (1957) found that rats could remember where they had been (east or west) on the preceding trial, but we also did not know what to make of it. A more important anticipation was the sudden appearance of ethological ideas in the early 1950s. Tinbergen's *The Study of Instinct* (1951) presented, in English for the first time, a mass of illustrations of releasers and fixed-action patterns. It demonstrated that an animal's innate behaviors lock it into its environment. And many of us who were in animal learning at that time read it and worried about it, because our behavioristic theories had not prepared us for such a thing. We could not assimilate it or relate it to what was happening in our labs. Indeed, there was a polarization: Us the psychologists and them the zoologists, us in our labs and them out in the field. Even in 1966, when

---

* You will be happy to know that Garcia continued to do research on what is called "conditioned taste aversions," and that within a few years this research attracted a great deal of attention and earned Garcia a great deal of recognition. The basic procedure was, to start with, a marvelously efficient new means of looking at conditioning in animals. Taste is the CS, illness is the US, and they become associated in one or two trials. Garcia ended up as a distinguished professor and learning theorist at UCLA, of all places. Garcia's story is not yet published; one way to get the story is to share a bottle of Rioja with him.

Breland and Breland said that to understand learning you have to understand your animal, very few psychologists paid any attention. A kind of liaison would only come when we began to explore a wider variety of experimental procedures, as Garcia did and as Olton did.

Spatial Learning

David Olton was impressed with the rat's remarkable ability to navigate in space, and began to explore that ability. Olton and Samuelson (1976) put a little food out at the end of eight long arms that radiated from a central platform. They started the rat in the middle and then asked: How many runs does the rat make in collecting all eight pieces of food? They found that after a few preliminary trials to learn the game, the rat makes only about 8.5 runs. Thus, about half the time it runs off in eight different directions without making an error (going back where it had been before). It looks random; there is certainly no obvious response strategy. The maze can be torn apart and reassembled between runs, and substantial delays can be introduced between runs, but nothing like that interferes with the rat's performance. A 17-arm maze begins to challenge the rat; it makes one or two errors in collecting the 17 bits of food. There are three important conclusions that can be drawn here, which will give us a pretty little model. One is that the rat starts with a *response bias*, it begins with a win-shift strategy, which makes Olton's task very natural and easy. The second conclusion is that the rat has an extraordinary capacity to *integrate spatial information*. It runs over here and runs over there, and then puts those experiences together so that, in effect, it knows where here and there are. This part of the task appears to be trivially simple for the rat because it starts with a bias for processing spatial information. Third, the rat *remembers* for many minutes that it has recently been here and there. Notice that these three conclusions are very informative about the animal; Olton has helped us to better understanding the rat. It is no longer just a device that learns, it has biases that we may assume help it to prosper in its natural world.

These three conclusions not only summarize the data and give us a better picture of the animal, they also constitute a cognitive model. And we can use that cognitive model, rough as it is, to devise new experiments. That is what cognitive psychology is all about, that is what it tries to do. Notice how easily the cognitive model is stated; it took five sentences. Now, by contrast, consider building an S–R reinforcement model that would generate the same conclusions. You would have stimuli at the start of each arm, stimuli at the end of each arm, food stimuli out there, all sorts of different stimuli. And you cannot use concrete stimulus elements, because recall that the maze can be taken apart and reconstructed between runs. You have orienting responses, locomotory responses, eating responses, all kinds of responses. And you have to worry about whether on a given run the rat is running forward because certain stimuli are present ahead of it, or whether it is running southeast. Then you will also have to invent a strange reinforcement mechanism because the rat rarely repeats a reinforced response. You cannot explain the behavior with inhibition because performance is poorly correlated with the time interval between runs. And you are going to have to minimize any discrimination learning, because the behavior appears after just a few trials. You are going to have a hell of a time building an S–R model to describe what falls so neatly into place with a cognitive model. That is what it is all about.

The Crisis for Reinforcement

Herb Jenkins was a Skinnerian, a student of Skinner's who had done a lot of nice work in the 1960s on visual discrimination learning in pigeons. He did some very creative things, but he always used conventional operant techniques, and always followed the operant orthodoxy. Jenkins was a believer. One day he and his student Peter Brown at MacMaster University were about to embark on a new project that required them to use naive pigeons, and young Mr. Brown was stuck with the chore of shaping up the new birds. Now I have to digress to note that operant conditioning people tend to use the same birds over and over in new experiments. This practice is justifiable because pigeons do not remember much about what they were doing a month ago, so they do not show much proactive interference. In addition, it is quite problematical and tedious shaping up naive animals. You have to go through successive approximations: You reinforce in turn being near the key, looking at the key, approaching the key, "thinking about" the key, "intentional" pecks, and tentative pecks, until you finally get the be-havior. It is a challenge. I have to digress further to note that the key the pigeon is supposed to peck is typically a one-inch plexiglas disk. In the work Jenkins was doing there would be colored lights, filters, or something behind the plexiglas disk to present the visual stimuli right on the key. Brown discovered a wonderful shortcut to the tedious shaping procedure. He discovered that all he had to do was put a white light on the disk for a few seconds and then give the birds food. Light–food, light–food for 30 minutes or so, and lo and behold they were pecking the key. You do not have to shape the animals with successive approximations, because they will shape themselves with the light–food procedure. Brown and Jenkins (1968) called it **autoshaping.** It looked like a methodological breakthrough, a great boon for hard-working graduate students.

But it turned out to be much more interesting and important than that. At the University of Pennsylvania David and Harriet Williams saw that Brown and Jenkins's birds had two good reasons to peck the key. One was operant; key pecks were reinforced with food. The other reason was Pavlovian; the recurring pattern of light and food would make the light a Pavlovian conditioned stimulus (CS). And perhaps a CS signaling food is very exciting for a hungry pigeon; perhaps hungry pigeons just peck CSs for food. In any case, the Williamses wanted to dissect experimentally the two factors that contributed to the behavior, so they reversed the operant contingency. The Pavlovian light–food business was still in place, but now if the bird pecked the key, the food was *withheld* on that trial. So rather than the Pavlovian and the reinforcement conditions both contributing to the behavior, they were working against each other. What they found (Williams and Williams, 1969) was that the reversal of the operant contingency made no difference, and that the behavior was being controlled mainly by the Pavlovian factor.

Now what was this? The behavior of pigeons in a Skinner box is not being controlled by the reinforcement contingency? That was unthinkable—but it was true. What appears to happen is that because of the many light–food trials, the light becomes a signal or symbol for food. Then the pigeon, along with many other animals, cannot keep from directing its eating responses at the symbol. Pavlov had reported that when a light bulb signaled food, his dogs would sometimes lick the bulb. Breland and Breland (1961) had reported a variety of such "misbehaviors" in different animals. Finally, Bruce Moore used strobe lights to take high-speed photographs of autoshaped key pecks. He found that his pigeons were obviously "eating" the key (Moore, 1973). Right around 1970 we were suddenly confronted with the awesome prospect that reinforcement had little to do with the behavior of pigeons in Skinner boxes.

Back in 1948 Skinner reported something interesting that resulted from a glitch that occurred in his lab one day. Something was wrong in the programming equipment such that the pigeons got food briefly from time to time regardless of their behavior. Although there was no explicit contingency in effect, different animals acquired different "bizarre" behaviors, including head waving, ground scratching, and feather puffing. Skinner concluded that if any such behavior just happened to be occurring at the time food came along, it would be slightly reinforced and more likely to be occurring when food came along in the future. Once any behavior gained a critical level of strength, it would be captured by the automatic, machine-like, response-strengthening effect of reinforcement, and become firmly established. Skinner (1948b) called it the *superstition effect*. Skinner's interpretation of the superstition effect was universally accepted for more than 20 years. And then John Staddon took another look at it.[*]

Staddon and Simmelhag (1971) looked at the acquisition and temporal distribution of bizarre superstitious behaviors. They found that they are only

---

[*] John Staddon was a student of Skinner's during the mid-1960s. It is a curious state of affairs that so many of the people who pulled the reinforcement rug out from under Skinner were his own students. We can count Keller and Marian Breland, Herb Jenkins, and John Staddon. What does that mean?

gradually acquired, and that they rarely ever occurred at the time food was presented! On the contrary, bizarre behavior usually occurred right after the last food was delivered, and was then replaced by perfectly reasonable food-oriented behavior (pecking at the covered food hopper) as the next food was due to be delivered. And the behavior is not bizarre. It is simple frustration behavior (there is the biology angle again). Barnyard chickens show similar behavior—they wave their heads, scratch the ground, and fluff up their feathers when their food is threatened by another chicken. What Staddon's animals had learned was to tell time. They were discriminating food time from no-food time. When food is due, they show food-oriented behavior; when food is not due, they show frustration behavior. If we can suppose that the temporal discrimination is Pavlovian, then reinforcement per se has nothing whatever to do with the superstition effect. Isn't that stunning.

Recall that a critical point in the development of Hullian theory was Mowrer's avoidance learning model. That was the source of the drive-reduction hypothesis, and Mowrer's popular two-factor theory. The model required that an avoidance response, such as running back and forth in a shuttle box, be reinforced by the reduction in conditioned fear that it produced. At the University of Washington we looked very carefully at that. We found that in avoidance learning everything depends on what avoidance response the rat is required to perform. If the rat is merely required to get out of a dangerous shock situation, then learning to do that is trivially easy, and does not depend on any of the common parameters such as intensity of shock, or the character of the warning signal (WS). On the other hand, if the rat is required to press a lever to prevent shock then it shows little or no learning, and the common parameters cannot keep it from being more of a challenge than the rat can handle. Even in the middle of the learnability spectrum, with the shuttle box, Mowrer's analysis was full of problems. It was not necessary to terminate the WS, it worked just as well to present a safety signal, or even to present a neutral feedback stimulus. Fear-reduction reinforcement did not seem to have much to do with avoidance learning in animals.

And fear-reduction reinforcement did not seem likely to have much to do with how animals avoid predation in nature, either. Wildebeests do not fear lions because they have been hurt by lions, they fear lions because their world requires it of them. Wildebeests that are fearless are all extinct. It seems likely that animals have species-specific defensive reactions (SSDRs) that help keep them alive in nature and that provide the basic response repertoire when we shock them in the laboratory. The rat's repertoire includes mainly freezing and running away. If the task allows either response to solve the problem then we get it immediately. If the task requires a response other than an SSDR then we get an animal that cannot cope. I gathered these ideas together in a paper (Bolles, 1970) suggesting that there is no need for a reinforcement mechanism in avoidance learning. The basic mechanism is Pavlovian: If it is dangerous and fearful over here, and relatively safe over there, then that is all the rat needs to learn, and it will go from here to there. After further consideration I was able to suggest (Bolles, 1972) that there is no place for a reinforcement mechanism anywhere in learned behavior.[1]

Classical Conditioning is Not What You Think

CLASSICAL CONDITIONING had always been seen as thoroughly mechanistic. Certainly that was how Pavlov saw it. And that was how Watson and almost everyone who followed him saw it. It was the automatic attachment of a response to an arbitrary CS. Some experimenters liked classical conditioning because they could condition responses such as GSR and nictitating membrane over which subjects had no voluntary control and for which there was no clear functional significance. The more meaningless the response the better it was. But then that image began to change. Leon Kamin (1965) reported a series of studies that developed a new methodology. Rats were trained up to a stable level of lever pressing for food. Then superimposed on this baseline were a few pairings of tone and shock. Then whenever the tone appeared lever pressing declined; it is said that fear was conditioned to the tone, and that the tone suppressed lever pressing. It was a very easy and efficient procedure, and it became a popular method for studying conditioning.

But Kamin was not done. He reported a series of studies (Kamin, 1969) on what he called **blocking**. After the fear had been conditioned to the tone, he ran another set of trials in which both the tone and a light were paired with shock. A test with the old tone revealed that it still suppressed lever pressing, but a test with only the light showed that it did not suppress lever pressing. Little or no fear had been conditioned to the light, even though it was paired with shock on a number of trials. Kamin ran all sorts of control groups and concluded that the prior conditioning of fear to the tone somehow *blocked* the conditioning of fear to the light that would otherwise be found.

The blocking phenomenon seems to call for some kind of cognitive interpretation, because the mechanistic principle of contiguity that had sufficed for decades was clearly not sufficient. Perhaps the rat pays no attention to the light when the tone is there. Perhaps the rat learns to attribute the shock to the tone. Kamin did not develop the idea, but he suggested that conditioning may occur to the extent that the shock surprises the animal. When tone and light come on together, the tone makes the animal expect shock, so its occurrence is not surprising—and so during that trial there is little additional conditioning to the tone and no new conditioning to the light.

340

Robert Rescorla and Predictiveness

Before going on with our story I want to note how the people in it seem to come in bunches; they tend to bunch in one place (like Leipzig or Harvard) or around a professor (like Stumpf or James). A modern-day bunching point is Richard Solomon, who was at Harvard for several years and then at the University of Pennsylvania for many more. Early on Solomon was a Hullian, and he followed Mowrer into the mysterious world of avoidance learning and did significant work on the avoidance problem. Solomon is also known for the great number of outstanding students who have worked with him over the years. Kamin was an early one who also worked on avoidance for some time before moving into fear conditioning. Earlier we met Seligman, who was another student about a decade later. Now we meet another Solomon student, Robert Rescorla.

Rescorla (1968) reported a conditioning study in which different groups had some fixed probability of being shocked in the presence of a warning signal (WS) while lever pressing for food. These were the control groups, and they showed that a lot of fear was conditioned to the WS. Then there were experimental groups that also had some chance of being shocked during the WS, but in addition had some chance of being shocked when the WS was not on. Among the various groups it was possible to look at fear conditioning in animals where the WS was not a predictor of shock because shock was just as likely in its absence as when it was on. Rescorla found no fear of the WS under those conditions. No predictiveness, no conditioning. It is evidently **contingency** (this depends on that) rather than contiguity (this and that occur together) that underlies conditioning.

By the early 1970s it had become common to think of Pavlovian conditioning in S–S terms: The CS and US become linked. This was not as mechanistic as the old Watsonian S–R formulation, but it was not necessarily cognitive, either. Actually, Pavlov was the first to think of it as a linking of sensory events. Some people, in part inspired by Rescorla's 1968 study, spoke of conditioning as though the CS *predicted* the shock. Others began to talk even more openly in a cognitive manner about the CS arousing the *expectancy* of the shock. There were many precedents for this usage, but it began to become popular around 1970. Then in 1973 Rescorla gave this movement a further twist; he said the CS aroused a *representation* of the shock. In effect, the cue brings the consequence to mind. This interpretation was based on a study (Rescorla, 1973) in which a tone CS was paired with a very loud, noxious noise US. After a few pairings the tone suppressed lever pressing. So the tone now brings the big noise to mind. At this point Rescorla presented the big noise by itself a number of times until the animal was pretty well habituated to it. When the tone was tested again it produced much less suppression than before. What this means, Rescorla said, is that the association was still intact, it had not been extinguished or otherwise weakened, but the representation

341

of the US has been diminished because of all the habituation trials. The CS now calls up a representation of a lesser US, so there is less suppression. That sort of model looks rather cognitive.[2]

Thus, in a few years just before and just after 1970, classical conditioning completely changed face. It had been mechanistic; it became cognitive. It had been S–R; it became something else, something that Alexander Bain would have understood: A stimulus arousing an idea. If that aroused idea is frightening, it will disrupt ongoing behavior. In these same few years all sorts of new conditioning phenomena were discovered, and new methodological tricks for studying them were devised (a number of them by Rescorla). This was a truly remarkable transition. But it was no more remarkable than the departure of reinforcement from the operant world or the discovery of cognitive and naturalistic themes in that world. The great behavioristic vision that had risen so dramatically with John Watson and then under Hull and Skinner gone on to become what seemed to be the paradigm for all of psychology collapsed just as dramatically and as quickly as it had risen. Animal-based learning theory had been the center of psychology, but now, suddenly, the old center was lost. But as it turned out, the rest of psychology was not revolving around that center anyway by 1970 but was going off in new orbits.

The Verbal Learning Tradition

WE MUST GO BACK in time a bit to look at the setting in which cognitive psychology arose. We have to see what human learning looked like before it turned cognitive. Beginning in the 1920s Thorndike was the key player in the verbal learning enterprise. His subjects learned lists of nonsense syllables, much as Ebbinghaus had used, or else long lists of words. But Thorndike had his own paired-associate method: The experimenter presents a word *table* and the subject guesses a matching number *3*. If nothing happens, the subject has about a .13 chance of giving *3* again when tested later (higher than .10 because subjects do not guess randomly). But if the experimenter responds with "Right!" to some response, then the repetition rate might jump up to .25. "Right!" is a reinforcer that strengthens the connection between stimulus *table* and the response *3*. Thorndike did hundreds of experiments on such matters as remote associations and learning without awareness or intention. When *table–3* gets appreciably stronger because it is reinforced, then a neighboring pair, *window–7*, gets a little stronger too, because it is a remote association. Afterward, one could ask if the *experimenter* also learns *table–3* and *window–7*. If so, then we have learning without the intention to learn. In all of his work on such questions Thorndike maintained that reinforcement was the only important determinant of associative learning.

The Dreary Period

A lot of people got involved in such studies over the years. It seemed important to be working on human learning and memory, and there was a lot of cleaning up to do. Apparatus had to be designed to present material precisely, statistical methods had to be standardized, and the nonsense syllables had to be graded in terms of meaningfulness. A number of effects had to be defined definitively, such as the serial position effect—the rapid learning of the ends of a list and the relatively slow learning of the middle. There was much to do.

What got done is described in great detail by McGeoch and Irion (1952) in a large book that was for many years the standard reference on verbal learning. Looking at it today, it describes a barren wasteland. Part of the problem was that McGeoch and Irion had no sense of history, and no concept of where they were going. Part of the problem was that there was no theory. What there was looked like old Thorndike. McGeoch and Irion had a long chapter on theory, but every bit of it was the animal-learning theory of Hull and his followers; there was no theory of verbal learning phenomena. And part of the problem was that McGeoch and Irion had a poverty of verbal learning phenomena; they cite endless studies of serial position effects, massed versus spaced practice, Thorndike's problems, and retention intervals. And that was about all that had been studied. The greatest verbal learners of all, children, had gone unnoticed by nearly all the experimental psychologists.

A sad part of this uninviting area is that it occupied the energies of some very capable people. E. S. Robinson had been among the last of the Chicago functionalists; he went to Yale and began to form a sort of network of verbal learners. Art Melton worked with him, and so did McGeoch. Ben Underwood became part of it. Thorndike was an independent entity, of course, as was Leo Postman, who came along a little later. And these people dominated the field. Early on Melton had proposed that the massive forgetting one generally finds in nonsense syllable studies was not true forgetting but rather the result of interference. It was reported, for example, that much more impressive retention is found if subjects sleep through the retention interval than if they go about their day-to-day, highly verbal business. And then a lot of new experiments had to be run to sort out retroactive and proactive interference. Those were some of the exciting highlights of that dreary period.

The Organization of Memory

Seemingly out of nowhere came a study by Bousfield (1953) that was different. Subjects got a list of words that included different categories of things, such as animals and vehicles. Then, rather than testing for remembered words one at a time, a *free recall* procedure was used that permitted subjects to recall what

343

they could at their leisure. It turned out that words were recalled in clusters. Once the subject got elephant, then horse, camel, and zebra usually followed immediately. Usually all the animals were recalled or none of them were. It appeared that subjects were not just learning elephant, they were also learning things like that there were animals on the list. The interesting thing here is that learning this higher level, or deeper layer, of meaning facilitates rather than interfering with remembering the specific words. It is not just associative, because subjects do not often give the most common animals, cat, dog, wolf, and cow, but rather the right ones, elephant, horse, camel, and zebra. Remembering the general category helps one remember the specific instances.

It took some time for all the implications to get sorted out and followed up; Bousfield had been so far ahead of his time he could not have known what he had found. Like Columbus, and like Lavoisier, he had discovered something wonderful but he did not know what it was. Bousfield's new method would in time generate a whole basketful of new phenomena and new concepts. One idea here is that stimulus material is coded in different ways at the same time. Elephant is stored as *elephant* but it is also in some way cross-indexed under the superordinate *animal*. One can imagine that words can be processed in a lot of different ways. If a number of the words referred to things that were gray, then elephant would also get indexed under *gray*. One can imagine that the categories are defined in part by prior experience and in part by the particular word presented to the subject. One can imagine endless possibilities.

Concept formation tasks had been studied by Thorndike and by Hull. To get rid of prior associations Hull had used what looked like Chinese characters, but most investigators were content to use meaningful concepts such as *small red triangle*. The conventional interpretation of results was almost always associative. The concept was nothing but the simultaneous activation of *small*, *red*, and *triangle* sensory impressions, and the associations were built up through reinforcement, just as Thorndike and Hull had contended. It was all very much according to the behavioristic paradigm. But then Bruner, Goodnow and Austin (1956) did it differently and gave it a new cognitive interpretation. They used four dimensions with three possibilities on each dimension. With the usual procedure the experimenter presents patterns to subjects one at a time, and waits for the correct concept to emerge gradually, which almost guarantees associative-looking, Thorndikian results. Bruner et al., on the other hand, displayed all the 81 possible patterns all at once in an organized matrix. The question they asked was, what do subjects do—where do they go next in the matrix—when they stumble onto an instance of the concept? How do they check it out? One common strategy that works well with a simple concept is to check the next one up, the next one over, and the corresponding one in the next panel. Often the subject can nail down the concept in a few seconds with a handful of tests. The exciting

J. S. Bruner

thing about this is that at least some of the time you can see what the subject is doing. You can see what strategy the subject is using, and when the strategy changes. And one thing is very clear: Subjects are not gradually, automatically, stamping in S–R connections. They are usually very busy doing different cognitive things.

Bruner was then at Harvard, where he had reported a variety of phenomena that confounded the establishment. For example, he had looked at the effect of motivation on perception. It seems that hungry people are more likely than satiated people to see food objects when the stimulation is ambiguous. Some have contended that Bruner was the founder of modern cognitive psychology. Certainly he was one of the founders, and certainly also one of the first to call himself a cognitive psychologist. That may have happened because Bruner was from the outset a maverick and definitely not part of the establishment. To prove it, he and George Miller splintered off from the psychology department in 1960 to form the Center for Cognitive Studies at Harvard. That might be said to be the start of cognitive psychology as a movement, that might be when it was first clearly self-conscious and wanting to call itself something new and attractive. But while the question of origin is one of those things that are fun to debate, it is not easily answered. All we can say for sure is that cognitive psychology got started some time around 1960.[3]

The Many Sources of Cognitive Psychology

WE HAVE TO BACKTRACK again to fill in some of the background that came not from the verbal-learning tradition but from elsewhere. Actually, a host of different sorts of people contributed to cognitive psychology, and some of them came from pretty far afield. Cognitive psychology is not something that psychologists created or did, it is more like something that happened to them.

A lot of it came from other disciplines. That is why the history of the movement is so difficult to track. The story is not one of marching forward, but rather of bumping into new influences and considerations and then moving in new directions. And it is like the early functionalist movement in that it is so permissive, and encourages so many different activities and lines of research that it seems at times to have no direction at all, only a growing mass. Hence, I do not pretend to be telling a coherent tale of these developments; I hope only to point to some of the new ideas that entered psychology and took hold.

The Electrical Engineers

Back in the 1940s, during and just after World War II, electrical engineers had worked out all the mathematical problems involved in transmitting energy over transmission lines. They had worked out the theory of feedback circuits. And they knew all about signal-to-noise ratios. The trouble was that the technology lagged far behind the mathematical understanding, so there was little general appreciation of what they had accomplished. But toward the end of the 1940s technology began to catch up. For example, some manufacturers began making audio output transformers that were greatly bigger (and more expensive) than anything ever seen before. These transformers had very little phase shift, and that permitted them to be used in audio amplifiers with a lot of **negative feedback.** All that feedback had two effects. One was that it lowered the amplifier's output impedance so that it "held onto" the loudspeaker and greatly reduced its distortion. The other effect was that it greatly reduced the distortion inherent in the amplifier. An engineer named D.T.N. Williamson figured out how to maximize the various parameters, and around 1950 people started buying or building Williamson amplifiers. And since these technical advances were matched by greatly improved FM transmission and by the development of LP records, it suddenly became possible to enjoy music in the home with sound quality that had been unimaginable just a year or two before. It was called *hi fidelity*, and it was miraculous. Negative feedback was wonderful.

Norbert Wiener had worked for the military during the war developing systems that would, for example, make torpedoes home in on their targets. The torpedo charges forward, and its two sound detectors, which point left and right, compare the loudness of their signals. If there is a difference that difference is fed back to a rudder on the torpedo that turns it until the sound is the same at both detectors. That points the torpedo at the sound—the sound of the enemy ship's engine. When the torpedo is launched this guidance system does not go into effect for 15 seconds or so (so that it will not turn around and go for the ship that launched it). This torpedo looks like it has a purpose, namely to get to the enemy ship. As the enemy ship carries out evasive action, the torpedo compensates and continues coming at it. If the torpedo overshoots the enemy ship it will stop and circle back to get it. The torpedo looks as though it is *motivated* to attack the enemy ship. But this evidence of purpose, this purposive behavior, is all a result of a negative feedback control system. Negative feedback really was wonderful. Wiener's *Cybernetics* (1948), which described a variety of such control systems, was quite influential. A little later George Miller, along with his colleagues (Miller, Galanter, and Pribram, 1960), would apply feedback loops to all sorts of human behavior, and get it organized in new ways.

If we think of behavior as coming from a system, one endowed with feedback loops that guide its behavior, then we have a very different sort of concept from the behaviorists' view that a system behaves in direct response to stimulation. The old idea, really, Descartes's idea, saw direct mechanical causation, while the new idea of a **cybernetic** system was much more subtle. While the response of the system still depends on stimulation, stimulation can be redirected by the behavior of the system. The organism makes its own contribution to the behavior because the feedback loop is a part of the organism. And we cannot understand that just by looking at stimulus and response; we have to consider the whole system (Dewey would have loved that). It was a different perspective from the total environmentalism and mechanical causation of the behaviorists.

Wiener is also important for his dictum that cybernetics, the analysis of control systems, could design a device that could mimic whatever feature of human behavior one might care to describe. Wiener observed, however, that the major problem in carrying out such work, and in designing an appropriate system, was always the difficulty in obtaining an accurate description of the behavior. Psychologists had so far done a poor job of describing human behavior. But once that was done it would be simple enough to build a robot that would mimic it. There was a lot of interest in robots around 1950. Ashby (1952) had a number of interesting comments on systems that would look motivated and generate purposive behavior. There was the famous robot, or at least a design for one, that would monitor its own batteries. When they got low the robot would abandon other activities and start searching for a wall socket—and then plug itself in.

But it was not the modeling of behavior that would come to fascinate cognitive psychologists, it was the organization of memory, which is to say, the processing of information. And it was not the robot that would be the paradigmic machine, it was the computer, the ultimate information-processing machine. We will meet the computer shortly, and take note of its part in all this.

Information Theory

Another dividend from the electrical engineers came from their work on signal transmission. Shannon and Weaver (1949) worked out in great detail the mathematics of transmission. A few psychologists became interested in what they called *information theory;* they found it useful for analyzing perceptual and behavioral data (e.g., Attneave, 1954). Anyone who has played the classic Twenty Questions game knows all about information theory: Your opponent thinks of anything and you try to discover what that thing is by narrowing down the possibilities with no more than 20 questions. You try to find questions that will split the universe of possibilities in half. Those optimum questions give you one bit of information. If you ask a bad question you get less than one bit of information. One actually wins the game by shrewd guesses based on personal knowledge of the opponent; a shrewd guess can provide several bits of information. Twenty optimum questions allow you to pick out the target from one million alternatives.

One of the first psychologists to take information theory seriously and do something important with it was George Miller. His marvelous paper "The magical number seven" (Miller, 1956) presented several sets of data indicating that our sensory systems seem to be limited in their ability to pass on usable information. Thus, the rainbow is a continuum of hues, but people can see at most seven distinct colors. With the rainbow different greens are lumped together and all called green. But if we restrict our attention just to greens, we can make out about seven of them between clearly yellow and clearly blue. The memory span for digits is about seven or a trifle more. The number seven pops up in so many different situations and with so many different procedures that it looks magical. Why can't we handle a full three bits of information (eight alternatives) all at once? Miller invited us to think about where the bottleneck is; is it in the sensory systems, in the way information is coded, or in short-term memory? In the next few years all these possibilities were examined with growing interest.

Increasing numbers of psychologists began to think about the transmission and especially the storage of information. The study of perception was rejuvenated during the 1960s by the search for encoding mechanisms. How do ganglion cells of the retina alter the spatial pattern of stimulation? How do they recode the visual information? Even without regard to machinery, the problem of perception became transformed into the question of how information about the external world gets conveyed to the observer, and how much and what kind of information gets conveyed. The study of memory, which is not so blessed with mechanisms or based on knowledge of neurology, was totally transformed by thinking of it as the holding of information. The mind was not only made of neurons and full of ideas, body stuff and mind stuff, it contained information, a new kind of stuff. We had discovered a whole new world.

By about 1970 there were several well-organized books dealing in systematic ways with information processing. Neisser (1967) was the first of these to integrate perception, concept formation, meaning, language, and thinking—almost all of human experimental psychology—with a handful of cognitive concepts. In effect, he defined cognitive psychology as the study of coding, storing, and retrieving information, which gave the cognitive movement at last some sort of structure. Lindsay and Norman (1972) did much the same using more linguistic concepts. Both were very appealing and influential books. Such books showed the cognitive movement well under way and gaining momentum by about 1970.

The Linguists

Some cognitive psychologists and virtually all linguists will say that the cognitive movement began in 1959 with Noam Chomsky's review of Skinner's 1957 book on verbal behavior. Skinner had, of course, viewed speech as operant behavior that was controlled by the reinforcement contingencies of the linguistic community, the family, or whatever. You say "Gimme salt," and no one gives it to you. You say "Please pass the salt," and you are pretty sure to get it and thus be reinforced by the better taste of your food. That is how we learn to talk, Skinner said. That is utter nonsense, Chomsky said. He said that much of the organization of language is innate. We understand at the outset that the names of things, the noun part, can be linked with what happens, the verb part. The infant understands *Daddy*, and understands *go*, which happens after breakfast when Daddy goes. One day the infant will volunteer "Daddy go." Even more impressive is the evidence for "good" errors, in the gestalt sense. The kid initially puts everything in the present tense, just as the adult tourist visiting Greece or Portugal does after going through Berlitz tapes. But there comes a point when the past tense is appreciated, and we see this most vividly when the child begins to say things like "Daddy goed." Chomsky says such errors demonstrate that the child has a general rule that is applied to all cases of past tense. The rule, or the idea of such a rule, cannot be learned by induction because there are too many irregular verbs; it must be already there in some sense.

Language is full of such rules. There is a sort of logical structure to it and much of the structure is innate. A given language might have its own way of doing plurals, and dealing with articles, but once the learner sees how it is done, the whole language gets more or less properly ordered. It does not have to be done piecemeal. Linguists like to represent structural rules in terms of logical paths, branches, and trees. Then they can plug this in here, that in there, make a decision or two, and describe an utterance. Adjectives are easy because of the roses are red, violets are blue type of rules, rules that hold trees together. There are phrase structures and phase spaces. It can be wonderfully logical.

Computer Simulation

It was inevitable that the logical analysis of language would be seen as similar to the logic of computer programming. One can construct a program routine that looks for all the world like a sentence-generating tree. One can therefore program a computer to produce sentences. One can construct routines for discriminating inputs from different objects, and therefore one can program it to produce sentences about those objects. Ask it questions about those objects and it will produce correct answers (Winograd, 1972).

One of the first people to get into such matters was Herbert Simon. But Simon gives a lot of credit to Otto Selz, so we should note him first. Back when Külpe left Würzburg and went to Munich, his former student and fellow Würzburger Karl Bühler went with him. And Selz was their student and collaborator. The three of them were almost alone at that time in worrying about thought processes. Back in 1913 Selz maintained that the meaning of a word had to include not only what it referred to but also the things superordinate and subordinate to it. Thus *dog* means not only dog but also animal, and perhaps spaniel and Rover. Selz also studied what people are doing cognitively when they play chess, and collaborated with de Groot on writing chess computer programs (see Frijda and de Groot, 1981).

Simon does not pay much attention to disciplinary boundaries. Thus, he got his degree in political science, he won a Nobel Prize in 1978 in economics, and we are looking at some of his contributions to psychology. The prize was for his analysis of the structure of bureaucratic organizations. Their structure is something like that of language! They show hierarchies, branching, and trees. But Simon was not so interested in language as in some of Selz's ideas. Simon was a computer expert back in the days when all computers could do was sort cards. And as they became more proficient, so did his programs. He had programs for solving logic problems. He had chess-playing programs. But his favorites were problem-solving programs, programs that could mimic all sorts of human cognitive activities. Computers could simulate what people do when they solve problems. Does this mean that we now understand people's behavior well enough that we can mimic it with a machine? Not necessarily; there are a lot of restraints in Simon's systems, and they generally only work in a limited context. But this sort of approach, **artificial intelligence,** is very appealing for its potential for illuminating cognitive processes.[4]

Hot New Trends and the Story of Little Red

My colleague Earl Hunt is a computer person and a cognitive psychologist. He tells me that when he is describing new cognitive developments to his students, he illustrates how things work with the dramatic story of young Red Ridinghood. We recall that Ms. Ridinghood went off into the woods one day with a basket of goodies for Granny. On the way there she bumped into Wolf and would have been in serious trouble except for the fortunate intervention of Woodsman. If we look at this well-known story properly, as a modern cognitive psychologist might, then we can understand the new connectionism, what parallel distributed processing is all about, and some other hot new trends in the cognitive movement.

First of all, little Red perceives the world around her. She is sensitive to and responds to things out there. She does not perceive things directly, of course, or understand reality, because she only detects certain features of things. She has a number of feature detectors, but we will not call them that because that is too old-fashioned. We will be cognitive about this and call them environmental interfaces, or better yet, *input nodes*. The story indicates that Red is sensitive to ears, and can distinguish big ones and little ones. In time she will learn that Wolf has big ears whereas Granny and Woodsman have small ones. We also know that she detects teeth, big ones like Wolf's and little ones like Granny's and Woodsman's. Finally, she notices fuzziness of face. Wolf is furry, Woodsman is bearded, and Granny is cleanshaven. Now when Red encounters one of the three characters, the information is there, enough information for her to respond differently to them. Certainly we could easily program a computer with a little AND logic to sort out the different patterns of input and respond differently to them. Red ought to be able to do that, too. The difference, of course, is that she has to learn to do so because she is not programmed with fixed outputs as our simple computer program is. Even fairy-tale people are more flexible than that.

All of the input nodes are tied to a second layer of nodes, which might be called intervening variables, or concepts, or ideas, but we will call them *hidden nodes*. They are hidden because they are not directly tied to input but rather depend on *patterns* of input. They are hidden because they lie functionally somewhere between the observable inputs and outputs. Watson had tried to tie responses directly to stimuli, and we know what a mess he made of that. Notice that Red does not have to check out ears, then teeth, and then face; she can do it all at the same time. That is a lot quicker and probably more realistic. It is called parallel distributed processing. Now when any combination of features is detected, then one of the hidden nodes is activated. In Red's world big ears and smooth face never occur together so that node is never activated, but there are three patterns that do recur, and it is those hidden nodes that concern us. When they are activated Red displays, for reasons of her own, certain index behaviors. She avoids Wolf, gives goodies to Granny, and flirts with Woodsman (perhaps Little Red is not as little as we thought).

We can even program the learning that goes on here, the learning that keeps Ms. Ridinghood out of trouble. Rather than have the nodes tied to each other in an all-or-none manner, we can link them (the input nodes with the hidden nodes) with a modest probability of transmission, something like .50. Then we can arrange it so that after each encounter with one of the characters there will be positive feedback following an appropriate response. The feedback mechanism increases the probability of transmission by a small amount, such as .05, and this increase occurs for whatever connections have just been firing. Over a number of trials the appropriate connections should get strengthened. According to Hunt, it works; his program has her learning to behave properly (although there may be an alarming number of trials where she flirts with Wolf).[5]

One thing we have to note about this model is that it is only concerned with the processing of information, how events in the real world are detected, discriminated, and coded into memory. The analysis is all on the input side, and it says very little about what happens after a hidden node is activated. We have no idea why Red gives goodies to Granny or flirts with Woodsman. We have no notion why those particular behaviors come about or how they are organized. Early on, Miller, Galanter, and Pribram (1960) had concerned themselves with behavior and proposed cognitive mechanisms to cope with it; but subsequent developments appear to have followed Neisser (1967) who said that questions of motivation and behavior belonged to "dynamic" psychology, which he contrasted with cognitive psychology. Today the overwhelming emphasis is on information processing, and behavior is left to take care of itself.

Another interesting feature of the Little Red model is that all its components and functions seem to be consistent with known neurological principles. The connections could be neural connections. The nodes could be neural systems, those lying just the other side of a synapse so that they can respond to summated inputs and inhibitory signals. The nervous system probably works something like that, so that the model is, as they say, biologically plausible. For some model builders that plausibility is very important, much more important than how things look to the observer. That is one kind of realism. Another kind of realism was shown by the gestaltists, who stressed how things look and then toyed with implausible brain models. A final consideration is that there appears to be something very conservative in some of these hot new trends. Associationism had been rejected by the gestaltists, by Tolman, by Bruner, by all the first cognitive people, but now it seems to be back. And it seems that atomism, the bane of the early cognitivists, is back too. Woodsman is nothing more than small teeth, short ears, and a fuzzy face. And Ms. Ridinghood has to learn about Wolf.

A Diversity of Opinion

THERE REMAINS A GREAT diversity of opinion on all these matters. Some cognitive people go at it like the behaviorists of old, trying to predict how different kinds of events will be responded to. Others try to be faithful to known neurological realities. Still others, including many of the computer people, are fascinated just by the logic of these things. They may ponder questions such as how to write a program that will recognize three-dimensional as against two-dimensional patterns. Some cognitive people run

Jean Piaget

subjects in experiments, others spend all day at the computer. Cognitive people may think of themselves as psychologists, or as linguists, computer scientists, or cognitive scientists. They may study artificial intelligence, memory, perception, almost anything. Some of these people will say they are studying the human mind, others say no, they are only simulating or modeling the activities of the mind. Others do not even talk about the mind but concern themselves with the intricacies of behavior. There is a marvelous diversity of cognitive people, but the label "cognitive" does not seem to mean anything very tangible anymore.

And while cognitive ideas were consuming the human experimental area, they were also taking over other areas of psychology. We have already seen how around 1970 they took hold in animal psychology, the area where behaviorism was born. But that was not all. In developmental psychology, for example, Jean Piaget had been observing children and describing their behavior since the 1920s. He invented a new lexicon of terms for his descriptions, and he had a set of developmental stages. It was a strongly cognitive and nativistic analysis, and for these and other reasons American psychology would have nothing to do with it in the early days when behaviorism was taking root. Then in the 1950s we started reading what Piaget had said 30 years before. By the 1960s there was a good deal of inter- est in his ideas, and we started checking them out experimentally. By the 1970s Piaget was really important. His time had finally come on this side of the ocean. The cognitive *zeitgeist* had caught up with him. And the cognitive spirit had caught up with all the diverse areas of our discipline.

The Cognitive Revolution

People who take part in a revolution like to think of themselves as revolutionaries. Certainly the gestaltists did, and the fact that their particular efforts were not totally successful does not matter; they were revolutionaries. The recent demise of old-fashioned behaviorism, and the ever-deepening cognitive mood looks like a revolution, a change in paradigm, a real Kuhnian event. Certainly some of the revolutionaries we have just met felt like revolutionaries. They came charging forth waving their swords. And having slain the enemy and taken over, the victors are certainly entitled to a little well-deserved celebrating. And they can be expected to fuss over just who led the charge. The linguists will attribute the revolutionary impulse to Chomsky, and he certainly was important. The memory people are inclined to give credit to Bruner and/or Miller, and both of them obviously deserve much credit. The computer people see it all as due to the wonderful new information machine, and that is a partial truth. But it is far from clear how the revolution was managed or who really led it.

The truth may be that we were not led by any particular general, and we may not have been led at all. It just happened. As Tolstoy said of wars, they are so complicated and involve so many people doing so many things that there may not be any pattern. The war just happens. History may sometimes be like that too, even when we try to sort it out.

A Final Look at the Unifying Themes

If we look at the major themes that characterized so neatly the behavioristic psychology of 1970, we find them all in disarray, and everyone seems to have drifted away from them. They do not unify us anymore. Some cognitive people are atomists. The binary digit or digital bit of information is an atom if ever there was one. The bit is the irreducible little piece. A handful of them is the molecular byte. A few bytes can give you a line of program. A bunch of lines and you are processing information, and doing something cognitive. But probably the majority of cognitive people work with molar units, things like strategies, expectancies, and images and perceptions. These concepts lack the clarity of a real atom, but they have the immense benefit of letting us describe complex psychological events very simply. The mood is mainly wholistic, but to do research one may be obliged to analyze, to search for atoms.

Some cognitive people are comfortable speculating about the machinery, the different kinds of neurons, or what is really happening in the hippocampus, for example. But probably the majority are model builders who try to get their hypotheses or equations to match the results they get from their subjects. Most psychologists are hypothesis testers, and are not too concerned with machinery. They are content to talk about the information coming in or being retrieved, without reference to the neural wherewithal that makes it happen.

A lot of cognitive people are comfortable with gestalts in perception, expectancies in behavior, and other sorts of nonassociative concepts, and there is now a vast variety of such concepts. On the other hand associationism is still quite popular. However, today's associations are very different from what they used to be. We have Rescorla's rat hearing a tone and then thinking about shock. We have Hunt's Little Red seeing a small tooth and then thinking about her Woodsman. These associations are used primarily to access memory, and not to generate responses. They are by no means the building blocks they used to be, and they usually have little to do with behavior. For the behaviorists there was nothing else in there except S–R associations, because that provided an explanation of behavior. Today associations are used by the cognitive people mainly because associations help them keep track of information.

Empiricism is no longer a central consideration. Learning is no longer the master key that unlocks all the mysterious doors of psychology. Learning in animals is found to depend on the animal, its species, its characteristics, and its lifestyle. A lot of learning occurs according to the animal's own peculiar agenda. And the human is no different. We each have our own agenda and our own priorities. For example, the rat spatializes everything while the human verbalizes everything. So while empiricism has been an essential part of psychology from its beginning, it seems to be slipping away.

Back near the beginning of our story we saw the empiricist John Locke propounding the view that all complex ideas are learned. They are built up slowly from simple ideas, he said. Near the end of our story I cannot resist mentioning the work of my colleague Andrew Meltzoff, who studies neonatal babies. In one study he shielded baby's mouth so that the baby could not see what was put into it. Sometimes it was a smooth pacifier and sometimes it was a bumpy pacifier. Then smooth and bumpy pacifiers were presented visually. The question is which one does the baby look at? It turns out (Meltzoff and Borton, 1979) that the baby looks at the one that had just been in its mouth. It appears that the idea of bumpy does not have to be built up of simpler ideas; the neonate already has the idea of bumpy. And it does not come from correlating visual and tactile sensations; the neonate already understands bumpy feeling and bumpy looking. And if you listen carefully you may hear the spirit of John Locke stirring.

Summary

IN THE 1960s, and that was not so long ago, psychology looked as though it had at long last found its paradigm. We had learned how to measure all sorts of things, how to test hypotheses, how to make our theories rigorous, and how to make ourselves look like scientists. We had the choice of being Hullians and being wrapped up in that sort of theory, or being Skinnerians and getting to work on behavioral applications. In either case one only had to control stimuli, measure responses, and dispense reinforcers. We would soon be able to explain everything in psychology as well as build a better world. It looked promising.

After the war, however, this peaceful picture was quietly being threatened by the introduction of many new ways of thinking about it all. The engineers were telling us that there is only so much information that can be pushed through a communication channel. Other engineers were telling us about the wonders of feedback; they were suggesting that no real line can be drawn between a machine and an organism, between a controlling mechanism and a reasoned purpose. They had machines that seemed to think, to contrast with the psychologists' subjects that were thinkers we treated like machines. The ethologists were telling us that the behavior of animals has a complex structure so that some behaviors were set while others might be flexible. Learning was no longer as universal as we had thought, nor as central or as important. The biologists were telling us things about Darwinian evolution that we had not properly appreciated before. Linguists, who should have been our allies, went to war with us, and with themselves. The computer was developing to the point where it could do some things faster and more accurately than we could. We were soon besieged on all sides by new ideas that were threatening our peaceful picture of psychology.

But the old ways of thinking were deeply ingrained, and what we had gained from the old way of thinking encouraged us to be conservative and hang on, to not be tempted by the new ways of thinking. And even for those who were receptive it took some time for the new ideas to be understood and sorted out and connected with what they were doing. It is perhaps not surprising, then, that some of the major movers in cognitive psychology were not psychologists at all but outsiders who did not have this inertia. We needed Wiener and Chomsky and Simon and Tinbergen to push us along. We needed the mavericks who never fit in with the establishment and never accepted the apparent paradigm, mavericks like Garcia and Bruner and Miller (who says that he hated the psychology he learned in college).

After a few years things began to shape up; we had people thinking about information processing and what it meant to think like that. Others started thinking about the biological aspects of learning, and what that implied. Others were running wild with their new high-performance computers. It is instructive perhaps that the cognitive movement has never had a leader. We fuss over who was in there first, but we rarely consider who was our leader because we understand that none of us was following anyone. Cognitive psychology is rather like the old functionalism in that respect. We can point to Dewey as the first functionalist, but did anyone follow him? Like functionalism, the cognitive movement is so open and so permissive that it really has no take-home message. Functionalism essentially gave psychologists license to flee Titchener's structuralism, but it did not tell them where to go. Cognitive psychology gives psychologists license to flee the behaviorism of Hull and Skinner, but it too does not indicate where they should go.

Notes

1. What is deficient here is the concept of reinforcement that had come to dominate psychology. What does not seem viable any longer is that there is a reinforcement *process* that strengthens behavior. There remains, of course, the reinforcement *procedure*, which does work, sometimes. If you want to control some person's or some animal's behavior it still makes sense to set up a reinforcement contingency, even if it does not work in the same way we used to think it did. My favorite reference on all these matters is Bolles (1979).

2. The appealing notion that classical conditioning is not what you think comes directly from Rescorla (1988). At the same time he was adopting a cognitive approach, Rescorla and Wagner (1972) also developed a purely descriptive, mathematical model, widely known as the Rescorla–Wagner model, for dealing directly with the blocking effect. The model has also proven extremely useful for dealing with situations where there is more than one conditioned stimulus, or where the environmental context is a factor. It is neat, but not cognitive.

3. There are several histories of the cognitive movement. Baars (1986) is interesting because it includes fairly lengthy interviews with many of the most prominent pioneers, letting us really meet them. Bruner (1983) is a delightful autobiography by one of the central figures in the cognitive movement. Gardner (1985) gives a very sophisticated look at the cognitive revolution, which looks far beyond psychology, and expresses little interest in psychology. Hunt (in press) provides another good look at these events, brings them up to date, and also puts them in a broad perspective.

4. The work of Simon and his colleagues first became well known to psychologists through the early paper by Newell, Shaw, and Simon (1958). A later, more developed account of their work, which basically defined the area of artificial intelligence, was Newell and Simon (1972).

5. My account of the fairy tale comes from Hunt (in press).

Chapter Fifteen

The Diversification
of Psychology

U P TO THIS POINT our story has focused on the major forces that have shaped psychology as a whole, and we have seen the different schools of thought that have contended for the hearts and minds of psychologists. We have seen psychology moving from a structuralist outlook to a more functionalist view. Then we saw it moving on to behaviorism, being tempted by the gestaltists, and more recently assuming a cognitive mood. Thus, we seem to have come to the end of the story. But there is another part of it. Up to this point we have been concerned primarily with the center of things, with the mean, one might say. The other part of the story is the variance, the spreading out of psychology. We will complete the story of psychology by looking briefly in this chapter at its diversification. Up to this point we have focused mainly on the science side of psychology; now we look more at the applied side of it.

We see a marvelous diversity, a broad spectrum with many different colors. Actually, I can make out about seven colors, and I will label them clinical, measurement, social, developmental, cognitive, animal, and physiological. Just as some people do not see indigo in the rainbow, some people might want to use other labels to partition psychology. But that is not critical because the dividing lines are by no means rigid. Their purpose is only to help us sort things out. We will start with clinical psychology, and see how it got started, and how it became such a large part of the whole.

Clinical Psychology

THE FIRST PERSON to call himself a clinical psychologist was Lightner Witmer (1867–1956). Witmer was a law student at the University of Pennsylvania in 1888 when Cattell got there from Wundt's lab. Perchance the law student took a class from Cattell, and that was it—Witmer was going to be a psychologist. He began looking at individual differences in reaction times. Cattell urged him, however, to finish his research with Wundt, which he did in 1892. Then when Cattell moved to Columbia that year, Witmer neatly took over his position at Penn.

Witmer's fascination with individual differences soon propelled him into clinical work. The story is that a child with a learning disability was brought to Witmer, and he was able to get the child going on a remedial program. That was the start. A psychological clinic was established at Penn in 1896, and it was the first in the world. Witmer was interested in the behavioral problems of children that disrupted their classes, and in the learning disabilities of kids that were not making it in school. He would involve teachers in working with such kids in new ways, and would often involve the family too. It was the sort of thing that today would be done by a school psychologist, but Witmer called it clinical psychology, and the name stuck.

Witmer was a good organizer. In 1907, he began the journal *The Psychological Clinic*, which he would edit and watch over for many years. For several reasons he thought it important to keep the clinic connected with the university. That would free the clinic from political pressures. Later, child guidance clinics, which were mainly concerned with delinquency, would be tied to local school districts. Witmer foresaw problems with such an arrangement. Moreover, staying within the psychology department meant there would be new clinical students, research projects, and the opportunity for the clinical movement to be firmly based and to grow. He had a number of outstanding students. Edwin Twitmeyer was an early student who specialized in speech defects; Morris Viteles came a little later and he originally specialized in vocational guidance. Viteles remained at Penn for many years and was a pioneer in industrial psychology.

We had a new kind of psychology that was applied rather than theoretical. We had a new helping profession, one that appealed to a lot of young psychology students because it got them away from the artificial world of the laboratory and out into the real world of people—people who needed help. Witmer's ideas gradually caught on, very slowly at first, because most psychologists were jealously guarding their young new science, making it free from philosophy, and making sure it was a science. Some of them no doubt saw the new clinical movement as tarnishing their fragile image. Witmer was considerably ahead of the *zeitgeist*. It was going to take a bit more of the functionalistic spirit to get the new movement flourishing, but in a few more years it was. By 1914 clinics modeled largely after the one at Penn had popped up at many universities (Wallin, 1914).[1]

Witmer's new clinical psychology looks rather like what we now call school psychology. But in time two developments totally altered its appearance. First, psychologists got deeply involved in the area of testing and measurement. Every possible attribute of personality got measured, but none more carefully or more thoroughly than intelligence. And it was Witmer's kind of people who did a lot of this measuring. Second, clinical psychologists gradually became involved in the mental health movement as it began to change and take on a more psychological look.

Some Help From Our Friends

All through the late 1800s psychiatrists had taken a strong mechanistic stand on mental illness. It was a mysterious disease of the nervous system, they said, that was caused by bad genes, or little lesions, or a toxin, or something of the sort. Treatment usually meant diet or rest or both. Take a vacation, it will do you good. An authority on these things was Emil Kraepelin (1855–1926), Wundt's early student, whose *Textbook of Psychiatry* was the standard text. First published in 1883, it reached its peak influence with the 1899 edition. The *Textbook* was strong on mechanistic faith but weak on how to help anyone. A lot of psychiatrists merely supervised the custodial care, or lack of it, given those wards of the state who had not shown any benefit from diet and rest. This was the mechanistic climate that Freud could not tolerate. And there were a few other protesters as well in the psychiatric community. One was Edward Cowles (1837–1919), a psychiatrist but also a former student of Stanley Hall at Hopkins and one of the founding members of APA. Even before the turn of the century Cowles began the tradition at McLean Hospital in Washington D.C. of having psychologists working with the medical people. By the time S. I. Franz (formerly a student of Cattell's but then a doctor) was at McLean in 1907 psychologists were routinely interviewing new patients. Franz relied on learning techniques for rehabilitation therapy, and his psychologists played a part in that, too.

Similarly, when the Swiss psychiatrist Adolph Meyer came to this country in 1895 (when he too made contact with Hall) he not only included psychologists on his team, he listened to what they had to say. Meyer moved to Johns Hopkins in 1910 and became a close friend of Watson; soon he was the director of the newly created Phipps Clinic at Johns Hopkins. There he said loudly and clearly that psychology had much of value to give to the mental health area. His approach to a new patient involved a psychiatric interview, and then a visit to the family to find out about the family history and to see what family support for treatment was available. It was perhaps the beginning of psychiatric social work. Renovation of the traditional doctor–patient relationship was also undertaken by William Healey in Chicago. Healey believed that juvenile crime was not a medical problem so much as a psychological problem. And when his new Juvenile Psychopathic Institute opened in 1909 he hired psychologist Grace Fernald, who appears to have been the first woman clinical psychologist.

It should be stressed, though, that while psychologists were getting their collective foot in the door, there should be no question of who was in charge. It was the psychiatrists' door and they were not about to fling it open. A few psychiatrists might listen to what a few psychologists were saying, but the door remained shut for many more years. Psychologists might do interviews, talk to the family, and give innumerable tests, but they were not doing therapy. And then slowly psychiatry began to change. It still took a pretty monolithic view of the organic basis of all ills. The difference is that rather than protect the body with diet and rest, they began to assault it with insulin shock, and electric convulsive shock, and other indignities. There was wild popularity and unbounded interest in these new techniques and thousands of research papers were published in the 1930s. Frontal lobotomies came along; the same kind of people were curing people's anxieties by removing the front of their brains as 50 years earlier had been curing women's hysterias by removing their uteruses.

But there was change, too. Freud's psychological ideas gained wide currency. And one did not have to be a psychoanalyst to understand that many mental health problems could reflect tensions, anxieties, conflicts, and pressures. Jung's ideas were circulating too. The concepts of criminality and degeneracy gradually got sorted out. Another major shift came with the influx of psychoanalysts to the United States in the 1930s. Many of them were orthodox Freudians, but some of them became less orthodox when they got over here. Thus, Karen Horney was a properly trained Berliner but she had only been here a few years when she began saying that much mental illness could be attributed to the breakdown of family values and economic security during the depression (Horney, 1937). Another Berliner, Erich Fromm (1941), said that we all feel cast adrift, as though we did not know where we belonged. Otto Fenichel (1945) was another purist, another orthodox Freudian from Berlin, but he said that the Oedipus thing was not universal, it depended on one's society. Everyone saw that sex was not the only source of the ego's problems and, moreover, that the ego with all its problems was much more important than Freud had led us to believe. Even daughter Anna saw that (A. Freud, 1936). The American psychiatrist Harry Stack Sullivan (for example, 1953) had none of the biologically inevitable Freudian spirit, and not much physiological causation either; he said we thrive or decline by virtue of our interpersonal relationships because they define who we are. In short, many psychiatrists started looking at mental illness in more psychological ways.

By the time of World War II clinical psychology was ready to redefine itself. No longer would the clinician be just working with troublesome schoolchildren and delinquents, no longer would the clinician be just administering endless tests, they would turn a historic corner and start being therapists. That only came about, however, through some curious political circumstances.

Politics and Professions

During the war academic and scientific psychology, the experimental stuff, almost came to a stop. The publication of conventional research papers fell to a small percentage of what it had been. The students had gone to war, and the psychologists went off to fight with them. Some were marching, sailing, and flying, but many more were testing, selecting, and training. Soldiers had to be tested to see who should go to officers' school. Sailors had to be selected for special duty because not everybody can live on a submarine. Pilots had to be trained. Communications people, spotters, riflemen, propaganda people, even spies had to be trained. With more enthusiastic optimism than anything else, psychology went to war.

Coordinating our efforts were some of our more distinguished experimentalists, people such as Robert Yerkes and Thorndike, and some of these old-timers were pretty smart politically. They knew how to run a lab, how to chair a department, how to get a grant, how to work their way around in APA, and how to get the ear of government. In 1944, in anticipation of the Allied victory, they made it clear to the administration and to Congress just how important the young science of psychology had been in getting our boys back home. They made it clear that there was a debt there. At the same time there was a major problem on the horizon. There was a Veterans Administration (VA) whose mission was to take care of veterans, including their psychiatric needs, but it was a relatively small operation and certainly could not deal with the millions of young men returning from the war. The VA would have to be vastly expanded. But even then the psychiatric community could not be expected to cope with the problem. The solution seemed to require a horde of new, quickly trained therapists. They would be trained with VA money given as grants to universities that would immediately set up clinical training programs.[2]

There were a lot of problems to be worked out. Would the new breed of therapists be licensed or be certified? Would those credentials be granted by the university or by the state? Would the new clinicians be held to the same standards as other graduate students at the university? Would they receive Ph.D.s, and if so would these be research degrees? A conference was held at Boulder, Colorado, in 1949 that served, tentatively, to answer such questions. The Boulder model proposed that the new clinicians would be university graduate students, and that they would be trained as psychologists first and clinicians second. They had to do a research Ph.D. as well as serve a clinical internship to demonstrate that they were indeed psychologists who were competent in research, diagnosis, and psychotherapy. There was some dissent at the conference because some older clinicians understood that most clinicians are basically not research people, so on them the research Ph.D. might look a little artificial. But the academics wanted to keep a grip on this new type of psychologist, and did not want to throw away the precious degree

CHAPTER FIFTEEN

on students who did not earn it. It was a tough fight that is still not completely resolved, but the compromise worked out at the Boulder conference prevailed, and for the most part it still prevails.[3]

There still remained the battle of the doctors. The M.D. psychiatrists were still in charge, even though the majority of them did not know the first thing about research. The lower-ranking Ph.D.s were skilled at research but made little impact when they all sat around the table to discuss a patient. And a lot of these Ph.D.s were also not very interested in research. But gradually the door got pushed open and psychologists became therapists. Psychologists could not do Freudian therapy; that was, unfortunately, regulated by the official psychoanalytic agencies, but they could do almost anything else. And as a side benefit of the system, one no doubt anticipated by its framers, a lot of the new clinicians stayed attached to the academic world of the university, did research on topics like therapeutic effectiveness, and taught graduate students how to be researchers and therapists. The new clinicians would reproduce themselves at the university.

There was another, perhaps unintended outcome of the Boulder conference, which was that it gave license to clinical psychologists to go into private practice. And a large percentage of the new clinicians did just that. Once past the Ph.D. and internship hurdles, they felt free of the academic rat race and could go into business for themselves. Given the right environment, they could specialize in marital or sexual or addiction therapy, or whatever they wished. A lot of these people, perhaps to help make ends meet, wrote popular books about their thoughts on adjustment and maturity, and these books stirred up widespread interest in therapy. This whole process snowballed so that in time ours became the therapy culture. It has gotten to the point where if you are not seeing a therapist you must be crazy.

A Diversity of Clinicians

There are some generalities. Most of the time your psychiatrist will tell you what your trouble is (they are very serious about the diagnosis part) and will give you pills. By contrast, your psychologist will just talk with you. Today some psychiatrists still believe in Freud or Jung, but most of them believe in pills. Today your psychologist may have a behavioristic background, and if so, may talk to you about desensitization, a technique first popularized by Wolpe (1952) who had a strongly Hullian approach. Or your psychologist might tell you when and how you can reward yourself, which would suggest a more Skinnerian approach. But you might also be urged to take responsibility for your life, and told that you are perfectly capable of doing it. That might suggest Carl Rogers (1942), one of the great free spirits in the clinical world, who early on gave us a variety of therapy that had nothing whatever to do with

Carl R. Rogers

Freudian matters. An appeal for you to get in better contact with your own feelings ("confront that hostility!" sort of approach) might suggest a Jungian influence. The wonder of it is that today you might encounter almost any kind of approach from your psychologist. The psychologist might try to restructure you cognitively, or help you to cope, or train you in some social skills, or almost anything. But it was not always so.

When clinical psychology began to boom late in the 1940s, there was Freud and very little else by way of theory. There were the neo-Freudians, for example, Horney and Sullivan, but while their ideas were widely discussed they were never widely accepted. Rogers intrigued a lot of clinicians with his straightforward, almost unintellectual approach, but while it described a therapeutic technique it offered little theory. Then at that moment of need there came the behaviorists offering a rigorous theory and an experimental approach to clinical problems. We remember that graduate students were obliged to do some kind of clinical research to earn their Ph.D.s, and the Hullians certainly pointed the way to research. So going into the 1950s the two dominant forces in clinical psychology were psychoanalysis and behaviorism.

Abraham Maslow (1908–70) argued that we needed a *third force*. Maslow had been trained as a behaviorist, but now was repudiating it. His dissertation was a study of dominance and sexuality in monkeys, and now he saw all such work as futile and without merit. Psychoanalysis was no good because it was so deterministic and mechanical in its orientation that it left no place for the human spirit. The third force would bring that spirit back; we would have a humanistic psychology. His would be a growth psychology emphasizing the heights that the human spirit can attain. There is a *hierarchy of human needs*, Maslow said, and the most primitive and least human of them are *physiological* needs, such as hunger. With growing confidence and maturity the individual

365

is no longer concerned about hunger but becomes concerned about *safety*. Further confidence and maturity moves the person up to *belonging*, which involves matters of family, home, and identity. Then there is the stage of *accomplishment and achievement*, which yields self-esteem and which makes it possible to move up to the lofty heights of the final stage, *self-actualization*. There we occasionally find something rather Aristotelian, people reaching their full human potential.

Maslow's motivational hierarchy, his analysis of self-actualization, and his great commitment to a humanistic approach attracted a lot of attention from clinicians and other psychologists as well. He was elected president of APA in 1967, and the validity of his efforts was recognized by the APA creating a new division of *humanistic psychology*.

And there were other voices. There were those who felt that the therapist invariably seeks to change the client in some way to make them more functional. The fault always lies with the client. No, they said, it might be the case that the client is trying to live in an unlivable environment. Harkening back to Adolph Meyer, they said that there might be family problems that are beyond the ability of the client to deal with, or a codependency relationship, or an impossible situation at work. Clients might be greatly aided by altering their environment, rather than by trying to alter their personality. Those who believed such ideas called themselves *community psychologists*, and they got their own APA division in 1967. There were those who maintained that people with psychological problems tend to come from families with psychological problems, and it is pointless to deal with them in isolation. It is more reasonable to deal with the whole family. And in time APA formed the division of Family Psychology. Some clinicians continued to work with hypnotic techniques and sought to join forces with those who were experimenting with hypnosis, and in due course APA formed a division of Psychological Hypnosis. Some clinicians are fiercely mechanistic and they certainly do not want to follow Maslow into humanistic psychology. Instead, they joined together and formed the divisions of Clinical Neuropsychology, and Psychopharmacology. There is a marvelous diversity of clinicians, who greatly diversify and enrich psychology.

There are more than eight kinds of clinicians, so they are hard to keep track of. And then there is a very large group who look rather like clinicians but call themselves Counseling Psychologists. The first counseling psychologist was clearly Frank Parsons, who opened the Boston Vocational Bureau in 1908. But after that the picture is rather murky. All these years counselors have struggled with who it is they are, what it is they do, what credentials they need, and how they differ from clinicians. There is further uncertainty because while many counselors come from psychology departments, a large percentage of them come from schools of education. Whitely (1984) has put their troubles in historical perspective.

Alfred Binet

Testing and Measurement

HERE WE WILL MEET a French experimental psychologist, and a very important one. He was Alfred Binet, and he measured intelligence more convincingly than anyone had done before. We saw in chapter 8 that Galton had worked with intelligence, but had equated it with accomplishment. That makes some sense when applied to adults, when we wish to judge their worth, perhaps, but it does not make much sense applied to children. All through the 1890s Cattell had tried to measure intelligence by giving children tests much like Galton's tests of sensory-motor coordination, reaction time, and so on. The thought was that a more intelligent person should be able to perceive better and respond more neatly than a less intelligent person. But by 1899 Cattell found out that kids' scores on his battery of sensory-motor tests did not correlate at all with their grades in school. Something fundamentally different was needed.

Binet's Concept of Intelligence

Alfred Binet (1857–1911) had been trained as a lawyer but never practiced law. Curiously, he never studied psychology, but he read a lot of it, and certainly was familiar with Galton. Binet was wealthy, did not need a salary, and evidently he never received one. Nonetheless he kept very busy. The young man approached the great Dr. Charcot to volunteer his time and energy, and began doing research with him on hypnosis. He became the doctor's protégé. Unfortunately, his research was pretty bad and when Delboeuf did his exposé of Charcot, hapless Binet was right there in the middle of it. It was a fiasco, but Binet learned some valuable lessons. One was how important suggestion was in producing hypnotic effects; he promptly switched over to the Nancy school's way of thinking about these things. He also learned to be more cautious and careful in his work.

In 1891 the Sorbonne University in Paris set up a new lab in physiological psychology and put Professor Henri Beaunis in charge of it. Binet offered his irresistible free services again and became Beaunis's assistant. When the professor died in 1894 Binet inherited the lab. So here he was with no training and no credentials but nonetheless in charge of a new lab in France's most distinguished university. He made the best of the opportunity by doing mountains of research on a wide variety of topics. He studied a little of everything. He studied suggestion, of course, but also did work on conformity that anticipated what we would see in social psychology many years later. He researched imageless thought, intelligence, and his own kind of case history analysis. He was enormously productive. It also looked as though Binet would get French experimental psychology organized. Thus, in 1895, only a few years after the first American journal, he founded the important journal *L'Année Psychologique*.

Soon Binet's work began to focus on intelligence in children. Binet was very fond of his two girls, and he did extensive research on them. They were his pilot subjects for many projects. When they were still very young the girls impressed him not by their genetic similarity but by their behavioral differences. Both were quite bright, but they had different styles, and were bright in different ways. One would solve a problem one way while the other would solve it in her own manner. From his girls Binet developed a profound respect for individuality. And he understood that intelligence was not a simple, one-dimensional thing.

In 1903 Binet wrote a book summarizing some of his experiments on intelligence and indicating how complex it was conceptually. That same year the French government, which had just enacted a law requiring that all children go to school, became concerned that the schools seemed to have many youngsters who could not or would not learn. Many children had behavioral problems, but many of them just seemed too unintelligent to learn in normal classes, which suggested that perhaps they should have special education. How can the system sort it out; how can we measure intelligence? Binet was at the time working with a student, Théodore Simon, and they got to work on the problem. In 1905 they published the famous Binet–Simon intelligence test. It was a short test including only 30 items, but the items reflected a variety of different intellectual skills. The items had all been tested against small groups of children of different ages. One item, for example, might be solvable by the majority of 7-year-olds but only a few 6-year-olds. At each age level there were a number of items to try to pick up some of the different dimensions of intelligence.

The Binet–Simon test provided an interesting mix of empirical work and theory. There were norms that had been carefully checked out, but the test also reflected Binet's basic belief that intelligence was a many-splendored thing. The test was never intended to measure intelligence in any quantitative sense but only to differentiate between normal kids who could survive the French school system and subnormal kids who could not. Binet also understood that the test was culture-bound; it only worked with children who had grown up in France. Binet, now pretty cautious, was quite clear about all of this (Binet, 1909). But, as we are about to see, there was trouble brewing, very great trouble. Binet further refined and expanded his tests, and extended them to somewhat older children in 1908 and again in 1911. After Binet died in 1911, the physiological psychology lab at the Sorbonne soon passed on to physiologists, and it has been so ever since. He was unique.[4]

Another Concept of Intelligence

Across the channel in England there was a brilliant young statistician named Charles Spearman, who was strongly in the tradition of Galton. Perhaps on his own, or perhaps challenged by Binet's 1903 book, or maybe just because he wanted to pursue Galton's mission, he started causing trouble. For ideological reasons Spearman wanted intelligence to be inheritable. He was a smart statistician and so he observed that all the items on an intelligence test are correlated with each other. He understood that if a person has a high verbal score, then they are likely to have a high mathematical score as well. Therefore, he concluded, this thing called intelligence is a single, unified, general factor, which he labeled g, that constitutes the major part of it. Certainly there may be special factors—one person may be exceptional in the verbal realm while another excels mathematically—but the fundamental differences among us are our differences in g. And because it is a unitary trait, g is no doubt determined genetically (Spearman, 1904).

More trouble came from Henry Goddard, the psychologist at the Vineland, New Jersey school for the feebleminded. One good thing Goddard did was translate the Binet–Simon test into English and begin using it at his school. A not so good thing was his insistence that delinquents and criminals are feebleminded, either intrinsically or through some sort of degeneracy. Then in 1912 he reported on his investigation of the Kallikak family. *Kallikak* was a contrived name meaning good and bad. Goddard reported that long ago a certain man whom he called Martin Kallikak got involved with a feebleminded girl, and they had a child who grew up, had a large family and eventually produced a horde of descendants. After his adventure with the bad girl, old Martin settled down with a good girl and in time they too had myriad descendants. Goddard sorted out the two families and found that the bad family was bad indeed and had included numerous criminals, drunks, prostitutes, and other bad sorts. By contrast, the good family was almost unblemished by such characters; they were all hard-working, church-going, upright citizens. The bottom line, Goddard said, is that feebleminded people have bad genes and should not be allowed to reproduce. Goddard was also instrumental in getting the immigration people concerned about bad genes. He was there with his intelligence tests at Ellis Island, where he discovered that a lot of those people coming from Eastern Europe did not test out very well. Bad genes again. Galton had died the year before, but the eugenics movement he had worked to promote was obviously thriving.

Lewis Terman (1877–1956) had studied with Hall at Clark and then spent much of his life at Stanford, working on intelligence. In 1916 he published a book that brought Binet's test up to date, standardized it on American kids, and built in Stern's concept of age ratio or *intelligence quotient*, or **IQ**. It was called the Stanford–Binet test, and it gave us pretty much our current IQ concept of intelligence. One feature of the new concept of intelligence was that it is permanent. You are pretty well stuck for life with that 110 or 124 or whatever they nailed on you back in the fourth grade. Binet had known better than that; for example, he understood that test scores often reflect a person's motivation at the time of taking the test, as well as his or her prior learning. Motivation and experience both change over time, and IQ score has to change with them. But we liked those numbers. They were handy markers. Perhaps they gave us the illusion we were measuring something.*

When the United States entered World War I the U.S. Army was somehow pursuaded that they should give IQ tests to all the troops. That would indicate who should be rejected (virtually no soldiers were rejected, however), who should be advanced to officer training programs, and so on. The task was organized by Robert Yerkes. He got together with Goddard and others and developed a group test, which was called the Army Alpha, and they administered it to a couple of million men—big-time testing. Probably none of the information had any impact on the army, but there were bits of data that were to have vast political repercussions. It turned out that the average white soldier had a mental age of only 13, showing no advance since eighth grade! It was apparently already too late for eugenics; we were doomed. And what should one make of the fact that the average black soldier scored reliably lower than 13? Very little dust has settled on these summary data; they are still quite controversial.[5]

The new British–American concept of intelligence was handy because it gave everyone a number label. That number was relatively permanent, and it was largely inherited. If you are stuck with a low number that means you

---

* There are some rather gruesome studies that illustrate the power of suggestion, and the danger of number markers. A schoolteacher is given a set of IQ scores for all the students in one class. But these scores are not the kids' actual scores—they have been randomized across kids. The gruesome finding is that the teacher's grades in the course may be more highly correlated with the fictitious IQ scores than with the kids' real scores. Sometimes it is not how smart you are, but what that magic number is that matters.

are cut out to be worthless, unteachable, and probably a criminal. You should be sent home where you came from. It was not a very good concept. But let us end this section on a happier note. Terman got a deal where he had almost as many subjects as Yerkes did! He measured IQs of all Californian schoolchildren. Then he picked out the brightest .6 percent of them, those scoring over 140, whom he put in the *genius* category. Terman then studied these kids exhaustively and carried out endless follow-up investigations on them. One might think that a genius is some sort of maladjusted, weird, intellectual person. But it is absolutely not so. Terman (1926) tells us that these young geniuses tend on average to be more attractive and healthier, more athletic, better liked, and happier than average children. The follow-up studies indicate that as these super-smart kids grew up and aged they continued to maintain all their statistical advantages. Thus, they end up wealthier than average.

Other Kinds of Tests

Intelligence testing grabbed everyone's imagination. There were all those political and sociological problems. There were so many inferences to be drawn, and so many misunderstandings to be straightened out. There was public policy to worry about. Nothing that psychology ever accomplished has stirred up so much fuss and furor. By comparison, any other kind of psychological test looks pretty dull. And that bias is still with us. If someone knows your score on a test for need Achievement, they do not pay much attention. But if they know your IQ, then they have some insight into the real you. I do not know why we dismiss the one test and take the other so seriously.

Hermann Rorschach had been a housepainter and his father was a painter; his nickname was Klex, which means blotch of paint. This is fitting, because in 1921 he devised the Rorschach ink-blot test. It was the first clinical diagnostic test, or at least the first popular test and one that is still used occasionally. The ink-blot test is interesting, too, because it was the first of what we call the *projective* tests. The examiner presents a standardized card showing symmetrical blobs of color, and the client or subject has to say what they see. The stimulus does not give much information; it looks for all the world like symmetrical blobs of color. Therefore, if the subject says he sees two men fighting, then that suggests that the fight image must come from the subject. It is something he projects on the external world. Because it comes from the subject and not from the stimulus, the clinician has learned something about the subject's inner dynamics. Rorschach was from Zurich and was quite familiar with Jung's views. Perhaps he thought that his clients could see things in the test that they could not openly express, things like aggression. The Rorschach test soon inspired a lot of research and even more discussion. Although it still has advocates, most therapists now believe the Rorschach is not very useful.

A second projective test came from Henry Murray and his colleagues at Harvard in 1938. Murray believed that all of our behavior is organized around motivational episodes and that one's personality is best defined in terms of the recurrent motivational themes that underlie one's particular behaviors. Thus, one person might be constantly affiliating while another person is usually achieving, and so on. The test presents a series of pictures of people, but they are vague, unclear pictures of people more or less just standing there. One young man is staring out the window. The subject is shown the picture and then asked to make up a story. Who is this young man, what has been happening, and how is it going to turn out? The subject might say that this guy wants to make up with his girl friend, and that he is afraid she will still be mad at him, but then he thinks of how to get out of trouble, and everything works out okay. Such a story sounds like affiliation, and if the subject gives a lot of such stories then we may suppose that affiliation is one of their major motivational themes.

Notice that Murray's test, the Thematic Apperception Test, or TAT, is not searching for hidden psychic forces, nothing like repressed aggression. Rather, it is trying to characterize what is already out on the surface. Affiliators usually do lots of affiliating, and they think about it a lot. So if they have to make up a story with almost no restraining stimulation, Murray was betting that they will reveal the affiliation theme again because they have to get a story from somewhere. Notice that both the TAT and Rorschach are what we can call *rational tests* because they were devised by pondering over what a person is likely to do in certain situations. There is a rationale for them. But there are tests that are purely empirical with no real rationale. The test designer starts with a big bunch of more or less random questions and administers them to various criterion groups to see which questions tend to discriminate the groups. A vocational guidance test, for example, might ask you if you would like to paint a fence. Most people say no, but curiously, truck drivers and bus drivers tend to say yes. Do you like to explain things to people? Not surprisingly, most teachers say yes. Some items might be transparent, but a good test will have enough items and enough different scales that the test as a whole is hard to fake.

The test that has undoubtedly received the most attention over the years is the Minnesota Multiphasic Personality Inventory, or MMPI. It was originally constructed by Hathaway and McKinley in 1940 but has been constantly revised, abridged, expanded, and restandardized in the subsequent 50 years. Originally it was standardized on a large group of normals and groups of sociopaths and hypochondriacs. Items were sifted through until the three groups could be easily distinguished. Now innumerable versions of the MMPI have been developed, and they can discriminate almost any kind of psychological disorder. And selections of MMPI items have been put together that can assess almost any sort of personality trait. Thus, it has been useful for all kinds of diagnostic work as well as personality research.

The testing and measurement area boomed when the rest of psychology did, right after World War II. All the new clinicians designed and used countless tests. The personality and social psychologists made many more of their own. The statisticians began working on the technical problems to make tests neat and orderly. They also invented new ways, such as factor analysis, to handle great masses of multidimensional data. And they worked out their own new theories of measurement. The majority of psychologists did not have to know much about the theory of measurement, but we all did have to understand about reliability and validity. Tests became one of psychology's major tools.

Social Psychology

THE FIRST PSYCHOLOGIST to title a book *Social Psychology* was William McDougall (1871–1938), and he did it in 1908. But *Introduction to Social Psychology* had little to say on the subject. It was intended to set the stage for his social psychology, but like Wundt and synthesis, although it was very important to him he never got to it. All behavior is motivated by instinctual forces, McDougall said, of which there are 20 or so. An instinct is known by three things that it does. An instinct: (1) determines how one perceives suitable objects in the world; (2) produces an emotional feeling—for example, the aggressive instinct makes us feel angry; and (3) prepares us to react (in the case of anger we are prepared to strike out and damage someone or something). Two different instincts can interact; one might like pizza for aesthetic reasons (it satisfies the aesthetic instinct) as well as for mundane nutritional reasons (it satisfies the hunger instinct). Then one would have a *sentiment* about pizza, a sentiment in favor of it. In such an example, as well as in most of life, we see innate predisposition and learning working together. It was an intriguing way to look at animal and human behavior, and it was a good antidote to the rising tide of mechanistic behaviorism. But psychology mainly ignored his message. McDougall's chief influence was on Tolman's cognitive psychology and not on social psychology.

McDougall undertook the impossible task of getting experimental psychology going in England. He started the British Psychological Society and founded the *British Journal of Psychology*, but he was at Oxford and they would not let him have a lab. He came to this country about 1920 but could not get along with the people at Harvard so he moved to Duke where he collected a crew of other outcasts. He was a wonderfully controversial character who fought with everyone. He was a great iconoclast who stood up for all the unpopular causes; he defended a cognitive behaviorism, Lamarckian evolution, and ESP. He was psychology's Don Quixote, a good man who had no chance of accomplishing what he set out to do.

373

The Beginnings

The first textbook of social psychology was written in 1924 by Floyd Allport. He was a behaviorist of the Watsonian variety, and he attempted to explain the small amount of research reported at that time in terms of conditioning mechanisms. He was particularly interested in the work that had been done on social facilitation. Back in 1898 Triplett had reported that people perform better when they are competing. It was soon discovered that people in groups outperformed individuals working alone. Several early experimenters had followed up on these leads, and Allport reviewed it all. In his own time, Allport's views were acceptable because they were behavioristic. But his notion that "others" are just another stimulus never took hold. Something was clearly missing. We were waiting for the gestalt influence.

We began to get some gestalt thought with Muzafer Sherif. In 1935 he reported work on the *auto-kinetic effect.* The subject is in a totally dark room except for one small light. The subject usually reports that the light moves around unpredictably, sometimes quite a bit. The auto-kinetic effect is an illusion because the light is actually fixed in space. It is explained by feedback from the neck muscles. If the light is up so that the muscles are basically uncomfortable then the effect gets more pronounced. But that is neither here nor there; subjects think they see the thing move. What Sherif did was add confederates, stooges, to the situation. Now if the stooges report the light moving to the right, then so does the subject! It was Wertheimer's game all over again: There is nothing out in the physical world that corresponds to what the observer is now seeing.

Sherif suggested that we have to think in terms of social perception; things are not seen because of what they are but as we have learned to see them. The individual forms a frame of reference in part because of the cultural group. We cannot account for such organizing processes in terms of conditioned reflexes, we have to do it by understanding both the external structure and our internal predispositions. Now *that* is beginning to sound like social psychology.

Social Psychology Takes Shape

During World War II there was a lot of work done on attitudes, and particularly on attitude change. There was more research done on propaganda and its effectiveness. The whole business of changing other people's belief systems was scrutinized. Much of this research was done from a behavioristic perspective, but the behaviorists were losing ground to the gestaltists, or those influenced by them. Some of their gain came from research in new areas, such as Lewin's work on group dynamics. Lewin and his people were studying group leadership (Lewin et al., 1939), and insisting that one cannot just select an effective leader of a group on the basis of personality, or analyze the situation just as a collection of stimuli. Instead one must regard people as moving within their own personal life space, as they see it, and as they are propelled by their own personal forces, as they feel them. It is the totality of the person in the situation that must be understood. John Dewey must have liked that.

Right after the war the students were back and they were mature, confident, dedicated students, the likes of which had probably never before been seen at the university. In chapter 12 we noted that this was the time when many of the young people who were to dominate social psychology were moving around in gestalt circles. They were moving around in that curious network of people that included the gestaltists and their sympathizers. The network included Solomon Asch, who soon startled everyone with his studies of *conformity*. Experimental stooges could get subjects to declare that the short line was really the longest (Asch, 1956). There was Fritz Heider, who was talking about something he called *balance*, that later he transformed into *attribution* (Heider, 1958). In the able hands of Leon Festinger, the idea of balance led to the idea of *dissonance* (Festinger, 1957), which explained the sour grapes effect, among other things. Richard Crutchfield collaborated with David Krech, who had also been at Swarthmore, on a textbook that spread the new ideas far and wide (Krech and Crutchfield, 1948).

The towering figure in all this was certainly Kurt Lewin, who gathered around him at MIT a dazzling collection of social psychologists. Festinger had earlier been his student. But Kelley, Cartwright, and Schachter were also there at MIT. Some of today's leading social psychologists were trained in the behavioristic tradition, but the gestalt influence appears to have been overwhelming.

In 1945 APA rearranged itself and formed divisions. One of them was social psychology. The first president of the division was Floyd's younger brother, Gordon Allport (1897–1967). Brother Gordon had contributed in many ways to the field. First of all, he had been the leader in the area of personality theory. The areas of social and personality have always had a symbiotic sort of relationship, as if neither one could make it on its own. Thus, sometimes they share journals, as with their most prestigious *Journal of Abnormal and Social Psychology*. Sometimes they share APA divisions, as today when we find that division 8 is Personality and Social. It is a funny relationship. Perhaps even more curious is the fact that prior to 1937 psychology had no theory of personality. Freud had told us what our problem is, but he had not told us who we are, or how we differ from each other. Apparently, no one, except of course for the astrologers, had thought about personality. Psychology types had worried about our knowledge (Hume), our morality (Reid), our perceptions (Wundt), our emotions (Darwin), and our behavior (Watson), but evidently no one before Allport had thought seriously

Gordon W. Allport

about the obvious fact that you and I are different folks. His book *Personality: A Psychological Interpretation* (Allport, 1937) begins with a definition. Actors in Roman times wore masks to tell the audience who they were. And these masks were called *persona*. The personality is, at least partly, the public mask one presents.

One might think that the personality is a private inner thing, and certainly it is that too, as William James described in distinguishing between the private self and the public self. But Allport persisted. The private, inner self is characterized by one's values and the variety of attitudes that one holds. One likes this and that, and is opposed to something else. But these likes and dislikes are precisely the basis of our social behavior. We welcome these folks and avoid those other folks. The study of attitudes is at the same time the study of personality and the study of social psychology. And for several years Allport and his students led the way on research on attitudes. Allport was also the editor of the hybrid *Journal of Abnormal and Social Psychology* for many years. Finally, Allport always stood in opposition to the behaviorists, and he made that antipathy very clear in his presidential address (Allport, 1947). He was an entirely appropriate first president.[6]

Socially Relevant Psychology

John Dewey was a social activist, so was Hugo Münsterburg, and so was Kurt Lewin. Part of the mission of the social psychologist, Lewin said, was to get out there to cause social change, to build a better world. And no sooner had APA set up divisions than one of them was called Society for the Psychological Study of Social Issues, or SPSSI. The original divisions of APA in 1945 included Industrial–Business, which I will discuss momentarily, and Psychologists in Public Service, which deals with political matters. Later years saw the splitting off of Consumer Psychology, Population Psychology, Psychology of Women, and the Psychology–Law Society. Recently APA has branched out to include the Society for the Psychological Study of Lesbian and Gay Issues and the Society for the Psychological Study of Ethnic Minority Issues, as well as Media Psychology. We see an amazing diversification of psychological interests, so that almost any aspect of society is now likely to attract the attention of some organized group of psychologists.

The oldest of these branches of applied psychology arose mainly through the efforts of Walter Dill Scott (1869–1955). Scott was the last American to get a Ph.D. with Wundt; he ended that era in 1900, right with the new century. There are some nice stories about Scott. One is that when he was only 12 he was plowing up a family field when it occurred to him that plowing was rather inefficient because he had to stop for 10 minutes every hour or so to let the horses rest. He saw that he was wasting his time while the animals were resting, so from then on he always took a book to read when he was plowing. Thus began, the story goes, Scott's life-long fascination with efficiency. There is another story: One day in 1901 the young psychologist was giving a talk in which he said that if the science of psychology could be applied to advertising, then it would be possible to sell anything. An advertising executive happened to be in the audience, he sought out the speaker, and then and there offered to set him up to research the advertising business. And so began Scott's life-long fascination with advertising.

When Scott entered the picture there was already in place the tradition of Frederick Taylor, the time-and-motion man. Taylor appeared to regard the factory worker as just another part of the machinery. To do his job efficiently his work should be laid out so as to minimize waste movement. Inefficiency was therefore reduced by designing better tools and work processes. More work in less time was his motto. The assumption was that the worker was motivated only for his pay, and was to be manipulated so as to increase productivity. Scott understood the need for productivity, but could not go along with the disregard for human welfare. The life of the worker had to matter too, he thought. The worker was a valuable resource that had to be protected.

Münsterburg (1913a) greatly popularized this emerging new attitude. He said that better working conditions benefit not only the employer through increased productivity, but even more so the employee who can use his best energies, work less, earn more, gain personal satisfaction from his work, and raise the quality of his life. Imagine if the whole nation could work like that, what a cultural advantage it would give us.

World War I provided industrial psychologists an opportunity to study the selection of personnel. The U.S. Army was selecting men for different sorts of duty, so they had to be tested and properly assigned. Scott, along with Angell's former student Walter Bingham, organized the army's efforts, and some of their tests provided the basis of personnel selection tests used not only in the military but throughout business and industry. The work of Scott and his allies met with tremendous success. The progress of these applied psychologists can be measured by the quick appearance of several new journals, including *Journal of Applied Psychology* (1917), *Journal of Personnel Research* (1922), and *Industrial Psychology* (1926).

Industrial and business psychology, as it used to be called, had started out looking for working conditions that would facilitate production. Then they got into advertising (your ads don't have to be believable, Scott said, but they have to be insistent and demanding). The war moved them very successfully into personnel problems. And then the next major move was back into productivity. Should there be background music, or more light, or maybe fresh air in the factory? They studied parameters of that sort. Around 1927 they were working for the Western Electric plant in Hawthorne (Chicago), and thought they should do a study of whether brighter lighting would be a good thing. They selected two groups of workers and interviewed them all at great length, gave them tests, and followed them up for some time. They also did the obvious experimental trick of giving one group, the experimental group, much brighter lighting. And as you might expect, the experimental group with the better illumination showed a big increase in productivity. That was nice, but the control group with their customary dim light showed a big increase, too!

My goodness. They repeated the study many times. They talked some more with the workers, gave them more tests and more follow-ups, and really got involved with this thing. And the more they got involved, the more they got the same strange results: The control group also showed great improvement. And apparently this went on for some time, because the answer to the puzzle was not published until many years later (Roethlisberger and Dickson, 1939). What these good people had discovered was the **Hawthorne effect,** which is that if you work in a factory near Chicago your life can be pretty dreary, and if folks come around to give you tests and talk with you about all sorts of personal matters, and if these folks really seem to care about your life and your work, then your life and your work become much more interesting and you work a lot harder. And it really does not matter very much how bright the lights are.

It was a major turning point. It said that the psychology of the worker really is important. It said that the worker is not just a part of the production machinery, not just a cog in a wheel of the machine. It was another déjà vu—I have to say it again—your behavior is not just a set of responses to stimuli out there, it also depends on inner stuff, like how you feel about yourself and how you believe others feel about you. It was a great day for psychology.[7]

Other Areas of Psychology

WE HAVE NOW MADE our way across the psychological spectrum to the point where we have covered, however briefly, the largest areas of applied psychology. We are back to the traditional experimental parts of psychology that we encountered earlier. But I need to say a little more about each of these experimental areas, first, because they have also diversified tremendously in recent years, and second, because they are no longer as clean and pure and scientific as we used to pretend they were.

Developmental Psychology

We have noted most of the stages of the development of developmental psychology at various points in our story. Here those odd pieces can be pulled together and put in chronological order. The study of children really began with Darwin's observations of his eldest child, William. This first baby diary was not published until 1877, however, and it was published then probably only because Taine had just reported in Bain's new journal *Mind* some observations on language learning in his own girls. Then we have just seen how Binet's observations of his own little girls around 1891 led him off for the rest of his life studying the intelligence of children.

It was at this same time that Stanley Hall turned his energies to the study of children. All through the 1890s Hall was making up questionnaires and giving them to kids and their parents. He was extraordinarily energetic and produced a huge number of questionnaires. And although his work appeared to have little direction, there was a theory behind it. The vaguely Darwinian theory had been articulated by Baldwin (1895). Roughly, the child's mind evolves in a manner parallel to how the human species evolved, from simple to complex. Thus, from the beginning the study of the child had a rightful place in American experimental psychology.

John Watson quickly moved his new behaviorism out of the rat lab and into the nursery. His subject Little Albert is no doubt better known to psychologists than any other infant in history. However, Watson's behavioristic approach to children does not look very appealing today; he left them without thought, feeling, or emotion. He made them out to be machines that did little more than associate Ss and Rs. John's book with Rosalie (Watson and Watson, 1928) seems particularly offensive today. A parent should not show affection toward their child, they say, it will make the child weak and dependent. The behavioristic paradigm set developmental psychology back in another way because it encouraged the idea that all learning is homogeneous. It discouraged the investigation of differences between little kids and big kids. In fact, it does not matter if you look at learning in rats or children or adults because all learning is the same.

379

While developmental psychology in this country was falling under the spell of behaviorism, it was advancing in new directions in Europe. There was a mystery man, mysterious because we know so little about him, Karl Bühler (1879–1963). We first met him as Külpe's assistant in 1907 in Würzburg, and then again still working with Külpe at Munich with young Otto Selz the cognitivist. After Külpe died, Bühler turned to developmental matters, and in 1918 wrote *The Mental Development of the Child*. He then went to Vienna as the professor of philosophy, but he also ran Vienna's Pedagogical Institute. Bühler with his wife, Charlotte, studied speech and cognitive development in children there for a number of years until the Nazis took over. All through the 1920s and into the 1930s Bühler held a commanding position, had many students, was highly productive, and must have had considerable influence. He must have been connected in some way with Binet, and then later with Piaget, but we do not know (see Weimer, 1974).

When the Bühlers came to this country in the 1930s, he essentially disappeared from view but Charlotte made a considerable mark on clinical psychology. She was almost alone in being interested in life-long motivational patterns, what she called *creative expansion*, and humanistic psychology. She followed Maslow as president of the new humanistic division of APA. Her presidential address (Bühler, 1971) is very instructive.

We saw that Binet never obtained a degree in psychology and never studied the subject. Neither did Jean Piaget (1896–1980) the French-speaking Swiss scholar. He was a biologist who published a lot of early papers on mollusks. About 1918 Piaget worked briefly with Théodore Simon testing children's intelligence. That got him hooked, and he spent the next 60 years studying children and trying to understand the way they think about the world. When Piaget tested a child he would not just add up a score, he would talk with the child to see what the child was thinking about. Gradually he began to understand how the child acquires information about the world. Piaget began to see that the child starts with a few reflexes, but these become elaborated with experience and form a cognitive structure. As this structure gets increasingly complex the child becomes less reflexive and more cognitive. The child interacts in different situations and has different experiences of the world. Those experiences that conform with the cognitive structure are said to be *assimilated*, understood, while those that do not conform lead to *accommodation*, which is a change in the structure. Piaget had a whole set of new concepts, and a new language to label them.

Piaget also understood that there are cognitive stages of development. Thus, for the first two years or so there is the *sensorimotor stage*, which involves few words and no symbols. After two the child moves ahead to the *preoperational stage*, where there can be symbols and the child can remember and compare concepts, but lacks logic. Piaget saw the cognitive structure becoming increasingly complex and changing in different ways as the child moves through the four stages. He saw different-aged children thinking in different ways. Piaget began writing about his complex system in the 1920s, and at least one of his many books, *The Language and Thought of the Child*, appeared in English as early as 1926. But we were committing ourselves to behaviorism back then and paid little attention to Piaget. When the cognitive mood began to deepen in the 1960s, however, we turned to his novel notions and started to check them out experimentally. Today Piaget's theory occupies a prominent place in developmental psychology.[8]

Experimental Psychology

We have been looking at experimental psychology all through our story. Perception was discussed in chapter 12. We outlined recent learning theory, the main occupation of animal psychologists, in chapter 13, and sketched the fateful transition from verbal learning to cognitive psychology in chapter 14. The other major part, physiological psychology, now needs to be mentioned. Before doing that, however, we should take note of the fact that experimental psychology used to stand in contrast to any kind of applied psychology, but that old distinction is now disappearing. To Titchener the distinction was very clear because there was his kind of experimental and everything else was applied. The line got fuzzy during World War II, however, when perception people were training the troops how to shoot guns, speech researchers were developing better communication systems, and the learning people were designing airplane cockpits. The line gets really blurry today when we can find learning theorists running groups of rats dosed with alcohol, and verbal learning researchers working with dyslectic kids. And what happens to the line when you find that some experimentalists do not do experiments, and many applied psychologists do? We suspect that there is no line, there is no distinction. Rather, it appears that the strong movement toward applied psychology is just a part of the modern mood, and that it runs through all of psychology.

In the old days, before applied psychology became acceptable, it seemed vitally important to many psychologists to ensure that their discipline was really a science. There were several ways that that was done. Wundt called his psychology a "physiological" psychology. There was nothing very physiological about it but that adjective meant that it was experimental, or nonphilosophical, or scientific. The great books by Bain and James talked a lot about the nervous system and what was happening in it during learning or emotion. These physicalistic references presumably gave scientific credibility to what they said about learning or emotion. In ridding psychology of the mind, Watson and the early behaviorists filled it with neurons. It was as if holding to a mechanistic philosophy made his behaviorism scientific. As later behaviorists developed a more mature view of the empirical character of science, they were able to get along quite well without any conceptual nervous system.

I take the position that what makes a physiological psychologist a scientist is not that he or she works with a real substrate, but that he or she measures a phenomenon and then analyzes the data until they make sense. There were ew significant physiological psychologists in the early days who did just t. Some—for example, H. R. Marshall, who was APA president in)7—studied cerebral brain mechanisms. Raymond Dodge, APA president 1916, worked for many years on vestibular mechanisms. In 1921 Dodge)orted that the compensatory eye movements that occur when you move ur head have zero latency. That shows that the eye movements are not ggered by an altered image on the retina, as Wundt's theory of local signs)uld require. Nor can they depend on vestibular information, as Watson's liance on feedback stimuli would require. The eye movements seem to be ·ganized and initiated at the same time the head movements are. That ggests something very interesting and very psychological about how we adjust to the environment.

For the most part, however, the early physiological psychologists worked on a narrow range of topics; they worked almost exclusively on sensory mechanisms. That reflected, no doubt, American psychology's structuralist beginnings. Something was needed to inspire interest in a broader range of topics, and apparently what did it was Watson's behaviorism. I think Watson's mechanistic philosophy was helpful but not critical; there is never a shortage of people who believe in the importance of the physiological world. What behaviorism did was focus attention on new questions, questions other than the sensory ones. It stressed learning, so one could now turn to the physiology of learning. It also focused attention on motivation, which is ironic because Watson sought to eliminate motivational concepts, or at least to reduce them to bodily stimuli. But the positive of that is that while one cannot easily study what the individual "wants," it should be possible to study the bodily stimuli that motivate behavior. And from these new questions there emerged a new physiological psychology.

The New Physiological Psychology

Karl Lashley (1890–1958) was a country boy from West Virginia, and was an undergraduate zoology student at the state university there. After a year at Pittsburgh, where he earned an M.A. in bacteriology, he advanced to Johns Hopkins, where he was with H. S. Jennings working with little animals that live in the water. Lashley's dissertation was a study of the genetics of such little animals, and he received his degree in genetics in 1914. Lashley was so bright and so energetic, however, that Jennings's department could not contain him, and he began to spend a lot of time over in the psychology department with John Watson. Watson was 12 years older than Lashley, and terribly busy with his department, the journal, and his own career, but even so they became close friends. They worked together on a number of studies.

Karl S. Lashley

They wandered off together to the Gulf of Mexico to study some birds that lived there. Lashley did the critical salivary conditioning study (with negative results) when Watson was trying to replicate Pavlov's work. Later, when Lashley had left Hopkins, he still came back to collaborate with Watson on several problems. Lashley became, in effect, Watson's student and protégé, even though it was all based on their friendship rather than any formal academic relationship. And at the same time he became a physiological psychologist, one of the first and one of the most important.

Lashley believed in behaviorism, but his attempts to test its physiological implications took him on a course much like that Külpe had taken. Shepherd Franz, in nearby Washington, D.C., was doing memory studies with animals, and in 1915 Lashley got a post-doctoral appointment with him. They trained animals on a discrimination task, and then after training they surgically removed different portions of the rats' cerebral cortex. They then tested the animals' performance on the task to see what part of the cortex was involved in memory. Watson believed that stimuli and responses are linked neurologically somewhere in the brain. Lashley just wanted to know where that happened. He was another Külpe.

In the lead-off paper of the new journal *Psychobiology*, Franz and Lashley (1917) reported that memories, what they called the *engram* of S–R connections, do not appear to reside in the frontal cortex because it did not seem to matter where their lesions were located there, they found only slight deficits in behavior. A second paper in the same volume of the journal indicated that no matter where the cortex was lesioned the engram still survived. Lashley worked on this conundrum for a dozen years and summarized all his findings in a book (Lashley, 1929) in which he was forced to conclude that the engram could not be localized. It did not seem to matter where on the cortex lesions were made, it only mattered how big they were. Big lesions caused more memory loss than small ones. Thus, we had Lashley's famous two hypotheses: *Equipotentiality* (one part of the brain can substitute for any other part) and *mass action* (it is only the amount of brain tissue that matters).

His behavioristic inclinations had led Lashley paradoxically to experimental results that had a very gestaltist look to them. Distressingly, it got worse. Later Lashley got into analyzing sequential behaviors. Consider a pianist practicing scales, whipping through a couple of octaves of A major. Watson would maintain that the execution of one response, B, produces feedback that controls the execution of the next response, C-sharp. But Lashley observed that the pianist can play the A-major scale so fast that there is simply not enough time for the feedback to get to where it is needed to control the next response. The whole thing has to be organized at some higher level. It has to be something like Dodge found, organized ahead of time. It has to be something like feedforward, which implies some higher level of organization, or something gestaltish. This conclusion must have hurt him to acknowledge, because he always wanted to believe in his friend Watson's view of things.

Lashley was respected by everyone who knew him or his work. He was elected president of APA in 1929, when he was only 39 years old, which made him one of the youngest presidents ever. Meteoric Watson had been 37. Franz, the physiological clinician, also gained from his collaboration with Lashley and was elected president of APA back in 1920.

We recall that Hall received his degree at Harvard from research done not with William James but with the physiologist Bowditch. Bowditch is notable for the fact that his was the first academic physiological lab in the United States. It was set up in 1871, and Hall was one of his first Ph.D. students. However, his most distinguished student was Walter B. Cannon, who then taught at Harvard and in due course inherited Bowditch's lab. In 1912 Cannon discovered that people could detect their own stomach contractions, and he called such sensations hunger pangs. These are the sensations of hunger, he said, but more than that, he maintained that these sensations *are* hunger. That is what hunger is, no more than these particular internal stimuli. It is not how much you need or want food, and hunger is certainly not the pleasure you anticipate from eating. All such conceptions are much too mentalistic to have a place in science. Translate motivation into stimuli, however, and then everything is okay because we can find the stimuli and do research on them.

Cannon's strategy here was very similar to Watson's when he dismissed motivational and emotional concepts. The difference was that Cannon continued to pursue research questions on both motivation and emotion (Cannon, 1915). It turned out, for example, that Cannon's stomach contractions were only poorly correlated with eating behavior, so the search began for the real stimuli. Some thought it was blood-sugar level. Later, others thought it was fats in the blood. A lot of people searched for a hunger hormone. People are still searching for that elusive hunger stimulus. During the 1950s the search focused on where in the brain the stimulus is detected rather than on what the stimulus is. Now, 80 years later, the search is for how that stimulus, whatever it is, changes neural transmitters.

Cannon also worked on emotion and on the concept he named *homeostasis*, the idea that the function of physiological adjustments is to maintain a stable, constant internal environment. Eating is part of that; the body falls apart if you don't eat. And presumably that unknown stimulus arises from the discrepancy between the momentary state of the body and how it should be. If the body needs salt the person can expect to have a *specific hunger* for salt. A lot of the research on consummatory behavior stems directly or indirectly from the early work of Cannon.

We conclude with mention of a unique, wonderful man. Curt Richter (1894–1988) had no graduate training and no training at all in psychology when he heard about behaviorism and found it interesting. He decided to pay John Watson a visit. The story goes that they visited, and Watson liked him so much that then and there he invited the young man to join him as a graduate student. Watson gave him a room over in the medical school, got him some rats, and just turned him loose. Richter loved to design and build crude-looking equipment that let him collect the sort of data he was looking for. He puttered, built equipment, and collected data in that same room for two years. That produced his famous dissertation in 1921, published the next year. Then Richter remained right there. *Remained* is the operative word here; you could come back to that same room in the medical school almost any time in the next seven decades and see that Richter was still there. All his long life Richter puttered, built equipment, and collected interesting data.

His dissertation was an extensive study of *spontaneous activity*, which is the seeming random moving about rats show when there are no particular stimuli to respond to. It is spontaneous rather than being elicited by the environment. Richter found that it depends on the apparatus the rat lives in. Rats are particularly active in running wheels. Activity declines with age and increases with food deprivation. And it is rhythmic, showing a strong daily cycle but many other cycles as well. Richter followed up on all these leads, and discovered a great host of other phenomena. Just to suggest the range of things he looked at, he worked on sex hormones, hunger, all sorts of cyclic behavior, salt appetite, food selection, nesting, wild versus domesticated rats, whiskers, and on and on. He began the study of many of the motivational phenomena that physiological psychologists still work on.

Richter did not have any systematic theoretical position, he had no compulsions, which might account for his wide-ranging enthusiasms. He offered many hypotheses, but always held them lightly. He was always more interested in collecting data to test new ideas than in defending old ones. He might do surgery and look at neural mechanisms, but a good part of his work was like his dissertation in looking at the behavior of intact and undisturbed animals, and how the animal adjusted to a physiological disturbance. So in a physiological psychology world dominated by people who fight for a mechanistic view of reality, we find this old gentleman exploring how the functioning animal adjusts to its world. He was a different kind of scientist.[9]

Even in physiological psychology, an area we might expect to be well-delineated by its scientific standards, we find great diversity of people, problems, and approaches. We find mechanists, as we might expect, but we also find functionalists, like Richter. We see researchers inquiring into new areas such as learning and motivation, in addition to the traditional neurological and sensory areas. This happened because of the rise of behaviorism. Watson stressed learning as the basis of all psychology. His friend Lashley went to work on the problem of where the learned association was localized in the brain. He never found what he was looking for, but he led the way into a very active area of research. Ironically, while Watson wanted to abolish from psychology everything motivational, his student Richter probably raised more intriguing motivational questions and introduced more techniques for studying them than anyone else. Watson's dismissal of motivation, by making it nothing but a stimulus, fit hand in glove with Cannon's desire to specify what the stimulus was. But the move to dismiss motivation blew up on them, because rather than being dismissed it became an active research area.

History never stops, it just keeps unfolding. But I must end my story, and I will do it here.

Recapitulation

WE BEGAN THE STORY with a review of science, and noted its social and political character, and we have certainly seen many instances of that character in the history of psychology. We have met some of the early scientists and some of the first modern philosophers. We noted the source of the basic themes. Thus, mechanistic ideas began to flourish with Descartes and Hobbes. Ancient atomistic ideas were revived by Gassendi and then were welcomed by many of his contemporaries. Locke made us believe that all knowledge comes from experience, and then Hume and Hartley got people thinking about the possibility that the mind is built up of little more than associations. There was a time when these themes seemed to be waiting for a psychologist to come along and put them together in an orderly manner.

Psychology might have started with Descartes's mechanism, or with Hume's associationism, but it did not turn out that way. Once the major themes were in place, the beginning of psychology looked imminent, even inevitable, but that did not happen. Actually, by 1800 or so the major themes were lost; they had been overwhelmed by other social and intellectual movements. At that time the prospects for an experimental psychology did not look good because its future was in the hands of ministers and poets. But German sensory physiologists began to rebel against the poets, and began to work on human perception. And while they made great strides, it gradually became clear by the 1860s that their mechanistic approach was not sufficient because too much of perception seems to depend on learning and other psychological variables.

Two problems were particularly challenging to the mechanistic sensory people. One was the reaction-time experiment, the personal equation, and the other was the host of phenomena indicating that people perceived their world much more accurately than seemed possible. Then came the breakthrough: Fechner, strange man that he was, figured out how to measure perception. Or so it seemed. Psychological variables were supposed to be beyond scientific measurement, but in 1860 Fechner showed the world how it could be done. In a few more years Wundt was using Fechner's methods to do research on reaction time and all of the other perception problems. Wundt also made experimental psychology a regular part of the curriculum in his philosophy department. Wundt wrote texts and papers, started a journal, started an official laboratory, supervised innumerable Ph.D.s, and did all the other things that had to be done to get psychology into the university. He was our founder.

A number of young Americans went to Wundt to get their degrees because our own university system, while rapidly transforming itself, was not yet able to meet the demand for degrees. But when the Americans returned home with their credentials they found Wundt's, and Titchener's, views of experimental psychology much too constricted. They wanted to open it up. Ebbinghaus had expanded experimental psychology by measuring memory. Galton had expanded it by measuring many psychological variables. Darwin had expanded psychology by giving us all a new naturalistic view of life and adaptation. Inspired by these developments, the pioneering American psychologists wanted to open up psychology even further. First, they agreed that psychology had to pull itself free of philosophy, and ironically that happened only after the philosophers James and Dewey gave us their views of reality. And then psychologists went on to opening clinics and studying developmental psychology. They began to measure personality; they certainly measured intelligence. From the beginning American psychologists showed great interest in applied psychology. They were not bound by any systematic view of the psychological world, and had no fixed way of regarding their science. They were free and open, and they followed the permissive message of the functionalists to go forth and take psychology off in all directions.

Early in the 1900s there were some conflicting schools of psychology vying for attention and commitment. Psychoanalysis, gestalt psychology, and behaviorism were the principal combatants. Psychologists were intrigued and fascinated by all these new ideas. Freudian ideas prevailed in the clinic and in personality theory, at least up to 1950. Gestalt ideas became very important, not early on in perception where they started, but later, after 1950, in cognitive and social psychology. In the interim, between approximately 1915 and 1965, systematic psychology was dominated by behaviorism. At first it was the mechanistic variety of Watson's, which was conceptually barren but rigorous and the right kind of stuff for those who wanted psychology to be a science. Watson's outlook was greatly altered by Tolman, Hull, and Skinner, but one or another of the new behaviorisms still seemed like the right kind of stuff. Indeed, it looked for a time (around 1970) as though psychology had finally found its long-sought paradigm. It looked as though psychology really was a science, as it had always wanted to be.

But after 1970 the idea of a unifying paradigm collapsed. Behaviorism was seen as too constraining, just as the American pioneers saw Wundt's psychology as too constraining. The pioneers had done one of two things: They either thought of themselves as functionalists and did what they wanted to do, or they went into applied psychology. After 1970 increasing numbers of psychologists, disenchanted by behaviorism, did one of two things: They either thought of themselves as cognitive psychologists, and did whatever they wanted to do, or they went into applied psychology. Cognitive psychology embraces the same sort of eclecticism that functionalism did; it seems to be completely loose and unsystematic.

And there is always the appeal of the real world. We saw in this chapter that many psychologists turned eagerly to the problems of real people. The clinicians began by looking at kids having trouble in school, and they tested them. Pretty soon they were testing everybody, and measuring personality. (What would Kant have thought about that?) We have seen that when the nation went to war, when there were real problems in the real world, psychologists responded promptly and in great numbers. They were testing, training, and helping out in many ways. After World War II clinicians started doing therapy and started to look as they do now. Clinicians work at hospitals, for the government, at universities, and in private practice. Their approach to their work has also diversified greatly. They can go at it like Freud did, or like Karl Marx might have.

This chapter took a quick look at many areas of psychology, but it also missed a lot of the smaller ones. There are also, for example, military psychologists, and environmental psychologists, and Christian therapists, and psychobiologists; there are all kinds. The best thing about psychology is its amazing diversity. Perhaps we do not need a paradigm. A paradigm is inherently constraining; it restricts the pool of intellectual genes. Perhaps it is more important in a rapidly changing world that psychology enjoy such a greatly diversified gene pool.

Notes

1. It is customary to begin the history of clinical psychology with an account of the great reformers, Phillipe Pinel (1745–1826) and Dorothea Dix (1802–87), who began the movement to clean up hospitals, asylums, and prisons in the 19th century. It is a great story, but I will not tell it again. A good history of all these things from a psychiatric point of view is Zilboorg and Henry (1941). For a psychological perspective see Reisman (1966). Reisman does a good job of tying the history of clinical psychology to other developments in psychology.

2. It was understood that there might be a great number of veterans with psychiatric problems and no one wanted to alarm the country with such a prospect. There was also a strong feeling of obligation to the veterans, so that nothing was too good for them; they should get cheap housing, free schooling, good medical service, and so on. Hence, there was no need for much public debate on these matters and so we do not know much about how the new psychological clinics were set up and paid for. We need someone who was an insider to tell us how it really happened. However it happened, it was a new awakening for psychologists.

3. The meeting at Boulder was by no means the first of its kind. Clinicians had been meeting to worry about professional matters every decade or so at least since 1911. The unique feature of the Boulder conference was that the stakes had been raised so high; there were momentous decisions to be made there. And clinicians continue to meet to worry about professional matters.

4. Wolf (1973) gives a sensitive biography of Binet, and in addition describes what was going on in France at the time. For example, she describes how Janet succeeded Charcot at the hospital, and how Janet charged that Freud had stolen his ideas. Fancher (1985, 1990) also delights us with Binet stories.

5. The intelligence controversy has many dimensions. They include empiricism versus nativism, nature versus nurture, and whether intelligence is learned or innate. These issues also overlap with the question of political policy, liberal versus conservative. The conservatives, represented by Goddard (1912), want the government to protect us from the dangers of bad genes. Liberals such as Fancher (1985) and Gould (1981) want to see better education for all.

6. The importance of Lewin, mainly because of his students and young post-doctoral associates, in the development of social psychology is clearly and correctly, I believe, indicated by Patnoe (1988). To outline the early history of the field we have a classic, written by the old man himself, the man who contributed in so many ways, the seasoned old pro Gordon Allport (1968). He tells the story with a little bias, to be sure, but also with much passion and with a great grasp of what had happened. There is also an excellent, more recent, and more detached history by Jones (1985). Another word on Allport: Before being president of the social division he had already been elected president of APA in 1939, no doubt because of the widespread appreciation of his unique book on personality theory (Allport, 1937).

7. My account of the early years of industrial psychology follows Viteles (1932). APA's division of industrial and business psychology became the division of industrial and organizational psychology in the reorganization of 1945. Actually, prior to 1945 APA did not have divisions; the academic experimentalists thought they were maintaining discipline over the applied areas by not recognizing any divisional lines. There had been a bunch of applied psychologists, including the clinical and industrial psychologists, who had seceded from APA back in the 1930s and formed the American Association of Applied Psychologists (AAAP) independently of APA. But in 1938 there was a reunification with no divisions, and then in 1945 a diversification into 19 divisions. This kind of political foolishness makes it difficult to keep track of things. The difficulty is illustrated by the curious fact that APA has divisions that never existed: Division 4 was set aside specifically for psychometricians, but they voted not to organize, and there never has been a division 4. At one time division 6, physiological, thought it was too small and so voted to join division 3. They promptly disappeared, but a few years later they changed their collective mind, joined forces with some animal psychologists and recreated division 6. All of which demonstrates that within the politics of APA, anything can happen to a division.

8. Piaget was an extraordinarily prolific writer, his productivity was comparable to Wundt's. Unfortunately I find his works hard to read—I have to accommodate too much. Evans (1973) describes the man and his ideas; the beginner could start with Fancher (1990).

9. Richter called himself a psychobiologist. His old room, together with some additional space, was called the Phipps Laboratory of Psychobiology. It appears that psychobiology emphasizes the adjustment of the whole, intact organism to its physiological problems. Blass (1976) includes some brief biographical sketches of Richter, plus several of his most interesting papers. It includes the 1922 report of his dissertation work on spontaneous activity, out of which gradually evolved a large part of the research on animal motivation.

Glossary

ERE ARE DEFINITIONS of and/or comments on a number of technical terms used throughout the book.

Act Psychology. Position popularized by Brentano that emphasizes mental activity. Even perception is an active process, it is something the mind does. The antithesis of act psychology is a psychology of mental content, such as structuralism.

Active powers of the mind. Phrase, and common book title, used by Scottish common sense school. It included emotion, motivation and behavior, and especially moral conduct.

Anecdotal method. Derogatory name given to Romanes's work in animal psychology where he collected stories, anecdotes, from pet owners to show how human-like animals are.

Animal magnetism. Ordinary magnetism had only recently been discovered, and no one understood it very well when Mesmer began manipulating what he believed was the flow of magnetic fluids in people to cure their neurotic problems.

Anthropology. The study of humankind through language, religion, and literature. Kant maintained that a science of psychology was impossible, but as a substitute he suggested anthropological methods to look at language, religion, and literature in different cultures.

APA. American Psychological Association; established in 1892 as a small group of academic researchers. It has grown to well over 70,000 members, most of whom are not academics and not researchers, which shows how large and diverse psychology has become.

Apperception. An old term in German philosophy that was emphasized by Wundt, it refers to a meaningful perception, one based on learned associations as well as prevailing sensations.

Artificial intelligence, or AI. Generally, computer programs that mimic human subjects solving problems. Ideally, the AI program should closely mimic a human subject because the more similar AI is the more likely it will shed light on human cognition.

Associationism. The important doctrine that one thing can be linked psychologically with another. At first it was ideas that were associated so that a sensation could arouse an idea. Then Hartley and James Mill linked in responses. Then the early behaviorists, through Hull, allowed only stimuli and responses to be linked.

Current behaviorists favor the position that a stimulus can arouse an idea of another stimulus.

Associationist. One who relies exclusively on associations to explain experience and/or behavior. The Scottish scholars believed in associations but did not rely on them, so cannot be properly labeled associationists.

Atomism. Philosophically, it is Democritus's doctrine that the visible world comprises very small, invisible particles. Psychologically, it is the faith that phenomena are best explained by breaking them up into their elemental parts, where the elements or atoms may be sensations, associations, or neurons. Locke, Titchener, and Watson were psychological atomists.

Aufgabe. A concept introduced by Külpe at Würzburg that means what the person is trying to do; it is something like set or intent. It can be influenced experimentally with instructions and demand characteristics.

Autoshaping. In 1968 Brown and Jenkins gave pigeons a number of trials with food following light on the key. This procedure, without the birds having been shaped, led to abundant key pecking, suggesting that the response depends on Pavlovian processes rather than reinforcement. It was grim news for the reinforcement people.

Autosuggestion. Self-hypnosis. The hypnotists at Nancy, and particularly Coué, discovered that one can hypnotize oneself and that this procedure can be used to produce relief from various bodily ills.

Behaviorism. The school of thought led by Watson. He held that everything mental should be dismissed from psychology, which should be concerned only with stimulus–response (S–R) associations. However, several other varieties of behaviorism have now been developed.

Bell-Magendie Law. Historically important because it was the first correlation of neural function with neural anatomy. The dorsal or rear branch of a nerve going to the spinal cord is sensory while the ventral or front branch is motor.

Binocular disparity. The fact that the two eyes have slightly different views of nearby objects. The disparity should produce a fuzzy perception, but instead it leads to objects being visually located in space.

Blind spot. Retinal nerve fibers gather together to leave the eyeball and form the optic nerve at a spot about 20 degrees toward the body center from the fovea, and at that spot the retina is nonfunctional. Thus, the right eye can see nothing 20 degrees to the right of where it is looking. But we never notice anything missing.

Blocking. Kamin (1969) discovered that if one stimulus is paired with shock, and then it together with a second stimulus is paired with shock, little or no fear gets conditioned to the second stimulus. Such conditioning is blocked even though the requirements for getting conditioning appear to be satisfied.

British empiricism. A handy label to encompass all the early British philosophers who were important in the history of psychology: Hobbes, Locke, Berkeley, and Hume.

Cartesian dilemma. The mind–body problem. How the mind and body interact became a special problem for Descartes because of his insistence that the body is a machine and yet it can be controlled by the mind.

Catharsis. Literally, the purging of emotion. When Breuer was treating Anna O. he found that the expression of real emotion in the hypnotic state drained the subconscious tensions causing her hysterical symptoms.

Cathexis. The value that becomes attached to some object. A person who satisfies our needs acquires value, and so does a place where we frequently eat, or sleep, or take drugs. Behaviorists have looked very carefully at reinforcement learning but have neglected value learning or cathexis learning.

Closure. According to gestalt theory, organizing forces pull our perceptions toward good figures, so given a stimulus with some defect, such as a circle with a break in it, we will be moved to see it as a complete circle.

Cognitive psychology. A widespread recent movement that is like functionalism in being loose, undisciplined, and very permissive. It is largely concerned with how information is learned, stored, and retrieved.

Common sense psychology. Descriptive name often applied to the Scottish psychology of Reid and his followers because their approach was sensible and practical rather than coming from philosophical subtleties.

Complication experiment. A reaction-time experiment in which the subject's task is complicated, and the subject's reaction delayed, by having to make some perceptual discrimination or judgment. Wundt believed that the delay indicated how long it took to make the judgment.

Context. The array of other stimuli, in addition to the central stimulus, that are present. The perception of or reaction to a stimulus may depend on the context just as much as on the stimulus itself. Context effects are stressed by both the gestaltists and modern learning theorists.

Contiguity. Literally, occurring together, as in the 48 contiguous states. A contiguity theorist, such as Pavlov or Watson, contends that learning depends only on the contiguity of stimulus and response and does not require an additional reinforcement process.

Contingency. An if–then kind of relationship between events. If the response occurs then reinforcement is given; if the tone comes on then an electric shock is given. These two kinds of contingency define operant and Pavlovian learning procedures respectively.

Creative synthesis. Wundt believed that the marvel of the mind was that it puts things together, and this was his term for the unifying process. For example, he believed that sensation, feeling, and volition always occur together.

CS. The conditioned stimulus in a Pavlovian conditioning procedure. Pavlov argued that almost any stimulus could serve as a CS as long as it was originally relatively neutral. Now we think the CS is like a signal, and we suspect that some stimuli make better signals than others.

Cybernetics. Term coined by Wiener to refer to control systems, generally ones using feedback loops. He argued that such systems are to be found in organisms as well as machines.

Daltonism. Red–green color blindness was for a long time named after the chemist Dalton, who discovered it about 200 years ago. Color blindness may occur in this form or in one of several less common varieties.

Deism. Natural religion, a personal religion based on reason rather than revelation. The most common form, English deism, believes in creation, and maybe a day of judgment, but that otherwise God does not intervene in human affairs.

Determinism. The principle that every event has some sort of cause. The difference from predestination is that the deterministic cause has to be specifiable and has to act here and now. Mechanical causation few could doubt; psychological causation few could understand until Freud spelled it out.

Determining tendency. Külpe's term for the organizing or motivational principle that makes a subject do one thing rather than another. The concept overlaps with aufgabe.

Diffusion. Bain believed that if stimulation had no ready means of being discharged, then it would spread around (diffuse) in the nervous system to cause emotion and other problems.

Distal stimulus. The distant stimulus, the stimulus object out in the environment, which the gestaltists contrasted with the proximal stimulus, which is the sensation or stimulation aroused by the object.

Dozent. A low-ranking, bottom-of-the-scale academic in the German university system. The *dozent* is equivalent to our lecturer or assistant professor, and in the old days received little or no salary.

Drive. A term coined by Woodworth to describe the fuel he thought had to be added to the machine, the body, to make it work—something had to be added to the behavioristic model. Drive is still thought of as a physiological disturbance, such as hunger or pain, that requires some behavior to make things right.

Dualism. The ancient doctrine that there are two realities, the world of the mind and the material world. Dualism was a dirty word for the early behaviorists, who wanted no mind, and the Skinnerians, who want no mind or matter.

Ego. In Freudian theory, the more or less conscious and rational part of the mind, which not only has to deal with the environment but also cope with the lustful id and the puritanical superego, neither of which is conscious or rational.

Empirical. For Brentano it meant based on personal experience, and was rather phenomenological. Now it means based on data that can be replicated by someone else, so it is rather scientific.

Empiricism. The doctrine promoted by Locke that our knowledge comes from experience and only from experience. The majority of psychologists have always endorsed this position, but there is now growing interest in the possibilities of nativism.

Epiphenomenon. Darwin's friend Huxley used the word to mean a phenomenon that is of no consequence. The flea riding on the elephant's back might think it is contributing to all the noise and dust, but it is an epiphenomenon.

Epistemology. The part of philosophy that deals with knowledge, what we can know, and how we come to know it. Piaget called himself an epistemologist because he studied the acquisition of knowledge in children.

Eugenics. The intellectual and political movement stimulated by Galton that worries about the genetic quality of the population. Galton said that the disadvantaged part of the population is reproducing faster than those of us who are advantaged, and something should be done about it.

Expectancy. Hobbes said it first: If we have seen B follow A a number of times, then when we see A again we will expect to see B. Tolman revived the word, but most behaviorists rejected it. Recent cognitive psychologists have revived it once again, however.

Extinction. The procedure, first described by Pavlov, of removing the contingency that originally produced learning. Thus, the CS is presented without the US. When the response drops away we sometimes, but imprecisely, say the response is extinguished.

Faculty psychology. A descriptive name for the Scottish psychology of Reid and his followers. Because they had no unifying theory they chose to refer to a person perceiving, comparing, remembering, reasoning, and so on. These different activities were the faculties of the mind.

Figure–ground. Rubin argued that we see figures against backgrounds, and the two are phenomenologically different in several ways. For example, the contour or edge appears to belong to the figure and not to the ground.

Folk psychology. The German word is *Folk*, but it is better described as cultural or ethnic psychology. Late in life Wundt began a systematic analysis of language, religion, folklore, and the like using Kant's anthropological approach.

Free will. We like to hold people responsible for their acts, but we do not do so if their actions are constrained. Constraint can come from other people or institutions; it was such political constraint that Locke deplored. There can be divine constraint—we are not free because God only lets us act—which was Edwards's concern. The more timely question is how much are we constrained by our genes, hedonics, Freudian forces, and our history of reinforcement? Many people worry about that. Others wonder if, rather than holding people responsible, it makes more sense just to try to change their behavior.

Functionalism. A school of thought that originated in Chicago and New York and spread throughout the country. It was based on the idea that consciousness as well as behavior must serve some function and have a purpose. Highly permissive, the functionalists encouraged applied, developmental, animal, and all sorts of psychology.

Gestalt psychology. A school of thought that began with three psychologists at Frankfurt, and became influential everywhere. It began with new ideas about the organization of perception but spread to other areas, most effectively in social psychology. Gestaltists were fundamentally opposed to structuralism and behaviorism.

Good figure. Figures such as circles and squares are easy to see, remember, and live with. The gestaltists call them good figures and assume that they are so because they are congruent with how the organizing forces of the mind operate.

Habilitation. In the German university system one goes from the lowly rank of *Dozent* to some sort of professor (equivalent in the United States to getting tenure) by presenting and defending some substantial body of work, the habilitation research.

Habit. For Bain and James it was a response that has occurred so often that it no longer needs conscious attention. For the behaviorists, who had no consciousness, all behavior is habitual.

Hawthorne effect. When psychologists began to pay a lot of attention to workers in the Hawthorne plant, they found a great increase in productivity, even when working conditions were not materially improved.

Hedonism. Originally the idea that pleasure is ethically good, it evolved into the psychological principle that one invariably does that which is anticipated to maximize pleasure.

Hypnosis. Generally thought to be an induced state of mind in which the subject is temporarily very confident, agreeable, and highly suggestible.

Hysteria. A disturbance in which mental stress or guilt or anxiety somehow causes the individual to have physical problems, aches, pains, or worse. It is still not very well understood.

Id. In Freudian theory, the part of the mind that is the source of primitive, lustful wishes and desires that are so terrible they get censored, repressed, and pushed into the subconscious, from where they emerge in disguised form, sometimes as dreams and sometimes as neurotic symptoms.

Idealism. Plato spoke of the reality of ideas. Later philosophers talked of ideal forms and spiritual matters. None of these views is very instructive to the psychologist. Berkeley is about the only idealist who has been discussed here.

Ideo-motor principle. James's name for his proposal that a voluntary act flows directly from the idea of its consequence. If that idea stands out clearly, then the response will follow.

Imageless thought. At Würzburg Külpe found that while his subjects could introspect on objects they were thinking about, they could report nothing about the thought processes themselves. Thought is invisible.

Incentive. A kind of animal motivation that complements drive. It is aroused by attractive external events rather than by disturbances of the body, and it is acquired rather than inborn, so it is basically psychological rather than physiological.

Individual differences. Political correctness notwithstanding, no matter how we are measured we all turn out to be different. Galton and Cattell began measuring those differences and correlating them with other measures, thus greatly enriching psychology.

Inhibition. Some neurons inhibit other neurons rather than excite them, and that idea has been useful in learning theory. Thus, Pavlov first proposed that a learned connection is not lost in extinction, it is only masked by inhibitory learning.

Insight. The gestaltist maintains that the solution of a problem can come all of a sudden, just as an ambiguous stimulus can suddenly get reorganized perceptually. The analogous conceptual reorganization is called insight.

Instrumental learning. Because they were all taken to be instances of learning by reinforcement, we can equate Morgan and Thorndike's trial-and-error learning, Hull's instrumental learning, and Skinner's operant conditioning.

Instrumentalism. Dewey's philosophy, which stressed practical, pragmatic questions rather than philosophical subtleties. Individuals must learn to deal effectively with their environment, he said.

Introspection. Loosely, looking within. For Titchener, it meant looking inward to see what sensations could be found after every semblance of meaning was stripped away. Subjects had to be carefully trained to do that.

IQ. The intelligence quotient, developed by Stern in 1911. If a 10-year-old child does as well on a standardized intelligence test as the average 12-year-old, then you can divide his mental age, 12, by his chronological age, 10, and multiply by 100 to get his IQ, 120.

Isomorphism. Literally, the same shape. It is Köhler's concept that what is happening in the perceptual field must look like what is happening in the brain field.

Ivy League. The prestigious old private universities—Harvard, Brown, Yale, Columbia, Princeton, Pennsylvania, Cornell, and Johns Hopkins.

J.N.D. Just noticeable difference. The basic building block in psychophysical scaling, it is commonly that difference that is correctly detected 75 percent of the time, that is, halfway between perfect (100%) and chance (50%).

James–Lange theory of emotion. James and Lange independently proposed that the feeling part of emotion arises because of responses we are making. I am in the woods and see a bear; my heart pounds and I start to run; then I feel frightened.

Law of effect. Thorndike's phrase referring to reinforcement. An S–R connection will be strengthened, he insisted, if the effect (consequence) of the response is something positive, such as food.

Libido. In Freudian theory libido is the energy from instinctual drives that motivates our behavior. Since most drives can be easily expressed they are not very interesting, but primitive sexual desires cannot be expressed, so libido builds up and has far-flung consequences.

Local sign. Lotze's concept to account for how we localize things spatially. Every stimulus conveys information about itself, what it is, and also about where it is, which is its local sign. We learn about space as we learn to respond appropriately to local signs.

Loyal opposition. In British politics they are the people out of power, and they deeply oppose those in power. In psychology we find first the structuralists and then the behaviorists in power, and then we find a line of academically related people from Brentano to Stumpf to Köhler, spanning nearly a century, who were deeply opposed to the people in power.

Materialism. The metaphysical position that only matter is real; other concepts, such as mind, can be dismissed. The materialist is usually also a mechanist. The subtle difference between the two is that the materialist is concerned about substances and their reality while the mechanist is more interested in how the machine works than in what it is made of. Materialists are perhaps not so distressed by looking at mental phenomena as they are by the prospect of the spiritual world, God and the like.

Mechanist. Mechanists share a common problem; they get unhappy when they don't have some sort of machinery to explain things. The ancients had those celestial spheres. Descartes found comfort in his vortices. Hartley had his little vibrations. Kraepelin had his little lesions. Watson had his little responses.

Mesmerize. To hypnotize, to put in a trance. Mesmer thought he was helping people with their troubles by directing their magnetic juices into healthy channels. He may very well have helped a lot of people with their troubles, but not for the reason he thought.

Metaphysical Society. A small collection of Harvard scholars who convened informally during the 1870s. Chauncy Wright was the leader, but James and several other notables were there, and together they began to shape American psychology.

Metaphysics. The part of philosophy that worries about reality. Is it ideas or matter or both or neither? Hume convinced many people that the question has no answer. Psychology is less interested in the reality question than in empirical matters.

Metatheory. Another word for paradigm. It establishes what kind of theory is permissible, what kind of data should be collected, and so on.

Mind–body problem. The dilemma of how a nonmaterial entity like the mind and a material entity like the body can contact each other. How can they affect each other?

Molar. Wholistic. A description of experience or behavior that looks at entire things, such as objects, persons, and episodes. Such an analysis tends to accept the everyday, common-sense definitions of things.

Molecular. Atomistic. The opposite of molar.

Moral sciences. A cute term from Hume's era that encompassed psychology, sociology, political science, and economics, none of which was established at the time.

Nativism. A philosophical doctrine that stresses innate features of the mind. It did not begin with Kant, but he gave it substance and set it in opposition to Hume's empiricism. Things like our sense of space and time are innately organized, Kant said.

Natural selection. The key part of Darwin's theory of evolution. It is not done by nature, although it is perfectly natural, and no one is selecting, although there are differential outcomes. A species gradually changes as the environment does because individuals with certain characteristics are better able to survive and reproduce.

Naturalism. The doctrine that the human species is just another one of nature's many marvels. Our great intelligence is distinctive, but does not set us apart from other animals. More importantly, there is nothing spiritual about us to set us apart.

Nature philosophy. A phase in German intellectual history that began about when Goethe wrote the Werther story in 1774 and lasted until about 1845 when Helmholtz and his friends got serious about science. It was the romantic era when science and philosophy were confused with poetry.

Negative feedback. Where the output of a system is fed back into the system to help control it. Distortion in an amplifier means that the output is not the same shape as the input. But then if part of the output is fed back and subtracted from the input, the result will be more nearly the same shape.

Normal science. Kuhn's term for what scientists do most of the time. They clean and tidy by writing better textbooks, improving the language, getting better data, and so on. They also grow by straightening out problems so the paradigm's generality is broadened.

Occasionalism. Malebranche's curious solution of the mind–body problem. You do something mental, such as make the decision to move your hand. On that occasion God intervenes and moves your hand for you.

Oedipus. The oracle told the king and queen that their baby would grow up to kill him and marry her, so they gave the baby away. But when Oedipus grew up he wandered unknowingly back home, and did those very things. The point of the story was that you cannot fight fate. Freud added that, like everyone else, Oedipus subconsciously wanted to do those things.

Operant conditioning. A procedure for increasing the rate of responding: Reinforcement is made contingent on the response's occurrence. A response that is modifiable in this way is called an operant. And someone who talks like this is called an operant person.

Paradigm. Kuhn's rather controversial term for the rules of a science. There are rules pertaining to acceptable data, experiments, language, and theories. With a scientific revolution there is a paradigm shift and all the rules change.

Parallelism. A curious solution of the mind–body problem, but one accepted by Wundt and many German scholars of the time. You do something mental, such as make the decision to move your hand. That mental event has absolutely no effect on anything. Nonetheless, at that precise moment, and for reasons of their own, motor neurons start firing and your hand moves. Mind and body are independent but run on the same time course, like two clocks.

Pavlovian conditioning. Classical conditioning. It is the pairing of a CS or signal with a US or important event such as food. After a number of pairings the CS by itself elicits salivation.

Perception. What we see depends only in part on sensory information. It also depends on who we are, what we pay attention to and think about, and all our prior experience as well as the present context.

Personal equation. The adjustment one could make to be rid of the mean error individuals show when they compare the timing of an auditory and a visual stimulus. Bessel's pioneering work on the problem was important historically as representing very early experimental psychology.

Phenomenology. The difficult business of looking at one's perceptions to see what one can see. One is supposed to look naively and exclude knowledge and meaning. But when Goethe, one of the first phenomenologists, saw red as warm, had he really excluded knowledge and meaning?

Phi phenomenon. The apparent movement Wertheimer saw when he viewed one line and then another a few milliseconds later. It was historically important because it revealed a failure of perception to mirror sensation.

Phlogiston. A great old concept defended by Priestley and attacked by Lavoisier. Phlogiston was the power to burn, which could be added to or taken away from a substance, thereby transforming it. Thus, phlogiston added to rust gives you iron, which can burn.

Phrenology. An amazingly popular fad of the early 1800s. The phrenologist would read your personality from analyzing the bumps on your skull.

Pragmatism. The philosophical doctrine originally developed by Peirce and James that holds that beliefs should be judged by their practical consequences rather than by a priori moral or logical criteria. Thus, if James wondered about free will, then he should have determined if believing in it made him happier, wiser, kinder, or better-looking.

Preparadigmic. Kuhn says that none of the social sciences has yet matured to the point where it has a paradigm. They are all preparadigmic and hence unable to undergo a scientific revolution.

Proximal stimulus. The term contrasts with distal stimulus, which is a stimulus object out in the environment. The proximal stimulus is up close, in the eyeball or inner ear. It is the pattern of sensory stimulation. The great puzzle is why our perception is more like the distal than the proximal stimulus.

Psychological determinism. We take for granted the lawfulness of rocks and planets and other things in the physical world, but we resist the idea that our experience and behavior are also lawful. The idea of such a thing was hinted at by Hume and clearly expressed by Freud, but still many people have trouble with it.

Psychologist's fallacy. James's label for the erroneous notion, which he says could only be subscribed to by a psychologist, that because it is possible to analyze our perceptions into little bits, they must in fact be built up out of those little bits.

Psychophysics. Fechner's beautiful child, conceived in 1850 and born in 1860, that showed that one could indeed measure the mind. Fechner's methods are no longer the center of psychology, but they are still being used.

Purkinje shift. As evening comes on, the spectral hue to which we are most sensitive shifts from yellow to green. Purkinje was a great phenomenologist who discovered this fact from noting the colors of things.

Purposive. Tolman (1923) argued that when it comes to describing animal behavior one must conclude that it looks as if it had purpose. Descriptively, it is purposive.

Reaction time. How quickly one can press a button, for example, when a particular stimulus is presented. The speed depends on many factors, such as whether there is a ready signal, the properties of the stimulus, and particularly (in Donders's work) whether the subject has to sort out the critical stimulus from other stimuli.

Rationalism. There are different kinds of rationalists, who are distinguished by what it was they were opposed to. Early rationalists of the modern era, like Locke, were opposed to revelation as a source of knowledge. Later rationalists, like Kant, were opposed to Locke's empiricism, so we have a rather tangled web.

Reductionism. Mechanists are uncomfortable with psychological phenomena, so when confronted by one they seek to reduce it to something mechanical. For example, if you have a serviceable law of reinforcement the mechanist will not let it stand but will try to locate some center in the midbrain that explains how it works.

Reduction screen. A device that reduces one's view to a small area, thereby reducing information from the field, or context. Köhler showed that such a screen dramatically alters our perception of things.

Reflex. Descartes's concept was that painful stimulation would be reflected back to the muscles of the hurt part so that it would be defended. The body is, at least in part, a machine. By the time of Pavlov and Watson the reflex idea had been expanded so that there was nothing but the machine.

Reinforcement. It is conceived as something in the environment that happens to the animal, namely, the giving of some stimulus such as food that acts to strengthen behavior.

Repression. The ego defends itself against trauma, Freud said, in several ways. Repression is the wiping out of consciousness particularly offensive material, such as inappropriate sexual feelings. Such thoughts may be removed from consciousness, but they still reside in the subconscious, Freud said.

Restraining forces. The gestaltists saw perception as a conflict between competing forces. The organizing forces always pull perception toward good figures, while the restraining forces, basically the sensory input, pull it toward what is really presented.

Rigorous. Applied to a theory, it is a loaded term that implies good. Applied to Hullian theory it meant that everything was defined and measurable, and therefore the theory was testable.

Royal Society. Distressed at how backward the universities were at the time, Boyle and his friends at first met informally to discuss new scientific developments and then in 1662 formed the Royal Society in London. Nearly all of the greatest British scientific figures have been members, but for a time so too were a number of politicians and business people.

S–R psychology. Until fairly recently most behaviorists held to the view that all behavior had to be analyzed into stimulus–response (S–R) terms. All learning consisted of new S–R connections. That was all there was.

Scholastic period. In the 13th century Catholic scholars were suddenly confronted with the new thought of the Arabians and the old thought of the Greeks, particularly Aristotle. All of this scholarly material had to be reconciled with their faith. Thomas Aquinas was the most notable and most successful of the scholastics.

Scottish school. A line of ministers–teachers–philosophers beginning with Reid, and going on through Stewart, Brown, and Hamilton. Their common sense or faculty psychology spread to this country with McCosh and others.

Seduction theory. Freud suggested that neurotics shared a history of childhood sexual abuse; that was the so-called seduction theory. But quickly he proposed instead that his patients' stories of abuse represented wishful fantasies, and he went from there directly on to psychoanalysis.

Sensation. Sensory input. The naive observer ordinarily ignores sensations per se and focuses on the people and things out in the environment. But one can learn to attend to sensations, as Titchener's subjects were trained to do.

Solipsism. The rather barren philosophical position that nothing exists except for one's own thoughts and perceptions. Berkeley was close to that view but slipped out of it.

Soul. For Aristotle it was the power that a thing had to do what it did. The soul of a plant makes it grow. The early Christian philosophers then reconceptualized the soul to make it the immortal, spiritual center of a person, so psychologists don't want to talk about it anymore.

Specific nerve energies. Müller's doctrine that all nerves are essentially the same, and that what produces our different sensations is that the nerves go to different places in the brain.

Stimulus error. Titchener wanted his subjects to report their sensations stripped of all meaning. If they reported any kind of meaning then they were guilty of making a stimulus error. They were reporting on the stimulus object and not the sensation.

Structuralism. Titchener's own type of experimental psychology, which sought above all else to catalog the contents of the mind and to determine its structure.

Subconscious. For Freud it was the home of the id with its instinctual drives and the superego with its strange sense of what was proper. Both were primitive, irrational, and troublesome parts of the personality.

Suggestion. The Nancy hypnotists believed that the hypnotized person was peculiarly open to suggestion, and in fact could not resist suggestion.

Transposition effect. Köhler believed that in a discrimination task animals learn relationships about the stimuli such as that this is darker than that. His research in which the stimuli were shifted, so that + and – got transposed, tended to support his position.

Unconscious inference. Helmholtz's description of how perception occurs. We compensate for the prevailing conditions, he said, and the adjustment is like an inference we make. But the inference is immediate, irresistible, and unconscious.

Uniformitarianism. The theory, hotly debated in the 1800s, that geological processes are always about the same. Fossils of sea creatures do not appear in the mountains because there once was a catastrophic flood, for example; they got there slowly over millions of years.

US. Unconditioned stimulus. Nearly always it is some biologically important event such as food or electric shock. It is an event worthy of signaling, and worth expecting.

Utilitarianism. The doctrine proposed by Bentham that in the just society there is the greatest pleasure for the greatest number of people.

Voluntary behavior. The great enigma. The physiologists say nothing about it. Behaviorists say it is behavior conditioned to subtle internal stimuli of some sort. They would be better off saying nothing about it, or like Watson, denying its existence. Everyone else just takes for granted that the mind can dictate our actions.

Wahrnehmung. A German word to describe what is left when you strip away all the learned associations from a meaningful perception. Artists have to do it when they paint, but they have lapses. For example, the moon is invariably rendered too large. Titchener's subjects tried to do it, but they kept making stimulus errors. It is hard to do.

Wholistic. Same as molar, and the opposite of atomistic. When wholists have to break things into pieces, they try to do it along the natural fault lines, so that they will not insult nature any more than they have to.

Würzburg. A lovely small city in Germany forever stuck in the psychologist's mind as the place where Külpe set out to look at thought but found that he couldn't see a thing. It was imageless.

Young–Helmholtz color theory. The old but still serviceable theory of color vision that holds that there are three different color receptors and that it is the balance of activation of them that determines what color we see.

Cast of Characters

H ERE IS A LIST of the 100 most important people in the story of psychology. The list includes various scientists and philosophers, and applied as well as experimental psychologists. Excluded from the list is anyone born after 1915, so that it consists mainly of the early folks, the anticipators, forerunners, and pioneers.

Alfred Adler (1870–1937). At first a close associate of Freud, he struck off on his own in 1912 and came to the United States in the 1920s. He practiced what he called individual psychology, which was a popular alternative to psychoanalysis. He stressed that we are all motivated to overcome our inherent sense of inferiority.

Gordon Allport (1897–1967). He believed that psychology should not be limited to hard science. He broke off from the Harvard department and helped form the department of Human Relations there in 1946. Before that he had been an important pioneer in social psychology, personality theory, and the humanistic psychology movement.

James R. Angell (1869–1949). While he did not originate functionalism at Chicago, he approved of it, presided over it, and he was the first to describe it clearly. His contribution was mostly this sort of administration rather than any particular research he carried out.

Thomas Aquinas (1225–74). The most distinguished and accomplished thinker of the scholastic period, and the most successful of those who sought to reconcile the "pagan" philosophy of Aristotle with the teachings of the Church. His own psychological ideas are still widely discussed and taught by Catholic scholars.

Aristotle (384–322 B.C.). The last of the great Greek philosophers and considered by many the greatest of all philosophers. He wrote extensively on logic, politics, and science, summarizing the work of others and then encompassing everything with his own system. In his system mind and matter fit together harmoniously.

Francis Bacon (1561–1626). English statesman, diplomat, and politician who also wrote extensively about how he believed science should be carried out. It should not make deductions from first principles as the philosophers do, he said, but proceed inductively by first getting lots of facts. Then the facts will arrange themselves.

Alexander Bain (1818–1903). Scottish writer, who had little background in psychology but still produced a remarkable book in 1855 that gave shape to the psychology that was to come. What he did was combine his understanding of neural machinery with the associationism that had been preserved by the Scots. When he added a number of his own insights, it looked like psychology.

Mark Baldwin (1861–1934). One of the American pioneer psychologists. He was a student of the Scottish McCosh and a supporter of research, but did none himself. He was mainly a theorist. He founded and edited *Psychological Review* as well as other journals, and he wrote extensively on many psychological topics. His career ended dramatically in 1908, when Watson replaced him as chairman at Johns Hopkins.

Jeremy Bentham (1748–1823). British philosopher and social activist who started the utilitarianism movement. He glorified hedonism and argued for the greatest pleasure for the greatest number of people. Because of his peculiar will, his mummified remains still sit where they can attend important meetings at the University of London.

George Berkeley (1685–1753). Irish clergyman and idealist philosopher who first clearly articulated associationistic principles. He did so as he developed an empiricistic account of how we learn to perceive things in visual space at the same time we learn to locomote in space. He is also remembered for his reliance on God to escape solipsism.

Hippolyte Bernheim (1840–1919). French psychiatrist at the University of Nancy. He was fascinated by a local doctor's work with hypnosis, and proceeded to develop his own hypnotic techniques. For a time around 1880, he was perhaps the only psychiatrist to use hypnosis, which he thought of as suggestion, to treat patients' neurotic symptoms.

Friedrich Bessel (1784–1846). German mathematician and astronomer, who found out that different observers made characteristic observational errors. He wanted to remedy the errors, and also figure out why they occurred. Thus, he was the first to pay attention to individual differences in perception, and to study such a thing experimentally.

Alfred Binet (1857–1911). French experimental psychologist who had absolutely no background in psychology, but who nonetheless studied a great number of psychological phenomena. He is best known for his testing of intelligence in children, which gave us the Binet–Simon test. It made its way to the United States and had amazing repercussions.

Emil du Bois-Reymond (1818–96). A German physiologist (in spite of the French name) who was a student of Müller, and whose great mission was to show that the nerve impulse was an electrical phenomenon. He showed that it was. Equally important to him was his mechanistic philosophy, which he shared with Helmholtz, Ludwig, and Brücke.

E. G. Boring (1886–1968). Harvard professor who arrived there just four years after James died. His long active life covered most of the history that he wrote about so authoritatively. He was at first a structuralist, then a student of perception, a student of psychology's history, something of a behaviorist, a journal editor, and then a wise old gentleman.

Robert Boyle (1627–91). English scientist, and one of the scientific leaders of his time. He and his friends started the Royal Society at London. He is a transitional figure because he links Hobbes the atomist with his friend Locke the psychological atomist, as well as with his friend Newton, who was a more physical sort of atomist.

Franz Brentano (1838–1917). Very early German psychologist who settled in Vienna. He started his career as a Catholic priest. He was a student of

Trendelenburg and became an Aristotelian. He was noted for his marvelous lectures. He developed what he called empirical psychology, which was a psychology of act rather than content or structure.

Joseph Breuer (1842–1925). A psychiatrist in Vienna who befriended Freud when he was just getting started. Breuer helped Freud in many ways, but the most important boost came from his experience with his patient Anna O. He found that if she expressed emotion under hypnosis, that could relieve her symptoms, and that was the start of psychoanalysis.

Thomas Brown (1778–1820). The third of the important philosophers in the Scottish tradition. He is notable because he weakened the associationistic doctrine by adding to the basic associationistic laws a number of secondary laws. His student Hamilton was the last of the Scottish line.

Jerome Bruner (b. 1915). A Harvard professor for many years, but now at Oxford, he is one of the pioneers and founders of cognitive psychology. Always something of a maverick, he began by doing research that behaviorists could not comprehend. He and Miller broke from the Harvard department in 1960 and formed an institute of cognitive studies.

Mary Calkins (1863–1930). An early student of James at Harvard who was denied the Ph.D. degree even though she had been an outstanding student. She made important contributions to the study of associative learning, such as designing the paired-associate procedure. In her later years she became an important philosopher.

J. McK. Cattell (1860–1944). One of the pioneering American psychologists, he had been one of Wundt's first American students, and his first lab assistant. He established the department at Columbia, studied individual differences, and went on to study personality and intelligence in children. Much of his energy went into running and editing journals.

Jean Charcot (1825–93). Distinguished French doctor. At the Salpêtrière, the famous old hospital in Paris, he started what was called the Salpêtrière school of hypnosis. He used hypnosis not to treat patients but to diagnose hysteria and other neurotic disorders. Hypnotically induced behavior looked like hysterical symptoms rather than the real neurological thing.

E. B. de Condillac (1715–80). French scholar who was a spokesman for empiricism and associationism. He is best remembered for his fanciful story about the statue equipped only with a sense of smell and the ability to learn associations that was able to build up an accurate conception of the world.

Nicholas Copernicus (1473–1543). Polish scholar who was perhaps the first to argue that the sun rather than the earth stood at the center of things. From analyzing the data of Regiomontanus he convinced himself that the system of Ptolemy would not work, and this reliance upon observation rather than the word of authority got modern science started.

John Dalton (1766–1844). Early English chemist whose faith in the existence of the atom enabled him to see how, and in what proportion, atoms of different substances combined. Thus, Lavoisier's concept of oxidation was substantiated, and thus modern chemistry began. He also discovered color blindness from his own peculiar sense of color.

Charles Darwin (1809–82). English biologist, the most important of all biologists. He produced abundant evidence for natural selection, which has endless implications. It means that there is continuity of man and animal, that we too are a part of nature, and that there are individual differences. It also suggests new ways of explaining natural phenomena, that none of us creatures has a fixed nature, and that we all have a history.

Democritus (460–370 B.C.). Early Greek philosopher whose works are now lost, but who lives on through his follower Epicurus. He advocated ethical hedonism, the doctrine that pleasure over the long term is morally right and should be maximized. He also advocated atomism, the idea that everything, mind and matter, is made up of tiny atoms.

René Descartes (1596–1650). Great French mathematician and philosopher and contributor in many areas. The first thoroughly modern scholar, he stood at the end of the old world and the beginning of the new. It is from him that psychology inherited a fascination with physiology, many of our views of emotion, the reflex, and the mind–body problem.

John Dewey (1859–1952). Early American psychologist, philosopher, educator, and social activist. His psychology soon evolved into functionalism, of which he can be said to be the father. His philosophy, instrumentalism, was highly practical and dealt with people's problems. His educational policy was antitraditional and very liberal. And he took all of this out into the real world.

F. C. Donders (1818–89). Dutch physiologist who began doing complication experiments in which subjects had to respond quickly after making some sort of judgment. Wundt saw this as a way to investigate the mental processes in judgment. The early date, 1868, of this research makes it among the first in experimental psychology.

Hermann Ebbinghaus (1850–1909). One of the first German psychologists, who is known mainly for his research in 1885 on memory. His work showed that not just perception but memory too could be studied experimentally. That opened the door and encouraged psychologists to experiment on all sorts of different things.

Gustav Fechner (1801–87). German physiologist who worked in many areas, including poetry. His great contribution to psychology was the insight, followed by a lot of research, that perceptual magnitudes could be systematically related to sensory magnitudes. The percept is basically the logarithm of the sensation. He called it psychophysics.

Wilhelm Fliess (1858–1928). A German doctor who studied and treated the nose. He is important to our story mainly because he was a very close friend of Freud during the critical years, the 1890s, when Freud was developing psychoanalytic theory. The letters Freud wrote to him are our best record of Freud's thoughts.

Sigmund Freud (1856–1939). Trained in the mechanistic medical tradition, he was at first a neurologist. Then dealing with his patients and his analysis of himself led him to think much more psychologically. Determinism was still there but the machinery was gone, replaced by dark motivating forces. Psychoanalysis was clearly recognizable by 1900. For the rest of his life he adjusted, expanded, and professionalized it.

Galileo Galilei (1564–1642). Italian physicist who first measured how fast objects fall, who first observed the moons of Jupiter, and who first understood that science is basically an empirical matter, that is, the collection and analysis of data. His observations shattered Aristotelian science and confirmed Copernicus's view of the heavens.

Francis Galton (1822–1911). English gentleman scholar who measured all sort of things. He was fascinated by data, and so measured everything he could think of.

He did important work in many areas, including mapping, weather, fingerprints, and statistics as well as psychology. He believed in the heritability of extraordinary talent and in eugenics.

Pierre Gassendi (1592–1655). French philosopher who was a key member of Mersenne's circle of friends. He was dedicated to popularizing the ideas of Epicurus. Thus, he revived and promoted the old Greek atomism, which he thought necessary for the new scientific era. He also believed in hedonism.

J. W. Goethe (1749–1832). Extremely influential German writer and thinker. His story of Werther in 1774 ushered in the romantic movement in Germany that swept through literature and the arts. He dominated German intellectual life through his own work and through his university connections. Thus, he virtually controlled the philosophers, who were bunched up at Jena.

Stanley Hall (1844–1924). Pioneering American psychologist who studied with James, taught at Johns Hopkins briefly, and then presided at Clark University for many years. He was a founder, much as Wundt was, who started journals, started APA, brought Freud over to visit, and got psychology organized. His main research was in developmental psychology.

David Hartley (1705–57). English doctor who in his spare time wrote a detailed psychology based entirely on mechanistic and associationistic concepts. He was the first complete associationist in the sense that he had no other explanatory concepts. He also expanded the doctrine to include responses, which he linked to stimuli and to ideas.

Hermann von Helmholtz (1821–94). The greatest of all sensory physiologists. A staunch mechanist, he said that many of the mysteries of vision could be explained by peripheral events in the eye. Even our sense of color was due to three hue-sensitive receptors in the eye. But space perception depended on experience and was psychological.

Ewald Hering (1834–1918). German sensory physiologist who followed in the phenomenological tradition of Goethe and Purkinje. He developed a nativistic theory of space perception and a new opponent-process theory of color perception. Both of these developments seriously challenged the work of Helmholtz.

Thomas Hobbes (1588–1679). Early English philosopher who combined the logical, deductive character of Euclid's geometry with the new atomism of Gassendi to build a new mechanistic view of society. In the process he outlined a mechanistic psychology that rejected free will and rationality. He said it is all just atoms moving in the head.

Clark Hull (1884–1952). Professor at Yale who was our most important behaviorist and learning theorist all through the 1940s and 1950s. His system was logical and deductive, and also very complex. But it was all explicit enough to invite experimental testing, and it did draw a lot of experimental attention. It started in animal learning, but many Hullians spread out into other areas of psychology.

David Hume (1711–76). Scottish philosopher who seems very congenial to psychologists because he often appears to be one. He doubted that we could be sure of reality, but, he said, we do have our world of experience and it is lawful. Thus, there are laws of association that explain why we think of one thing and then another.

William James (1842–1910). Harvard professor who was the leading philosopher of his time. For several years he was very interested in psychology and wrote a wonderful book on it, but he never really got into it. Still, because of his position and personal charisma, and because of his book, he was enormously influential in early American psychology.

Carl Jung (1875–1961). Swiss psychiatrist whose ideas were originally quite similar to Freud's. For a few years they were close, and Freud probably hoped that Jung would follow in his footsteps. But he went his own way in 1914 and promoted a type of therapy that emphasized dreams, symbols, and the expression of the total personality.

Immanuel Kant (1724–1804). Great German philosopher who was "roused from his slumbers" by Hume. While accepting the empiricistic idea that we learn from experience, he insisted that there were innate or a priori categories of thought that experience had to fit into. He argued, too, that not all of our knowledge comes from experience.

Johannes Kepler (1571–1630). German mathematician who spent many years analyzing Brahe's excellent data on the apparent motion of Mars, and concluded that its orbit was an ellipse rather than a circle, and that Mars and earth were both moving about the sun. Copernicus had been right, and Aristotelian astronomy had been wrong on all counts.

Kurt Koffka (1886–1941). One of the original gestalt psychologists, and the first to come to this country and promote the cause here. He settled at Smith College. He was the first to apply gestalt concepts to developmental psychology, and he also wrote the definitive statement of gestalt principles.

Wolfgang Köhler (1887–1967). One of the original gestalt psychologists, and later on the leader of the movement. He applied gestalt principles to animal learning, and to behavior problems more generally. He did much research on perception, some of it with the purpose of defending his theory of how the brain generates perception.

Oswald Külpe (1862–1915). An early student of Wundt and for several years his assistant. He went on to Würzburg, where he tried to extend Wundt's introspection methodology to higher level processes, that is, thinking. What he found, to everyone's surprise and consternation, was imageless thought: Thoughts do not seem to be available for introspection.

G. T. Ladd (1842–1921). He was a professor at Yale and one of the American pioneers. He was particularly sensitive to what German physiological psychologists were doing, and wrote extensively on their work. His physiological textbook was a classic. He was elected the second president of APA.

Christine Ladd-Franklin (1847–1930). A mathematician by training, she developed an important theory of color vision, a theory similar to Hering's. She was the first woman to have a major impact on psychology. Despite never receiving the Ph.D. that she had earned or ever holding a meaningful academic position, she made her mark.

J. O. La Mettrie (1709–51). Often credited with being the first completely mechanistic philosopher. The credit might not be deserved because he was too humorous to be taken seriously, he mainly developed the ideas suggested by Descartes, and he was entirely anticipated by Hobbes.

Karl Lashley (1890–1958). Important physiological psychologist, and one of the first. He was an associate of Watson, and tried to locate where in the brain the all-important learned S–R associations were stored. His research forced him to conclude that they were not located anywhere, and that, in fact, they had a rather gestalt quality to them.

408

Antoine Lavoisier (1743–94). Early French chemist who is generally credited with discovering oxygen and thereby establishing modern chemistry. The truth is more nearly that he had little idea of what he had when he discovered it, and that modern chemistry gradually emerged over the next few decades. Even so, he was a landmark scientist.

Kurt Lewin (1890–1947). Trained at Berlin in the gestalt tradition, he worked on motivation for many years, and proposed a number of motivation concepts. After coming to the United States in 1935, he turned increasingly to social psychology, and he and his associates came to dominate that field.

John Locke (1632–1704). Great English philosopher who stressed more than anything else the concept of empiricism. Indeed, he could be said to be the father of the empiricist doctrine. Because of his liberal values and his distrust of authority he insisted that our knowledge must come from experience rather than from authority or revelation.

Hermann Lotze (1817–81). German philosopher who focused on physiological mechanisms and psychological problems. His early book on medical psychology paved the way for a lot that was to follow. He had two very important students, G. E. Müller and Carl Stumpf.

Abraham Maslow (1908–70). Originally an experimental animal psychologist, he became increasingly disenchanted with that approach and turned in a humanistic direction. He was instrumental in developing the humanistic third force in psychology and getting it recognized as legitimate. He is known for his hierarchy of human needs.

William McDougall (1877–1938). British psychologist who later came to Duke University. He emphasized behavior, and the important part played in it by emotion and motivation, which he believed sprang from basic human instincts. Always a heretic, he believed in purpose, in Lamarckian evolution, and in ESP at a time when they were all scientifically taboo.

Marin Mersenne (1588–1648). An early French scholar whose circle of friends included Descartes, Galileo, Gassendi, and Hobbes. It was through him that they (especially Descartes) kept in contact. He was mainly a mathematician, but he also studied the physical character of sound.

Franz Mesmer (1734–1815). An exorcist who developed techniques he thought involved redirecting people's magnetic fluids. Actually, it appears that his famous treatments were based on the hypnotic states he was producing. He gathered a wide following, however, and some of his followers gradually clarified what hypnosis was.

James Mill (1773–1836). He studied with Stewart of the Scottish tradition but later protested against it. He was a well-known writer, historian, and social commentator. His 1829 book presented a thoroughly associationistic psychology, one that bridged the old work of Hartley and the forthcoming work of Bain, which began psychology proper.

John Stuart Mill (1806–73). Son of James Mill and himself a very distinguished literary and intellectual figure. However, he felt torn between his devotion to literature and the arts on the one hand and his fascination with the new psychological sciences on the other, and never did resolve the conflict.

Neal Miller (b. 1909). One of the first and most important of the neo-Hullians. Always mechanistic in orientation, he has studied drug effects, food intake, and biofeedback. Always interested in motivation, he has studied Freudian mechanisms, conflict, and acquired drives. Always the theorist, he has clarified issues in all these areas.

Lloyd Morgan (1852–1936). Professor at Bristol, England, who was instrumental in arousing interest in animal learning and behavior. For animals, he believed in simple associative learning rather than something like human thought processes, and he carried out a number of ingenious studies to demonstrate associative learning.

O. H. Mowrer (1907–84). One of the original neo-Hullians and one of the most creative. His analysis of anxiety in the lab and in the clinic was critical not only for Hullian drive-reduction theory but for many people's theories. In his later years he turned increasingly to more cognitive models of behavior, and to clinical problems.

G. E. Müller (1850–1934). German psychologist at Göttingen who was second only to Wundt in having an early lab, in the number and caliber of his students, and in his general impact on experimental psychology in Germany. He was a strong methodologist who helped straighten out psychophysics, human memory work, and perception.

Johannes Müller (1801–58). Nicknamed here "the professor." He was professor of physiology at Berlin, and he and his many great students dominated the field for years. Not so much himself, but his students were militant mechanists, and they helped to spread the faith throughout the continent.

Hugo Münsterberg (1863–1916). One of Wundt's first psychology students who antagonized the old man and ended up at Harvard, where James just turned everything over to him. Enormously energetic, he ran the psychology part of the department almost singlehandedly, and in addition branched out to become active in many fields of applied psychology.

Isaac Newton (1642–1727). A towering figure in English science. He worked out the main features of the calculus and the problem of gravity while at home on vacation from college, and then spent 25 years working out the details. The *Principia* treats a great variety of physical phenomena from a mathematical point of view.

Ivan Pavlov (1849–1936). The star of Russian physiology. He received the Nobel prize for his early work on digestion, and then having discovered classical conditioning spent the rest of his long life studying it. The great body of research he produced has only recently been appreciably enlarged. He gave learning theorists much of their language and many of their concepts and procedures.

Jean Piaget (1896–1980). Swiss developmental psychologist who had absolutely no background in psychology, but shook it to its roots anyway. In the 1920s he began describing the cognitive development of children using new terms and concepts with a strong nativistic flavor, just what the behaviorists would not permit. But as they fell from their glory, Piaget's ideas have ascended.

Joseph Priestley (1733–1804). British clergyman and intellectual who is included here only to demonstrate that while a person may be badly wrong about one thing, such as the phlogiston theory of combustion, they may still be a good person who does good things, such as bringing the Unitarian church to the United States, and keeping associationism alive by revising Hartley's old book.

Thomas Reid (1710–92). The first of the Scottish school of philosophers, who brought out a common sense psychology, which is also called faculty psychology. He was, like his opponent Hume, an engaging writer who made his point effectively. He was also important because he began a long tradition of like-minded academics in Scotland.

410

Curt Richter (1894–1988). Psychobiologist at Johns Hopkins for many years. He studied a great variety of behavioral phenomena, but there was a common theme. Nearly always he was looking at some kind of behavioral adjustment to a physiological challenge. For example, he found that rats become very active when they are made hungry, and they consume salt avidly when their adrenal glands are surgically removed.

Carl Rogers (1902–87). Clinical psychologist who completely rejected the methods and concepts of psychoanalysis, and developed his own technique based on helping—allowing—clients to help themselves. It begins with unconditional acceptance and approval. He was at Ohio State and Wisconsin but never really settled down.

George Romanes (1848–94). English biologist who was closely associated with Darwin. He tried to promote Darwin's idea of the continuity of species by looking for signs of human-like intelligence in animals. Unfortunately, he used the anecdotal method, which consists mainly of collecting stories from pet owners, and his results seem foolish.

Ivan Sechenov (1829–1905). Pioneer Russian physiologist who transplanted the mechanistic philosophy of Western Europe back to Russian soil, where it flourished. He emphasized particularly the importance of inhibition in reflexive behavior; inhibition makes behavior hard to predict.

Charles Sherrington (1857–1952). Great English physiologist who by 1906 had worked out many details of reflexive behavior. The nervous system integrates behavior, he said. He was also important in developing such concepts as the final common pathway and the synapse.

B. F. Skinner (1904–90). Harvard professor who worked independently of other behaviorists to develop his own view of things. He called it radical behaviorism because it looked neither to the mind nor the nervous system to explain behavior. He soon turned to practical matters, behavior in the real world, or behavioral engineering, which attracted a great many followers.

Kenneth Spence (1907–67). An early student and staunch ally of Hull who always defended Hull's metatheory, although he developed his own particular theory. He was chairman at the University of Iowa for many years. He had innumerable students and directed a great deal of research to test out his ideas.

Herbert Spencer (1820–1903). British writer who was a contemporary of Bain and who wrote some very similar work. He stressed evolution; we, our brain, our society, have all evolved, he said. He used his mechanistic psychology to build an evolutionary and mechanistic social philosophy rather reminiscent of Hobbes.

Dougald Stewart (1753–1828). The second of the line of Scottish philosophers in the common sense tradition. He wrote little but was a charismatic and influential teacher. His most notable students were Brown, who succeeded him, and James Mill, who rebelled and became an associationist.

Carl Stumpf (1848–1936). Professor at Berlin who studied the psychology of music. He was the connecting link between Lotze and Brentano before him and the later gestaltists, who were all his students. There is a continuity here in their shared opposition to all of our unifying themes, mechanism, atomism, empiricism, and associationism.

E. L. Thorndike (1874–1949). Professor at Columbia who was the first American learning theorist. He anticipated behaviorism by insisting that all behavior was built of S-R units. He anticipated the later behaviorists by insisting that these

411

units are learned through a reinforcement mechanism. He was a pioneer in many areas, including educational psychology.

E. B. Titchener (1867–1927). Professor at Cornell for 35 years, he was the power behind structuralism. He was structuralism. Even if he had changed Wundt's system for his own purposes, he was, like it or not, our main link with German psychology and our experimental history.

Edward Tolman (1886–1959). Professor at Berkeley who presented a cognitive variety of behaviorism at a time (1932) when behaviorism had become overwhelmingly mechanistic. He introduced terms such as expectancy, sign-gestalt, and cognitive map, and showed in the animal laboratory what they meant.

F. A. Trendelenburg (1802–72). Philosopher in the history department at Berlin who studied Aristotle. He converted Brentano to Aristotle. Most remarkable is that so many of the people who were to be early psychologists studied with him as undergraduates. We suspect that it was not just coincidence.

Margaret Washburn (1871–1939). Titchener's first student, who at first followed structuralist doctrine, but later turned to animal psychology, wrote about the animal mind, and studied animal motivation. She was the first woman anywhere to be awarded a Ph.D. in psychology.

John B. Watson (1878–1958). Professor at Johns Hopkins and the founder of behaviorism. Fiercely mechanistic, he sought to rid the head of thoughts, consciousness, feelings, and motives, and replace them all with learned S–R associations. To his credit, he did the first classical conditioning studies in the United States.

Ernst Weber (1795–1878). Early sensory physiologist at Leipzig. He studied the sense of touch, but is actually best known for his research on lifting weights, which is muscle sense. The data from this work inspired his former student Fechner to go off into psychophysics.

Max Wertheimer (1880–1943). One of the original three gestalt psychologists. He authored the phi-phenomenon study that launched the gestalt movement. He came to the United States in the 1930s, settled at the New School in New York, and applied gestalt principles to problem solving—what he called productive thinking.

Lightner Witmer (1867–1956). The first clinical psychologist, originally concerned mainly with problem schoolchildren. He was a professor at Pennsylvania where he opened the first clinic and started the first clinical training. He started the first clinical journal, and generally got the area founded.

R. S. Woodworth (1869–1962). The grand old man at Columbia who helped create the functionalistic mood there. Originally very physiological, he moved into various other experimental areas. Perhaps his greatest contribution was his many books—outstanding texts on introductory, general experimental, and the history of psychology.

Wilhelm Wundt (1832–1920). The founder. The man who took psychology away from the philosophers and made it an experimental science. At Leipzig for many years, he introduced the first experimental laboratory there in 1879. He is known for his complex theory, something like structuralism, and for his multitude of students.

References

Abrams, M. H. (1953). *The mirror and the candle.* London: Oxford University Press.

Allport, F. H. (1924). *Social psychology.* Boston: Houghton Mifflin.

Allport, G. W. (1937). *Personality: A psychological interpretation.* New York: Holt.

Allport, G. W. (1947). Scientific models and human morals. *Psychological Review,* 54, 182–192.

Allport, G. W. (1968). The historical background of modern social psychology. In G. Lindzey & E. Aronson (eds.), *The handbook of social psychology,* 2d ed. Reading, Mass.: Addison-Wesley.

Altschuler, G. C. (1990). *Better than second best.* Urbana: University of Illinois Press.

Angell, J. R. (1903). The relations of structural and functional psychology to philosophy. *Philosophical Review,* 12, 243–271.

Angell, J. R. (1904). *Psychology.* New York: Holt.

Angell, J. R. (1907). The province of functional psychology. *Psychological Review,* 14, 61–91.

Angell, J. R. (1936). In C. Murchison (ed.), *A history of psychology in autobiography,* vol. 3. Worcester, Mass.: Clark University Press.

Angell, J. R., & Moore, A. W. (1896). Reaction-time: A study in attention and habit. *Psychological Review,* 3, 245–258.

Asch, S. E. (1956). Studies of independence and conformity: A minority of one against a unanimous majority. *Psychological Monographs,* (Whole No. 416).

Ashby, W. R. (1952). *Design for a brain.* New York: Wiley.

Attneave, F. (1954). Some informational aspects of visual perception. *Psychological Review,* 61, 183–198.

Baars, B. J. (1986). *The cognitive revolution in psychology.* New York: Guilford.

Babkin, B. P. (1949). *Pavlov: A biography.* Chicago: University of Chicago Press.

Bacon, F. (1620). *Novum Organum.*

Bain, A. (1855). *The senses and the intellect.*

Bain, A. (1859). *The emotions and the will.*

Bain, A. (1875). *Mind and body.*

Bain, A. (1882a). *J. Mill.*

Bain, A. (1882b). *J. S. Mill.*

Bain, A. (1904). *Autobiography.*

Baldwin, J. M. (1889–91). *Handbook of psychology,* vol. 1, *Senses and intellect,* vol. 2, *Feeling and will.*

Baldwin, J. M. (1895). *Mental development in the child and the race.*

Baldwin, J. M. (1901). *Dictionary of philosophy and psychology.*

Baldwin, J. M. (1913). *History of psychology.* London: Watts.

Baldwin, J. M. (1926). *Between two wars, 1861–1921.* London: Stratford.

Barlow, N. (1958). *The autobiography of Charles Darwin.* New York: Harcourt, Brace.

Bartlett, F. C. (1932). *Remembering.* New York: Macmillan.

Baudouin, C. (1920). *Suggestion and autosuggestion.* London: Allen & Unwin.

Beardslee, D. C., & Wertheimer, M. (1958). *Readings in perception.* New York: Van Nostrand Reinhold.

Bechterev, V. M. (1913). *La psychologie objective.* Paris: Alcan.

Bell, C. (1806). *Anatomy of expression.*

Benjamin, L. T. (1986). Why don't they understand us? A history of psychology's public image. *American Psychologist,* 41, 941–946.

Bentham, J. (1789). *Theory of legislation.*

Berkeley, G. (1709). *Essay towards a new theory of vision.*

Berkeley, G. (1710). *Treatise concerning the principles of human understanding.*

Berkeley, G. (1721). *De motu.*

Berkeley, G. (1732). *Alciphron.*

Bernfeld, S. (1944). Freud's earliest theories and the school of Helmholtz. *Psychoanalytic Quarterly,* 13, 341–362.

Bernheim, H. (1884). *Suggestion in the hypnotic state and in the waking state.*

Bernheim, H. (1886). *Suggestive therapeutics,* 2d ed. Transl. by C. Herter. New York: Putnam's, 1897.

Binet, A. (1903). *The experimental study of intelligence.*

Binet, A. (1909). *Modern ideas about children.* Transl. by S. Heisler. Albi, France: Presses de L'Atelier Graphique, 1975.

Blass, E. M. (ed.) (1976). *The psychobiology of Curt Richter.* Baltimore: York Press.

Blumenthal, A. L. (1975). A reappraisal of Wilhelm Wundt. *American Psychologist,* 30, 1081–1088.

Blumenthal, A. L. (1979). The founding father we never knew. *Contemporary Psychology,* 24, 449–453.

Boakes, R. (1984). *From Darwin to behaviorism.* London: Cambridge University Press.

Bolles, R. C. (1970). Species-specific defense reactions and avoidance learning. *Psychological Review,* 77, 32–48.

Bolles, R. C. (1972). Reinforcement, expectancy, and learning. *Psychological Review,* 79, 394–409.

Bolles, R. C. (1979). *Learning theory,* 2d ed. New York: Holt.

Boring, E. G. (1927). Edward Bradford Titchener: 1867–1927. *American Journal of Psychology,* 38, 489–506.

Boring, E. G. (1933). *Dimensions of consciousness.* New York: Appleton.

Boring, E. G. (1935). Georg Elias Müller. *American Journal of Psychology,* 47, 344–348.

414

Boring, E. G. (1937). Titchener and the existential. *American Journal of Psychology*, 50, 470–483.

Boring, E. G. (1950). *A history of experimental psychology*, 2d ed. New York: Appleton.

Bousfield, W. A. (1953). The occurrence of clustering in the recall of randomly arranged associates. *Journal of General Psychology*, 49, 229–240.

Bowlby, J. (1990). *Charles Darwin*. New York: Norton.

Breland, K., & Breland, M. (1961). The misbehavior of organisms. *American Psychologist*, 16, 681–684.

Breland, K., & Breland, M. (1966). *Animal behavior*. New York: Macmillan.

Brentano, F. (1874). *Psychology from an empirical standpoint*. Transl. by L. McAlister. New York: Humanities Press, 1973.

Brett, G. S. (1912). *A history of psychology*. London: George Allen.

Bringmann, W. G., Balance, W. D. G., & Evans, R. B. (1975). Wilhelm Wundt. *Journal of the History of the Behavioral Sciences*, 11, 287–297.

Bringmann, W. G., & Tweney, R. D. (eds.) (1980). *Wundt studies*. Toronto: Hogrefe.

Brown, P. L., & Jenkins, H. M. (1968). Auto-shaping of the pigeon's key-peck. *Journal of the Experimental Analysis of Behavior*, 11, 1–8.

Brown, T. (1820). *Lectures on the philosophy of the human mind*.

Bruner, J. S. (1983). *In search of mind*. New York: Harper.

Bruner, J. S., Goodnow, J., & Austin, G. (1956). *A study of thinking*. New York: Wiley.

Bühler, C. (1971). Basic theoretical concepts of humanistic psychology. *American Psychologist*, 26, 378–386.

Bühler, K. (1918). *Mental development of the child*. Transl. by O. Oeser. London: Kegan Paul, 1930.

Burnham, J. (1968). On the origins of behaviorism. *Journal of the History of the Behavioral Sciences*, 4, 143–151.

Burnham, W. H. (1924). *The normal mind*. New York: Appleton.

Cabanis, P. J. G. (1799). *Relations of the physical and moral in man*.

Cannon, W. B. (1915). *Bodily changes in pain, hunger, fear and rage*. New York: Harper.

Carini, L. (1970). A reassessment of Max Wertheimer's contribution to psychological theory. *Acta Psychologica*, 32, 377–385.

Carpenter, W. (1844). *Human physiology*.

Carr, H. A. (1925). *Psychology: A study of mental activity*. New York: Longmans, Green.

Carr, H. A. (1936). In C. Murchison (ed.) *A history of psychology in autobiography*, vol. III. Worcester, Mass.: Clark University Press.

Cattell, J. McK. (1890). Mental tests and measurement. *Mind*, 15, 371–381.

Cattell, J. McK. (1929). Psychology in America. In *Proceedings and papers: Ninth international congress of psychology*. Princeton, N.J.: Psychological Review Co.

Chomsky, N. (1959). Review of *Verbal Behavior* by B. F. Skinner. *Language*, 35, 26–58.

Cogan, D., & Capaldi, E. J. (1961). Relative effects of delayed reinforcement and partial reinforcement on acquisition and extinction. *Psychological Reports*, 9, 7–13.

Cohen, D. (1979). *J. B. Watson: The founder of behaviourism*. London: Routledge & Kegan Paul.

Colp, R. (1977). *To be an invalid: The illness of Charles Darwin*. Chicago: University of Chicago Press.

Conant, J. B. (1947). *On understanding science.* New Haven: Yale University Press.

Conant, J. B. (1950). The overthrow of the phlogiston theory: The chemical revolution of 1775–1789. *Harvard Case Histories in Experimental Science,* case 2.

de Condillac, E. B. (1748). *Essay on the origins of human knowledge.*

de Condillac, E. B. (1754). *Treatise on the sensations.*

Copernicus, N. (1543). *De revolutionibus orbium coelestium.*

Danziger, K. (1980). The history of introspection reconsidered. *Journal of the History of the Behavioral Sciences,* 16, 241–262.

Darwin, C. R. (1839). *Voyage of the Beagle.*

Darwin, C. R. (1859). *On the origin of species.*

Darwin, C. R. (1871). *The descent of man.*

Darwin, C. R. (1872). *The expression of the emotions in man and animals.*

Darwin, C. R. (1877). A biographical sketch of an infant. *Mind,* 2, 285–294.

Darwin, F. (1887). *Life and letters of Charles Darwin.*

deFord, M. A. (1948). *Psychologist unretired: The life pattern of Lillien J. Martin.* Stanford, Calif.: Stanford University Press.

Derry, T. K., & Williams, T. I. (1961). *A short history of technology.* New York: Oxford University Press.

Descartes, R. (1637). *Discourse on method.*

Descartes, R. (1641). *Meditations.*

Descartes, R. (1644). *Principles of philosophy.*

Descartes, R. (1649). *Passions of the soul.*

Descartes, R. (1662). *Treatise on man.*

Descartes, R. (1664). *The world.*

Dewey, J. (1886). *Psychology.*

Dewey, J. (1896). The reflex arc concept in psychology. *Psychological Review,* 3, 357–370.

Dewey, J. (1922). *Human nature and conduct.* New York: Holt.

Diamond, S. (1980). Wundt before Leipzig. In R. W. Rieber (ed.) *Wilhelm Wundt and the making of a scientific psychology.* New York: Plenum.

Dollard, J., & Miller, N. E. (1950). *Personality and psychotherapy.* New York: McGraw-Hill.

Donders, F. C. (1868). On the speed of mental processes. Transl. and reprinted in *Acta Psychologica,* 1969, 24, 412–431.

Dreyer, J. L. E. (1953). *A history of astronomy from Thales to Kepler,* 2d ed. New York: Dover.

Dunlap, K. (1922). *Elements of scientific psychology.* St. Louis: Mosby.

Dunlap, K. (1923). The foundations of social psychology. *Psychological Review,* 30, 81–102.

Durant, W. (1953). *The story of philosophy,* 2d ed. New York: Simon & Schuster.

Ebbinghaus, H. (1885). *On memory.* Transl. by H. A. Ruger & C. E. Bussenius. New York: Columbia University Press, 1913. Reprinted by Dover, 1964.

Ebbinghaus, H. (1902). *An elementary text book of psychology.* Transl. by M. Meyer. Boston: Heath, 1908.

Edwards, J. (1746). *Treatise on religious affections.*

Edwards, J. (1754). *Freedom of the will.*

von Ehrenfels, C. (1890). Excerpted in *Psychological Review*, 1937, 44, 521–524.

Eiseley, L. (1958). *Darwin's century*. New York: Norton.

Ellenberger, H. F. (1970). *The discovery of the unconscious*. New York: Basic Books.

Elliotson, J. (1843). *Numerous cases of surgical operations without pain in the mesmeric state*.

Elliott, M. H. (1928). The effect of change of reward on the maze performance of rats. *University of California Publications in Psychology*, 4, 19–30.

Elliott, M. H. (1929). The effect of change of "drive" on maze performance. *University of California Publications in Psychology*, 4, 185–188.

Ellis, W. D. (1938). *A source book of gestalt psychology*. London: Routledge & Kegan Paul.

Evans, R. I. (1973). *Jean Piaget: The man and his ideas*. New York: Dutton.

Eysenck, H. J. (1952). The effects of psychotherapy: An evaluation. *Journal of Consulting Psychology*, 16, 319–324.

Eysenck, H. J., & Wilson, G. D. (1973). *The experimental study of Freudian theories*. London: Methuen.

Fancher, R. E. (1973). *Psychoanalytic psychology: The development of Freud's thought*. New York: Norton.

Fancher, R. E. (1985). *The intelligence men: Makers of the IQ controversy*. New York: Norton.

Fancher, R. E. (1990). *Pioneers of psychology*, 2d ed. New York: Norton.

Fay, J. W. (1966). *American psychology before William James*. New York: Octagon.

Fearing, F. (1930). *Reflex action: A study in the history of physiological psychology*. New York: Hafner.

Fechner, G. (1860). *Elements of psychophysics*. Transl. by H. E. Adler. New York: Holt, 1966.

Fechner, G. (1876). *Vorschule der aesthetik*.

Fenichel, O. (1945). *The psychoanalytic theory of neurosis*. New York: Norton.

Festinger, L. (1957). *A theory of cognitive dissonance*. Evanston, Ill.: Row-Peterson.

Fisch, M. (1964). Was there a metaphysical club in Cambridge? In E. C. Moore & S. Robin (eds.) *Studies in the philosophy of Charles Sanders Peirce*. Amherst, Mass.: University of Massachusetts Press.

Franz, S. I., & Lashley, K. S. (1917). The retention of habits by the rat after removal of the frontal portion of the cerebrum. *Psychobiology*, 1, 3–18.

Freud, A. (1936). *The ego and the mechanisms of defence*. London: Hogarth, 1937.

Freud, A., et al. (eds.) (1954). *The origins of psychoanalysis, letters to Wilhelm Fliess, drafts and notes: 1887–1902*. New York: Basic Books.

Freud, S. (1895). Project for a scientific psychology. In *The origins of psychoanalysis*. New York: Basic Books.

Freud, S. Most of Freud's works cited here are in the *Standard Edition*, edited by J. Strachey and others, as well as in many other collections and reprintings.

Freud, S. (1940). *An outline of psychoanalysis*. New York: Norton.

Freud, S., & Breuer, J. (1893). *On the psychical mechanism of hysterical phenomena: Preliminary communication*.

Freud, S., & Breuer, J. (1895). *Studies on hysteria*.

Frijda, W. R., & de Groot, A. D. (1981). *Otto Selz: His contribution to psychology*. The Hague: Mouton.

Fromm, E. (1941). *Escape from freedom.* New York: Holt.

Fullerton, G. S., & Cattell, J. McK. (1892). On the perception of small differences. *Philosophical Series,* Series No. 2. Philadelphia: University of Pennsylvania Press.

Galileo, G. (1610). *Sidereus nuncius.* Transl. by A. van Helden. Chicago: University of Chicago Press, 1989.

Galileo, G. (1632). *Dialogue on the two chief systems of the world.*

Galileo, G. (1636). *Dialogues on the two new sciences.*

Galton, F. (1869). *Hereditary genius.*

Galton, F. (1874). *English men of science.*

Galton, F. (1883). *Human Faculty.*

Galton, F. (1889). *Natural inheritance.*

Galton, F. (1908). *Memories of my life.* London: Methuen.

Garcia, J., & Koelling, R. A. (1966). Relation of cue to consequence in avoidance learning. *Psychonomic Science,* 4, 123–124.

Gardner, H. (1985). *The mind's new science.* New York: Basic Books.

Garvey, C. R. (1929). List of American psychology laboratories. *Psychological Bulletin,* 26, 652–660.

Gassendi, P. (1649). *The life and death of Epicurus.*

Gay, P. (1988). *Freud: A life for our times.* New York: Norton.

Gay, P. (1989). *The Freud reader.* New York: Norton.

Gibson, J. J. (1950). *The perception of the visual world.* New York: Houghton Mifflin.

Gigerenzer, G., et al. (1989). *The empire of chance.* Cambridge: Cambridge University Press.

Goddard, H. H. (1912). *The Kallikak family: A study in the heredity of feeble-mindedness.* New York: Macmillan.

Goethe, J. W. (1774). *The sorrows of young Werther.*

Goethe, J. W. (1810). *Theory of color.* Transl. by C. L. Eastlake, 1840. Reprinted by Dover, 1970.

Gottschaldt, K. (1926). Excerpted in Ellis (1938).

Gould, S. J. (1981). *The mismeasure of man.* New York: Norton.

Guthrie, E. R. (1935). *The psychology of learning.* New York: Harper.

Haldane, E. S. (1905). *Descartes: His life and times.* London: Murray.

Haldane, E. S., & Ross, G. R. T. (eds.) (1955). *Descartes' philosophical works.* New York: Dover.

Hale, M. (1980). *Human science and the social order: Hugo Münsterberg and the origins of applied psychology.* Philadelphia: Temple University Press.

Hall, G. S. (1904). *Adolescence.* New York: Appleton.

Hall, G. S. (1912). *Founders of modern psychology.* New York: Appleton.

Hall, G. S. (1922). *Senescence.* New York: Appleton.

Hall, G. S. (1923). *Life and confessions of a psychologist.* New York: Appleton.

Hamel, I. A. (1919). A study and analysis of the conditioned reflex. *Psychological Monographs,* 27 (Whole No. 118).

Hamilton, W. (1852). *The psychology of Thomas Reid.*

Hamilton, W. (1859). *Lectures on metaphysics.*

Hartley, D. (1749). *Observations on man.*

Hartmann, G. W. (1935). *Gestalt psychology.* New York: Ronald.

Hathaway, S. R., & McKinley, J. C. (1940). *The Minnesota multiphasic personality inventory.* New York: The Psychological Corporation.

Heidbreder, E. (1933). *Seven psychologies.* New York: Appleton.

Heider, F. (1958). *The psychology of interpersonal relations.* New York: Wiley.

von Helmholtz, H. (1856–1866). *Handbook of physiological optics.* Transl. by J. C. P. Southall, 1925. Reprinted by Dover, 1962.

von Helmholtz, H. (1863). *On the sensations of tone.* Transl. of 4th ed. by A. J. Ellis, 1885. Reprinted by Dover, 1954.

Helson, H. (1925). The psychology of Gestalt. *American Journal of Psychology,* 36, 342–370, 494–526.

Helson, H. (1926). The psychology of Gestalt. *American Journal of Psychology,* 37, 25–62, 189–223.

Helvetius, C. A. (1758). *On the mind.*

Henle, M. (1983). Mary Henle. In A. N. O'Connell & N. F. Russo (eds.) *Models of achievement.* New York: Columbia University Press.

Hering, E. (1864). *Beiträge zur Physiologie.*

Hering, E. (1874). *Outline of a theory of the light sense.* Transl. by L. M. Hurvich & D. Jameson. Cambridge: Harvard University Press, 1976.

Hilgard, E. R., et al. (1991). The history of psychology: A survey and critical assessment. *Annual Review of Psychology,* 42, 79–107.

Hobbes, T. (1650). *Human nature.*

Hobbes, T. (1651). *Leviathan.*

Hobhouse, L. T. (1901). *Mind in evolution.*

d'Holbach, P. H. T. (1761). *Christianity unmasked.*

d'Holbach, P. H. T. (1770). *System of nature.*

Holmes, O. W. (1881). *The common law.*

Holmes, S. J. (1911). *The evolution of animal intelligence.* New York: Holt.

Holt, E. B. (1914). *The concept of consciousness.* New York: Holt.

Holt, E. B. (1915). *The Freudian wish.* New York: Holt.

Holt, E. B. (1931). *Animal drive and the learning process.* New York: Holt.

Horney, K. (1937). *The neurotic personality of our time.* New York: Horton.

Hull, C. L. (1930). Knowledge and purpose as habit mechanisms. *Psychological Review,* 37, 511–525.

Hull, C. L. (1935). Special review: Thorndike's Fundamentals of learning. *Psychological Bulletin,* 32, 807–823.

Hull, C. L. (1943). *Principles of behavior.* New York: Appleton.

Hull, C. L. (1952a). *A behavior system.* New Haven: Yale University Press.

Hull, C. L. (1952b). In E. G. Boring et al. (eds.) *A history of psychology in autobiography,* vol. IV. Worcester, Mass.: Clark University Press.

Hull, C. L. (1962). Passages from the "idea books" of Clark L. Hull. *Perceptual and motor skills, Monograph Supplement,* 15, 807–852.

Hume, D. (1739). *A treatise of human nature.*

Hume, D. (1748). *An enquiry concerning human understanding.*

Hume, D. (1752). *Political discourses.*

Hume, D. (1754). *History of England.*

Hume, D. (1779). *Discourses concerning natural religion.*

Humphrey, G. (1951). *Thinking: An introduction to its experimental psychology.* New York: Wiley.

Hunt, E. B. (in press). *Thoughts on thought.* Hillsdale, N.J.: Erlbaum.

Hunter, W. S. (1949). James Rowland Angell, 1869–1949. *American Journal of Psychology,* 62, 439–450.

Jaffe, B. (1957). *Crucibles: The story of chemistry.* Greenwich, Conn.: Fawcett.

James, W. (1890). *The principles of psychology.*

James, W. (1892). *Psychology: Briefer course.*

James, W. (1897). *The will to believe and other essays in popular philosophy.*

James, W. (1902). *The varieties of religious experience.*

James, W. (1907). *Pragmatism.* New York: Longmans, Green.

Jennings, H. S. (1906). *The behavior of lower organisms.* New York: Columbia University Press.

Joncich, G. (1968). *The sane positivist: A biography of E. L. Thorndike.* Middletown, Conn.: Wesleyan University Press.

Jones, E. (1953). *The life and work of Sigmund Freud.* New York: Basic Books.

Jones, E. E. (1985). Major developments in social psychology during the past five decades. In G. Lindzey & E. Aronson (eds.) *The handbook of social psychology,* 3d ed. New York: Random House.

Kahl, R. (1971). *Selected writings of Hermann von Helmholtz.* Middletown, Conn.: Wesleyan University Press.

Kamin, L. J. (1965). Temporal and intensity characteristics of the conditioned stimulus. In W. F. Prokasy (ed.) *Classical conditioning: A symposium.* New York: Appleton.

Kamin, L. J. (1969). Predictability, surprise, attention, and conditioning. In B. A. Campbell & R. M. Church (eds.) *Punishment and aversive behavior.* New York: Appleton.

Kant, I. (1781). *Critique of pure reason.*

Katz, D. (1911). *The world of colour,* 2d ed., 1930. Transl. by R. B. MacLeod & C. W. Fox. London: Kegan Paul, 1935.

Kepler, J. (1609). *Commentaries on the motion of Mars.*

Kepler, J. (1619). *The harmony of the world.*

Kimble, G. A., et al. (1991). *Portraits of pioneers in psychology.* Washington, D.C. and Hillsdale, N.J.: American Psychological Association and Erlbaum.

Koffka, K. (1921). *The growth of the mind.* Transl. by R. M. Ogden. London: Kegan Paul, 1924.

Koffka, K. (1922). Perception: An introduction to the Gestalt-theorie. *Psychological Bulletin,* 19, 531–585.

Koffka, K. (1935). *Principles of gestalt psychology.* New York: Harcourt, Brace.

Köhler, W. (1917). *The mentality of apes.* Transl. by E. Winter. New York: Harcourt, Brace, 1925.

Köhler, W. (1920). *Die physischen Gestalten.* Erlangen: Weltkreisverlag.

Köhler, W. (1929). *Gestalt psychology.* New York: Liveright, 1947.

Köhler, W. (1942). *Dynamics in psychology.* London: Faber & Faber.

Köhler, W. (1967). Gestalt psychology. *Psychologische Forschung*, 31, xviii–xxx.

Köhler, W. (1969). *The task of gestalt psychology*. Princeton, N.J.: Princeton University Press.

Köhler, W., & Wallach, H. (1944). Figural after-effects: An investigation of visual processes. *Proceedings of the American Philosophical Society*, 88, 269–357.

Kraepelin, E. (1883). *Textbook of psychiatry*, 6th ed., 1899.

Krafft-Ebing, R. (1886). *Psychopathia sexualis*.

Krech, D. (1962). Cortical localization of function. In L. Postman (ed.) *Psychology in the making*. New York: Knopf.

Krech, D., & Crutchfield, R. S. (1948). *Theory and problems of social psychology*. New York: McGraw-Hill.

Kuhn, T. S. (1957). *The Copernican revolution*. Cambridge, Mass.: Harvard University Press.

Kuhn, T. S. (1962). *The structure of scientific revolutions*. Chicago: University of Chicago Press.

Kuklick, B. (1977). *Rise of American philosophy, Cambridge, Mass. 1860–1930*. New Haven, Conn.: Yale University Press.

Külpe, O. (1893). *Outline of psychology*. Transl. by E. B. Titchener. New York: Macmillan, 1895.

Ladd, G. T. (1887). *Elements of physiological psychology*.

Ladd, G. T., & Woodworth, R. S. (1911). *Physiological psychology*. New York: Scribner's.

Ladd-Franklin, C. (1929). *Colour and colour theory*. New York: Harcourt, Brace.

Lakatos, I., & Musgrave, A. (eds.) (1970). *Criticism and the growth of knowledge*. Cambridge: Cambridge University Press.

La Mettrie, J. O. (1748). *Man a machine*. Transl. by G. C. Bussey & M. W. Calkins. La Salle, Ill.: Open Court, 1912.

Langfeld, H. S. (1937). Carl Stumpf. *American Journal of Psychology*, 49, 316–320.

Lashley, K. S. (1916). The human salivary reflex and its use in psychology. *Psychological Review*, 23, 446–464.

Lashley, K. S. (1929). *Brain mechanisms and intelligence*. Chicago: University of Chicago Press.

Lewin, K. (1917). Kreigslandschaft. *Zeitschrift für Psychologie*, 12, 212–247.

Lewin, K. (1922). Das problem der Willensmessung der Assoziation. *Psychologische Forschung*, 1, 191–302; 2, 65–140.

Lewin, K. (1926). Vorsatz, Wille und Beduerfnis. In D. Rapaport (ed.) *Organization and pathology of thought*. New York: Columbia University Press, 1951.

Lewin, K. (1935). *A dynamic theory of personality: Selected papers*. New York: McGraw-Hill.

Lewin, K. (1936). *Principles of topological psychology*. New York: McGraw-Hill.

Lewin, K. (1938). *Conceptual representation and the measurement of psychological forces*. Durham, N.C.: Duke University Press.

Lewin, K., Lippitt, R., & White, R. K. (1939). Patterns of aggressive behavior in experimentally created "social climates." *Journal of Social Psychology*, 10, 271–299.

Ley, R. (1990). *A whisper of espionage*. Garden City, N.Y.: Avery.

Lindsay, P. H., & Norman, D. A. (1972). *Human information processing.* New York: Academic Press.

Locke, J. (1690). *Essay concerning human understanding.*

Loeb, J. (1918). *Forced movements, tropisms, and animal conduct.* Philadelphia: Lippincott.

Lotze, R. H. (1852). *Medical psychology.*

Lotze, R. H. (1886). *Outlines of psychology.* Transl. by G. T. Ladd. Boston: Ginn, 1886.

Macfarlane, D. A. (1930). The role of kinesthesis in maze learning. *University of California Publications in Psychology,* 4, 277–305.

Malcolm, J. (1984). *In the Freud Archives.* New York: Knopf.

Malthus, T. (1798). *Essay on the principle of population.*

Marrow, A. J. (1969). *The practical theorist: The life and work of Kurt Lewin.* New York: Basic Books.

Marshall, M. E. (1969). Gustav Fechner, Dr. Mises, and the comparative anatomy of angels. *Journal of the History of the Behavioral Sciences,* 5, 39–58.

Martin, L. J. (1906). Experimental study of Fechner's principles of aesthetics. *Psychological Review,* 13, 142–219.

Maslow, A. H. (1954). *Motivation and personality.* New York: Harper.

Masson, J. M. (1984a). The persecution and expulsion of Jeffrey Masson. *Mother Jones,* 9, 34–47.

Masson, J. M. (1984b). *The assault on truth: Freud's suppression of the seduction theory.* New York: Farrar, Strauss, & Giroux.

Masson, J. M. (1990). *Final analysis: The making and unmaking of a psychoanalyst.* Reading, Mass.: Addison-Wesley.

Mateer, F. (1918). *Child behavior: A critical and experimental study of young children by the method of conditioned reflexes.* Boston: Badger.

McDougall, W. (1908). *Introduction to social psychology.* London: Methuen.

McGeoch, J. A., & Irion, A. L. (1952). *The psychology of human learning.* New York: Longmans, Green.

Meltzoff, A. N., & Borton, R. W. (1979). Intermodal matching by human neonates. *Nature,* 282, 403–404.

Mersenne, M. (1646). *Universal harmony.*

Mill, J. (1821). *Elements of political economy.*

Mill, J. (1818–1830). *History of British India.*

Mill, J. (1829). *Analysis of the phenomena of the human mind.*

Mill, J. S. (1843). *A system of logic.*

Mill, J. S. (1865). *An examination of Sir William Hamilton's philosophy.*

Mill, J. S. (1873). *Autobiography.*

Miller, G. A. (1956). The magic number seven, plus or minus two: Some limits on our capacity for processing information. *Psychological Review,* 63, 81–97.

Miller, G. A., Galanter, E., & Pribram, K. H. (1960). *Plans and the structure of behavior.* New York: Holt.

Miller, N. E., & Dollard, J. (1941). *Social learning and imitation.* New Haven, Conn.: Yale University Press.

Mills, E. S. (1969). *George Trumbull Ladd, pioneer American psychologist.* Cleveland: Case Western Reserve University Press.

Moore, B. R. (1973). The role of directed Pavlovian reactions in simple instrumental learning in the pigeon. In R. A. Hinde & J. Stevenson-Hinde (eds.) *Constraints on learning.* New York: Academic Press.

Morgan, C. L. (1890). *Animal life and intelligence.*

Morgan, C. L. (1894). *An introduction to comparative psychology.*

Mowrer, O. H. (1939). A stimulus–response analysis of anxiety and its role as a reinforcing agent. *Psychological Review,* 46, 553–564.

Mowrer, O. H. (1960). *Learning theory and behavior.* New York: Wiley.

Müller, G. E. (1878). *Zur grundlegung der psychophysik.*

Müller, J. (1833–1840). *Handbook of human physiology.* Transl. by W. Baly as *Elements of physiology,* 1842.

Münsterberg, H. (1908). *On the witness stand.* New York: McClure.

Münsterberg, H. (1909). *The eternal values.* Boston: Houghton Mifflin.

Münsterberg, H. (1913a). *Psychology and industrial efficiency.* Boston: Houghton Mifflin.

Münsterberg, H. (1913b). *American patriotism.* New York: Moffat, Yard.

Münsterberg, H. (1914). *Psychology general and applied.* New York: Appleton.

Münsterberg, M. (1922). *Hugo Münsterberg: His life and work.* New York: Appleton.

Murray, H. A. (1938). *Explorations in personality.* New York: Oxford University Press.

Neisser, U. (1967). *Cognitive psychology.* New York: Appleton.

Newell, A., Shaw, J. C., & Simon, H. A. (1958). Elements of a theory of human problem solving. *Psychological Review,* 65, 151–166.

Newell, A., & Simon, H. A. (1972). *Human problem-solving.* Englewood Cliffs, N.J.: Prentice-Hall.

Newton, I. (1687). *Mathematical principles of natural philosophy.*

Nietzsche, F. (1880). *Human all too human.*

Nietzsche, F. (1883). *Thus spake Zarathustra.*

Nietzsche, F. (1887). *Genealogy of morals.*

O'Connell, A. N., & Russo, N. F. (eds.) (1983). *Models of achievement.* New York: Columbia University Press.

Olton, D. S., & Samuelson, R. J. (1976). Remembrance of places past: Spatial memory in rats. *Journal of Experimental Psychology: Animal Behavior Processes,* 2, 97–116.

Osgood, C. E., & Heyer, A. W. (1952). A new interpretation of figural aftereffects. *Psychological Review,* 59, 98–118.

Ovsiankina, M. (1928). Die Wiederaufnahme unterbrochener Handlungen. *Psychologische Forschung,* 11, 302–379.

Patnoe, S. (1988). *A narrative history of experimental social psychology: The Lewin tradition.* New York: Springer-Verlag.

Pavlov, I. P. (1897). *Lectures on the work of the digestive glands.* Transl. by W. H. Thompson. London: Griffin.

Pavlov, I. P. (1927). *Conditioned reflexes.* Transl. by G. V. Anrep. London: Oxford University Press.

Pearson, K. (1911). *The grammar of science*, 3d ed. London: Black.

Pearson, K. (1914–1930). *Life, letters and labours of Francis Galton*. Cambridge: Cambridge University Press.

Perry, R. B. (1935). *The thought and character of William James*. New York: Oxford University Press.

Peters, R. S. (1956). *Thomas Hobbes*. Harmondsworth, England: Penguin.

Petrinovich, L., & Bolles, R. C. (1957). Delayed alternation: Evidence for symbolic processes in the rat. *Journal of Comparative and Physiological Psychology*, 50, 363–365.

Pfungst, O. (1907). *Clever Hans: The horse of Mr. van Osten*. Transl. by C. C. Rahn. New York: Holt.

Piaget, J. (1926). The language and thought of the child. London: Routledge.

Preyer, W. (1882). *Mind of the child*. Transl. by H. W. Brown. New York: Appleton.

Puglisi, M. (1924). Franz Brentano. *American Journal of Psychology*, 35, 414–419.

Reid, T. (1764). *Inquiry into the human mind*.

Reid, T. (1785). *Essays on the intellectual powers of man*.

Reid, T. (1788). *Essays on the active powers of the human mind*.

Reisman, J. M. (1966). *The development of clinical psychology*. New York: Appleton.

Rescorla, R. A. (1968). Probability of shock in the presence and absence of CS in fear conditioning. *Journal of Comparative and Physiological Psychology*, 66, 1–5.

Rescorla, R. A. (1973). Effect of US habituation following conditioning. *Journal of Comparative and Physiological Psychology*, 82, 137–143.

Rescorla, R. A. (1988). Pavlovian conditioning: It's not what you think it is. *American Psychologist*, 43, 151–160.

Rescorla, R. A., & Wagner, A. R. (1972). A theory of Pavlovian conditioning: Variations in the effectiveness of reinforcement and nonreinforcement. In A. H. Black & W. F. Prokasy (eds.) *Classical conditioning: II. Current research and theory*. New York: Appleton.

Rieber, R. W. (ed.) (1980). *Wilhelm Wundt and the making of a scientific psychology*. New York: Plenum.

Robinson, D. N. (1989). *Aristotle's psychology*. New York: Columbia University Press.

Roethlisberger, F. J., & Dickson, W. J. (1939). *Management and the worker: An account of a research program conducted by the Western Electric Company, Chicago*. Cambridge: Harvard University Press.

Rogers, C. R. (1942). *Counseling and psychotherapy: Newer concepts in practice*. Boston: Houghton Mifflin.

Romanes, G. J. (1882). *Animal intelligence*.

Romanes, G. J. (1883). *Mental evolution in animals*.

Romanes, G. J. (1888). *Mental evolution in man*.

Ross, B. (1991). William James: Spoiled child of American psychology. In G. A. Kimble, et al. (1991).

Rostenstock, G. G. (1964). *F. A. Trendelenburg: Forerunner to John Dewey*. Carbondale: Southern Illinois University Press.

Royce, J. (1885). *Religious aspects of philosophy*.

Rubin, E. (1915). *Synsoplevede figurer*. Copenhagen: Gyldendal.

Rudolph, F. (1962). *The American college and university*. New York: Knopf.

Russell, B. (1927). *An outline of philosophy*. London: Allen & Unwin.

Scarborough, E., & Furumoto, L. (1987). *Untold lives: The first generation of American women psychologists*. New York: Columbia University Press.

Schachter, S., & Singer, J. E. (1962). Cognitive, social, and physiological determinants of emotional state. *Psychological Review*, 69, 379–399.

Sears, R. R. (1943). *Survey of objective studies of psychoanalytic concepts*, Bulletin 51. New York: Social Science Research Council.

Sechenov, I. M. (1863). *Reflexes of the brain*. Transl. by S. Belsky. Cambridge, Mass.: Massachusetts Institute of Technology Press.

Segall, M. H., Campbell, D. T., & Herskovits, M. J. (1966). *The influence of culture on visual perception*. New York: Bobbs-Merrill.

Seligman, M. E. P., & Hager, J. (eds.) (1972). *The biological boundaries of learning*. New York: Appleton.

Shakow, D. (1930). Hermann Ebbinghaus. *American Journal of Psychology*, 42, 505–518.

Shannon, C. E., & Weaver, W. (1949). *The mathematical theory of communication*. Urbana: University of Illinois Press.

Sherif, M. (1935). A study in some social factors in perception. *Archives of Psychology* (No. 187).

Sherrington, C. S. (1906). *The integrative action of the nervous system*. New Haven, Conn.: Yale University Press.

Shinn, M. W. (1900). *The biography of a baby*. Boston: Houghton Mifflin.

Shipley, T. (1961). *Classics in psychology*. New York: Philosophical Library.

Singer, C. (1959). *A short history of scientific ideas to 1900*. New York: Oxford University Press.

Skinner, B. F. (1931). The concept of the reflex in the description of behavior. *Journal of Genetic Psychology*, 5, 427–458.

Skinner, B. F. (1936). The reinforcing effect of a differential stimulus. *Journal of Genetic Psychology*, 14, 263–278.

Skinner, B. F. (1937). Two types of conditioned reflex: A reply to Konorski and Miller. *Journal of Genetic Psychology*, 16, 272–279.

Skinner, B. F. (1938). *The behavior of organisms*. New York: Appleton.

Skinner, B. F. (1948a). *Walden two*. New York: Macmillan.

Skinner, B. F. (1948b). "Superstition" in the pigeon. *Journal of Experimental Psychology*, 38, 168–172.

Skinner, B. F. (1956). A case history in scientific method. *American Psychologist*, 11, 221–233.

Skinner, B. F. (1961). The flight from the laboratory. In *Current trends in psychological theory*. Pittsburgh: University of Pittsburgh Press.

Skinner, B. F. (1972). *Cumulative record*, 3d ed. New York: Appleton.

Skinner, B. F. (1979). *The shaping of a behaviorist*. New York: Knopf.

Smith, N. K. (1941). *The philosophy of David Hume*. London: Macmillan.

Smith, S., & Guthrie, E. (1921). *Chapters in general psychology*. Seattle: University of Washington Press.

Sokal, M. M. (1973). APA's first publication. *American Psychologist*, 28, 277–292.

Spearman, C. (1904). "General intelligence," objectively determined and measured. *American Journal of Psychology*, 15, 201–293.

Spence, K. W. (1956). *Behavior theory and conditioning.* New Haven, Conn.: Yale University Press.

Spencer, H. (1855). *Principles of psychology.*

Spencer, H. (1904). *An autobiography.* New York: Appleton.

Staddon, J. E. R., & Simmelhag, V. L. (1971). The "superstition" experiment: A reexamination of its implications for the principles of adaptive behavior. *Psychological Review,* 78, 3–48.

Stevens, S. S. (1956). The direct estimation of sensory magnitude—loudness. *American Journal of Psychology,* 69, 1–25.

Stewart, D. (1792–1827). *Elements of the philosophy of the human mind.*

Stewart, D. (1828). *The philosophy of the active and moral powers of man.*

Stones, G. B. (1928). The atomistic view of matter in the XVth, XVIth, and XVIIth centuries. *Isis,* 10, 445–465.

Stumpf, C. (1873). *Ober den psychologischen Ursprung der Raumvorstellung.*

Stumpf, C. (1883–1890). *Psychology of tone.*

Sullivan, H. S. (1953). *The interpersonal theory of psychiatry.* New York: Norton.

Sulloway, F. J. (1979). *Freud, biologist of the mind.* New York: Basic Books.

Suppe, F. (ed.) (1970). *The structure of scientific theories.* Urbana: University of Illinois Press.

Terman, L. M. (1916). *The measurement of intelligence.* Boston: Houghton Mifflin.

Terman, L. M. (1926). *Genetic studies of genius.* Stanford, Calif.: Stanford University Press.

Thorndike, E. L. (1898). Animal intelligence: An experimental study of the associative processes in animals. *Psychological Review Monograph Supplement,* 2 (No. 8).

Thorndike, E. L. (1911). *Animal intelligence.* New York: Macmillan.

Thorndike, E. L. (1913). *Educational psychology.* New York: Teacher's College Press.

Thorndike, E. L. (1932). *The fundamentals of learning.* New York: Teacher's College Press.

Tinbergen, N. (1951). *The study of instinct.* London: Oxford University Press.

Tinker, M. A. (1932). Wundt's doctorate students and their theses. *American Journal of Psychology,* 44, 630–637.

Tinklepaugh, O. L. (1928). An experimental study of the representative factors in monkeys. *Journal of Comparative Psychology,* 8, 197–236.

Titchener, E. B. (1896). *An outline of psychology.* New York: Macmillan.

Titchener, E. B. (1898). The postulates of a structural psychology. *Philosophical Review,* 7, 449–465.

Titchener, E. B. (1899). Structural and functional psychology. *Philosophical Review,* 8, 290–299.

Titchener, E. B. (1901–1905). *Experimental psychology: A manual of laboratory practice.* New York: Macmillan.

Titchener, E. B. (1909). *A textbook of psychology.* New York: Macmillan.

Titchener, E. B. (1917). Professor Stumpf's affective psychology. *American Journal of Psychology,* 28, 263–277.

Titchener, E. B. (1921). Wilhelm Wundt. *American Journal of Psychology,* 32, 161–178.

Titchener, E. B., & Geissler, L. R. (1908). A bibliography of the scientific writings of Wilhelm Wundt. *American Journal of Psychology,* 19, 541–556.

Tolman, E. C. (1920). Instinct and purpose. *Psychological Review,* 27, 218–233.

Tolman, E. C. (1923). The nature of instinct. *Psychological Bulletin,* 20, 200–218.

Tolman, E. C. (1932). *Purposive behavior in animals and men.* New York: Appleton.

Tolman, E. C. (1951). *Collected papers in psychology.* Reprinted in 1966 as *Behavior and psychological man.* Berkeley: University of California Press.

Tolman, E. C. (1952). In E. G. Boring et al. (eds.) *A history of psychology in autobiography,* vol. IV. Worcester, Mass.: Clark University Press.

Triplett, N. (1898). The dynamogenic factors in pacemaking and competition. *American Journal of Psychology,* 9, 507–533.

Veysey, L. R. (1965). *The emergence of the American university.* Chicago: University of Chicago Press.

Viteles, M. S. (1932). *Industrial psychology.* New York: Norton.

Vrooman, J. R. (1970). *René Descartes: A biography.* New York: Putnam's.

Wallin, J. E. W. (1914). *The mental health of the school child.* New Haven, Conn.: Yale University Press.

Warren, H. C. (1921). *A history of the association psychology.* London: Constable.

Warren, R. M., & Warren, R. P. (1968). *Helmholtz on perception: Its physiology and development.* New York: Wiley.

Washburn, M. F. (1908). *The animal mind.* New York: Macmillan.

Washburn, M. F. (1916). *Movement and mental imagery.* Boston: Houghton Mifflin.

Watson, J. B. (1903). *Animal education.* Chicago: University of Chicago Press.

Watson, J. B. (1913). Psychology as the behaviorist views it. *Psychological Review,* 20, 158–177.

Watson, J. B. (1914). *Behavior: An introduction to comparative psychology.* New York: Holt.

Watson, J. B. (1916). The place of the conditioned reflex in psychology. *Psychological Review,* 23, 89–116.

Watson, J. B. (1917). The effect of delayed feeding upon learning. *Psychobiology,* 1, 51–59.

Watson, J. B. (1919). *Psychology from the standpoint of a behaviorist.* Philadelphia: Lippincott.

Watson, J. B. (1924). *Behaviorism.* Chicago: University of Chicago Press.

Watson, J. B., & Rayner, R. (1920). Conditioned emotional reactions. *Journal of Experimental Psychology,* 3, 1–14.

Watson, J. B., & Watson, R. R. (1928). *The psychological care of infant and child.* New York: Norton.

Watson, R. I., & Evans, R. B. (1991). *The great psychologists,* 5th ed. New York: HarperCollins.

Weber, E. H. (1834). *On touch.* Transl. by H. E. Ross. In *The sense of touch.* New York: Academic Press.

Weber, E. H. (1846). The sense of touch and common sensibility. Transl. by D. J. Murray. In *The sense of touch.* New York: Academic Press.

Weimer, W. B. (1974). The history of psychology and its retrieval from historiography: I. The problematic nature of history. *Science Studies,* 4, 235–258.

Weiss, A. P. (1925). *A theoretical basis of human behavior.* Columbus: Adams.

Welby, F. A. (1906). *Hermann von Helmholtz.* Oxford: Clarendon Press. Reprinted by Dover, 1965.

Wertheimer, M. (1912). Experimentelle Studien uber das Sehen von Bewegungen. *Zeitschrift für Psychologie,* 61, 161–265.

Wertheimer, M. (1945). *Productive thinking.* New York: Harper.

Whitely, J. M. (1984). *Counseling psychology: A historical perspective.* Schenectady, N.Y.: Character Research Press.

Whyte, L. L. (1960). *The unconscious before Freud.* New York: Basic Books.

Wiener, N. (1948). *Cybernetics: On control and communication in the animal and the machine.* Cambridge, Mass.: Massachusetts Institute of Technology Press.

Williams, D. R., & Williams, H. (1969). Auto-maintenance in the pigeon: Sustained pecking despite contingent non-reinforcement. *Journal of the Experimental Analysis of Behavior,* 12, 511–520.

Williams, K. A. (1929). The reward value of a conditioned stimulus. *University of California Publications in Psychology,* 4, 31–55.

Winograd, T. (1972). *Understanding natural language.* New York: Academic Press.

Wolf, T. (1973). *Alfred Binet.* Chicago: University of Chicago Press.

Wolpe, J. (1952). Experimental neurosis as learned behaviour. *British Journal of Psychology,* 43, 243–268.

Woodward, W. R. (1972). Fechner's panpsychism: A scientific solution to the mind–body problem. *Journal of the History of the Behavioral Sciences,* 8, 367–386.

Woodworth, R. S. (1918). *Dynamic psychology.* New York: Columbia University Press.

Woodworth, R. S. (1921). *Psychology.* New York: Holt.

Woodworth, R. S. (1931). *Contemporary schools of psychology.* New York: Ronald. 3rd ed., with M. Sheehan, 1954.

Woodworth, R. S. (1938). *Experimental psychology.* New York: Holt.

Wundt, W. (1863). *Lectures on human and animal psychology,* 2d ed, 1892. Transl. by J. E. Creighton & E. B. Titchener. London: Swan Sonnenschein, 1901.

Wundt, W. (1874). *Principles of physiological psychology,* 5th ed., 1902. Transl. by E. B. Titchener. London: Swan Sonnenschein, 1904.

Wundt, W. (1886). *Ethics.* Transl. by E. B. Titchener, J. H. Gulliver, & M. F. Washburn. New York: Macmillan, 1897.

Wundt, W. (1896). *Outlines of psychology.* Transl. by C. M. Judd. New York: Stechart, 1902.

Wundt, W. (1920). *Erlebtes und Erkanntes.* Leipzig: Verlag.

Young, P. T. (1961). *Motivation and emotion.* New York: Wiley.

Zeigarnik, B. (1927). Excerpted in Ellis (1938).

Zilboorg, G., & Henry, G. W. (1941). *A history of medical psychology.* New York: Norton.

THE STORY OF PSYCHOLOGY: A THEMATIC HISTORY

Credits

THE PHOTOGRAPHS in this book are courtesy of the following sources: pages 2, 19, 26, 37, 39, 48, 54, 57, 64, 81, 87, 90, 122, 145, 164, 165, 189, 240, 243, 261, 270, 324, 353, 365, 367, and 376, The Bettmann Archive; page 12, Burndy Library; page 110, Keystone; pages 112, 114, 127, 153, 157, 172, 198, 201, 204, 215, 217, 315, and 345, Archives of the History of American Psychology; page 231, Wellesley College; pages 177 and 272, National Library of Medicine; page 249, Shigeko Ikari; pages 271, 306, and 318, Clark University Press; page 283, *The Mentality of Apes* by W. Kohler, Routledge and Kegan Paul, London; page 285, Wide World Photos; pages 301 and 383, Yale University Press; page 334, John Garcia.

Index

A

Aberdeen, University of, 84, 176, 178
Abriss, 147
Ach, N., 159
Actions, intentional, 285–286
Active powers, mind, 82
Act psychology, 151
Adjustment, method of, 115
Adolescence, 203
Aesthetics, Introduction to, 117
A History of Experimental Psychology, 128
Alexander the Great, 49
Allport, F. H., 374
Allport, G. W., 375
Alpha test, U.S. Army, 370
American Association of University Professors, 216
American Civil Liberties Union, 216
American Journal of Psychology, 202
American Men of Science, 205
American Naturalist, 205
American Philosophical Association, 231
American pioneers
　American University, 185–188
　James, 188–197
　Münsterberg, 197–199
American Psychoanalytic Association, 258–259
American Psychological Association (APA), 202, 226–228, 291, 309–310
　divisions of, 376–377
American psychology, 225–228
American University, 185–210, 227

Analytical geometry, 26
Anatomy of Expression, 178
Anecdotal method, 296–297
An Enquiry Concerning Human Understanding, 63
Angell, F., 225
Angell, J. R., 216–219
Animal electricity, 35
Animal Intelligence, 296, 304
Animal magnetism, 239–240
Animal Mind, The, 232
Animal Psychology, 124, 382–386
Anna O. case study, 251–252
Anomalies, perceptual, 106–113
Anschauungen, 104–105
Anthropology, 89, 123
Anthropometric lab, 174
Antioch College, 200
APA. *See* American Psychological Association
Apperception, 104, 136
Aquinas, T., 50
Aristotle, 10, 16, 48–50, 83
Asch, S. E., 375
Ashby, W. R., 347
Association, secondary laws, 83–84
Associationism
　defined, 47, 68
　French, 78–79
　German influence, 86–92
　Hartley and, 72–76, 81
　Hume and, 63–67
Astronomy, 10, 14–22
Atomism, 47, 51–53, 59–60, 67